Communication Theories in Action

From the Wadsworth Series in Communication Studies

Communication Theories in Action

AN INTRODUCTION

JULIA T. WOOD

The University of North Carolina at Chapel Hill

Wadsworth Publishing Company

I(T)P® An International Thomson Publishing Company

BELMONT   ALBANY   BONN   BOSTON   CINCINNATI   DETROIT   LONDON   MADRID   MELBOURNE

MEXICO CITY   NEW YORK   PARIS   SAN FRANCISCO   SINGAPORE   TOKYO   TORONTO   WASHINGTON

Communication Studies Editor: Todd Robert Armstrong
Editorial Assistant: Michael Gillespie
Assistant Editor: Lewis DeSimone
Marketing: Joanne Terhaar and Elaine Cline
Production: Vicki Moran
Print Buyer: Barbara Britton
Text Design: Janet Wood
Permissions Editor: Robert Kauser
Copy Editor: Melissa Andrews
Composition: Thompson Type
Printer: Quebecor Printing/Fairfield

Photographs: page 2, © Leslie Shipnuck, 1995; page 10, © Mickey Pfleger/Photo 20-20, 1983; page 42, © Leslie Shipnuck, 1995; page 70 and cover, © Leslie Shipnuck, 1995; page 106, © Leslie Shipnuck, 1995; page 124, © Richard Bloom, 1987; page 158 and cover, © E. Williamson/The Picture Cube, 1994; page 186, © Comstock, Inc.; page 216 left, © Bruce Kliewe/The Picture Cube; page 216 right, © Comstock, Inc.; page 246, © Frank Siteman/The Picture Cube, 1993; page 280, © Leslie Shipnuck, 1995; page 310 and cover, © Ben Ferris, 1979; page 342, © Comstock, Inc.

Printed on acid-free
recycled paper

Printed in the United States of America
1 2 3 4 5 6 7 8 9 10

For more information, contact Wadsworth Publishing Company:

Wadsworth Publishing Company
10 Davis Drive
Belmont, California 94002, USA

International Thomson Publishing Europe
Berkshire House 168-173
High Holborn
London, WC1V 7AA, England

Thomas Nelson Australia
102 Dodds Street
South Melbourne 3205
Victoria, Australia

Nelson Canada
1120 Birchmount Road
Scarborough, Ontario
Canada M1K 5G4

International Thomson Editores
Campos Eliseos 385, Piso 7
Col. Polanco
11560 México D.F. México

International Thomson Publishing GmbH
Königswinterer Strasse 418
53227 Bonn, Germany

International Thomson Publishing Asia
221 Henderson Road
#05-10 Henderson Building
Singapore 0315

International Thomson Publishing Japan
Hirakawacho Kyowa Building, 3F
2-2-1 Hirakawacho
Chiyoda-ku, Tokyo 102, Japan

Library of Congress Cataloging-in-Publication Data

Wood, Julia T.
    Communication theories in action / Julia T. Wood.
       p. cm.
    Includes bibliographical references and index.
    ISBN 0-534-50668-2 (hard cover)
    1. Communication—Philosophy. I. Title.
P90.W59   1996
302.2'01—dc20   95-50322

For Frances, who is family and more. She has always been, and she remains, an important presence in my life.

About the Author

Julia T. Wood is the Nelson R. Hairston Distinguished Professor of Communication Studies at the University of North Carolina at Chapel Hill. Since completing her Ph.D. (Pennsylvania State University) at age 24, she has conducted research and written extensively about communication in relationships and about gender and communication. In addition to publishing more than 40 articles in major journals, she has authored or co-authored twelve books and edited six others. The recipient of four awards for outstanding teaching and three awards for her scholarship, Professor Wood divides her professional energies between writing and teaching.

Professor Wood lives with her partner, Robbie Cox, who is also a professor of Communication Studies at the University of North Carolina and is the current president of the Sierra Club. When not writing and teaching, Professor Wood enjoys traveling, legal consulting, and spending time with friends and family.

Contents at a Glance

Contents

Chapter Nine

Theories About Communication Cultures   247

Chapter Ten

Theories of Mass Communication   281

Preface

I wrote *Communication Theories in Action* because I wanted to show students that communication theories, as well as the process of theorizing, are practical, interesting, and relevant to everyday life.

Goals

One goal of the book is to introduce students to theories that provide insight into everyday communication. A second goal is to acquaint students with the process of theorizing as both a formal activity and an informal practice in which we all engage. By emphasizing that theories are paths to understanding experience, this book invites students to understand, evaluate, and use communication theories in their lives.

For years, I have been troubled by students' perception that theories are obscure and removed from "real life." This perception may be fueled by the ways in which theories are presented in many recently published communication theory textbooks. Some textbooks employ technical language and advanced concepts that are not translated for students who have no background in the study of theories. The level and the language of these books confirm introductory students' impression that theories have little to do with their lives. Other theory textbooks cover such a range of theories that students can easily be overwhelmed. When a great many theories are presented without highlighting interrelationships among them, students may perceive that there is little coherence to the field of communication.

In *Communication Theories in Action,* I present selected communication theories in ways that students can understand and use. The book is written in an accessible and engaging style appropriate for introductory students. I avoid jargon whenever possible and provide clear definitions of specialized terms. To further animate writing, I offer practical examples that relate to students' concerns, relationships, and everyday activities.

The theories included in this book represent the breadth of the field and call attention to relationships among important theories. Rather than overwhelming students with encyclopedic coverage of theories, this book focuses on 20 selected theories that are prominent in the field of communication. Introductory students should be able to understand and apply this limited number of theories. I believe the accessibility and the selective coverage make *Communication Theories in Action* teachable for faculty and interesting for students.

Distinguishing Features

I have already mentioned two features that distinguish *Communication Theories in Action* from other communication theory textbooks: accessible discussions and discriminating selection of theories. In addition to these features, this book is distinct in the following ways:

Personal Involvement   Examples relevant to students' lives and examples from my own life demonstrate the relevance of theory to everyday life and invite students to engage in the material personally.

Practical Application   Each chapter includes several "Try It Out" features, which are short exercises that allow students to discover how a theory works in action. The Try It Outs may be used as in-class activities or assigned as homework or entries for a journal.

Reflections   Each chapter includes a number of "Reflections," which are questions that encourage students to think further about ideas that have been discussed.

Coherent Organization   The book is divided into two sections. Chapters 1–3 introduce the field of communication and discuss foundations of theorizing and criteria for evaluating theories. Chapters 4–11 present theories that share a focus on a particular type of communication (mass media), a specific context of communication (organizations, relationships), or an aspect of communication (creating meaning, critiquing social praxis). This organization helps students appreciate the connections among theories and the "multiple truths" that coexist in human experience.

Critical Evaluation   Presentation of each theory is followed by critical assessment of its strengths and weaknesses. This encourages students to adopt critical attitudes when thinking about theories. The Reflections that punctuate each chapter further invite critical thinking about theories.

Emergent Theories   In addition to covering historical and established theories of communication, I have included a number of theories that have emerged only in recent years. These include cultural studies theories, critical theories, feminist theories, and standpoint theory. The final chapter introduces students to postmodern and poststructural theories, which mark the frontiers of current theorizing in the field of communication and elsewhere.

To assist in the teaching of this book, I have written an *Instructor's Guide*. It includes suggestions for organizing the course, creating an engaging classroom climate, and developing major assignments. In addition, I have included activities to apply material in every chapter and sample test items. Also available are computerized testing and a Student Companion book with exercises, activities, chapter summaries, and self-test items so that students can evaluate their command of material covered.

Acknowledgments

Although I am listed as the author of this book, many others contributed to it. I am particularly grateful to my colleagues at the University of North Carolina at Chapel Hill and to other communication scholars around the nation whose research and theorizing inspired *Communication Theories in Action*. I hope I have done justice to the creativity and quality of their ideas.

I am also grateful to the superb publishing team at Wadsworth. They are true professionals who blended imagination and rigor in developing this book. Especially, I thank Todd Armstrong, the Communication and Media Studies editor at Wadsworth. Both his personal support and his editorial talents have greatly enriched this book. In addition to Todd, others at Wadsworth who contributed to this book include Vicki Moran, production editor; Melissa Andrews, copy editor; Bob Kauser, permissions editor; and Lewis DeSimone, assistant editor.

I acknowledge the generous and insightful reviews of drafts of this book that were provided by Bill Balthrop, the University of North Carolina at Chapel Hill; Judy Bowker, Oregon State University; James Chesebro, Indiana State University; Bill Owen, California State University–Sacramento; Jack Perella, Santa Rosa Junior College; Charles Roberts, East Tennessee State University; James Sahlman, Angelo State University; Donna Vocate, Boston University; and Denice Yanni, Fairfield University.

Finally, I thank the people to whom I am most close. Invariably, my work reflects the support and stimulation I receive from my intimates. At the top of that list is Robbie Cox, my partner for 22 years and we hope for many more to come. Along with Robbie, my friend Nancy and my sister Carolyn enrich my life and my work with their support, challenges, and thoughtful responses to my ideas.

Julia T. Wood
NELSON HAIRSTON PROFESSOR OF COMMUNICATION STUDIES
The University of North Carolina
Chapel Hill, North Carolina

Part One

Thinking About Communication and Theory

Opening

Opening

When I was a child, my father devoted much time and energy to making sure I knew our family history. He told me vivid stories of his spirited and strong mother, Miss Sal, whom I never met. I heard about Luther and Mary, who were important members of his family, though unrelated by blood. I became very fond of my father's brother Arch, who died young but not before he stirred up considerable mischief, which my father claimed was a talent I had inherited directly from Arch. I learned about his father, who stoically endured the Great Depression, and his grandfather, who taught him to respect animals and to value compassion in dealing with others.

Sometimes I was bored by my father's narratives of people long dead, and I wondered why I had to know about them. With the impudence and ignorance of a young child, I once demanded, "What do any of these people and stories have to do with me?" His reply was fast and firm: "To understand who you are, you have to know your family history." Although I didn't fully appreciate his wisdom at the time, in the years that followed I listened with greater respect to the steady stream of family stories that poured forth from my father. As a result, I feel I *know* personally many of the people he brought alive for me. Today, I realize that my own identity is intricately tied to those of my foremothers and forefathers.

Reprinted by permission of Tribune Media Services.

Just as we learn our family histories to understand who we are, we learn the history of an intellectual field to appreciate its present identity and character. An academic field of study bears the traces of the people, ideas, and events that have been part of it. To understand the modern discipline of communication, then, it's necessary to explore the people and ideas that have contributed to its historical and current character.

Communication, like all fields, has constructed a history of its identity—the people, ideas, and events that have shaped what it is today. Central to the history of the field's identity are the theories that define its scope and that cultivate insight into human interaction. The concerns and knowledge of the communication discipline reflect a history of discoveries, conceptual developments, and modes of inquiry. Consequently, what the field is today can be fully appreciated only by understanding its historical journey and the theories that were developed along that journey.

Values of Studying Communication Theories

Knowledge of the Field

There are many reasons to study communication theories. I've already noted that one value is better understanding of the field's present concerns and knowledge. The disciplines in the modern university do not exist in isolation of their histories. Instead, every discipline that exists today can be fully understood only within the context of what has come before. Learning about the theories that have historically influenced the communication field will enhance your insight into the issues, principles, and problems that characterize the discipline today. By extension, learning about theories that are influential now will help you understand current foci and anticipate future developments in communication research and teaching.

Practical Value

In addition to expanding your knowledge of the field, studying theories has practical value. Because theories of communication describe and explain what happens when people interact, they will enlarge your understanding of experiences in your personal life and patterns in the larger social world. In other words, communication theories are directly pertinent to real life.

What you learn in this book will have immediate, practical value to you. You will gain skill in developing and testing theories in your own everyday life. If that statement surprises you, it may be because you share the common misunderstanding that theorizing is restricted to academic scholars. Actually, all of us—academics, attorneys, clerks, salespeople, parents—are theorists who are continuously trying to describe, explain, understand, and control our experiences in communicating with others.

Perhaps in your relationships you've sometimes been confused by competing desires to be close to and separate from another person. If so, dialectical theory (Chapter 7) will help you understand that both autonomy and connection are normal and constructive impulses that surface in most personal relationships. Maybe you've noticed there are ritualized patterns of communication at mixers ("Hi, what year are you?" "What's your major?" "Do you like this band?"), in exchanges with store clerks ("How are you today?" "Fine—you?" "Thank you; have a nice day"), and on first dates ("Where are you from?" "Do you like Chinese food?"). Rules theory (Chapter 6) describes these sorts of regularities in interaction so that we understand why they occur and what they mean.

If you've ever wondered why many men and women tend to differ in some of their communication behaviors, then you'll want to pay particular attention to Chapter 9. In that chapter, we discuss standpoint and speech communities theories, both of which shed light on gendered dynamics in communication. If you have ever noticed that some public figures are more skillful than others in generating commitment to them and their ideas, then you'll want to read about Kenneth Burke's work. His dramatistic theory focuses on ways that people use symbols, primarily language, to create identification with others. Each theory that you will study in this book is relevant to your interactions with others. Consequently, learning about communication theories empowers you to understand and function effectively in your own life and to appreciate more fully the complexities of communication in society as a whole.

Although everyone is a theorist, not everyone is equally skilled at theorizing. Like any other activity, theorizing can be done well or poorly. Effective theorizing is based on knowing what theories are, how to test them, and how to evaluate their validity and value. In the chapters that follow, you will learn how to test and assess theories. In turn, this will allow you to be more effective in your theorizing about communication in your life. Thus, you will enlarge your ability to understand and control what happens in your interactions with others.

The Focus of *Communication Theories in Action*

Communication Theories in Action provides a history of many theories that have charted the communication field's evolution and led to its current status as one of the most vibrant and socially relevant areas of study and practice in our society. As you learn about theorizing and specific theories of communication, you should gain an enlarged understanding of the complex, multifaceted process of human communication in its many forms and contexts.

Selective Focus on Theories

The history provided in this book, like all histories, is partial. Over the years, communication scholars have advanced hundreds of theories. Don't worry—you won't encounter all of them in the pages that follow! Rather than trying to cover expansive territory lightly, I've chosen to concentrate more selectively on a limited number of theories that have shaped the character of the field. I believe the 20 theories discussed in this book will give you a good introductory understanding of the breadth of the field and the diversity of approaches, concerns, and assumptions that communication theorists make.

Attention to the Process of Theorizing

Beyond what you will learn about specific theories presented in this book, you may develop an appreciation of the *process* of theorizing as an intellectual activity. As a result of your study, you should gain insight into the concerns and goals that motivate scholars to develop theories. You will also learn about the special challenges and constraints that confront scholars as they generate and test theories in the real world of practical situations and concrete activities.

Tensions Among Theories

In learning about the process of theorizing, you will discover that theories and theorists vary widely not only in what they study, but also in the fundamental assumptions they make about human nature, knowledge, communication, and the goals of theory. Although I point out disagreements among theories, I've made no effort to disguise differences in order to fabricate a false consensus among communication scholars. Rather, I encourage you to struggle with tensions among theories so that you may appreciate the multiple, sometimes conflict-ing, views of human beings, communication, and theorizing that co-exist within the field.

Each theory that we will explore (as well as many that we won't cover in this book) offers us valuable tools for understanding our everyday lives, our relationships with others, and the ways in which communication shapes and reflects cultural values. This highlights the fact that theory and practice are not distinct concerns. Good theories inform and improve practical life, and practical activities are the focus of theories.

I firmly believe that theories are not dull, irrelevant abstractions, of value only to academics. I see theories as vibrant, fascinating perspec-tives on personal and social life. In writing *Communication Theories in Action,* I've tried to bring important communication theories to life for you so that you may share my excitement about their value, inter-est, and relevance. Perhaps some of the theories you study in this book will become as real and alive to you as Miss Sal and Uncle Arch are to me. If so, then you'll have a living link to your academic family history.

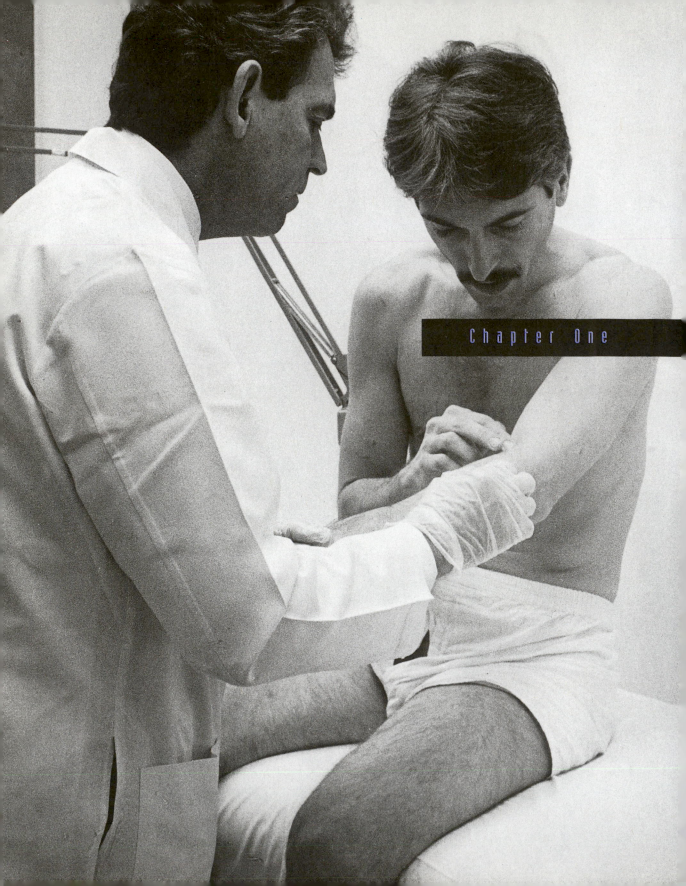

Chapter One

Communication as a Field of Study

Cass stumbles across the room to silence her alarm clock. Last night she moved it away from the bed so that she wouldn't cut it off and go back to sleep as she did the last three mornings she had chemistry class. Yawning, Cass promises herself that she not only will make it to the class today, but also will keep her attention focused on what the professor is saying. Her mind always seems to wander in that class. As Cass showers, she thinks about Jason, her boyfriend. Sometimes she feels so close to him and can't see enough of him, but at other times she feels crowded and wants some distance. That just doesn't make sense if she really loves him.

Cass cuts on the television so that the news can be heard in the background. Hearing the reporter recount two assaults, Cass shrugs and thinks to herself, "So what else is new? It's a mean world out there." While she dresses, Cass runs through the schedule for the day: first, the chemistry class and then classes in anthropology and communication. Later in the afternoon, she'll meet with the project group in her psychology class. She dreads that meeting because one member of the group, Nelson, is so overbearing and dominant; he always pushes his ideas on others. He is from a very well-off family, and he acts like someone who has always had influence and status. Cass is intimidated by Nelson's style of communicating, and she becomes

11

virtually silent when she's around him. The final item on her list for today is a presentation to the residence hall association for programming this spring. She has only 5 minutes to explain her ideas, and she's not sure how to be effective.

Cass wonders if her problems with Jason, the group, and the privileged students like Nelson mean that there's something odd about her. Sometimes she feels like a real misfit at this school. She comes from a poor family that lives in a small rural town in the South, and most everyone here is middle or upper class. And white. Cass is African American, and she just doesn't feel part of the mainstream. Do her communication problems with Nelson and others on this campus stem from differences in race and class?

Like most of us, Cass is involved in communication continuously. We talk with ourselves to organize our time and prod ourselves to do what we should (like pay attention in chemistry class), interact with friends and romantic partners, tune into mass communication, work in groups, and present our ideas to others. Communication is fundamental to our everyday lives.

Because you've been communicating all of your life, you might wonder why it's necessary to study formally something you already do. One answer is that the better we understand something, the more effective we can be. For example, some individuals have a natural aptitude for singing or playing basketball. Their innate talent allows them to sing or play basketball fairly well. They become even more effective, however, if they take formal voice training or study theories of offensive and defensive play. Likewise, even if you already communicate well, learning about communication will make you still more effective in your everyday communication activities.

Another reason to study communication theories is that they help us to make sense of interaction. You may think you don't want to learn any theory because it is boring and removed from real life. Before you decide this, however, consider how helpful theories can be in everyday life. For instance, Cass is confused by her contradictory feelings about her boyfriend, Jason. Sometimes she loves being with him, yet at other times she wants her own space. Relational dialectics, a theory we'll discuss in Chapter 7, explains that it is normal for Cass to feel what she does. All of us have needs for intimacy, or closeness, on the one hand, and for autonomy, or independence, on the other hand. Understanding and managing the tension between these conflicting needs are constant challenges in personal relationships.

Cass might also figure out why she becomes quiet around people like Nelson if she learns about muted group theory (Chapter 11), which explains that dominant social groups tend to silence members of nondominant groups. Theories of symbols and meaning, such as Burke's dramatism and Fisher's narrative theory (Chapter 5), could help Cass design a persuasive presentation for the residence hall association. Theories about speech communities and standpoint theory, which we'll explore in Chapter 9, could shed light on the reasons Cass sometimes feels out of place with people of different races and socioeconomic classes. And cultivation theory, which you'll study in Chapter 10, would inform Cass of ways in which violence on television persuades many people to believe the world is more violent than it is.

Reflection

How do you think race and class affect your communication?

Cass can maximize her effectiveness in each communication activity in her day by gaining theoretical insight into different kinds of communication. She can understand more about what is happening and what might happen based on choices she could make about how to communicate and respond to the communication of others.

Because communication is basic and important, we need to understand how it works and how it affects personal, interpersonal, professional, and cultural life. *Communication Theories in Action* will help you gain those understandings by increasing your insight into how communication works, or doesn't work, in a wide range of contexts. In Part I, we will lay the foundation for thinking about communication theories. This chapter and the following two introduce you to the field of communication, the nature of theorizing, and the process of building, testing, and evaluating theories.

In Part II, we'll look at a variety of communication theories that provide perspectives on meaning, language, interaction in relationships, communication dynamics, mass communication, and the reciprocal influence between communication and culture. Studying these theories will enhance your understanding of human communication and your ability to communicate effectively in your everyday life.

In this opening chapter, our goal is to gain a broad understanding of the field of communication. Later chapters will expand and build on ideas introduced here. To introduce the field, we'll pursue five questions: What is communication? What are the values of communication? What is included in the field? What are the foci of scholarship and teaching in communication? What careers are open to individuals with strong backgrounds in communication?

A Definition of Communication

So far we've been using the word *communication* as if it means the same thing to everyone. That's probably not very wise, since there are a great many different definitions of communication. In 1970, Frank Dance, a communication theorist, counted over 100 definitions of communication proposed by experts in the field. In the two and a half decades since then, even more definitions have emerged. So that we have a shared understanding of communication, let's begin with a definition. **Communication*** is a systemic process in which individuals interact with and through symbols to create and interpret meanings.

The first important idea in this definition is that communication is a **process,** which means it is ongoing and always in motion. It's hard to tell when communication starts and stops, since what happened long before we talk with someone may influence interaction, and what occurs in a particular encounter may have repercussions in the future. The fact that communication is a process means it is always in motion,

---

* Boldfaced terms are in the glossary at the end of the book.

moving ever forward, and changing continuously. We cannot freeze communication at any one moment.

Communication is also **systemic,** which means that it involves a group of interrelated parts that affect one another. In family communication, for instance, each member of the family is part of the system. In addition, the physical environment and the time of day are elements of the system. People interact differently in a formal living room and sunning on a beach, and we may be more alert at certain times of day than others. Communication is also affected by the history of a system. If the family in our example has a history of working out problems constructively, then a son is unlikely to raise defensiveness by saying "There's something we need to talk about." On the other hand, if the family has a record of nasty conflicts and bickering, then the same comment might arouse a high level of defensiveness. A lingering kiss might be an appropriate way to communicate affection in a private setting, but the "same" nonverbal behavior would raise eyebrows in an office. To interpret communication, we have to consider the entire system in which it takes place.

The third key idea in our definition is **symbols,** which are abstract, arbitrary, and ambiguous representations of other things. Symbols include all of language and many nonverbal behaviors, as well as art and music. Anything that abstractly signifies something else can be a symbol. We might symbolize love by giving someone a ring, saying "I love you," or taking someone out for a special dinner. Later in this chapter, we have more to say about symbols. For now, just realize that human communication involves individuals who use symbols to interact with themselves and each other.

Finally, our definition focuses on **meanings,** which are the heart of communication. As we will see later in this chapter, as well as ones that follow, meanings are not intrinsic in experience. Instead, we create them, typically in the process of communication. We talk with others to clarify our own thoughts, decide how to interpret nonverbal behaviors, and put labels on feelings and hopes to give them reality. In all of these ways, we actively construct meaning by working with symbols. By the end of this chapter, you'll more fully grasp our definition of communication.

Values of Communication

We spend more time communicating than doing anything else. We talk, listen, have dialogues with ourselves, watch television and listen to radio, participate in group discussions, browse the World Wide Web, interview or are interviewed, send electronic mail messages, and so forth. From birth to death, we communicate to meet personal, professional, relationship, and social goals.

Personal Impact

George Herbert Mead (1934), whose theory we'll encounter in Chapter 5, said humans are talked into humanity. He meant that we gain personal identity through communicating with others. In the earliest years of our lives, our parents told us who we were. "You're so strong." "You're so attractive." "You're such a funny one." Mead theorized that we first see ourselves through the eyes of others, so their messages are extremely important in forming the foundations of self-concept.

Later in life, we interact with peers and teachers, who communicate how they see us, and we filter their impressions into our own self-image. Interactions with friends and romantic partners provide additional insight into how others see us and, thus, how we come to see ourselves. Mass communication, including radio, television, and films, also influences our understandings of ourselves and the world.

The profound connection between identity and communication is dramatically evident in children who are deprived of human contact. Case studies of children who were isolated from others reveal that they seem to have little sense of themselves as humans, and their mental and psychological development is severely hindered by lack of language.

One of the most extraordinary cases was Ghadya Ka Bacha, or "the wolf boy." In 1954, outside of a hospital in Balrampur, India, a young boy was found. He had calloused knees and hands as if he moved on all fours, and he had scars on his neck, suggesting he had been dragged about by animals. Without interaction with others, children cannot learn what it means to be human and cannot develop their identity as humans. Ramu, which was the name the hospital staff gave the child, showed no interest in people, but became very excited when he visited a zoo and saw wolves. Ramu lapped his milk from a glass instead of drinking as we do, and he tore apart his meat. Some of the doctors who examined Ramu concluded he was a "wolf boy" who had grown up with wolves and who himself acted like a wolf, not a person (Shattuck, 1980). Others thought Ramu had not been raised by wolves, but clearly had been deprived of interaction with other humans.

Reflection

Was Ramu human? What does your answer imply about your definition of human nature?

Communication with others not only affects our sense of identity, but also directly influences our physical well-being. People who lack close friends have greater levels of anxiety and depression than people who are close to others (Hojat, 1982; Jones & Moore, 1989). Heart disease is also more common among people who lack strong interpersonal relationships (Ruberman, 1992). Steve Duck (1992), a scholar of interpersonal communication, reports that people in disturbed relationships tend to have low self-esteem, headaches, alcoholism, cancer, sleep disorders, and other physical problems. Clearly, healthy interaction with others is important to our physical and mental health.

Relationship Impact

Communication also critically affects our relationships. We build connections with others by revealing our private identities, remembering shared history, planning a future, and working out problems and tensions. Marriage counselors have long emphasized the importance of communication for healthy, enduring relationships (Beck, 1988; Gottman & Carrere, 1994; Scarf, 1987). They point out that troubles and problems are not the primary reason some marriages fail, since those are common to all relationships. A primary distinction between relationships that endure and those that collapse is effective communication. Couples who have worked at understanding each other and who talk through problems have the potential to adjust and refine their relationships so that they remain healthy over time. Good communication in intimate relationships involves being a skillful listener, expressing your own ideas clearly, and responding with empathy and understanding.

But communication is important as more than a way to solve problems or make personal disclosures. Steve Duck (1994b, p. 52), who studies personal relationships, says that "talk is the essence of relational maintenance." The mundane, routine talk between friends and romantic partners continuously weaves their lives together. More than the big moments, such as making the first statements of love or surmounting a major crisis, it is the unremarkable, everyday interaction between partners that sustains the "conversation of marriage" (Berger & Kellner, 1964). Through small talk, gossip about mutual acquaintances, nonverbal exchanges, and discussions of clothes and other mundane topics, partners embody their relationship. For this reason, couples involved in long-distance romances say the biggest problems are missing the nonverbal communication that occurs in face-to-face interaction and not being able to share small talk (Gerstel & Gross, 1985).

Reflection

Why is "small talk" important in linking intimates?

Professional Impact

Communication skills affect professional success. The importance of communication is obvious in professions such as teaching, business, law, broadcasting, sales, and counseling, in which talking and listening are central. Many attorneys, counselors, businesspeople, and teachers major or minor in communication before pursuing specialized graduate training. What they learn about ways to present their ideas and respond to the communication of others allows them to be persuasive, effective professionals.

In other fields, the importance of communication is less obvious, but nonetheless present. Even highly technical work such as computer programming, accounting, and systems design requires a variety of communication skills. Specialists have to be able to get along with others and to explain their ideas, particularly technical ones, to people who lack their specialized knowledge. An IBM manager stated that when he considers applicants for positions as computer programmers, he looks for abilities to get along well with people and to express themselves effectively. The manager went on to point out that if applicants lack skills in computer programming, they can learn those on the job, but no company is prepared to teach employees how to deal with people and communicate effectively (McBath & Burhans, 1975).

Success in most professions requires communication skills. Members of work teams must learn to coordinate meanings so that they share understandings, an issue that is of primary concern in rules theory (Chapter 6). In addition, they must understand the rituals and specialized language that define their group, a topic considered by organizational culture theory (Chapter 9). Individuals in caregiving professions must be able to empathize and respond in ways that provide comfort. This topic has been explored in depth by research relying on constructivist theory (Chapter 6). Careers involving organizing—from grassroots level to political campaigning—require an understanding of power relationships in society and ways that the existing power hierarchy can be challenged. This is the primary focus of cultural studies theories, which we consider in Chapter 11. It's virtually impossible to think of a career that doesn't involve communication and that can't be more successfully pursued by studying theories relevant to that profession.

Cultural Impact

Communication skills are also important for the health of our society. To be effective, citizens in a democracy have to be able to express ideas and to evaluate the ideas of others. A routine event in presidential elections is one or more debates between candidates. To make informed judgments, viewers need to listen critically to candidates' arguments and responses to criticism and questions. We will also be more enlightened as citizens if we're familiar with communication theories that explain how media shape our perceptions of events, people, and issues. We'll consider two theories of mass communication in Chapter 10.

Beyond the political realm, good communication skills are the essence of social life. Particularly as our culture becomes increasingly pluralistic, we must all learn to interact with people who differ from us and to learn from them in the process. This means we need to understand the different verbal and nonverbal communication styles that are learned in distinct communication cultures. In Chapter 9, we consider speech community theory, which sheds light on the different ways that women and men and people of different ethnic backgrounds learn to communicate. We should also be critical of media representations of social groups, since sometimes these are stereotyped and distorted. Our study of cultivation theory in Chapter 10 will sharpen your awareness of how media shape perceptions. Both civic and social life depend on our ability to listen thoughtfully to a range of perspectives and to communicate in a variety of ways.

Communication, then, is important for personal, relationship, professional, and cultural reasons. Because communication is a cornerstone of human life, your choice to study it will serve you well. To understand what's involved in communication, let's now discuss the scope of the field.

 **readth of the Communication Field**

More than 2,000 years ago, when the study and teaching of communication began, the field focused almost exclusively on public communication. Aristotle, a famous Greek philosopher, believed effective public speaking was essential to citizens' participation in civic affairs. He taught his students how to develop and present persuasive speeches to influence public and political life. Although public speaking remains a vital skill, it no longer marks the boundaries of the communication field. The modern field of communication includes seven major areas.

Intrapersonal Communication

Intrapersonal communication is communication with ourselves, or self-talk. You might be wondering whether intrapersonal communication is just jargon for thinking. In one sense, intrapersonal communication does involve thinking, since it is a cognitive process that goes on inside of us. Yet, because the process relies on language, it is also a kind of communication. Intrapersonal communication involves dialogues we have with ourselves—those conversations that continuously go on in our heads. This area of the field is reflected in many books, most recently one by Donna Vocate (1994), that focus exclusively on intrapersonal communication.

One school of counseling focuses on enhancing self-esteem by changing how we talk to ourselves about negative feelings (Ellis & Harper, 1977; Rusk & Rusk, 1988; Seligman, 1990). For instance, you might say to yourself, "I blew that test, so I'm really stupid. I'll never graduate and, if I do, nobody will hire a klutz like me." This kind of talk lowers self-esteem by convincing you that a single event (blowing one test) proves you are totally worthless. Therapists who believe that what we say to ourselves affects our feelings would encourage us to challenge negative self-talk by saying, "Hey, wait a minute. One test is not a measure of my intelligence. I did well on the first test in this course and have a good overall record at the college. I shouldn't be so hard on myself." What we say to ourselves can enhance or diminish self-esteem.

Pay attention to the way you talk to yourself for the next day. When some-thing goes wrong, what do you say to yourself? Do you put yourself down with negative messages that blame you for what happened? Do you gener-alize beyond the specific event to describe yourself as a loser or as inadequate?

The first step in changing negative self-talk is to become aware of it. The second step is to challenge it when it occurs.

We engage in self-talk to sort out feelings and ideas, plan our lives, rehearse different ways of acting, and prompt ourselves to do or not do particular things. For example, Cass used self-talk to motivate her-self to listen more attentively in her chemistry class. Intrapersonal com-munication is how we remind ourselves to eat in healthy ways ("No saturated fats"), show respect to others ("I can't let my boss see that I'm peeved at her"), and check impulses that might be destructive ("I'll wait until I've cooled off to say anything").

Intrapersonal communication also helps us rehearse alternative sce-narios to see how each might turn out. Cass might consider telling Nelson to shut up, suggesting the group adopt a rule that everyone should participate equally, and taking Nelson out for coffee and pri-vately encouraging him to be less domineering. She'll think through the various ways to approach Nelson, weigh the likely consequences of each, and then choose one to put into practice. We engage in internal dialogues continuously as we sort through ideas and test out alternative courses of action.

Interpersonal Communication

A second major emphasis in the modern field of communication is **interpersonal communication,** which deals with communication between people. In one sense, all communication is between people, so all communication is interpersonal. Such a broad definition, how-ever, doesn't create any useful boundaries for the area of study.

There is growing consensus that interpersonal communication is not a single thing, but rather exists on a continuum from highly impersonal to highly interpersonal (Wood, 1995b). The more personally we interact with another as a distinct individual (versus communicating in a general social role), the more interpersonal the communication is. Using this criterion, we would say that a deep conversation with a friend is more interpersonal than a casual exchange with a sales clerk.

Since the late 1960s, interest in interpersonal communication has mushroomed, making it one of the most vibrant branches of the field. Scholars focus on how communication creates and sustains relationships (Duck, 1994a,b; Spencer, 1994), how partners communicate to deal with the normal and extraordinary challenges of maintaining intimacy over time (Canary & Stafford, 1994; Duck & Wood, 1995; Wood & Duck, 1995a,b), and how media shape our expectations of and communication in relationships. Of particular concern to scholars of interpersonal communication are the ways romantic partners and close friends use communication to create and sustain intimacy. Research indicates that communication is the lifeblood of close relationships, since it is how friends and couples develop intimacy and how they continuously refashion relationships to meet their changing needs and preferences. Intimates who learn how to understand and talk with each other have the greatest chance of enduring over time.

Interpersonal communication researchers also study how communication is influenced by gender (Wood, 1986, 1993c,d, 1994a,b, 1996a; Wood & Inman, 1993), ethnicity (Gaines, 1995; Houston & Wood, 1996), and sexual orientation (Huston & Schwartz, 1996; Wood, 1994c). Interpersonal communication is one of the fastest growing areas in the field.

Group and Team Communication

A third important area of the field is communication in small groups or teams. Small group communication involves a range of topics, such as leadership, member roles, group structure, task agenda, and conflict.

Several of the theories we'll consider in this book shed light on how communication affects various aspects of groups and teams.

One of the most prominent scholars in this area is Dennis Gouran, who has devoted more than 30 years to studying small group decision making. Gouran's research and teaching concentrate on enhancing the rationality of group decision making. He has identified communication tendencies that both foster and interfere with rational decision making, and his work provides guidance to teams that want to make effective decisions (Gouran, 1982).

Other scholars of small group communication have concentrated on communication processes that transform a collection of individuals into a cohesive group. In this area, the work of Ernest Bormann and his associates is particularly important (Bormann, 1975; Bormann, Putnam, & Pratt, 1978). According to this line of study, group cohesion and identity often crystallize through **fantasy themes,** which are chains of ideas that spin out in a group and capture its social and task themes. The talk of politicians often suggests they view their parties as warring opponents. When politicians speak of "attacking" the other side's plan, "defending" their agenda, and "refusing to give ground," they create a fantasy chain that defines the parties as warring factions. Fantasy themes frame how group members think about what they are doing and how they define success. A compromise is less attractive if parties define themselves as at war where only one side wins than if they define themselves as collaborating to create resolutions that work for everyone.

Public Communication

Although public speaking no longer defines the scope of the field, it remains an important branch of communication theory, research, and practice. Even though most of us may not seek careers that involve frequent formal speaking, all of us will have opportunities to speak to others. My editor speaks to his sales representatives to explain what his books are about and how to spotlight important features to faculty and students. I recently coached my doctor who was asked to address her colleagues on an important development in treatment of renal disease. My sister relies on public speaking skills when she's trying cases in court and when she's persuading companies to support the battered women's center in Atlanta, Georgia. My plumber talks with his staff about new developments in plumbing and new regulations that affect what they do. He once told me that the main reason his business has grown while others went under is that he takes time to develop good talks to inform his staff. My editor, doctor, sister, and plumber don't consider themselves public speakers, but public speaking is a part of their lives, and doing it effectively is important to their success.

Scholars of public communication focus on the related subjects of critical evaluation of speeches and principles for speaking effectively. Rhetorical critics study important communication events such as the Reverend Martin Luther King, Jr.'s "I Have a Dream" speech and public arguments for and against reproductive freedom. Critics often take a role in civic life by evaluating political debates and speeches to help voters understand how well candidates support their positions and respond to challenges from opponents.

Scholars of public communication are also interested in discovering and teaching principles of effective public speaking. By now we have learned a great deal about what makes speakers seem credible to listeners and how credibility affects persuasion. Research has also enlightened us about the kinds of argument, methods of organizing ideas, and forms of proof that listeners find effective. If Cass had studied this body of research, she would glean useful guidelines for preparing her remarks for the residence hall association.

Media and New Technologies of Communication

One of the most exciting areas of the modern field of communication is media and new technologies. For some time, communication scholars have studied mediated communication such as films, radio, and television. From substantial research, we understand a great deal about how different media work and how they represent and reproduce cultural values. For instance, our culture's ideal for women centers on youth and beauty. This feminine ideal is perpetuated by media practices such as having young and beautiful women as news reporters and anchors. In fact, several women who crossed the forbidden age line of mid-thirties were fired and replaced by younger women. Media also reinforce cultural stereotypes about race and ethnicity. For example, African Americans are most often cast in supporting roles, rather than principal roles. In addition, black males are frequently portrayed as lazy and unlawful and are typically cast as athletes or entertainers (Evans, 1993; "Sights, Sounds, and Stereotypes," 1992). Hispanics and Asians seldom appear in prime time; when they do, it is usually as villains or criminals (Lichter, Lichter, Rothman, & Amundson, 1987). Robert Entman (1994), a communication professor at Northwestern University, points out that major networks are more likely to show black defendants in mug shots without names, but to offer multiple pictures and names of white defendants. This difference may contribute to perceptions of blacks as an undifferentiated group.

Reflection

Do media have any responsibility not to foster stereotypes of social groups?

To the extent that media shape our understandings of ourselves and our society, misrepresentations can be dangerous. Communication scholars who study media heighten our awareness of how they inform and entertain us, as well as how they sometimes distort reality. In Chapters 10 and 11, we'll explore theories that describe and criticize the ways that mass communication functions and affects us.

A more recent focus in the area of media is new and converging technologies of communication. We are in the midst of a technological revolution, which provides us with the means to communicate in more and more ways, faster and faster, with greater and greater numbers of people throughout the world. How do new technologies and the accelerated pace of interaction influence how we think, work, and form relationships? Some scholars caution that new technologies might undermine the kind of human community formed through face-to-face talk (Hyde, 1995), whereas others celebrate the increased social contact and productivity technology allows (Lea & Spears, 1995). Still others claim that new communication technologies will fundamentally transform how we think and process information (Chesebro, 1995a).

Reflection

To what extent do media affect the content, as well as the form, of communication?

The verdict on media's effects is not in and will not be for some time. Meanwhile, all of us struggle to keep up with our increasingly technological world. Ten years ago, students typed papers on type-writers. Today, any student without access to a computer is at an academic disadvantage. Five years ago, we relied on letters and phone calls to communicate across distance. Today, FedEx, faxes, and electronic mail make it possible for us to communicate almost immediately with people on the other side of the world. Whereas previous generations of students had to physically go to libraries to conduct research, today's students often rely on the Internet and World Wide Web to find and read reference works. Communication scholars will continue to study whether emerging technologies merely alter how we communicate or whether they actually change how we think about interaction and the human connections we build.

Organizational Communication

Communication in organizations is another growing area of interest in the field of communication. As we saw earlier in this chapter, communication skills facilitate advancement in most careers. Communication scholars have identified verbal and nonverbal communication skills that enhance professional success and have traced the impact of various kinds of communication on morale, productivity, and commitment in organizations. For many years, scholars of organizational communication have studied aspects of work life such as interviewing, organizational structure, leadership, and decision making.

In addition to continuing to study these topics, organizational scholars have begun to focus substantial attention on organizational culture and personal relationships in professional settings. **Organizational culture** refers to understandings about identity and codes of thought and action that are shared by members of an organization.

Some organizations think of themselves as families. This understanding of who they are is reflected in rules for how to interact with each other and how to work together.

Another example of how organizational culture affects patterns of work life comes from the tragic Colorado wildfire in July of 1994, in which 14 firefighters lost their lives. A detailed investigation revealed that a primary contributor to the loss of lives was a "can do" culture among firefighters. Trained to believe they can do what others cannot and that they can perform heroic feats, the firefighters didn't observe known and essential safety regulations. Ironically, the can do culture essential for such a dangerous job also led to disregard for important cautions and the subsequent loss of 14 lives.

Studies of organizational culture also shed light on the continuing problem of sexual harassment. In many institutions, there is a culture that normalizes sexist comments and treatment of women as sex objects. Mary Strine (1992), a critical scholar in communication, has shown how some institutions trivialize complaints about sexual harassment and sustain abusive environments by adopting a culture that says "This is how we do things around here." Other communication scholars have identified ways that organizational cultures allow or discourage sexual harassment (Bingham, 1994; Conrad, 1995; Taylor & Conrad, 1992).

Another area of increasing interest for organizational scholars is personal relationships among co-workers. As we expand the hours we spend on the job, it is natural for personal relationships among co-workers to increase. Further, since the majority of women work full- or part-time today, there is increased opportunity for romantic and sexual relationships to unfold. Obviously, this adds both interest and complications to life in organizations.

In one excellent example of a study in the area of personal relationships among co-workers, communication scholar Ted Zorn (1995) reports on "bosses and buddies"—people involved in friendships in which one friend is the boss of the other. Zorn discovered a number of ways people cope with the often contradictory rules for communication between friends and between superiors and subordinates. He also points out both potential values and hazards of friendships in which one person has formal power over another.

Personal relations on the job also require that women and men learn to understand each other's language. In a number of ways, women and men communicate differently, and they frequently misunderstand one another (Wood, 1993c,d, 1994a, 1995b, 1996a). For example, women tend to make more "listening noises" such as "um," "uh huh," and "go on" than men. If men don't make such noises when listening to women colleagues, the women may think the men aren't paying attention. Conversely, men are likely to misinterpret the listening noises women make as signals of agreement, rather than indicators of interest. Such misunderstandings can strain professional relations and performance. Some scholars of organizational communication study and conduct workshops on effective communication between the sexes (Murphy & Zorn, 1996).

Try it out   Interview a professional in the field you plan to enter to discover what kinds of communication perspectives and skills she or he thinks are most important for success. Which of the perspectives and skills do you already have? Which ones should you learn more about? How can you use this book and the course it accompanies to develop the understandings of communication that will help you be effective in your career?

Intercultural Communication

Finally, intercultural communication is an important focus of research, teaching, and training. **Intercultural communication** refers to communication between people from different cultures, including distinct cultures within a single country. Although intercultural communication is not a new area of study, it is one whose importance has grown in recent years. Demographic shifts in the last decade have enlarged the diversity that has always marked life in the United States.

Increasing numbers of Asians, Indians, Latinas and Latinos, and people of other nations are immigrating to the United States and making their homes here. With them they bring cultural values and styles of communicating that differ from those of citizens whose heritage is European American. Understanding different modes of verbal and nonverbal communication can help us learn how to live, socialize, and work effectively with an ever-increasing range of people.

Scholars of intercultural communication increase awareness of different groups' communication goals, styles, and meanings. For example, a Taiwanese woman in one of my graduate classes seldom spoke up and wouldn't enter the heated debates that characterize good graduate classes. One day after class I encouraged Mei-Ling to argue for her ideas when others challenged them. She replied she could not be so impolite. In her culture, unlike in the West, it is disrespectful to argue with others or to assert oneself. I would have been mistaken to interpret her deference as lack of confidence or involvement in the class.

Reflection

If communication differs in different cultures, can we have universal criteria for effectiveness in communication?

A particularly important recent trend in the area of intercultural communication is research on different communication cultures within a single society. Cultural differences are easy to perceive in communication between a Nepali and a Canadian. Less obvious are cultural differences in communication between people who speak the "same" language. Within the United States, there are distinct communication cultures based on race, gender, affectional preference, and ethnicity.

Two of the leading writers about intercultural communication are Larry Samovar and Richard Porter (1994). Their book, *Intercultural Communication,* reveals distinctive styles of communication for women, men, blacks, whites, Native Americans, gays, individuals with disabilities, and other groups in our country. For example, women more than men tend to disclose personal information and to engage in emotionally expressive talk in their friendships (Wood, 1993c, 1994a,d). African Americans belong to a communication culture that encourages dramatic talk, rappin', verbal duels, and signifying (indirect comments), which have no equivalents in Caucasian speech communities (Houston & Wood, 1996). Recognizing and respecting different communication cultures increases effectiveness in a pluralistic society.

Reflection

How do culture and communication shape one another?

After reading about the major branches of the modern field of communication, you might think that the field is made up of a collection of separate and unrelated areas of interest. Actually, this isn't at all the case. The overall field of communication is unified by a persisting interest in language, nonverbal behavior, and the process by which we construct meaning for ourselves and our activities.

The Heart of Communication Research

Seemingly disparate areas such as intrapersonal, organizational, and relational communication are unified by central concerns with symbolic activities and meaning. These two themes underlie research and teaching in different branches of the communication field.

Symbolic Activities

Symbols are the basis of language, thinking, and much of our nonverbal behavior. You may recall that we defined symbols as arbitrary, ambiguous, and abstract representations of other phenomena. For instance, a wedding band is a symbol of marriage, the name *Julia* is a symbol for me, a smile is a symbol of friendliness, and the word *cat* is a symbol for one species of animal. Symbols represent, or stand for, other things, but they are not the things for which they stand. In other words, a map represents a territory, but it isn't itself the territory.

Symbols are abstract, which means they aren't concrete or tangible. On a map, the term *New York* is not the concrete state, but it is an abstract representation of that state. Symbols are also arbitrary, which means they have no intrinsic, or natural, relation to what they represent. There's no natural reason to call one of our northeastern states New York; we could just as easily call it Oregon or Kalamazoo. Similarly, there's no necessary connection between your name and the person you are and no intrinsic reason why shaking hands is a form of greeting in the United States and kissing cheeks is a form of greeting in other countries. Symbols are arbitrary conventions that allow us to agree on what things mean. Finally, symbols are ambiguous, which means their meaning is less than clear-cut. Imagine you ask a friend if a course in Third World film is tough. *Tough* might mean the course is challenging, the tests are demanding, a major paper is required, or the course is graded on a strict bell curve. What *tough* means is not transparent. We have to think about the word and assign meaning to it.

Symbols allow us to name experiences, which is a primary way we give meaning to our lives (Wood, 1992a). It's hard to think about and understand things we cannot name. For instance, prior to the 1970s, there was no name for unwanted and unwelcome sexual attention. A number of people, especially women, were subjected to sexist comments, demeaning suggestions, unwanted touching, and overt propositions for sexual activity. However, there was no term to name what was happening, so victims of unwelcome sexual attention tended to think "He went too far," or "What have I done to invite this?" (Wood, 1992b). When the term *sexual harassment* was coined, victims had a socially recognized label for their experiences, one that blamed the harasser. The social reality of sexual harassment has been further established as a result of media's use of the term and the showcasing of the Hill–Thomas hearings. Similarly, in the 1970s, we didn't have the terms *date rape* or *marital rape,* though dates and wives were sometimes forced to have sex with their partners. Language gives social reality to experiences. In addition, language allows us to reflect in ways we cannot without words.

Because we humans are symbol users, we are not confined to the concrete world of the here and now. Symbols make it possible to call up memories and to dream of the future. We cast ourselves into real and possible futures when we speak about "after I graduate," "next summer," and "when I win the lottery." We revisit former moments when we talk about "yesterday" and "when I was a child." Symbols enable us to live continuously in all three dimensions of time and to do so simultaneously so that past and future infuse the present (Dixson & Duck, 1993).

Symbols also allow us to reflect on ourselves and to monitor our own activities. Many philosophers and academics claim that humans are the only species capable of self-reflection. We are able to think about who we are, to have a self-concept, and to view ourselves and our activities from the perspectives of others. Feelings such as shame and pride, self-pity and self-confidence are possible because we can reflect on ourselves. Symbolic interactionism, a theory we'll consider in Chapter 5, concentrates on explaining the relationships between symbols and self-identity.

Monitoring is observing and managing our own thoughts, feelings, and actions. As you sit in class, your mind wanders, you realize the teacher could think you're not paying attention, and you refocus your eyes on her or him and nod understanding. This is an example of monitoring. You looked at how you were acting and decided to adjust your behaviors to project the image you wanted—in this case, an attentive student. We monitor all the time: reminding ourselves not to interrupt, prodding ourselves to be more assertive, warning ourselves not to raise our voices, checking an impulse to criticize a friend, suppressing a look of disapproval or a snicker. We audit our communication continuously and adjust it so that we can be more effective. Monitoring is possible because we think symbolically and point out our behaviors to ourselves, reflect on them, and modify them as appropriate.

Finally, symbols allow us to share ideas and feelings with others. Because symbols provide names for things, we can share things with others that they have not directly experienced. Words allow us to tell others about events and people in our lives and to express how we feel

"Learn to communicate, Marmaduke...just 'woof, woof, woof' me for the remote."

about them. A friend may not know your parents, but she or he can understand how you feel about them if you explain what happens between you and your parents and how you feel. If we couldn't communicate, each of us would have our own private experiences, but we'd have no way to share them with others. Thus, we couldn't build many of the connections that allow people to understand and care about one another.

Reflection

Can you think about something without relying on symbols?

Whether we are interested in intrapersonal, group, organizational, or intercultural communication, symbols are always central to what happens. Thus, symbols and the mental activities they allow are a unifying focus of study and teaching about all forms of communication. Symbolic interaction theory, dramatism, and semantics are theories we'll study that focus especially on symbols as an essential foundation of meaning.

Meaning

Closely related to the communication field's focus on symbols is its persisting concern with **meaning.** Meaning is significance that is conferred on experiences and phenomena. The human world is one of meaning. We don't simply exist, eat, drink, sleep, and go through motions. Instead, we imbue every aspect of our lives with significance, or meaning. When I fill my cat Scrambles's dish, she eats her food and then goes about her feline adventures. For her, eating is a necessary and enjoyable activity, but not one that has layers of meaning beyond consuming food.

For humans, however, food and the activity of eating are layered with significance. Food often symbolizes special events or commitments. For example, kosher products reflect commitment to Jewish heritage, eating turkey with all the trimmings is a widely followed Thanksgiving ritual in the United States (though vegetarians have to generate alternative ways to symbolize the holiday), eggnog is a Christmas tradition, and Mandel Brot is a Hanukkah staple. Birthday cakes celebrate an individual, and we may fix special meals to express love for others.

Some families consider meals the time when they come together and share their days, while in other families meals are battlefields where family tensions are played out. A meal can be a way to conduct business (power lunches, for instance), or a romantic engagement (candles, wine), or a personal struggle to stick to a diet, or an excuse to spend 2 hours talking with a friend. Unlike Scrambles, for us the activity of eating takes on significance as a result of how we define what we are doing and what it means.

Because we are symbol users, we actively interpret events, situations, experiences, and relationships. Many communication theorists argue that humans don't react passively or unthinkingly to our worlds, but we proactively construct its meanings (Wood, 1992a, 1995b). Symbols are the foundation of meaning because they enable us to name, evaluate, reflect, and share experiences, ideas, and feelings. Using symbols, we can construct organized systems (called schema) for perceiving and making sense of our experiences. In the process of communicating with others we define our relationships: Do we have a friendship or something more? How serious are we? Is this conflict irresolvable or can we work it out and stay together?

To study communication, then, is to study how we create meaning in our lives. Communication scholars see relationships, groups, cultures, media, and organizations as human constructions that we create and assign meaning to in the process of interaction (Andersen, 1993; Wood, 1992a, 1995b). Leslie Baxter (1987, p. 262) says that "relationships can be regarded as webs of significance" spun as partners communicate. In Chapter 5, we'll look at three theories that focus specifically on communication and meaning, and we'll also see attention to meaning in many of the theories covered in other chapters.

 areers in Communication

Studying communication is good preparation for a wide array of careers. As we've seen, most professions require understanding of communication and good communication skills. In addition, there are a number of careers for people whose primary backgrounds and interests are in communication.

Research

Communication research is a vital and growing field of work. A great deal of study is conducted by academics who combine teaching and research in faculty careers. In this book, you'll learn a good deal about how academic research is designed and conducted, as well as about what we learn from doing it.

Businesses also conduct research to determine how people respond to different kinds of advertisements, logos, and even labels for products. Before naming a new cereal or beer, companies extensively test market reaction to various names. Their bottom line depends on understanding how customers will interpret different communication strategies. In addition, businesses research the audiences reached by different media such as newspapers, magazines, radio, and television. Individuals who understand communication and who have research skills may pursue careers in communication research.

Public Relations and Advertising

Communication specialists are also in demand for careers in advertising and corporate public relations. Professionals who understand how communication works can use their knowledge to help companies develop effective strategies for media advertising. Expertise in communication also allows individuals to pursue careers in public relations in which the "product" to be advertised is a particular company or corporation. In recent years we've heard a great deal about the dangers of silicone breast implants. Dow-Corning was one of the major manufacturers of silicone breast implants, and the company has engaged in a vigorous media effort to redeem its image as a careful company that consumers can trust. In 1994, Intel's much-touted pentium chip was revealed to have a defect. To control the damage, Intel ran full-page ads in major newspapers assuring customers that it stood behind its product and would make repairs or exchanges for any pentium-powered computers. The corporate image of Intel was restored because an event that could have impugned the company's integrity was managed well. Public relations professionals help companies define their images and protect them when there are problems.

Education

Teaching others about communication is another exciting career path for individuals with extensive backgrounds in the field. Clearly, I am biased toward this profession, since I've had a 20-year love affair with teaching communication. I find nothing more exciting than opening students' eyes to the power of communication and working with them to improve their skills. Across the nation there are growing opportunities for communication teachers at all levels. There are communication classes and often whole curricula in secondary schools, junior colleges, colleges, universities, technical schools, and community colleges.

The level at which a person is qualified to teach depends on how extensively she or he has pursued the study of communication. Generally, a B.A. in communication education plus certification by the Board of Education are required to teach in elementary and secondary schools. A master's degree in communication qualifies a person to teach at community colleges, technical schools, and some junior colleges and colleges. The Ph.D., or doctoral degree, in communication is generally required for a career in university education, although some universities offer short-term positions to individuals with master's degrees.

Although generalists are typically preferred for many teaching jobs, at the university level individuals can focus on areas of communication that particularly interest them. For instance, my research and teaching focus on gender and communication and on communication in personal relationships. My partner, who is also on the faculty in my department, specializes in environmental advocacy and social movements. Other faculty members concentrate in areas such as oral traditions, intercultural communication, family communication, organizational dynamics, performance of literature, and symbolic development in children.

Not all communication educators make their homes in academic departments of communication. In recent years, more and more individuals with advanced degrees in communication have taken positions in medical schools and business schools. Good doctors have not only specialized medical knowledge, but also good communication skills. They know how to listen sensitively to patients, how to explain complex problems and procedures, and how to provide comfort, reassurance, and motivation. Similarly, good businesspeople not only know their business, but also know how to explain it to others, how to present themselves and their company or product favorably, and so on. Because communication is essential for doctors and businesspeople, increasing numbers of medical and business schools are creating permanent positions for communication specialists.

Consulting

Consulting is another field that increasingly welcomes individuals with backgrounds in communication. Businesses want to train employees in effective group communication skills, interview techniques, and interpersonal interaction. Some large corporations such as IBM have entire departments devoted to training and development. Individuals with communication backgrounds often join these departments and work with the corporation to design and teach courses or workshops that enhance employees' communication skills.

In addition, communication specialists may join or form freelance consulting firms, which offer to provide particular kinds of communication education to a variety of businesses. One of my colleagues consults with corporations across the country, training men and women in how to understand each other's language and work together effectively. Another of my colleagues consults with organizations to help them develop work teams that interact effectively. Other communication specialists work with politicians to improve their presentational style and sometimes to write their speeches.

I consult with attorneys on cases of sexual harassment and sex discrimination. I help attorneys understand how particular communication patterns and actions create hostile, harassing environments, and I collaborate with them to develop trial strategy. In addition, I sometimes testify as an expert witness on whether sexual harassment or sex discrimination occurred. Other communication specialists work with attorneys to make jury selections and to advise about dress and nonverbal behaviors that might affect jurors' perceptions.

Human Relations and Management

Because communication is the foundation of human relations, it's no surprise that many communication specialists build careers in human development or human relations departments of corporations. Individuals with solid understandings of communication and good personal communication skills are effective in careers such as personnel, grievance management, customer relations, and development and fund raising. In each of these areas, communication skills are the primary requirements.

For the same reason, communication degrees may open the door to careers in management. The most important qualifications for successful managers are not technical skills, but abilities to interact with others and to communicate effectively. Good managers are skilled in listening, expressing their ideas, managing conflict constructively, creating supportive work environments, team building, and balancing task and interpersonal concerns in dealings with subordinates and peers. These are all communication skills, so specializing in this field provides a firm foundation for a career in management.

ummary

In this chapter, we've taken a first look at the field of human communication. We discussed the pervasiveness of communication in our lives and the value of theory in helping us understand how communication works and how we can be effective in our own communicative endeavors. We also explored the personal, relationship, professional, and cultural values of communication. Third, we surveyed the breadth of the communication field, noting that it ranges from intrapersonal to public and organizational to intercultural.

What holds these seemingly diverse areas of study together is abiding interest in symbolic activities and meanings, which together form the foundation of personal, interpersonal, and social life. Finally, we considered some of the many career opportunities open to individuals who choose to specialize in communication. The modern field of communication is growing, and it offers an array of exciting career paths.

Chapter Two

Understanding Communication Theories

Recently, I visited my 5-year-old niece, Michelle. One morning she brought me an apple and then asked if she could have the bracelet I was wearing. I asked her if she thought giving me the apple would make me give her my bracelet. With childlike candor, she replied "yes."

———

Two years ago my partner, Robbie, was elected president of the national Sierra Club. His responsibilities as president require him to travel much of the time, so we are separated more than we typically have been in our 22 years of marriage. In the past, we've tended to work on our individual projects on weekends, but now we usually spend time together any weekend he is home.

———

In 1993, I served as an expert witness in a sexual harassment trial. The facts of the case were ambiguous: There had definitely been some sexist treatment of a woman hired to lead an organization, but whether that explained her dismissal was unclear. Jennifer, the attorney with whom I consulted, wove all of the evidence and known facts into a coherent story that painted her client as the victim of a systematic campaign of sexual harassment. Opposing counsel offered other explanations of individual pieces of evidence, but he didn't create an overall story that convincingly offered a counter-explanation. We won the case. Later, Jennifer told me that she always prepared her closing statements in cases in the form of a story. She said, "You have to give jurors an account that makes sense and holds together; whichever attorney creates the better story is going to win."

43

Each of these situations involves communication theory. Each situation also shows that people act on theories, often without realizing it, in their everyday lives. Michelle's strategy for getting my bracelet reflects exchange theory, which claims that people like equal rewards in relationships. Although she didn't realize she was using a theory, Michelle nevertheless applied the principles of exchange when she reasoned that giving me an apple might induce me to give her my bracelet (I did).

The changes in my relationship with Robbie can be explained by dialectical theory, which asserts that people have needs both for connection or closeness and for distance or autonomy. As long as Robbie and I lived together most of the time, our connection needs were satisfied by our normal daily interaction. Once his work took him away from our home, however, our needs for connecting were unsatisfied, and we had to generate other ways to be together.

The attorney with whom I consulted relied on narrative theory, which maintains that human beings have a natural capacity to tell and listen to stories. In other words, we think in terms of characters, settings, plots, and motives. Although Jennifer had not formally studied narrative theory, she had learned from experience that jurors were most persuaded by a good story that provided a coherent explanation for the evidence and what happened in a case.

Jennifer, Michelle, Robbie, and I use communication theories in our daily lives. You also use communication theories, whether or not you realize it. All of us are everyday theorists. This means that in taking a course in theories, you are not studying something that is removed from your normal life. The formal study of theory allows you to be more careful and effective in your own theorizing. As we'll see in this and later chapters, theories are directly relevant to practical life. Theories guide how we act, respond to others, and make sense of our experiences.

In this chapter, we'll explore the nature of theorizing. We'll ask what theories do, why they matter, and how we can use them in our lives. In addition, we'll consider how to evaluate the worth of theories. By the time you have completed this chapter, you should have a good, basic understanding of what theories are, what they do, and how to judge them. This will provide you with a firm foundation for reading Chapters 4–11, in which we consider specific communication theories.

The Goals of Theory

The simplest way to define theories is to say that they are attempts to make sense of things. A **theory** offers an account of what something is, how it works, what it produces or causes to happen, and what should be the case. Put another way, theories are human constructions—symbolic ways we represent phenomena. The fact that theories are human constructions implies that they are not objective descriptions of reality, nor are they necessarily true. Instead, theories represent points of view. As we'll see, however, not all points of view are equally sound. We'll discuss ways to evaluate the quality of various theoretical points of view.

Theories pursue one or more of four basic goals: description, explanation, prediction or understanding, and reform. We'll consider each of these objectives and see how it operates in the context of particular theories.

Description: What Is It?

The foundation of a theory is **description,** which is a process of using symbols to represent phenomena. Before we can figure out how something works, we must first describe what it is. Thus, the first task in building a theory is to identify features of some phenomenon and describe any variations in them. Descriptions, of course, are not neutral reflections of some objective reality. They are necessarily subjective, since what a theorist perceives and emphasizes is affected by personal background, sensory skills, values, and so forth. Ecologists identify important features of environments and describe how they may vary. For example, a wetlands area includes marshes and the vegetation and animal life supported by the marshy environment. The marshes and the life they support vary in response to rainfall, erosion, and weather. Geneticists have identified 23 pairs of chromosomes as the basis of individual characteristics. Chromosomes vary in response to the chromosomal structure of parents and other factors.

Like environmental scientists and geneticists, communication theorists begin by identifying key features of communication and describing how those features may vary. For example, elsewhere (Wood, 1995b) I have described personal relationships as made up of five features: individuals, social contexts, communication, relational culture (the private world of intimates), and time. Each feature in this model of relationships affects all others. Thus, when Robbie travels frequently and meets new people, communication between us changes. As Robbie's involvement with the Sierra Club accelerates, we place greater emphasis on time together than when we were continuously together in the same place.

In the 1940s, Claude Shannon and Warren Weaver developed one of the earliest models of the communication process. At the time Shannon and Weaver were working on their theory, the United States was captivated by scientific ideas in general and by mechanical and technical explanations in particular. We would expect a theory developed in this historical context to emphasize information flow and accuracy. That is precisely what the Shannon and Weaver model of communication did.

Claude Shannon was a research scientist who worked for Bell Telephone, and Warren Weaver was a member of the Rockefeller Foundation and the Sloan–Kettering Institute on Cancer Research. With Shannon working out the mathematics behind the theory and Weaver in charge of translating it into understandable language, the two men developed a model that described what happens when people communicate. They described communication as the flow of information

The Shannon—Weaver Model of Communication

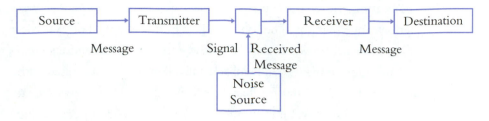

from one person's mind (a source) to the mind of another person (a destination). The person who is a source creates a message and transmits it by voice or with the aid of a telephone or microphone or other transmitting equipment. The message is then received by an ear or a piece of receiving equipment, and it is interpreted by the person who is a destination. As messages move from source to destination, there is a potential of loss of information due to noise in the communication system. Noise could be static on phone lines, competing sounds such as television or stereo, or distractions such as smoke or odors in the environment of one or both communicators.

Reflection

What do you perceive as the strengths and limitations of Shannon and Weaver's description of the communication process?

Since 1949, when Shannon and Weaver published their comprehensive statement on the information theory of communication, there have been many criticisms. One of the strongest indictments is that this model misrepresents communication by portraying it as a one-way process in which information flows in a linear sequence from a source to a receiver. The model also labels each communicator as either a sender or a receiver, instead of acknowledging that all communicators are both senders and receivers. When Sharon talks with Molefe, he smiles, frowns, wrinkles his brow, and nods. All of these nonverbal messages are communication. When Michelle is bargaining with me for my bracelet, she is watching my nonverbal behaviors as she speaks, and I am sending her cues as I listen.

In 1967, Norbert Weiner, an MIT scientist, published a book that refined Shannon and Weaver's model. Weiner added two new features to the description of communication his predecessors had developed.

First, he emphasized feedback as an essential feature of effective communication. In Weiner's view, feedback was information about past performance that could be used to adjust future activity. For example, if I wrinkle my brow and shake my head when Robbie mentions a trip he's planning to make, that feedback will tell him I'm not pleased with his plan. Based on my feedback, he may adjust what he says next: Perhaps he'll suggest I join him for the trip, propose doing something together before he leaves, or explain why it is important for him to make this particular trip.

Weiner's second addition to the information model of communication was an emphasis on ethics. He was very concerned that technological systems of communication could be used to control and manipulate human beings, and he saw this as undesirable. In his book *The Human Use of Human Beings* (1967), Weiner cautioned that technical systems of communication should be used to control only things, not people.

A second criticism of the Shannon–Weaver model, one that hasn't been resolved by later research, is that a communication theory that focuses only on information overlooks important dimensions of human communication. Shannon and Weaver's theory doesn't describe or help us understand feelings, motives, needs, history, and other factors that affect how we communicate and how we interpret the communication of others. The fact that Shannon and Weaver's research was funded by Bell Telephone labs may explain the mechanical focus of their theory. The model they offer represents telephone communication rather well. What is more debatable is whether it offers a useful description of other kinds of communication, such as romantic interaction, team building, mass media, and conflict management.

The Shannon–Weaver model of communication is one of many ways to describe the features of communication. Other theories that we will encounter later provide alternative descriptions of what happens when people interact. For example, Leslie Baxter's theory of relational dialectics, which we'll discuss in Chapter 7, offers a far more dynamic and interactive view of communication than the Shannon and Weaver model does. Ethical aspects and uses of communication are of primary concern in critical theories, which are covered in Chapter 11. Although theorists offer different descriptions of what communication is, all theories begin with a description of features of communication and how they vary.

Explanation

The second objective of theory is **explanation,** which is an effort to clarify how and why something works. After describing what makes up communication, a theorist turns to the question of how the parts interact and work together. An ecologist might explain how commercial development causes specific damage to wetlands environments. A geneticist might explain how certain drugs affect chromosomal structure in developing fetuses. And a communication theorist wants to explain why communication works as it does: Why does Michelle's strategy to get my bracelet succeed or fail? Why and how does Robbie's travel affect communication between us? Why are juries persuaded by a good story?

Mary Lund (1985) wanted to explain what caused commitment between romantic partners. Previous research had focused on love as the basis of enduring relationships, and love was viewed as the result of receiving rewards in a relationship. Thus, the common belief was that we love and stay with people who reward us with positive experiences, support, and other things we value. Lund, however, thought that love might not be the real glue of romantic relationships. In a sophisticated study, Lund discovered that commitment, which she defined as the intention to continue in a relationship, was a better predictor of whether a relationship lasts than was love. Lund also found that commitment is heightened by investments in a relationship, whereas simply receiving positive outcomes may not enhance commitment. To explain why relationships endure or fail to endure, Lund said that personal choices to invest time, energy, material resources, and feelings heighten commitment, and commitment, in turn, predicts relational continuity. Although love often accompanies commitment, it is not the basic glue of lasting intimacy.

Lund's theory offers a convincing explanation of why some relationships endure and others wither. In addition, Lund's work provides a good example of the practical value of theory. You can use her theory to analyze your own relationships: What have you invested? What has your partner invested? Have the two of you invested equally? Asking these questions is a way for you to apply one theory to your everyday life.

Reflection

How does Lund's theory add to your understanding of a current or past romantic relationship in your life?

Understanding, Prediction, and Control

A third objective of theories is to allow us to understand and/or predict and control what will happen. **Prediction** involves projecting what will happen to a phenomenon under specified conditions or when exposed to particular stimuli. **Control** is the use of explanations and predictions to govern what a phenomenon actually does. For some theorists, prediction and control are primary objectives. Scholars who adopt this position believe that a good theory is one that allows us to forecast what will happen under certain conditions and/or if certain other actions are taken. Prediction is related to control, since we can control outcomes if we can predict what causes them. An environmental scientist could construct a theory to predict what will happen in wetlands areas if commercial development takes place. Control would be exercised by allowing or precluding commercial development adjacent to wetlands areas. Similarly, geneticists have been able to predict the probability that children will have various genetic qualities (ranging from hair color to conditions such as Tay-Sachs) based on the genetic structure of their parents. Narrative theorists explain that stories are persuasive because they provide coherence and bring order to a jumbled set of facts.

Other scholars, often ones who define themselves as humanists, are less interested in prediction and control for their own sake. Instead, their goal is understanding, which may not require prediction and control. They evaluate the value of a theory by its ability to provide insight into why something is as it is or why certain things happen. For this group of scholars, a good theory is one that provides **understanding** or insight into a particular situation, process, or phenomenon. An environmental scientist would want to understand in detail how wetlands are altered by natural and human interventions. A geneticist would seek to understand why chromosomes occasionally deviate from the XY and XX structure for males and females, respectively; why do some individuals have XO, XYY, or XXY sex chromosomes, and what do these variations mean? A communication theorist might try to understand why humans seem to like fairness in their relationships and why they count certain exchanges as fair or unfair.

Different communication theories place more or less emphasis on the objectives of prediction, control, and understanding. For example, assume that two communication theorists are interested in the relationship between parent–child interaction and a child's self-concept. The scientific theorist who seeks prediction and control will be satisfied only if she or he discovers how to use communication to enhance self-concept. The humanistic theorist would more likely focus on understanding why some children develop more positive self-concepts than others and the subjective impact of differing self-concepts.

Reflection

What is your personal evaluation of the goals of prediction, control, and understanding?

The goals, though distinct, are not necessarily incompatible. Prediction and control, on the one hand, and understanding, on the other hand, can and often do overlap. Understanding how parents' communication affects children's views of themselves is the basis of being able to predict and control parent–child interactions. Conversely, even if understanding is all a theorist seeks, the understanding she or he gains may inform predictions.

Despite the fact that understanding and prediction often go hand in hand, the two goals are distinct. The goal of science is objective explanation, whereas humanism strives for subjective understanding of humans and how they operate. Although these distinct goals can go together, sometimes they do not. For example, suppose you notice that a friend of yours likes it when you talk about how she feels about a problem but doesn't appreciate it when you give her advice on how to solve a problem. Maybe you don't understand or even care why she likes to talk about feelings more than solutions to problems. Just being able to predict that she will be hurt if you offer solutions when she shares a problem with you is sufficient for you to interact effectively with her.

It's also possible to understand something that you cannot predict or control. For instance, I understand that Robbie and I have needs for both autonomy and togetherness, and I know we become uncomfortable whenever either need is unsatisfied. Even with this understanding, however, I can't always predict or control when we will seek more distance from each other or more intimacy with each other. Also, I understand the typical stages in children's development, so I have insight into some of Michelle's antics, but I have virtually no control over her developmental patterns.

Reform

A fourth goal of some theorizing is **reform,** or active pursuit of positive social change. At the outset of discussing this goal, we need to recognize that not all theorists and not all theories are interested in reform. Many theorists see description, explanation, prediction, and control as the proper goals of theorizing. These scholars believe theorists have no responsibility and possibly no right to try to change social behavior. It is primarily critical theories, which we'll explore in Chapter 11, that regard social change as a major goal of theorizing.

Reflection

Do you believe theorists should try to affect social policy and social life?

Emphasis on reform is a relatively new trend in theoretical scholarship. Traditionally, description, explanation, and prediction were the foci of theory. That is because historically, theorizing has been regarded as an objective process in which a theorist is and should be detached from what he or she studies. In recent years, however, a number of scholars have challenged these conventional views of theorizing. Many current scholars argue persuasively that theories should make a difference in the real world—that they should improve the lives of humans in concrete ways. In addition, many theorists today reject the idea that scholars are or should be removed from what they study. Instead, they believe that scholars are part of the world—not removed from it—and that their work is informed by who they are and the experiences they have had (Wood & Cox, 1993).

Critical theorists study how communication oppresses or liberates individuals and social groups. One impressive line of critical theorizing has come from feminist scholars who have shown how prevailing communication practices often silence women (Campbell, 1995; Foss & Foss, 1991; Kramarae, 1981). Another important focus of critical theorizing is the impact of the media in sustaining a social order that privileges some people and oppresses others (Hall, 1982, 1989). Other subjects of critical theory are communicative structures and practices that make sexual harassment seem normal and acceptable (Bingham, 1994; "Telling Our Stories," 1992) and that sustain patterns of abuse between intimates (West, 1995). In each case, the theories attempt to point the way to reform of social practices that are oppressive and sometimes deadly. Critical theorists believe that it is not enough to describe, explain, or even predict the incidence of wife battering. We also need to change the social and personal circumstances that allow it to happen.

It's important to realize that theorists interested in the goal of reform seldom dismiss the values of more traditional theoretical goals. Although critical theorists don't consider description, explanation, prediction, and control to be sufficient theoretical goals, they often find them necessary to their larger goal of inducing positive social change. After all, it's very difficult to reform a process unless we first understand what it is and how it works. It's also the case that reform can be thought of as a kind of control—an effort to influence what happens.

In summary, we've discussed four goals that may guide theory. The first two goals, description and explanation, are objectives of all theories, since understanding what communication is and how it works is the basis of any further theoretical work. A third goal of theory is either to predict and control communication or to understand communication. Although these two can overlap or work in tandem, they aren't synonymous or necessarily joined. We can understand phenomena that we can't predict or control, and we can predict and control phenomena that we don't fully understand. The final goal of theorizing, one that is most often sought by critical theorists, is social change or reform. This goal goes beyond prediction and even control to focus on theorists' responsibilities to better the world, an objective that requires a firm foundation of understanding.

You might stop for a moment and reflect on how you view different goals of theorizing. Do you value prediction and control more than understanding? Do you think theorists have a moral responsibility to be agents of positive social change? As you read later chapters in this book, you'll discover that how you answer these questions has considerable bearing on which theories you appreciate and which ones you find uninteresting or pointless.

Try it out

Now that you're familiar with the goals of theory, put them in practice by constructing a theory of your own. Develop a theory of communication in your communication theory classroom.

1. **Identify and describe the most important features of communication in your classroom.**

2. **Explain how the features interact and what happens as they do.**

3. **Offer an understanding of what the communication in your classroom means and how it is subjectively experienced by individuals in the class.**

4. **Predict what will happen in the future, and define ways you could control future events in the classroom.**

5. **Identify what should be the case for communication in your class. Are there any communication practices that oppress or discriminate against certain members of the class? If so, what needs to be changed to end or reduce the disadvantage? Does the communication that takes place support the goals of learning fully? If not, how should it be changed to improve learning?**

**S**tandards for Evaluating Theories

Now that we understand what theories are and the goals they pursue, we can turn to the question of how to evaluate theories. How can you tell whether a theory is good or bad, important or trivial, helpful or useless, sound or defective? Over the years, theorists have developed five criteria for evaluating theories.

Scope: How Much Does the Theory Describe and Explain?

The first question to ask about any theory is how large a scope it has. **Scope** refers to the range of phenomena a theory describes and explains. Theories vary in their scope, with some focusing on very narrow realms of communication and others advancing grand perspectives on all human communication. Symbolic interactionism and dramatism, which we discuss in Chapter 5, are among the broadest in the field of communication: Each of them claims to offer a theory of communication in general, that is, a range of diverse contexts. Interactional theory (Chapter 7), on the other hand, has a much more limited scope—it attempts to describe and explain only communication in the context of families. The theories discussed in Chapters 4–11 will give you opportunities to examine theories of diverse scope.

A good theory is one that provides a good description and explanation of events, processes, or behaviors. Although descriptions and explanations don't offer completely objective representations of phenomena, we can still assess the value of the particular representation of communication a theory offers. To do so, we ask how well a theory answers the *what* question (What is it?) and the *how* or *why* question (How does it operate? Why does this happen?).

In providing a description of a communication phenomenon, a theory clarifies what it considers essential in communication. For example, Shannon and Weaver's information model concentrated on features such as source, message, noise, and destination. Shannon and Weaver cast the spotlight on only a few of the many factors that are part of communication and that affect how it works. In so doing, they directed our attention to those features and not others. My model of personal relationships focuses attention on five features: individuals, social systems, communication, relational culture, and time. It does not emphasize other aspects of relationships such as partners' feelings or rewards and costs.

All theories are partial in focusing on some aspects and not others of a phenomenon. The question for the critic is whether the features a theorist highlights are the most important ones. As we saw, Shannon and Weaver's model was criticized for not including feedback and ethical considerations that are part of communication. If you, like Norbert Weiner, believe that feedback and ethical implications are important in communication, then you, too, would judge Shannon and Weaver's description of communication as inadequate.

We also evaluate theories by how well they explain communication. Generally, a theory that provides incomplete description will be weak in its explanatory power. A theory that rests on a good descriptive base, however, may or may not result in a satisfying explanation. A good explanation requires not only that we understand what's involved in communication, but also that we know how the parts work together and what results follow from how they interact.

Theorists use two broad types of explanations. One relies on universal laws to explain why things happen. **Laws-based explanations** argue that anytime x happens, y will follow; or x and y are always related. This form of explanation seeks to discover universal laws that explain human communication in a wide range of situations. For example, one communication theory claims that uncertainty (not knowing what is happening in a relationship) fosters increased communication (efforts to figure out what is happening). This is a law about communication.

Reprinted by permission of Levin Represents.

Laws-based explanations may be either **causal** or **correlational.** A causal law states that x causes y or y happens because of x. For example, we might say uncertainty causes communication. A correlational claim, on the other hand, says only that two things go together, but does not assert that one causes the other. We might note, for instance, that uncertainty and increases in communication go together. It's possible that uncertainty actually causes communication; alternatively, it's possible that uncertainty causes some other factor (interest, curiosity), which, in turn, results in increased communication. It is also possible that one or more other factors cause both uncertainty and communication—different cultural backgrounds, for example, might increase both uncertainty in interaction and efforts to communicate. If two things go together but the cause is unclear, then the relationship between the two things is correlational. If it can be demonstrated that one thing directly causes another, then the relationship is causal.

In *The Structure of Scientific Revolutions* (1970), a highly influential book on the nature of theory, Thomas Kuhn contended that a mature science has a universal paradigm, theory, or model that explains its phenomena. For many years, communication scholars, as well as academics in other fields, tried to achieve the universal theories that Kuhn claimed were the earmark of a mature science. However, their attempts to produce universal laws of communication failed. It seems that communication, like other human activities, is so complex and varies so greatly across situations that it cannot be covered by universal laws.

A second form of explanation identifies rules that explain why people in particular circumstances communicate as they do and why certain consequences follow. **Rules-based explanations** do not claim to offer any universal laws about human communication. Instead, they aim to articulate the patterns that describe and explain what happens in a specific type of communication situation or relationship. Thus, rules have a more restricted scope than laws. For example, there are rules (or regularities) that friends follow in their communication, but these rules may not surface in communication between members of work teams.

Don't make the mistake of thinking that rules explanations are entirely idiosyncratic and can only account for what happens in a single case. Therapists may be concerned only with understanding and helping a particular client, but theorists have broader aims. A theorist who relies on rules-based explanations attempts to explain how communication operates in a defined sphere of activity. For example, theorists of group decision making don't claim that the communication rules in groups necessarily extend to public speaking situations. They do, however, believe that there are some communication rules common to how most groups function. Similarly, theories of communication between romantic partners may not tell us a great deal about political rallies and speeches.

Reflection

Can you state some laws of human communication that are universal?

When evaluating how well a theory explains communication, we should ask whether it provides an account that incorporates all known data and that makes sense. One basic question to ask about any theory is this: Does it make sense? A good theory should make sense and provide a reasonable account of all known data.

Testability: Is It Testable?

A second important criterion for evaluating theories is **testability,** which asks whether the claims advanced by a theory can be investigated to determine whether they are accurate or not. If a theoretical claim or prediction is faulty, we should have a way to detect this. We should also be able to verify theoretical predictions that are correct. If we can't test a theory, we can rely only on faith, guesswork, or personal experience to evaluate its accuracy.

A testable theory is clearly and specifically stated. For example, we can test the proposition that increased communication always accompanies uncertainty. The accuracy of the theory can be tested by conducting observations or experiments to determine whether communication always follows uncertainty and whether increased communication ever occurs when uncertainty isn't present. On the other hand, it would be difficult to test the proposition that honesty is a good thing in relationships. We'd have trouble testing this claim because we don't have a precise definition of "a good thing"—is it something that makes partners feel good, something that is right by particular moral precepts, or something that has concrete effects on trust, love, and commitment? We also don't have a clear definition of "relationships"—does this refer to romantic relationships, friendships, family connections, professional associations, or all of these? Finally, our ability to test the claim that "honesty is a good thing in relationships" requires us to evaluate honesty, which might prove very challenging. How could we tell for sure whether a person was being honest or dishonest? It is extremely difficult to test predictions that are general, vague, or ambiguous.

Reflection

Can you think of ways other than testing to assess a theory's accuracy? What assumptions of Western culture underlie the idea that testing determines accuracy?

Let's return to Lund's (1985) theory of commitment. She predicted that the greater the investment a person makes in a relationship, the higher will be the person's level of commitment to continuing the relationship. She also predicted that investment would be a stronger influence than love on relational continuity. To test these predictions, Lund studied college students. Because college romances are most likely to deteriorate during times of transition, Lund measured the students' reported feelings of love and commitment in February of their senior year and in the summer following their graduation. Her findings were very clear: Those students who expressed the greatest intention to continue a relationship (commitment) in February were most likely to be together the following summer. The amount of love expressed by students in February was not nearly as good a predictor of which couples would remain together. She tested her prediction empirically and found convincing support for its accuracy.

Reflection

Look back at the theory of classroom communication that you developed. Reflect on whether it can be tested. If it is too vague or general to be tested, how might you revise it to make it testable?

Parsimony: Is It Appropriately Simple?

When it comes to theory, complexity is not necessarily desirable. The term **parsimony** refers to appropriate simplicity. Among theorists it is widely believed that the best theory is the simplest one that is capable of describing, explaining, understanding, and perhaps predicting future events or instigating change. This doesn't mean that theories should be simplistic or omit important ideas. What it does mean, however, is that a theory should be as simple as possible without sacrificing completeness. Thus, if we have several theories that provide equally useful explanations, the most parsimonious one is the best.

Sometimes theorists get caught up with complexity and offer explanations that are more involved than is necessary to understand the phenomena that interest them. Of course, a theory must be complete in order to meet the criterion of providing sound description and explanation. However, theories that are unnecessarily cumbersome fail to meet the criterion of parsimony. As you encounter theories in this book, you can ask whether they include irrelevant material and whether they are more complex than they need to be. The general rule is that if there are two theories that shed equal light on the same phenomenon, the simpler one is better.

Utility: Is It Useful?

Theories are also measured by their **utility** or practical value. Years ago, a distinguished social psychologist named Kurt Lewin said that there is nothing so practical as a good theory. By this Lewin meant that a good theory should have practical use. Because the goals of theories are to increase understanding, prediction, and/or quality of life, then it's fair to ask how well a given theory does that.

How we evaluate the practical utility of a theory should be based on the goals of that particular theory. A theory that seeks to predict and control communication is measured by how well applying it achieves the desired results. A theory that seeks to understand subjective aspects of communication, however, is not appropriately measured by whether it allows prediction and control. Instead, a theory that aims to enhance understanding is gauged by whether it achieves that. The practical value of critical theories rests on their ability to motivate or actually direct positive social change.

Reflection

What is the practical value of your theory of classroom communication? What does it do that matters?

Heurism: Does It Generate New Thought or Insights?

The final criterion for evaluating a theory is **heurism,** which refers to the degree to which a theory provokes new ideas, insights, thinking, and research. A theory is judged to be heuristic if it sparks new thinking. Some scholars regard heurism as the most advanced quality of theories (Wood, 1992a, 1995b), since a theory that extends thinking fuels further research and theorizing. By this criterion, Shannon and Weaver's information theory was good because it generated an enormous amount of research on how communication works. Weiner's emphasis on feedback and communication ethics might never have surfaced if Shannon and Weaver hadn't introduced their theory. Lund's theory of commitment also has triggered substantial research that has elaborated knowledge about the bases of commitment and relational endurance.

1. Does the theory provide a full description and explanation of communication?

2. Can the theory be tested?

3. Is the theory as simple as it can be?

4. Does the theory have practical utility?

5. Does the theory generate new thinking?

Balancing Criteria for Evaluating Theories

We have discussed five criteria for evaluating theories. It may have occurred to you that a particular theory can be good on some of the criteria and fare poorly on others. For instance, Shannon and Weaver's information theory doesn't offer a full description of communication, yet it is highly heuristic. It is not unusual for a theory to meet some evaluative standards better than others.

As an analogy, think about how we evaluate apples, broccoli, pizza, bagels, and eggs. One criterion might be low fat and cholesterol: The apples, bagels, and broccoli would come out well on this measure. A second criterion for evaluating foods is sodium content: Again, the apples, bagels, and broccoli fare well and so do eggs. We might also assess a food by the amount of protein it supplies: The egg and the pizza come out best by this measure. Finally, we might judge the foods by how tasty they are: Which ones rate most highly on this will depend on individual tastes (I'd pick the bagel). Which is the best food? It depends on which criterion or set of criteria you consider most important in evaluating the foods. This implies that evaluating theories is not an objective activity. Instead, the criteria we use to judge theories reflect our subjective values, preferences, perspectives, and goals.

Theories, like foods, can be assessed in different ways that lead us to different conclusions about their merit. Ideally, a good food would be low in sodium, fat, and cholesterol and high in protein and taste. Ideally, a good theory would provide full description and explanation and also would be easy to test, parsimonious, useful, and heuristic. However, just as most foods don't meet all criteria for merit, most theories don't entirely satisfy all five criteria for value. This is one reason why scholars often disagree about the worth of a particular theory: They use different measuring sticks to assess it.

Each criterion we discussed measures theories along one dimension. No one criterion is the only or the most important standard. As you study theories in this book, keep in mind all five criteria and apply them to each theory. Doing this will give you insight into which criteria you consider most important in judging the worth of theories.

Reflection

How would you rank-order the five criteria for evaluating theories?

A Perspective for Studying Theories

So far we've examined the various goals that motivate theory and the standards for evaluating the worth of theories. Drawing from what we've already discussed, we can develop guidelines for thinking about the theories that you'll encounter in subsequent chapters. As you consider specific theories, you may find it useful to keep in mind that theories are points of view, not absolute truths. You'll also want to remember that any theory is limited in scope and that different theories may fit well together.

Theories Reflect Points of View

Students who are new to the study of theory often find it confusing that there are different theories of communication. They want to know which is "the right" one, which is the truth. The desire to know which theory is right is understandable, but it isn't a realistic or useful attitude to hold when studying theories.

A theory expresses a point of view. It is a way of making sense of experiences, situations, events, or other phenomena. A majority of scholars recognize that theories do not (and cannot) offer capital-T

Truth. Instead, theories offer perspectives on reality, and those perspectives reflect the particular human beings who build theories and the specific historical and cultural contexts in which theories are built.

Because human beings create theories, the theories include points of view that keep them from being absolutely objective descriptions of reality. Let's consider just a few of the ways in which theories reflect the particular interests, values, assumptions, and contexts of the people who develop them. In working to understand communicative phenomena, individual theorists make choices about which phenomena to emphasize and which to neglect. The choice of what to study involves several kinds of decisions. First, theorists choose which kind of communication to focus on—talk between intimates, interaction in groups, public speaking, cross-cultural communication, mass media, and so forth.

Second, theorists make different choices about what they will focus on in studying a particular kind of communication. For example, Leslie Baxter and Steve Duck both concentrate on communication in personal relationships. Yet Baxter (1990, 1992, 1993, 1994) rivets her attention on the tensions between contradictory impulses such as the need for autonomy and the need for togetherness. Duck (1994a,b), on the other hand, focuses his energy on understanding how ordinary, routine talk between intimates creates the meaning of relationships. Both Baxter and Duck are theorists of communication in personal relationships, but they emphasize distinct facets of intimate interaction. Recall that Shannon and Weaver emphasized the flow of information in their theory of communication. Other relationship scholars have focused on different aspects of interpersonal communication, including sharing meaning, creating identification between people, and developing feelings of trust and commitment.

Theorists also vary in the goals they pursue. A scholar interested in prediction and control will develop a theory quite different from a scholar whose primary interest is understanding. Critical theorists, who see the ultimate goal of theory as producing positive social change, will not be satisfied to develop a theory that describes, explains, and predicts how communication works, but does nothing to change it so that it is more constructive for humans.

Finally, theorists differ in what they regard as a good explanation. Whereas some theorists adhere to the traditional quest for universal or near-universal laws, others seek to understand rules that guide communication in specific contexts. A lawful explanation will not be persuasive to a theorist who believes there are no universal laws of human behavior. Conversely, a rule-based explanation will seem inadequate to a theorist who thinks science requires universal laws.

Because different theorists focus on different types of communication and different facets of communication within each type, the theories they generate are naturally distinct. Consequently, we shouldn't be surprised to find that there are many different theories of communication, each reflecting the views, values, and interests of the person or persons who developed it. As you study the different theories in this book, try to resist the urge to pick one as the right one. Instead, approach each theory on its own terms and consider when, where, and for whom it might be useful. Each theory we will study offers a perspective that can help us understand particular aspects of what happens when certain people communicate in defined situations.

Different Theories Are Not Necessarily Incompatible

We've already seen that theories, even theories about a single kind of communication, vary. This leads to the question of whether different theories are compatible or separate and irreconcilable perspectives. The answer to that question is, "It depends."

Some theories cannot work together because they reflect fundamentally oppositional views of human beings or of knowledge. We'll look more closely at these issues in Chapter 3. For now, it's important for you to understand that when the foundations of two or more theories are inconsistent, they are incompatible. Let's consider a concrete example to clarify this point. Scholars who believe humans have no free will try to identify the external stimuli that cause human behaviors. Operating from the assumption that human behavior is determined, a scholar might develop a theory that claims the external factors of job stress and middle age cause male midlife crisis. A theory of this sort would suggest that we should lessen job stress to reduce the incidence of male midlife crisis.

A theorist who believes that humans have free will would reject the idea that male midlife crisis is caused by external factors. Instead, a theorist who believes in free will might explain the increasing incidence of middle-aged men who have identity crises as the result of cultural attitudes that undercut personal responsibility for one's actions. If individuals internalize cultural views that we aren't responsible for what we do, then they are more likely to act in ways that could be judged irresponsible. The theorist who believes human behavior is determined focuses on external stimuli that precede certain actions, while the theorist who believes in free will concentrates on the meanings and values that individuals have for what they do. The two perspectives are not compatible.

Reflection

To what extent do you think humans act from free will?

Yet some theories do work well together. This is the case when the theories are concerned with the same kind of communication and when they have common fundamental assumptions about human nature and knowledge. For example, in Chapter 5, we will examine symbolic interactionism, which is very broad. The value of this theory is that it provides an overall perspective on the process whereby individuals learn the symbols and the meanings of their culture. What symbolic interactionism doesn't do is explain precisely how individuals create meaning in various specific contexts. Two other theories covered in Chapter 6, constructivism and rules theory, supplement the general view of symbolic interactionism with more detailed explanations of how individuals create meanings. Rules theory highlights the personal, relationship, and social rules that structure communication between people. Complementing this emphasis is constructivism, or attention to the cognitive processes individuals use to organize and interpret communication. These three theories work well together, and in combination, they provide a fuller understanding of the human process of creating meaning than does any of the theories on its own.

Theories Have Limited Focus and Scope

A theory asks particular questions. Its scope is defined by the specific aspects of communication it seeks to describe and explain. No theory can address all communication or even all facets of a single type of communication. Brant Burleson's (1984, 1986, 1991) work on comforting behaviors provides enormous insight into the ways we communicate comfort and support to others. It tells us nothing, however, about constructive methods of managing conflict or ways of dealing with power and manipulation. Burleson isn't trying to explain power or conflict, and it's not appropriate to judge his scholarship by whether it sheds light on power and conflict. Those issues are beyond the scope of his theory.

A theory should be considered and evaluated on how well it does what it sets out to do. It's entirely reasonable to decide that a certain theory's focus doesn't interest you or isn't of value in your life. It is not reasonable, however, to criticize a theory for not doing something it doesn't attempt to do. The fact that there are hundreds of theories of communication tells us that any theory is limited in scope. Thus, each theory should be appraised in terms of whether it enlarges our knowledge about the particular contexts and facets of communication that are its focus.

As you consider theories in this book, keep in mind that theories are human constructions and, therefore, they reflect points of view, not statements of objective truth. Also realize that theories with compatible basic assumptions often work well together to provide richer understandings of human communication than any single theory can offer. Third, you should recognize that theories have limited scope and can be judged only on whether they increase knowledge about the specific domain of communication that is the theory's focus. Finally, I hope you'll keep an attitude of curiosity as you study communication theories. Learning about many different perspectives on human communication introduces you to points of view and modes of understanding other than your own. This allows you to grow personally and intellectually.

 ummary

In this chapter, we've considered the foundations of communication theory. We began by examining the goals that guide theory. Description and explanation are the basic building blocks of all communication theories. Beyond those two goals, theories also attempt either to predict and control or to increase understanding of communication phenomena. A fourth goal, most often embraced by critical theorists, is to produce positive social change. As we noted, these are not mutually exclusive goals; they often work together. Description is necessary for explanation; explanation allows prediction, control, and/or understanding; and positive social change grows out of a foundation of understanding.

The second section of the chapter concentrated on criteria for evaluating theories. To judge the value of a theory, we ask five questions: (1) Does it offer a full description and explanation of the communication it studies? (2) Is it testable? (3) Is it appropriately parsimonious, or simple? (4) Does it have practical utility? (5) Is it heuristic in generating new thoughts, research, and/or insights? Most theories will not fully meet all five of these evaluative criteria. Thus, you will have to decide which criterion or criteria are most important to your evaluations of theories.

In the final pages of this chapter, we discussed guidelines for studying theories in this book. Perhaps the most important one is to realize that communication theories are human constructions. As such, they reflect individuals' perceptions, values, needs, experiences, and goals, as well as the social, temporal, and intellectual currents of particular contexts in which theorists live and work. Realizing this allows us to understand that theories are not objective truths, but rather they are perspectives on reality.

A second guideline for your study of theories is to recognize that different theories that share common fundamental assumptions may complement one another and work well together. Theories with contradictory views of human nature and knowledge, however, are not compatible. Third, it's important to recognize that theories have limited scopes. No communication theory explains all communication in all contexts, and it would be unrealistic to expect this of a theory. What is reasonable is to ask whether a given theory does a good job of explaining and enhancing knowledge about the communication on which it focuses. Finally, I've suggested it's valuable to adopt an attitude of curiosity toward the range of theories we'll discuss in this book. You're most likely to gain new insights into your own communication, as well as communication in general, if you keep your mind open to points of view that differ from your own. This allows you to learn about people and contexts that are beyond your current personal experiences.

In Chapter 3, we will continue considering how theories are developed and tested. There we will examine different assumptions that underlie and shape theories and ways of doing research to test theories. Following this are eight chapters that introduce a variety of communication theories. As we discuss each theory, we will describe its goals and scope, examine research that has tested the theory, and critically assess strengths and weaknesses of the theory. This should provide you with a solid basic understanding of each theory and some insight into its particular values and limitations.

Chapter Three

Building and Testing Theory

f you tell a 2-year-old child that the world is round or that the moon will not appear tonight, the child is likely to ask "How do you know?" or say "Prove it."

Children's skeptical attitude toward claims is very much like the attitude scholars take toward theories. We don't accept an account of communication just because someone advances it. Instead, we ask "How do you know?" and we demand "Prove it." The question of how you know concerns how the theory was developed and what assumptions the theorist made. The demand to prove it asks for evidence that supports the claims a theory makes.

In this chapter, we'll trace the process of theorizing to see how theories are developed, refined, and tested. We'll begin by discussing the building blocks of theory: Assumptions about human beings, knowledge, and the research process. Next, we'll consider diverse methods that scholars use to test and refine theories. By the end of this chapter, you should have a good working understanding of alternative foundations on which theories are built and various methods by which they are tested.

Building Blocks of Theory

Do theories of human communication describe how humans actually communicate, or do they reflect individual theorists' perceptions and perspectives? When people communicate, are they reacting to external stimuli or making personal choices? Are theories based on objective knowledge or subjective interpretations? Do they tell us about communication behaviors or about the meaning of communication? Do they provide universal truths or situated accounts? Each of these questions is answered in different ways by various theorists. Just as there is no single theory of communication, there is no single view of the foundations of theory. In this section, we will consider four building blocks of theories and varying points of view on each of them.

Reflection

As a framework for reading the rest of this chapter, state your personal opinions regarding the preceding questions.

Views of Human Nature

The most basic foundation of any theory is the view of human nature that guides it. A theory about human activity necessarily reflects a particular view of what humans are and how they operate. Different theorists subscribe to different views of human nature, and you will find you agree with some views more than others.

One of the continuing controversies in philosophy concerns **ontology,** or views of human nature. The crux of the controversy is whether or not humans have free will and, if so, how great the latitude of free will is. How you answer this question makes a great deal of difference in the theories you find credible and in how you act in everyday life. For example, if you think people don't have free will, it makes no sense to blame individuals for bad behavior or praise them for good behavior. In neither case do they control what they do. On the other hand, if you think that humans do have free will, you're likely to hold people responsible for their actions.

Despite all of the effort and energy devoted to figuring out the nature of human beings, we still don't know whether we have free will and, if so, how much. There is no conclusive answer—at least not yet. Consequently, the assumptions theorists make about humans can't be proven or disproven scientifically. They are matters of faith or belief. Theorists are divided in terms of whether they assume individuals react to external stimuli or act from free will and, thus, exercise intentional choices.

Reflection

What practical difference does it make whether we believe human behavior is determined or personally willed?

Determinism   Those who believe that our behavior is caused by external stimuli subscribe to a deterministic view of human nature. **Determinism** assumes that human behavior is governed by forces beyond individual control, usually the twin forces of biology and environment. Whatever we do is the inevitable result of genetic inheritance, environmental influences, or a combination of the two.

Freud is famous for having said, "Biology is destiny." By this he meant that biology determines sex and sex determines phenomena such as fear of castration in males and penis envy in females. From this point of view, each of us is prewired by sex chromosomes to have certain feelings and fears. How we behave is inevitable and unavoidable, given the determining force of biological sex.

Many more modern thinkers draw a sharp distinction between sex and gender (Basow, 1992; West & Zimmerman, 1987; Wood, 1993c, 1994a,e, 1995a). Sex refers to biological qualities determined by the sex chromosomes (XX or XY usually) and hormones (estrogen, testosterone, androgen). Sex describes whether a person is biologically male or female. Gender, on the other hand, refers to socially constructed views of men and women—that is, the meanings assigned to the sexes at a particular time in a given society. Gender refers to whether people see themselves as masculine or feminine and whether they embody what a particular society prescribes for masculinity and femininity. Most scholars of gender believe that the vast majority of differences between women and men are learned (a matter of gender), not biologically determined (a matter of sex). Thus, to explain differences between the sexes, they focus on social practices that prescribe how women and men are expected to think, feel, act, and be.

Although both biological and environmental causes can be viewed as determining individual behavior, there is an important difference between the two causes. Biologically determined qualities and behaviors are difficult and sometimes impossible to alter, whereas environmental causes of behavior are more amenable to change. Even with all the wonders of modern medicine, we can't substantially raise the intelligence of individuals with Down syndrome, and we can't transform genetically determined skin color. We can, however, work to change social attitudes toward people of different colors and mental abilities.

In some cases, biologically determined conditions and behaviors can be hidden or altered. For instance, a person who doesn't like her or his inherited hair color or nose can use dye or undergo plastic surgery to create the desired hair color or nose shape. Injections of testosterone promote the growth of body hair in males who produce less than average amounts of that hormone. In addition to disguising or remaking biological characteristics, in some cases we can chemically alter them or their consequences. Individuals with inherited inclinations toward bipolar personality, hyperactivity, or depression can be helped with medications. Similarly, people who have inherited diabetes can control many of the consequences of the condition with insulin and/or diet. At the extreme of tampering with biological dictates are radical measures such as sex change operations. Through cosmetic, chemical, or surgical means we can alter or camouflage much of our biological destiny. Even so, biological blueprints are probably the most difficult to change.

Environmental determinists believe that social factors cause human behavior. From this perspective, a man who feels inferior because he has small pectoral muscles or a woman who feels inadequate because she has small breasts would be explained with reference to prevailing social beliefs of what makes men and women attractive. Rather than looking for ways to control, or change, the physiology of the individuals, environmental determinists might seek ways to alter the social context and the gender expectations it imposes on women and men. Despite differences between them, both environmental and biological determinists believe that human behavior is controlled by something other than individuals themselves.

Free Will   At the other end of the ontological spectrum is the belief that humans have free will and that they make choices about how to act. Theorists who believe in free will assume individuals interpret experiences and create meanings that then guide what they think, believe, say, feel, and do. These theorists reject the idea that human behavior is an unthinking, automatic response to conditions and stimuli around us.

Belief in free will is sometimes misunderstood as the notion that people have complete control over their lives. Most scholars and lay persons who assume individuals have free will are not so naive as to believe will is boundless and unqualified. Instead, the majority of theorists who assume humans have and exercise will recognize that we do so within definite constraints. In writing about the impact of social structures on personal relationships, Graham Allan (1989) noted that our relationship choices are not entirely free. Instead, he pointed out, we make them within the limitations of biological and social forces that undeniably affect our lives and how we perceive our options in any situation. Realizing that biological and social forces *affect* what we do is quite different from assuming they determine what we do.

Many years before Graham Allan's time, the philosopher Martin Heidegger (1927/1962) advanced the idea that individual freedom is constrained by what he called "thrownness." For Heidegger, **thrownness** refers to the fact that we are thrown into a multitude of arbitrary conditions that influence our lives and our opportunities. For example, a Caucasian woman born in the United States in 1812 would not have been allowed to pursue professional training, own property, or vote. Those constraints on her choices would have resulted from the fact that she was thrown into an era that radically limited women's rights. African Americans born in Alabama in 1850 were automatically slaves, an identity that severely restricted their life chances and opportunities. A woman with extrasensory perception would have been burned, hung, or drowned if she had been thrown into Salem in the late 1600s. A woman born in India at the turn of this century, and in some regions of India today, would be thrown into the custom of arranged marriage. In each of these cases, the free will of individuals is constrained by their thrownness—the arbitrary social conditions of the time and place in which they live. Each of us is also affected by our thrownness into a society that has particular beliefs about gender, race, age, sexual orientation, ethnicity, physical ability, socioeconomic class, and so forth.

Reflection

Describe your thrownness. How does it limit your ability to exercise will?

Those who believe in human will do not think the fact that will is constrained means it is nonexistent. Instead, they argue that within the constraints of biological and social influences, there remains substantial latitude for us to make choices about what we believe and do and to shape our own destinies. How we are thrown into the world is not within our control. Each of us does, however, have some control over what we do with our thrownness.

Individual control over how to deal with thrownness is evident in the different choices individuals with similar social and biological constraints make. For example, in the early 1800s, women were legally defined as property of fathers or husbands. Many women accepted social views of them as dependents and as inferiors to men. Yet other women responded differently to their thrownness. Individuals, such as Elizabeth Cady Stanton and Susan B. Anthony, challenged prevailing restrictions on women's identity and rights. Eventually their actions, along with those of hundreds of others who didn't accept existing views of women, altered the legal rights available to women and the spheres of society in which they could participate.

Another example of exercising choice within the constraints of thrownness comes from the actions of key figures in the 1960s civil rights movement. In the United States, blacks, like women, were treated as subordinate members of the society. They were not given equal opportunities in careers, and they were forced to attend less well supported schools, ride in the back of buses, and use separate eating, lodging, and restroom facilities. Although many blacks were resigned to the racist attitudes that held sway at the time, others refused to accept them. The Reverend Martin Luther King, Jr., was one of the leaders who emerged to champion the cause of racial equality. His choice to challenge racism influenced what thousands of other African Americans saw as their options for resisting racism. Even among those who argued against racial discrimination there were differences. The Reverend Martin Luther King, Jr.'s advocacy of civil disobedience and passive resistance was far removed from the confrontational rhetoric of Malcolm X, or the fiery politics of Stokley Carmichael, or the quiet, behind-the-scenes organizing of Ella Baker. Each individual made distinct choices about how to challenge racial discrimination and how to instigate change in society.

In addition to presenting historical examples of outstanding individuals, proponents of free will have marshaled persuasive evidence that ordinary individuals make choices that have concrete impact on them and their activities. Recent research demonstrates that individuals adopt different perspectives on their relationships and that the perspectives they choose affect how they see themselves and how they act in relation to others (Duck & Pond, 1989; Fletcher, Rosanowski, & Fitness, 1992; Honeycutt, 1993). We also know that people who choose to focus on positive aspects of relationships and to downplay dissatisfactions have more comfortable and gratifying relationships than partners who choose to concentrate on negative features and to downplay what is good about their relationships (Bradbury & Fincham, 1990; Fletcher & Fincham, 1991). This implies that we can change how we see our relationships by changing how we think about them.

In summary, the most basic foundation of any theory is its ontological premise. Whether theorists view human behavior as determined by social and/or biological forces or as personally willed, within the constraints of thrownness, is a choice that affects all other aspects of theorizing. What theorists study and how they explain their findings inevitably echo the assumptions they make about human nature.

Ways of Knowing

At some time in your life, you probably entertained this question: If a tree falls and nobody hears it, does it make a sound? That question is part of a larger philosophical debate about the nature of knowledge. **Epistemology,** the branch of philosophy that deals with knowledge, is concerned with how we know what we know. Epistemologists ask whether knowledge is based on the existence of phenomena (the falling tree) or on human perceptions (hearing it fall). As you might suspect, there are different opinions about what counts as knowledge and how we come to know what we think we know.

Bizarro   by Dan Piraro

Epistemological assumptions are the second building block of theory. Along with ontological premises, all theories include epistemological propositions that state what knowledge is and how we acquire it. The continuum of epistemological assumptions ranges from the notion that there is an objective, real truth that humans discover to the idea that humans create their own meanings and, therefore, many meanings are possible. We'll consider each end of the epistemological continuum.

Discovering Truth   Some people, both scholars and individuals removed from academia, believe that there is a singular truth. This viewpoint is called **objectivism,** which is the belief that reality is material and external to the human mind. For objectivists, truth or reality is material, external, independent of feelings, and the same for everyone.

For the ancient philosopher Plato, the ultimate truth was the idea or ideal of something, rather than any concrete instance of the thing. For others, truth is external, resolute reality. Those who believe in a singular, objective truth assume that it is independent of human feeling and motives and is discovered through direct observation. In other words, through our senses, we should be able to see, hear, taste, smell, and/or touch the reality of what is "out there." Our senses do not alter or affect objective reality. Within this perspective, knowledge is assumed to be objective and discovered by humans.

Scholars who assume there is an objective truth also regard theorizing and research as objective activities. **Objectivity** is the quality of being uninfluenced by values, biases, personal feelings, and other subjective factors when perceiving material reality. According to researchers who believe inquiry can and should be objective, a theorist's values and subjective feelings should not affect science. Instead, good scholars detach themselves from their values in order to maintain objectivity and discover reality. The result of detached scholarship, these individuals think, is real knowledge that is uncontaminated by human subjectivity.

Believers in a singular truth presume that the nature of communication can be objectively determined. Thus, they would claim that particular communication acts have fixed meanings. For example, they might agree that "You look wonderful today" is objectively complimentary communication, that calling someone "queer" is inarguably derogatory, and that saying "I love you" is always affectionate. If someone suggested that those words don't always mean the same things to everyone, believers in singular truth might respond that people who don't understand the "right" meanings are simply misguided. The truth of the communication doesn't vary and isn't affected by what individuals feel. Thus, people may perceive things differently, but only one perception is ultimately correct, or true. Only one is consistent with the "real world."

Creating Meaning   At the other end of the epistemological spectrum are people, again both scholars and nonacademic individuals, who do not believe in an objective truth. Instead, they assume there are multiple views of reality, no one of which is intrinsically more true than any other. They believe that what we call reality is a subjective interpretation, rather than an objective truth. Because individuals have different experiences, values, perceptions, and life situations, their realities and their meanings vary widely. Further, even with great effort we may not be able to uncover all of the meanings people have, since some of them are less than conscious and others may be ones they conceal to avoid embarrassment.

Let's return to the examples of three statements that we discussed above. In some situations you might interpret "You look wonderful today" as a compliment. However, if it were said by Tom Clarence, who has a history of sexually harassing Hillary Ann, then Hillary might perceive the words as threatening, debasing, and cause for alarm. Calling someone a "queer" might be interpreted as an insult in most circumstances. In recent years, however, many gays have reappropriated that word as a positive self-description that they use among themselves. What calling someone "queer" means differs depending on whether it is uttered by a straight person or said by one gay man to another. Finally, most of us would agree that "I love you" is generally affectionate communication. Yet, in some circumstances it can be manipulative. For example, children often proclaim love when they want something from the person they claim to love. Individuals who batter their spouses often follow violence with pledges of love that are intended to keep the abused partner from leaving or reporting the crime. In this context, "I love you" might not be regarded as an expression of affection.

Those who believe that there are multiple realities would regard it as entirely reasonable that different people interpret communication in varying ways. A good illustration of this perspective is found in **standpoint theory,** which we will discuss in detail in Chapter 9. The starting premise of standpoint theory is that the material, social, and symbolic circumstances of a social group shape what its members experience, as well as how they think, act, and feel (Harding, 1991; Wood, 1993e, 1995a). Thus, someone from the underclass has experiences with deprivation, hunger, and poor housing that a middle- or upper-class person doesn't have. The two individuals have different knowledge about what it means to be hungry, homeless, and so forth. Similarly, in the United States, members of racial minorities have experience with prejudice and discrimination that most European Americans don't have. Can different racial groups have the same knowledge of what racism is and means?

One group of communication scholars ("Telling Our Stories," 1992) explored the multiple meanings of sexual harassment. Their analyses dramatically illustrated the difference between what women and men in general consider sexually harassing. One reason that women are more likely to be offended by sexually oriented remarks and nonverbal behaviors is that they have been the victims of harassment more often than men. The danger that offensive remarks and behaviors may lead to more serious kinds of sexual intrusion may also be more salient to women than to men. The sexes' disparate standpoints explain some of the differences in how they interpret communication of a sexual nature.

A second example of different interpretations that people make comes from analysis of communication misunderstandings between people of different races (Houston & Wood, 1996). Assume you are playing a game of cards and your opponent in the game says, "My 2-year-old sister plays better than you." Would you take the comment as an insult or a deliberate attempt to hurt you? You might be offended if you are a European American. If you are African American, however, you might regard the comment as a normal and friendly type of verbal play. A good response would be a matching taunt such as "Yeah, well then maybe *you* should take lessons from her to improve your game!" The words uttered by the other player mean different things, depending on your social standpoint and the ways it teaches you to interpret communication.

For theorists who assume there are multiple, legitimate realities, differences in interpretation are normal and to be respected. They are not evidence that some people don't perceive capital-T Truth.

Reflection

Where do you stand on the question of whether truth is singular or multiple? What difference does a point of view on this issue make?

Building and Testing Theory

The epistemological question of how we know is a foundation of theories. Some individuals believe truth is an objective phenomenon that humans can discover through careful observation or other scientific methods. Other people think that reality is ultimately subjective and that what we know is intimately tied up with who we are. The stances theorists take on this issue influence how they conduct research, interpret findings, and advance claims.

Purposes of Theory

The third building block of theory concerns the purpose of theory. We first encountered this issue in Chapter 2, and now we will examine it in greater detail. A basic controversy about the purpose of theory is whether theories should generate universal laws that apply in a broad range of circumstances, or whether theories should articulate rules that describe patterns in more limited spheres of activity.

Universal Laws   As we saw in Chapter 2, some theorists believe there are universal laws of human behavior. A **law** is an inviolate, unalterable fact that holds true across time and space. For example, you are familiar with the law of gravity, which states that objects are pulled toward the earth. The law of gravity explains everything from the fact that a pen dropped from your hand hits the floor to the fact that an airplane whose engines fail falls to the ground. The law of gravity is true across all situations within the scope of the earth's atmosphere (but the law of gravity doesn't hold in outer space). It's also universally true that mixing two molecules of hydrogen and one molecule of oxygen will unvaryingly produce water. Consuming large quantities of arsenic will inevitably cause death. These are all laws that remain true across a variety of circumstances.

The question is whether human communication is as lawlike as the movement of physical objects. Are humans no different from billiard balls or physical particles? Theorists who believe in universal laws assume that human behavior is as much subject to laws as physical entities are.

Beliefs about the purpose of theory are related to ontological assumptions, which we discussed earlier in this chapter. If human behavior is determined by biological and social forces, then we would expect to be able to predict behavior with relative certainty. In other words, if human behavior is determined by something other than personal will, then patterns of behavior will occur in response to specific stimuli; they will not vary as a result of personal wishes, commitments, or perceptions.

Situated Rules   Some theorists scoff at the idea that theories of human behavior should generate universal laws. Instead, they assume there are no laws that explain human communication across all time and circumstances. Theorists who adopt this position tend to see the purpose of theory as articulating rules that describe patterns in human behavior, rather than laws that explain its causes.

As you'll recall from our discussion in Chapter 2, a second way to explain human behavior is by identifying rules that guide how we act in particular situations. Rules-based explanations of communication aren't assumed to hold true across all situations and people. Instead, they are believed to describe regularities in how some people act in specific circumstances. For example, most of us follow turn-taking rules when we talk with others (Nofsinger, 1991). When we are speaking, we expect not to be interrupted; when we're through speaking, we signal this by looking at others to indicate the conversational floor is open again. When we want to speak, we wait until the person speaking finishes. Within Western culture, it is considered rude for one person to monopolize a conversation and not let others have their say. The turn-taking rule is a convention that we learn in the process of becoming socialized. Children aren't born knowing this rule, however, and often they don't follow it. Moreover, turn taking isn't a pattern that is equally important in all cultures. Thus, theorists who believe in rules regard turn taking as a rule-governed activity, not a behavior caused by any universal law.

Just as faith in universal laws is related to ontological assumptions, so too is belief in rules connected to views of human nature. Theorists who rely on rules to describe human activity tend to assume humans have at least some degree of free will. They argue that our behavior is guided by rules or follows rules, rather than being absolutely determined by laws beyond our control. This suggests that our actions represent choices, rather than automatic responses to external stimuli. Presumably, we could communicate differently by adopting different rules to guide us. Rules-based accounts assume that regularities in human behavior reflect rules that are arbitrary, learned, and subject to change. Thus, they search not for lawlike explanations, but for reasons that shed light on why people follow particular patterns in their communication.

Focus of Theorizing

The final building block of theory that we will consider is the focus, or content, that theories address. Once again, we'll see there are different schools of opinion on this matter. We'll also see that where a theorist stands on the issue of the focus of theory is related to her or his ontological and epistemological assumptions.

The basic divide on this issue is whether theories should focus on behavior, meanings behind behavior, or a combination of the two. Most theorists who believe human behavior is determined and knowledge is objective also believe that the proper focus of theories is behavior. Theorists who assume human behavior is sculpted by free will and that knowledge is subjective and variable are more likely to see the appropriate focus of theories as meanings. This doesn't necessarily mean that theorists who assume a degree of free will ignore behaviors, since studying behaviors may help us understand meanings. Many theorists who focus on observable behavior do not assume that this is all there is to humans.

Reflection

In your everyday theorizing about communication, do you tend to focus on behaviors themselves, the meanings you think underlie behaviors, or both?

Behavioral Focus   Traditionally, science has been concerned with observable phenomena. Thus, scientists have sought to describe, explain, predict, and control behavior. Many researchers focus on observable behaviors, but do not necessarily assume that there is nothing other than what can be observed. Some scientists assume, however, that behaviors are all there is or all that matters. This explains the label **behaviorism,** which refers to a form of science that focuses on observable behaviors and that assumes meanings, motives, and other subjective phenomena either don't exist or are irrelevant. Behaviorists believe that scientists can study only concrete behaviors such as what people do or say. Human motives, meanings, and intentions are beyond the realm of behavioristic investigation. In fact, behaviorists would consider such explanations idle speculation, rather than scientific activity.

B. F. Skinner (1971) was a staunch behaviorist who believed that human behavior is a response to external stimuli. Skinner is particularly well known for referring to the mind as a "black box," the contents of which cannot be known and which are irrelevant to science. Skinner believed that understanding what happens in the human mind is not necessary for a theory of human behavior. The mind and its activities, such as wanting, hoping, dreaming, intending, fearing, and so forth, are irrelevant.

Skinner regarded free will as a romantic illusion that many people find comforting but that really has nothing to do with how we behave. He thought concepts such as human freedom and responsibility and feelings such as pride, shame, hope, and commitment were humanistic fictions that allow people to believe they control their fates when, in fact, they do not. This may explain why Skinner (1971) titled his book on behavioral science *Beyond Freedom and Dignity.* For Skinner, as well as other behaviorists, all that matters and all that can be measured is concrete, objective behavior. Meaning, motive, and intentions, if they even exist, aren't measurable, so they aren't within the province of science.

It would be erroneous to assume that all researchers who study behaviors are strict behaviorists who think internal human activities are irrelevant. Skinner was a radical behaviorist; that is, he studied only outward behavior and also argued that any unobservable behavior (if it exists) is unimportant. Many communication scholars who study observable phenomena do not share Skinner's assumption that human mediation and intention are romantic fictions. These scholars study behavior because it can be observed and measured, whereas feelings, motives, and other internal activity are not outwardly visible. They do not, however, share Skinner's assumption that subjective experiences are nonexistent and/or irrelevant.

Meanings Many scholars aren't convinced that behaviorism is desirable. They reject both behaviorism's ontological assumptions and the idea that science should confine itself to the study of observable, concrete behaviors. Theorists who reject behavioral views of science believe that the crux of human activity is meaning, not behaviors themselves. Because this group of scholars claims to be interested in what is distinctively human—namely, free will, ability to make choices, and capacity to create meanings—they are often called humanists, and the form of science they pursue is called **humanism.**

Humanists see external behaviors as the outward signs of mental and psychological processes. For them, what we perceive, think, and feel directly affect what we do and what we assume it means. Thus, the reasons for human behavior lie with what happens inside of us. These scholars believe that cognitive and psychological processes offer the most insight into why we do what we do and into what our behaviors mean.

A number of years ago, a scholar named John Searle (1976) wrote an important book called *Speech Acts.* In this small volume, he made the distinction between brute facts and institutional facts. **Brute facts** are objective, concrete phenomena—the observable behaviors that behaviorists study. **Institutional facts,** in contrast, are what brute facts mean—what humanists wish to study. To illustrate the difference between these two kinds of facts, or activities, Searle used the example of a football game. He offered this amusing account of the brute facts an observer would use to describe what football is:

> *Our observer would discover the law of periodical clustering: at statistically regular intervals organisms in like colored shirts cluster together in a roughly circular fashion (the huddle). Furthermore, at equally regular intervals,*

circular clustering is followed by linear clustering (the teams line up for the play), and linear clustering is followed by the phenomenon of linear inter-penetration (p. 52).

This account does describe the observable behaviors in a football game. Yet, as Searle pointed out, no matter how much data of this sort we collect and no matter how many inductive generalizations we make from the data, we cannot describe football by relying on these raw behaviors. Brute facts alone tell us little about what the game means. To understand the meaning of football, we turn to institutional facts that explain the social meanings of head and shoulder gear, lines on the field, the conical object, and so forth.

In a sharp repudiation of behaviorism, Searle asserted that brute facts offer little insight into human activity because behaviors alone have no intrinsic meaning. Instead, humans assign meanings to them, and this requires interpretation. Interpretation is not evident in concrete behaviors, and it cannot be reduced to physical motion.

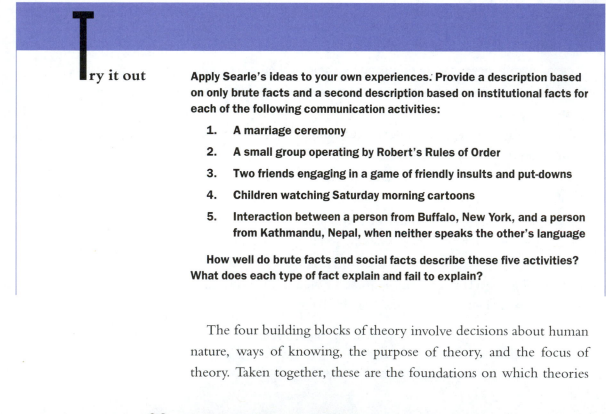

Try it out

Apply Searle's ideas to your own experiences. Provide a description based on only brute facts and a second description based on institutional facts for each of the following communication activities:

1. **A marriage ceremony**

2. **A small group operating by Robert's Rules of Order**

3. **Two friends engaging in a game of friendly insults and put-downs**

4. **Children watching Saturday morning cartoons**

5. **Interaction between a person from Buffalo, New York, and a person from Kathmandu, Nepal, when neither speaks the other's language**

How well do brute facts and social facts describe these five activities? What does each type of fact explain and fail to explain?

The four building blocks of theory involve decisions about human nature, ways of knowing, the purpose of theory, and the focus of theory. Taken together, these are the foundations on which theories are developed. We turn now to a discussion of how theories are tested. This will acquaint us with alternative ways of doing research and the kinds of data and knowledge that each method generates.

Testing Theories

Let's assume that as a theorist you have worked out your starting assumptions. You have clear ideas about human nature and knowledge, and you have decided what the purposes and focus of theories should be. Based on your starting assumptions, you develop a theory.

Hypotheses and Research Questions

Perhaps you have heard that women and men have different communication styles, but your own experience doesn't support that. Thus, you want to develop and test your theory that women and men engage in conversation in similar ways. The first step in developing and testing theory is to pose some hypotheses or questions for study. **Hypotheses** are testable predictions about relationships between communication phenomena. As a theorist, your goal is to develop hypotheses that allow you to test whether the sexes talk in similar or different ways:

H_1: Women and men interrupt with equal frequency.

H_2: Women and men make equally frequent efforts to involve others in conversation.

H_3: Women and men find it equally satisfying to talk about issues in a shared relationship.

If you don't have a clear basis for making predictions, then you might prefer to avoid formal hypotheses. A second option for studying men's and women's communication is to generate **research questions,** which specify the phenomena of interest but do not predict relationships between the phenomena. For instance, you might generate these research questions to guide your study:

RQ₁: How frequently do women and men interrupt in dialogues with each other?

RQ₂: How frequently do women and men make efforts to involve others in conversation?

RQ₃: How do women and men feel about discussing their relationship and issues in it?

Before moving ahead with your research, you have one further task: You need to define terms in your hypotheses or questions. So that others can understand your research, you need to specify exactly what you are studying. Pertinent to the study in our example, we need to define terms such as *interruption* (Is it any comment made when another is speaking or only comments that initiate new lines of talk?), *satisfaction* (Is it defined by individuals, a research instrument, or another measure?), *efforts to involve others in conversation* (Do these include verbal only or both verbal and nonverbal efforts? Questions of others, comments to others, or both?), and *discussing their relationship* (Do discussion topics cover problems, good features, small talk, history?).

Operational definitions are precise descriptions that specify how to observe the phenomena of interest. For example, operational definitions for your theory would define what counts as an interruption, satisfaction, and so forth. If the concepts of interest in a theory have been studied by others, it's a good idea to consider their definitions. This allows different researchers to use concepts in the same way and, thus, their findings can be compared and related. To grasp the importance of consistent operational definitions for research concepts, consider the confusion that can result when researchers in a particular area rely on diverse definitions. In a recent report, Mary Rohlfing (1995) noted that various researchers have defined the concept of "long-distance relationships" as living more than 250 miles apart, visiting less than once a month, and being in situations in which partners find it difficult to see each other every day. Given these discrepant definitions, it's no wonder that some researchers report that long-distance couples are frustrated (those living many miles apart) and other researchers report that long-distance couples are content!

Now that you know your basic assumptions and have generated three testable hypotheses or researchable questions with key concepts operationally defined, you confront the question of how to find out if your predictions are accurate or not. In this section, we'll consider three broad types of research that scholars use to test theories. As we examine each approach to research, we'll discuss examples related to the three hypotheses and questions we just generated.

Quantitative Research

Many scholars use **quantitative methods** to conduct research. They gather information that can be quantified and then interpret the data to make arguments about what the numbers reveal about communication behaviors and relationships among communication phenomena. Three of the most popular quantitative methods are descriptive statistics, surveys, and experiments.

Descriptive Statistics   As the name implies, **descriptive statistics** describe human behavior with numbers. They describe populations, proportions, and frequencies of behavior. To investigate your first hypothesis or question, which focused on the frequencies of interruptions by women and men, you might observe natural conversations and count the number of interruptions made by members of each sex. This simple frequency count would give you information about how often each sex interrupts. Communication researcher Victoria DeFrancisco (1991) did just that in her study of interruptions that occur in conversations between wives and husbands. She found that husbands interrupt wives far more often than wives interrupt husbands. Relationship therapist Aaron Beck (1988) observed the same pattern in couples he counseled.

But suppose you want to know whether the pattern of interruptions DeFrancisco and Beck found holds true in contexts other than marital conversations. To discover the scope of your findings, you would need to count interruptions in a variety of situations. Work by other communication scholars shows that the interruptions DeFrancisco and

"I TELL YOU, MR. ARTHUR, THIS SURVEY HAS NO WAY OF REGISTERING A NON-VERBAL RESPONSE!"

Reproduced by Special Permission of *Playboy* magazine: Copyright © 1977 by Playboy.

Beck noted between spouses also occur in group communication (Baird, 1976; Eakins & Eakins, 1976) and face-to-face interaction between men and women who aren't married (Brandt, 1980; Mulac, Wiemann, Widenmann, & Gibson, 1988). Numbers are like brute facts—alone they mean very little. We attribute meaning to numerical data, deciding whether it is important that men interrupt more often than women do. Numerical observations are meaningless until we interpret them.

You could also use descriptive statistics to test your second hypothesis or pursue your second question, which concerns the frequency of women's and men's attempts to include others in conversation. You might count the number of times women and men in varying communication contexts invite others into conversations. Existing research indicates that women are more active than men in doing what is called "conversational maintenance," which is involving others in conversations (Beck, 1988; Fishman, 1978; Tannen, 1990). Descriptive statistics aren't very helpful in testing your third hypothesis (women and men find it equally satisfying to talk about relationship issues). We can't count satisfaction, since it isn't an overt behavior.

Descriptive statistics are useful to describe patterns and frequencies in communication behavior. Although they can't tell us much about the causes of communication or about subjective states such as satisfaction, descriptive statistics can give us valuable profiles of what happens.

Surveys   A second quantitative method is surveys. Surveys are instruments, questionnaires, or interviews that ask respondents to report on their experiences, feelings, actions, and so forth. You could devise a questionnaire to get data relevant to all three of your questions or hypotheses. You might ask 100 women and 100 men to report how frequently they interrupt others, how often they try to include others in conversations, and how satisfying they find it to talk about relationship issues with partners. Alternatively, you could survey 100 members of each sex about their perceptions of men's and women's conversational behaviors. Because both self-reports and observers' perceptions are fallible, collecting both forms of data would provide you with greater information than either form of data alone.

Responses to surveys are raw data. We have to do something with them to understand their significance. In other words, scholars construct the meaning of significance. They have established a number of statistical tests that can be used to determine whether there are significant differences in quantitative data about perceptions of women's and men's conversational styles. A basic statistics course or textbook will explain these tests to you.

There are definite limits to what survey research can tell us. Surveys can demonstrate patterns and even relationships such as an association between interruptions and satisfaction with relationship talk. As we noted in Chapter 2, however, correlational data can't prove causation.

Thus, finding that satisfaction is lower in relationships in which there are many interruptions doesn't tell us whether interruptions cause dissatisfaction, whether dissatisfaction causes interruptions, or whether the two simply accompany each other while some other variable such as relationship history causes both of them.

Reflection

Can you think of correlational phenomena in your communication? What is the value of recognizing correlational patterns?

A popular form of survey is self-reports in which respondents report on their activities, feelings, perceptions, and so forth. Some scholars consider self-reports suspect for several reasons. First, there is the possibility of a social desirability bias, which occurs when people give responses that are socially acceptable rather than ones that are honest. Second, participants may want to "help" researchers and may provide the responses they think researchers want. Third, respondents may have inaccurate or selective perceptions of what they and others do, feel, and so forth. We might selectively notice all of the times people interrupt us, but fail to perceive instances in which we interrupt others. Despite these limitations, self-reports provide valuable insight into how individuals perceive themselves, others, and communication encounters.

Finally, surveys often ask respondents to recall past behaviors and feelings. There is the possibility that respondents edit retrospective experience to fit with current knowledge. For example, if you have read reports that say men interrupt more frequently than women, then this knowledge may affect how you recall your own experiences with interruptions. This doesn't mean that retrospective data are useless. Quite the contrary. As Steve Duck and Kris Pond (1989) have pointed out, retrospective accounts are very important sources of information about how people currently think about, feel, and perceive experiences. Retrospective data may not accurately reflect what actually happened in the past, but they can tell us how people presently perceive their experiences. Particularly if you assume that there is no singular, absolute reality, then retrospective data are good sources of information.

Experiments   **Experiments** are controlled studies that systematically manipulate one thing (called an independent variable) to determine how that affects another thing (called a dependent variable, since what it does depends on the independent variable). One of the greatest strengths of experimental methods is that they provide control so that only the variables of interest are present. This is also a major limitation of experiments: Because human interactions are seldom controlled, relationships found in a laboratory where so many conditions are controlled may not tell us much about what happens in real communication.

Reflection

In what ways are experimental findings relevant or irrelevant to everyday communication in which laboratory control is not present?

Linda Acitelli (1988) conducted an experiment that provides information about the third hypothesis. She had men and women read descriptions of talk between husbands and wives. Half of the situations were ones in which the couples discussed a conflict or problem in their relationship. The other half of the situations involved talk about the relationship in general when no particular problem was present. After participants in her experiment had read the descriptions, Acitelli asked them how satisfying they thought the husbands and wives in the descriptions found the conversations. Her assumption was that participants would rely on their own feelings and experiences to rate the satisfaction of the spouses in the scenario.

Acitelli found that both partners were satisfied with conversation about the relationship when there was a problem. When no conflict or difficulty existed, however, the wives in the scenarios were perceived as being more satisfied with conversation about the relationship. This finding by Acitelli is consistent with a great deal of research that reports that in general women enjoy talking about relationships more than men do (Aries, 1987; Schaef, 1985; Wood, 1993, 1994a,c, 1995b, 1996a).

Qualitative Analysis

Not all communication can be measured quantitatively, and quantitative data are not able to provide substantial insight into the texture and meaning of experiences. **Qualitative methods** of research are valuable when we wish not to count or measure phenomena, but to understand the quality of an experience, particularly how people perceive and make sense of their communication experience. This involves interpreting meanings and other unobservable dimensions of communication. We will consider two widely used forms of qualitative research.

Textual Analysis   Textual analysis, also called interpretive analysis, involves describing communication **texts** and interpreting their meaning. In scholars' vocabulary, texts are more than written documents or presented speeches. Texts include all symbolic activities that are written, oral, or nonverbal. Examples of texts are a presidential address, a discussion between friends, the AIDS quilt, the Vietnam Veterans War Memorial, cartoons, and secret handshakes exchanged between members of a club.

Textual analysts aim to mine the meanings of texts by studying them closely. Linguist Deborah Tannen (1990) uses textual analysis to understand gendered conversational dynamics. By scrutinizing interactions between women and men, Tannen has discovered a number of sex differences in conversational behaviors. Relevant to our research topic, Tannen's analysis of conversational texts reveals that men do interrupt more often than women and that women invest greater effort than men to include others in conversations.

Textual analyses are especially powerful in identifying overall patterns in communication and for interpreting what those patterns mean to individuals. For instance, William Foster Owen (1984, 1985) and a research group to which I belonged (Wood, Dendy, Dordek, Germany, & Varallo, 1994) used thematic analysis of texts to discern broad patterns of meaning and significance in romantic partners' accounts of their relationships. Our goal wasn't to identify and classify particular communication acts, for which quantitative methods might have been more useful. Instead, we wanted to decipher threads of meaning that ran through intimates' perceptions of their relationships.

Textual analysis can also inform us about what different people mean by particular behaviors. Using textual analysis, several communication scholars have identified differences in the kind, or quality, of interruptions that women and men typically make. Men, it seems, often interrupt to challenge others or to assert themselves. Women's interruptions are more likely to support others or to indicate interest in what others are saying (Aries, 1987; Mulac et al., 1988; Stewart, Stewart, Friedley, & Cooper, 1990). This finding enriches our understanding of the brute fact of interruptions by helping us recognize qualitative differences in what interruptions do and mean.

Ethnography   Another qualitative method that is gaining increasing popularity is **ethnography,** which is an interpretive approach to meaning (Geertz, 1973). Ethnography attempts to discover what things mean to others by sensitive observation of human activity. Typically, ethnographers rely on **unobtrusive methods,** which are means of gathering data that intrude minimally on naturally occurring interaction. Rather than constructing an artificial experiment or interrupting natural interaction with a survey or other instrument, unobtrusive data gathering takes place within the existing flow of activity. The goal is for the researcher to fade into a situation so that participants act as they normally do when not being observed. For example, a researcher might sit in the break room of a company every day for 2 weeks before formally gathering data on communication in the break room. By making herself or himself part of the setting, the researcher's presence is less obtrusive.

The guiding principle of ethnography is to discover what behaviors mean to people on their own terms, not those of the researcher. Thus, ethnographers try not to impose their perceptions, meanings, and views on the activities of others. Instead, their interest is understanding the meanings that others attach to communication, which may be quite different from their own meanings. This implies that they need to do more than record brute facts of communication. In addition, they need to become enough a part of interactional settings to have insight into institutional facts that shed light on how participants in the scene attribute meaning to particular activities (Philipsen, 1992).

Ethnographic studies have long been a mainstay in anthropological research. Because anthropologists seek to understand other cultures, they must avoid imposing their views, values, and perceptions on people in societies different from their own. In other words, the brute facts of particular customs and rituals in a culture become meaningful only when we have insight into cultural perspectives that establish institutional facts. Only by understanding the perspective of members of other cultures can we learn the meaning and social significance of activities.

In recent years, ethnographic methods have been increasingly adopted in fields outside of anthropology. Many communication researchers find ethnography an especially valuable way to gain insight into communication practices of diverse social groups. For example, Westerners regard eye contact as a sign of respect and interest, so making eye contact is considered polite. In other cultures, including many Asian ones, eye contact is regarded as rude and intrusive. If an American researcher judges Nepalese nonverbal communication by American standards, she or he will misinterpret the lack of eye contact. Instead, the researcher must figure out what eye contact means to Nepalese people.

Reflection

What epistemological stance and what view of the goals of research seem most consistent with ethnography?

Ethnographic research directs attention toward rituals, myths, stories, customs, beliefs, and speech patterns that reflect meanings shared by members of particular social groups. Relying on ethnography, communication researchers have been able to identify distinctive communication practices typical of feminine and masculine speech communities (Tannen, 1990; Wood, 1994a, 1995a,b, 1996a), differences in how women and men experience and express closeness (Riessman, 1990; Wood & Inman, 1993), and dissimilar meanings that women and men attach to talk about relationships (Acitelli, 1988; Beck, 1988; Tannen, 1990; Wood, 1994). We risk misinterpreting masculine communication if we evaluate it according to standards of feminine speech communities. Conversely, we may misunderstand the meaning of much feminine communication if we judge it by criteria appropriate for masculine talk.

Critical Scholarship

A third approach to research is **critical analysis.** An increasing number of communication scholars believe that research should not be confined to the ivory tower, but should make a real difference in the lives of human beings. Critical scholarship is one important way to change oppressive or wrong practices in the world. Thomas Nakayama (1995, p. 174) insists that "communication scholarship can (and should) make a difference in the everyday lives of people." These critical theorists aren't satisfied to understand what happens in communication or even the meanings of various communication practices. Instead, they see the goal of their research as critiquing communication practices that oppress, marginalize, or otherwise harm people. Criticism raises awareness of inequities and problems and, thus, can motivate change. In addition, critical scholarship can illuminate paths to change by identifying and arguing for alternatives to present conditions, practices, and processes.

Critical theorists often begin with other research methods to determine what is happening and what it means. However, they go beyond description and explanation of communication to argue for changes in communicative practices that disadvantage some social groups. For example, assume our tests of the hypotheses on women's and men's conversational styles revealed that men interrupt women and don't make efforts to include them in conversations. We might use what we learned about techniques of dominance to suggest how men should alter their communication styles to be more egalitarian, and/or to advise women on ways they might resist efforts to interrupt their communication.

Scholars committed to challenging and changing sexist social practices have conducted critical analyses of communication behaviors that support sexual harassment and make it seem normal (Strine, 1992; Taylor & Conrad, 1992; Wood, 1994b). Lana Rakow (1992), another critical scholar, has analyzed television advertisements to reveal the ways in which they oppress women by holding them to impossible standards of beauty as measures of their worth. Critical theorists have also exposed and critiqued communication practices that oppress minority groups and working-class individuals (Houston, 1994; Lee, 1993; Wood & Cox, 1993).

Analysis that reveals how communication supports unjust social relations instigates change on two levels. On a personal level, knowledge of oppressive practices allows individuals to notice and resist subtle communicative manipulations. On a social level, understanding of oppressive strategies can be used to revise social policies and practices. Deliberately and unapologetically partisan, critical scholars engage themselves in their work and aim for positive social change.

Reflection

How does involvement with social problems enhance and limit researchers' insights into communication?

Assessing Research

A theory isn't necessarily good simply because researchers have conducted a series of studies and reported their findings. We have to judge how the research was framed, conducted, and interpreted to decide how useful it is and whether it supports a theory. The scholarly community has developed three basic criteria for judging both individual research projects and theories.

Validity   **Validity** refers to the truth or accuracy of a theory in measuring what it claims to measure. Concern with validity does not imply an objectivist ontology, since multiple truths can be regarded as reasonable. The basic issue of validity is whether a theory studies and tests what it intends to study and test.

There are two forms of validity. **Internal validity** refers to whether the design and methods used to test a theory actually measure what they claim to. In regard to our example, we might ask how we know that asking questions is a means of including others in communication. Could questions equally reflect a kind of pressure or conversational dominance? Another example of internal validity concerns research on communication apprehension. For years, many scholars studied communication apprehension by measuring how much individuals communicated in various situations. Then a key distinction was made between being unwilling and being unable to communicate. A person who isn't motivated to communicate may speak infrequently but may not actually be apprehensive about communicating. Thus, an internally valid test of communication apprehension has to measure anxiety about communicating.

External validity refers to the generalizability of a theory across contexts, especially ones beyond the confines of experimental situations. In other words, the concern of external validity is whether a theory applies in the real world. The artificiality of an experimental laboratory may affect how we behave, so that actions observed in an experiment may not generalize to real life. For example, people may be less likely to interrupt when they are being observed than in ordinary conversations. If so, then a laboratory study of interruptions might lack external validity.

Reliability　A second criterion for evaluating theoretical research is **reliability,** which concerns the accuracy of measurement. Accuracy is generally defined as consistency of occurrence of a given relationship, behavior, or pattern. If the speedometer in your car registers 60 mph when you are driving 50 mph, 60 mph, and 70 mph, it is unreliable (it may also earn you a speeding ticket). If your doctor's arm cuff registers 150/110 as your blood pressure one day, 100/80 a second day, and 190/138 a third day, then something is wrong. It is possible that your blood pressure is actually fluctuating substantially. It's also possible that your doctor's pressure cuff is unreliable because it doesn't measure your blood pressure accurately on different occasions. Developing good communication theories demands that we use reliable methods of research—ones that measure communicative phenomena with consistent accuracy.

Significance　A third criterion for evaluating research and theory is **significance,** which refers to the conceptual or pragmatic importance of a theory. A good theory is useful. It allows us to do something we could not do without the theory. The utility of a theory depends on whether it allows us to explain, predict, control, or change communication behavior and/or conditions that affect it. Research might discover that laughing is correlated with crinkled eyes, leading to the theory of eye crinkling. Even though the theory might accurately describe and predict a behavior, we would be likely to raise questions about the significance of the theory. What difference does its claim make to anyone other than perhaps a plastic surgeon?

Quantitative research, qualitative study, and critical analyses are all valuable methods of learning about communication. Each form of research tends to be most useful in providing particular kinds of insight and limited in revealing other information. The research method or methods scholars use should be appropriate to the questions they are asking and the assumptions they hold about human beings, knowledge, and the research process. Thus, when you read a research report, you should ask whether it is based on methods that suit the goals of that specific investigation.

Summary

In this chapter, we've learned how theories about communication are developed and tested. The building blocks of theories are fundamental assumptions that frame researchers' perspectives on human beings and their activities. The most basic assumption a theorist makes concerns ontology, or the nature of humans. Whereas some scholars believe human communication is determined by social and biological forces, others assume it reflects the free will, or intention, of sentient agents. The second assumption underlying theories is an epistemological belief either that knowledge is the discovery of objective truth or that it is the interpretation of multiple realities. Third, theorists make assumptions about whether the purpose of research is to generate universal laws of human communication or situated accounts of communication practices in particular circumstances. Finally, theorists differ in whether they assume the focus of research and theory building is communication behavior itself (brute facts) or the meaning of communication behaviors (institutional facts). These four assumptions are the foundations that support theory.

We also considered the process of testing theories to determine whether they provide credible accounts of human communication. We examined three broad approaches to research: quantitative, qualitative, and critical methods. The methods differ in what they can tell us and in the fundamental theoretical assumptions with which they are compatible. Despite differences among them, all of the methods we discussed are valuable tools for unlocking knowledge about human communication. Each way of doing research helps us test and refine theories so that they are continuously bettered.

Part Two

Communication Theories

Chapter Four

A First Look at Communication Theory

In this chapter, we'll make an initial foray into the world of communication theories by examining one of the first theories advanced in the field. Because this is our first effort to consider a specific theory, we will examine only one. Chapters 5 through 11 explain and analyze two or more theories. As you read this chapter, keep in mind the various goals of theories and the criteria for evaluating them. These are tools that will help you make sense of theorizing in general and specific theories in particular.

General Semantics

The field of communication in the 1920s was much different than it is today. In Chapter 1 we noted that the modern discipline has a broad scope that includes everything from dialogues with ourselves (intrapersonal) to organizational and intercultural communication. In the second decade of this century, however, the scope of the field was much narrower. Rhetoric was the unquestioned center of the communication field, and professors studied great speeches and speakers and devoted their primary teaching energies to improving students' public speaking skills.

In this era, young I. A. Richards was a novice member of the field who found himself at odds with its emphasis on public speaking. Richards regarded oratory as contemptible, because in his opinion, public rhetoric had sunk to a low level of quality. He also believed that studying classical rhetoric and historical speeches was largely a waste of time. As for teaching, Richards disdained the idea of teaching public speaking, whether in classes to students or in workshops for professionals. He was skeptical of what in later years (1955) he called "sales talk" and equally skeptical of those who would teach persuasive skills.

Despite his criticism of the prevailing emphasis in his field, Richards was not uninterested in communication nor was he uncommitted to teaching communication skills. He believed, however, that the field needed to redirect its energies to study misunderstandings that plague everyday communication and to discover ways to fix them. Richards criticized the focus on public speakers and the process of persuasion and instead advocated a focus on listeners and the process of understanding.

Richards's challenge to trends in the field in the 1920s was instrumental in altering the directions, emphases, and content of both scholarship and teaching in communication. His insistent criticism of the narrow focus on public rhetoric expanded thinking about the scope of communication contexts. His disinterest in persuasion paved the way for studies of a fuller range of communicative processes.

Richards was one of many scholars who are called general semanticists. This group of theorists embraced the goal of improving everyday communication by discovering the ways in which words distort, obscure, and complicate understanding between people. If they could discover the sources of misunderstanding, general semanticists thought they could develop ways to avoid or correct them and, thus, improve communication. To understand the point of view of Richards and other general semantic theorists, we'll explore their primary ideas about language and some of their proposed remedies for misunderstanding.

The Special Character of Symbols

When a cat hisses, it's a signal of anger and warning of possible attack. Red berries are signals that a plant is poisonous. Lightning is a signal of thunder. In each of these cases, the signal (hissing, red berries, lightning) is directly connected to what it signifies. Signals, then, are naturally related to what they represent. Because of this natural relationship between signals and their referents, little effort is needed to understand signals—their meanings are relatively clear, unvarying, and unambiguous.

Symbols Are Arbitrary

General semanticists recognized that symbols are different from signals. Symbols such as words, art, and music have no direct or natural relationship with what they represent. The word *cat* is not intrinsically related to furry critters like Scrambles, who is sitting on my shoulder as I write. We could as easily call her a kudzu, hetap, or magpie. *Cat* is an arbitrary symbol that we use to refer to a particular species of animal. Like the word *cat,* all symbols are conventions that members of a culture agree to use to represent other things. As such, they are arbitrary ways of representing reality, not necessary or natural ones.

In their book *The Meaning of Meaning* (1923), Ogden and Richards used the semantic triangle pictured in Figure 4.1 to illustrate the arbitrary and indirect relationship between words and their referents. Notice that the line between the symbol "cat" and the actual referent of a particular cat is dotted to indicate the two are only indirectly related. There is no natural, absolute connection between the symbol and the referent. The other two lines in the triangle, however, are unbroken. This reflects the direct linkage between our thoughts and both symbols and referents. Once someone who likes cats thinks the word *cat,* she or he has fond thoughts about friendly pets. Because humans tend to

Figure 4.1

The Semantic Triangle

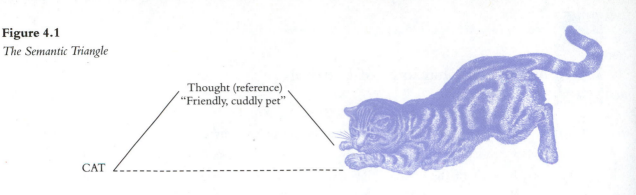

Thought (reference)
"Friendly, cuddly pet"

CAT

think in words and images, our thoughts (references) are directly connected to the words we've learned to use to describe phenomena. Likewise, our thoughts about cats are directly connected to the actual furry creatures we call cats, which are the referents for the word *cat* and thoughts about cats. But the relationship between the word *cat* and the actual referent of the furry animal is arbitrary. Symbols are connected to referents only by indirect, agreed-on conventions of how to use words.

Symbols Are Abstract

In addition to being arbitrary, symbols are abstract (Wood, 1992a, 1995b) because they are not concrete or tangible. They stand for ideas, people, situations, and so forth, but they are not themselves the concrete ideas, people, and situations. Instead, symbols are imperfect, partial ways of designating the raw reality of experience. When we rely on symbols to refer to actual phenomena, we abstract or move away from those phenomena.

Abstractness is a matter of degree, so symbols can be more or less abstract, depending on how general and removed from concrete referents they are. Because there are concrete referents for it, the word *table* is less abstract than words like *love, honor,* and *dignity,* which don't refer to tangible phenomena. To illustrate varying levels of abstraction in language, general semanticists used the model of the ladder of abstraction (Hayakawa, 1978) (see Figure 4.2).

Calvin and Hobbes

by Bill Watterson

Symbols Are Ambiguous

Symbols are also ambiguous because their meanings are unclear and variable (Wood, 1992a, 1995b). Whereas signals such as red berries have uniform and absolute meanings, the meaning of a symbol is not absolute and fixed. The word *cat* means one thing when used in reference to an animal, and it means something quite different when used to describe a person. We say "I love you," "I love broccoli," and "I love this course," but the word *love* means different things in each usage.

Try it out   **Write your definitions for each of the following words:**

1. **Marriage**
2. **Faith**
3. **Prejudice**
4. **Feminist**
5. **Welfare**
6. **Affirmative action**

Compare your definitions with those of other students in your class. How do your meanings differ?

Figure 4.2

The Ladder of Abstraction

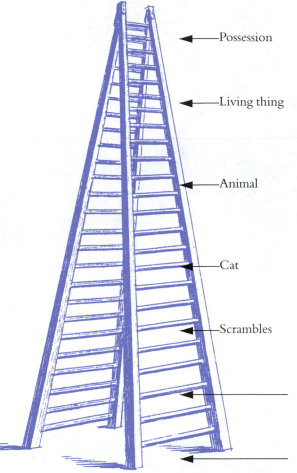

Possession — A very abstract way of describing the particular cat Scrambles. At this level of abstraction, we've left out almost all references to the features of the specific cat.

Living thing — *Living thing* is an even more abstract term than *animal*. This label calls attention to what Scrambles has in common with all living phenomena, but fails to specify how she differs from dogs, people, trees, or flowers.

Animal — At this level of abstraction, the label is even more general. The word *animal* recognizes what Scrambles has in common with all other animals, but fails to note what is distinctive about her or even her species of animal.

Cat — This species label abstracts what is common to all members of the species known as cats. It, thus, is a more abstract, or less specific, designation of Scrambles.

Scrambles — The name we give to the particular cat. The name captures only some of the qualities that we perceive in her and obscures other features of her that we could notice.

The cat Scrambles as we perceive her. Out of the totality that she is, we abstract only certain features that we identify as Scrambles.

The chemical, biological, and physical creature that is Scrambles has specific qualities and makeup that cannot be fully appreciated by the human eye.

Symbols are arbitrary, abstract, and ambiguous. These three qualities account for the mystery, majesty, and power of language. At the same time, as we will see, these qualities explain the potential for misunderstandings when we use words to communicate.

Reflection

Would we be better off if we developed a language that was concrete, clear, and based on natural ties between referents and symbols?

Meanings Are Contextual

General semanticists claimed that the arbitrariness, abstractness, and ambiguity of symbols accounted for why people have different meanings for the same words. This led to a still popular communication axiom: Meanings are in people, not words. Richards (1936) argued that the key to understanding (and misunderstanding) is context because the meanings change as symbols move from one context to another.

For Richards and other general semanticists, context was a very broad concept. It refers to more than specific sentences or communication situations. Context also includes thoughts and feelings we have in a situation, history between communicators, the relationship in which communication occurs, and so forth. Context, then, is the entire field of experience that is related to communication. To complicate matters, each person has her or his unique field of experience. Because no two individuals have precisely the same field of experience, it's impossible for them to have exactly the same meanings for words.

If fields of experience shape our interpretations of communication, then perhaps we could decrease misunderstandings by working on our fields of experience. General semanticists were interested in this solution to misunderstanding. Among them was Alfred Korzybski, a Polish American scientist, linguist, and philosopher who founded the Institute for General Semantics in Connecticut in 1929. One of the better known ideas from the general semanticists is captured in their phrase "The map is not the territory," which is meant to emphasize the difference between concrete referents (the territory) and symbols that represent them (the map).

Korzybski's training as a physical scientist inclined him to appreciate the precision of science and the importance of careful, empirical observation. That scientific perspective is embodied in Korzybski's book *Science and Sanity* (1958), which attempted to use scientific principles to reduce misunderstandings in communication. A major emphasis of this book, as well as much of the work by general semanticists, was finding ways to distinguish maps from territories in our thinking and communication.

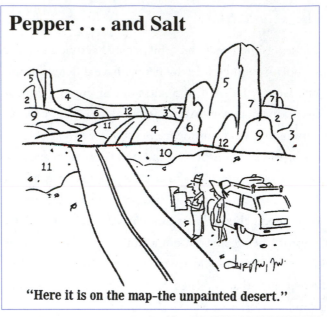

Pepper . . . and Salt

"Here it is on the map-the unpainted desert."

Reprinted from THE WALL STREET JOURNAL
by permission of Cartoon Features Syndicate.

Korzybski believed that communication problems often occur when we rely on our maps, or words, to assign meanings instead of referring back to the territories, or actual phenomena of experience. To distinguish between these two routes to meaning, Korzybski referred to intensional and extensional orientations. **Intensional orientations** to communication and meaning are based on internal factors or what's inside of us—our own definitions, associations, and fields of experience related to words we speak, hear, and read. **Extensional orientations,** in contrast, are based on observation and attention to objective particulars that distinguish phenomena from one another. Korzybski believed we would have fewer misunderstandings if we adopted more extensional orientations and kept "checking the facts" behind words. In other words, Korzybski thought the problems caused by intensional orientations were inherent in language—we could escape them only by getting out of language and back into the extension world to which language refers. For example, intensional language such as "She's politically liberal" should be replaced with more extensional language such as "She supports efforts to reduce

Intensional	Extensional
Notices generalities and classes	Notices particulars and uniqueness
Relies on preset beliefs and values to assign meaning	Observes reality to determine what it is and means
Begins with assumptions about meaning	Begins with observations of phenomena
Doesn't question the assumed meaning of words	Compares words with concrete referents

Table 4.1

Intensional and Extensional Orientations

Source: Adapted from Korzybski, A. (1958). *Science and sanity: An introduction to non-Aristotelian systems and general semantics.* Lakeville, CT: Institute of General Semantics.

discrimination and to lessen the difference between haves and have nots in society." Table 4.1 summarizes the differences between the two orientations to communication.

Perhaps you've had the experience of being fooled by language because you didn't check back to see what the territory was. For example, a group of communication researchers (Stacks, Hill, & Hickson, 1991, p. 85) recounted a clever advertising tactic invented by a fast-food store. Noticing that many customers refused to order milkshakes because they were fattening, this store named its milkshake a "Skinny Shake." Sales of milkshakes/Skinny Shakes soared because people who wanted to avoid high-calorie foods assumed the label "Skinny Shake" meant the beverage was appropriate for them. In reality, the very same ingredients in milkshakes were used to make Skinny Shakes.

A less amusing example of being fooled by words because we don't check back on the facts occurred in the early 1990s. At that time, Congress was debating a bill designed to increase job opportunities. The Republicans who opposed the bill dubbed it the "quota bill," and it was soundly defeated. When questioned about the reasons for their votes, many politicians reported that they were against quotas and wouldn't support any legislation that imposed quotas on hiring. A check of the extensional facts, the actual language in the bill, however, revealed that the bill did not mandate quotas. In fact, there was a

Reflection

What ethical implications do you perceive in using language that inaccurately represents "the facts"? Can symbols ever be really "accurate"?

provision in the bill that explicitly banned quotas. In this case, the label "quota bill" shaped meanings more than the facts did.

Remedies for Misunderstanding

Unlike some of the theorists we'll encounter later who focus on pure theory, the general semanticists were firmly committed to practical application of their ideas. They believed that the value of a theory of communication was its ability to reduce misunderstandings between people. Consequently, general semanticists generated a number of practical techniques for improving the clarity of communication. We've already encountered several of these. Adopting an extensional orientation, for example, allows us to ground meanings in observations, facts, and actual referents, rather than in abstract language and personal fields of experience. Reminding ourselves that "the map is not the territory" is a similar procedure to ensure we check the facts behind words.

Because the remedies proposed by general semanticists are numerous, we cannot discuss them all. We will, however, discuss three of the more popular techniques for understanding that they advocated.

Etc.

Because symbols are abstract, they don't capture all of the referent they attempt to represent. Remember our example of Scrambles/cat/ animal/living thing/possession. All of these symbols refer to the cat Scrambles, but they are progressively more abstract, leaving out more and more of the particulars of the one cat named Scrambles. Even the most precise word, *Scrambles,* doesn't represent all of the subtleties and details of the individual cat.

According to general semanticists, we get ourselves in linguistic trouble when we forget that symbols are abstract and, therefore, partial representations of phenomena. We can never say all there is to say about anything. To remind ourselves of the incompleteness of symbols, we should use the term *etc.* continuously. For example, we should say "That was a great class, etc.," "I met an interesting person, etc.," "General semantics theory is exciting, etc." Using *etc.* is a way of indicating to ourselves and others that we know we haven't said all that can be said about a class, person, or theory. Reminding ourselves that language abstracts only part of reality was so important to general semanticists that they named their professional journal *Et Cetera*.

Indexing

Have you ever been frustrated because someone, perhaps a parent, refers to you in a way that reflects who you used to be but not who you are now? As a child and teenager, I was not responsible with money. If someone gave me a dollar, I spent it as fast as I could on some short-lived pleasure such as ice cream. In my twenties, however, to put myself through college and graduate school, I worked 40 hours a week. This experience taught me to budget, save, and be financially responsible. Yet, well into my thirties, my father continued to lecture me about savings and to refer to any purchases I made as frivolous extravagances. I felt hurt and angry that he didn't recognize the financial responsibility I had developed.

General semanticists would say that my father's misunderstanding of me was a common problem that resulted from the use of a single, unchanging word to refer to phenomena that change and evolve. The word *Julia* labeled me at 5, 15, 25, and 35 years of age. Because my parents had an unchanging label for me, their thoughts about me were similarly fixed (notice this reflects an intensional orientation). To remedy the fixity of symbols, general semanticists recommended that we index terms to specific dates, situations, and so forth. For example, we could say that $Julia_{1958}$ was irresponsible with money, but $Julia_{1970}$ was responsible about finances. Using the dates reminds us that when we refer to Julia or others, we are referring to them at particular times, and people change. We can also index situations. We might say that $Zuri_{in\ social\ situations}$ is outgoing and dynamic, but $Zuri_{in\ one-to-one\ conversations}$ is quiet and pensive. **Indexing** terms is a way to remind ourselves that meanings vary and change across time and circumstances.

Feedforward

You've heard the term *feedback*, which refers to a response to communication. General semanticists coined the term **feedforward** to describe the process of anticipating the effects of communication and adapting to these anticipated effects in advance of actually communicating with others. Their thinking was that if we were more thoughtful in planning communication, we would have fewer misunderstandings that require repairing.

Nearly half a century after he began his career, at the age of 75, Richards (1968) reflected on the most important things he had learned in his career. Of all the insights he had gained into communication and all the solutions to misunderstandings he and others had developed, feedforward was the one that seemed most valuable to Richards. He wrote that feedforward is a method of taking into account the field of experience of those with whom we communicate and adapting our communication accordingly. Feedforward, in other words, is anticipatory feedback.

Richards advised us to take the perspective of others, to think through what we plan to say and how we plan to say it, and to ask whether the planned communication will mean to others what we intend it to mean. If Jerome walks into his apartment planning to hole up to write a paper that's due tomorrow, he might feel angry on hearing his roommate's stereo blaring. Jerome might immediately think, "I'm going to tell him to shut that ★★!!!##! music up so that I can work." Using feedforward, however, Jerome would realize that demanding and cursing may express his personal feelings, but they are unlikely to motivate his roommate to cooperate, much less to preserve friendly relations. Thus, Jerome might modify his communication and say to his roommate, "Hey, guy, could you turn it down for tonight? I have to get a paper written in time for my 9 A.M. class tomorrow." This request is likely to be more effective than the original communication that Jerome conceived.

Reflection

What aspects of situations and particular relationships affect the ability to engage in feedforward?

Although general semantics is no longer a dominant communication theory, the idea of feedforward has survived rather well. Using varying language, many theorists emphasize the importance of considering the perspectives of those with whom we communicate as a prerequisite for creating effective communication. In several books, I have used the term *dual perspective* to capture the idea that good communication requires awareness of our own and others' perspectives (Phillips & Wood, 1982; Wood, 1992a, 1995b). I have also written of monitoring, which is observing, evaluating, and adapting our communication throughout the communication process. Constructivism, which we will discuss in Chapter 6, uses the concepts of person-centeredness and perspective taking to emphasize the same process. George Herbert Mead, whose theory of symbolic interactionism we'll study in Chapter 5, wrote about taking the role of the other in order to interact effectively. Theories that we will examine in later chapters also stress the importance of considering others' viewpoints.

Critical Assessment of General Semantics

The heyday of general semantics was the 1920s through the 1940s. Since then, it hasn't prospered nor does it receive much attention from a majority of modern scholars and teachers. This is somewhat surprising, since many of the basic ideas that originated with general semantics inform current theory and teaching. For instance, the notion that the map is not the territory is an axiom found in current textbooks, and the advice to distinguish between facts (extensional orientation) and inferences (intensional orientation) is a basic premise taught in many introductory communication courses. Given the endurance of some of the concepts that general semanticists developed, why has the theory not withstood the test of time?

Too Simplistic

One reason general semantics no longer has many followers is that many scholars regard the theory as simplistic. They charge that general semantics oversimplifies communication and advises quick and easy fixes for highly complex problems. Further, some critics assert that for all of its commitments to practical applications, the theory is not very practical at all. How realistic is it to follow every noun we think or say with "etc."? The same criticism can be made of indexing and other remedies that general semanticists proposed. They may make sense theoretically, but they don't work in everyday communication.

Misrepresents the Character of Symbols and Language

A second and particularly important criticism of general semantics is that the theory misrepresents the complex character of symbols, specifically language in the case of this theory. From what you've read, you realize that general semantics views language as representing the extensional world, or concrete reality. Thus, theorists who adopt this perspective seem to suggest that all language does is represent what is—what already exists.

Many communication scholars reject the view that language is only representational (Billig, 1987; Shotter, 1993; Stewart, 1991; Wood &

Calvin and Hobbes

by Bill Watterson

Duck, 1995a). Instead, they argue, language is also presentational in that it presents images, ideas, and perspectives. In other words, language not only reflects reality; it also creates the reality in which we believe. From this point of view, one of the most powerful functions of language is to create meanings—this is far different from the general semanticists' presumption that language represents a concrete and objective reality. When you say "I love you" for the first time to another person, something happens. You are not just describing an objective phenomenon. You are bringing into existence a feeling, an identity, and a new kind of relationship. This suggests that identities and social experiences arise in discourse. If language is presentational, not merely representational as general semanticists claimed, then this theory fails to offer a good description of communication.

Lacks Applied Value

Related to the criticism that general semantics neglects the presentational power of language is the charge that some of the correctives advised by general semanticists can't be applied to a substantial portion of human communication. Why might this be so? Because symbols are inherently abstract and ambiguous, they often do not have extensional referents. For example, what are the concrete referents for symbols such as love, honor, idea, loyalty, friendship, family values, arrogance, and fear? What these symbols mean to you depends on your own experiences, values, and perceptions, and those may not be the same as others' experiences, values, perceptions, and meanings for the symbols. Meaning, in other words, often isn't based on concrete, material phenomena. Thus, it isn't always possible to follow the general semanticists' advice to "check the facts" by referring to objective, concrete phenomena.

Try it out

Can you specify extensional referents for the following terms?

1. **Betrayal**
2. **Fun**
3. **Compassion**
4. **Challenge**
5. **Fairness**
6. **Exploitation**
7. **Prejudice**
8. **Conservative**
9. **Ethical**
10. **Evil**

Check your definitions and referents for these terms with those of others in your class. What do differences among meanings imply about the practical value of the general semantics claim that extensional orientations are desirable?

Summary

Even though general semantics is no longer influential in the field of communication, it made and makes valuable contributions to our understandings of what happens when people talk to one another. Basic ideas such as "The map is not the territory" and "Meanings are in people" are shorthand references for very important insights. If we realize that words are slippery and have great potential for multiple meanings, then we are more likely to use them carefully and to check with others to see whether meanings are shared.

The general semanticists were concerned about misunderstandings that arise because of the slippage in language. Their goal was to discover and teach methods of enhancing clarity and reducing misunderstandings in communication. Because general semanticists saw context in the broad sense as the source of meanings, their theorizing focused on describing and explaining contextual sources of misunderstanding, and the practical applications they generated emphasized habits of thought and communication that minimize misunderstandings between people. As we explore more modern theories of communication in later chapters, keep in mind the central concerns of general semanticists. You will see the issues that commanded their attention resurface in various ways in theories developed in more recent years.

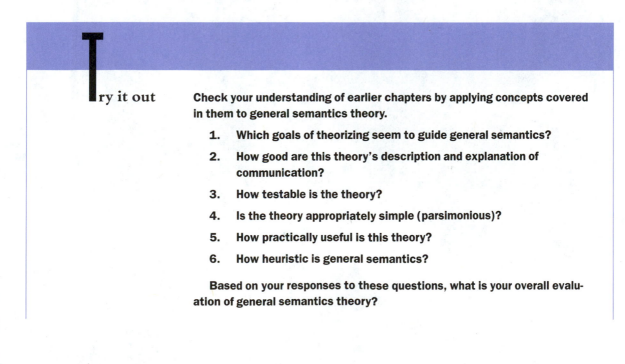

Try it out   Check your understanding of earlier chapters by applying concepts covered in them to general semantics theory.

1.   Which goals of theorizing seem to guide general semantics?

2.   How good are this theory's description and explanation of communication?

3.   How testable is the theory?

4.   Is the theory appropriately simple (parsimonious)?

5.   How practically useful is this theory?

6.   How heuristic is general semantics?

Based on your responses to these questions, what is your overall evaluation of general semantics theory?

Chapter Five

Theories About Symbolic Activity

Because symbols are at the heart of communication, scholars have generated many theories about symbolic activity. In this chapter, we'll consider three that, although distinct, are compatible in their basic assumptions about human nature and the importance of symbols in human experience. Although the theories differ in important aspects, they share a common interest in understanding the ways in which we use, misuse, and abuse communication.

Symbolic Interactionism

Although George Herbert Mead never completed his Ph.D., for many years he lectured at the University of Chicago, which was a hub of intellectual life in the United States in the 1920s and 1930s. Trained in both philosophy and social science, Mead was fascinated by the human ability to use symbols. His observations and reflections over many years led Mead to believe that human symbolic activities account for the distinct character of human thinking, for individual identity, and for the persistence of society through the behaviors of individuals.

Mead thought that symbols were the basis of individual identity and social life. In his opinion, individuals can acquire identity only by interacting with others. As we do so, we learn the language and the perspectives of our social communities. Because Mead regarded symbols as the foundation of both personal and social life, the theory he developed is called symbolic interactionism.

Throughout his academic career, Mead continuously refined his ideas about the ways humans create meaning for objects, situations, experiences, others, and themselves. During his lifetime, Mead was an enormously popular teacher and a widely respected intellectual leader. Given his influence, it is odd that Mead himself published very little during his life. After his death, however, his students collaborated to create a book based on Mead's lectures. That book, *Mind, Self, and Society* (1934), is the bedrock of symbolic interactionism. In the 60 years since Mead formulated symbolic interactionism, the theory has continued to inspire scholars in a range of fields, including communication. To understand Mead's ideas, we'll examine five of the key concepts in symbolic interaction theory.

Mind

Mead believed that at birth humans have neither minds nor selves. Both, he argued, are acquired in the process of interacting with others. In the earliest period of life, infants can interact with others only by behaving and responding to the behaviors of others. There is no way for a 4-week-old baby to share ideas with others. Once a child learns language, however, she or he can communicate meanings with words. Instead of using the behavior of crying to signal a desire for food, an infant who has acquired language can say "food," "din din," or some other symbolic code to communicate the desire for food. Also, once a child understands language, others can communicate ideas to him or her. Instead of punishing a child for throwing food after the fact, a parent can issue a verbal warning, "If you throw your food, you're going into quiet time."

Mead defined **mind** as the ability to use symbols that have common social meanings. As children interact with family, peers, and others, they learn language and, concurrently, they learn the social meanings attached to particular words. In Mead's view, social life and communication between people are possible only when we understand and can use a common language. The ability to use symbols that have common meanings allows individuals to share ideas and to communicate about ideas, rather than simply to behave toward one another as animals do (Wood, 1992).

Because language expresses social meanings, in learning language, individuals also learn the meanings of a society. Every culture has its own meanings for various feelings, actions, concepts, and other phenomena. In Western society, the word *dog* means a four-footed animal that is usually friendly and often a cherished pet. In Korea, however, dogs are often eaten. Thus, a Korean child and an American child might both learn the symbol for dog, but they would learn different meanings for it. In Western society, the word *individualism* has positive connotations of personal strength, initiative, and self-reliance. Most Asian cultures emphasize family and community above individuals, so individualism is considered selfish and unbecoming (Ferrante, 1995). In the process of acquiring language, individuals learn the common meanings of their culture. This is what it means to acquire a mind.

Self

Like mind, **self** doesn't exist at birth. Also like mind, self is developed through interaction with others. Mead regarded self as the ability to reflect on ourselves from the perspective of others. Before children develop a concept of themselves, they first experience others acting toward them, labeling them, defining them. Children learn how others see them when children hear comments such as "You're a good boy," "You're always creating trouble," "You're smart," "You're dumb," "You were an accident," or "You're the apple of my eye." The views of us that others communicate are the basis of our initial meanings for ourselves—our understanding of who we are.

The concept of **looking glass self** clarifies Mead's view of the human self. Symbolic interactionists explain that we learn to see ourselves in the mirror of others' eyes. In other words, our perceptions of how others see us are lenses through which we perceive ourselves. We learn to see ourselves in terms of the labels others apply to us. Those labels shape our self-concepts and behaviors.

Mead's views of self explain the phenomenon of **self-fulfilling prophecy** in which individuals live up to the labels others impose on them. Perhaps you have known people who believe they are unattractive, although you think they're nice looking, or who think they are not very smart, although you perceive them as bright. How others see us may be so powerful that it dictates how we see ourselves and how we live our lives, regardless of whether others' perceptions are reasonable.

I and ME

In analyzing the self, Mead was fascinated by the fact that humans have the distinctive ability to be both the subjects and the objects of their experience. We can both act and observe ourselves in the process of acting. Mead referred to the part of the self that is an acting subject as the **I.** The I is impulsive, creative, spontaneous, and generally unburdened by social rules and restrictions. Thus, the I is the source both of creative genius and individuality and of criminal and immoral behavior. The **ME** is the socially conscious part of the self who reflects on the I's impulses and actions. The ME is analytical, evaluative, and, above all, aware of social conventions, rules, and expectations. The I might think it would be great fun to go skinny dipping on a crowded beach, but the ME would probably remind the I that skinny dipping is not socially approved. The I may wish to tell off a friend or parent, but the ME imposes social guidelines.

Mead saw the I and the ME as complementary, not opposing, parts of the self. He emphasized that the I is the source of personal creativity and social invention and progress. The I's impulsive, imaginative talents are important to individuals and societies. At the same time, Mead thought, if we acted only from personal whim, desire, and impulse, collective life would not be possible. We would live in anarchy or chaos. When the two parts of the self work well together, the ME edits and channels the I's creativity in socially acceptable ways, and the I refuses to let the ME turn it into a carbon copy of other people.

Reflection

How do your I and ME show up in your everyday activities?

Role Taking

According to symbolic interactionists, the ME, or the socially aware aspect of the self, consists of the perspectives of others. As we interact with others, we come to understand the meanings they attach to situations, behaviors, people, ideas, values, and so forth. We then import, or take inside ourselves, the perspectives of others, which become our (the ME part of us) own perspectives on the world.

Symbolic interactionists claim that our meanings for things reflect the perspectives of both particular others and the generalized other. **Particular others** are individuals who are significant to us. The first particular others for most of us are family members. Later, friends, romantic partners, and work associates may also become significant people in our lives. As we interact with particular others, we gain an understanding of what things mean to them and how they make sense out of various experiences, situations, and people. Once we internalize the perspectives of particular others, we are able to see the world through their eyes. In other words, we invoke the perspective of a particular other or several particular others to guide how we think and act. The process of internalizing others' perspectives and viewing experience from their perspectives is called **role taking.**

My mother was a very compassionate woman who remains one of my models for caring for others. I often rely on my mother's perspective when I am trying to comfort a friend or student. My father was an accomplished negotiator and a very creative prankster. I find myself taking his perspective when I am negotiating business and when I am plotting a practical joke. The cast of particular others in my head also includes a teacher whose perspective I often assume when thinking about teaching, a friend whose knowledge of art is excellent and whose perspective I use when I look at works of art, and a partner whose sense of social responsibility has formed much of my own view of social issues and my contributions to my community and the planet. All of these particular others are included in the ME aspect of my self. They provide lenses through which I view both the world and myself.

Reflection

Which particular others' perspectives have you imported into your own perspective?

In addition to particular others, individuals also use the perspective of the **generalized other** to decide what things mean. Mead defined the generalized other as the viewpoint of a social group, community, or society as a whole. It includes rules, roles, and attitudes that are shared by members of the society or community in which an individual lives (Wood, 1992, p. 164). The generalized other is an organized composite of all of the particular others who are significant to us. In addition, the generalized other reflects our understandings of society in general based on direct interactions with others, exposure to media, and observations of social life.

To clarify how particular others and the generalized other are distinct, as well as how they work together, Mead relied on the analogy of a baseball game. He noted that at first a new player understands only his or her own role in the game. The player recognizes what's required to be a pitcher, first-base player, or catcher. Gradually, the new player grasps the perspectives of other particular players in the game. Even when our player is in the role of batter, she or he understands the role of pitcher enough to know that the pitcher will try to get her or him to strike at bad balls. At this point, the player grasps the perspectives of particular others. Finally, said Mead, our novice player understands the game of baseball as a whole. This involves realizing how all of the players interact and how their coordinated activities create the overall game. When our player comprehends the big picture, she or he understands and can use the perspective of the generalized other.

Let's consider an example to illustrate the symbolic interactionist view of how individuals create meanings for their activities. One of my closest friends is a man. We both understand that our relationship is neither romantic nor sexual, but is a very warm friendship. Both Bert and I are people who express affection by touching, so we're inclined to hug each other and engage in other nonverbal communication to symbolize our fondness for each other.

Our friends and families understand what our relationship is and is not, and they all realize that we are each firmly committed to other romantic partners. Because we know the particular perspectives of our families and friends, Bert and I don't worry about being misinterpreted if we embrace or touch each other when we are with these people. Yet when we are together in public settings with people who don't know us well, we restrain nonverbal expressions of affection. We understand that the perspective of the generalized other in Western society is that a man and a woman who are physically affectionate are romantically and/or sexually involved. Because we realize that is the perspective of the generalized other, we edit our behavior in public contexts. When we adopt the generalized other's perspective on nonverbal signs of affection between women and men, we understand that others would be likely to misinterpret hugs between us. Like Bert and me, all of us learn to see ourselves and our communication from the perspectives of particular others and the generalized other.

Let's summarize the symbolic interactionist view of how individuals create meaning. First, symbolic interactionists believe that people act on the basis of what things mean to them. Thus, meanings are the basis of behavior, including communication. Second, symbolic interactionists claim that meanings are formed in the process of interacting symbolically with others in a society. This implies two important ideas: (1) Symbols are the foundation of meaning; and (2) individuals' meanings aren't strictly personal, but always carry social overtones. Third, symbolic interactionists believe that the meanings individuals have for experiences, feelings, events, activities, other people, and themselves reflect the internalized perspectives of particular others and the generalized other.

As you may have realized, symbolic interactionism views individuals as interpretive beings whose mental activities, rather than external stimuli, are the source of their behaviors. Herbert Blumer (1969), a theorist who extended Mead's original work, insists that individuals construct their actions through a process of personal interpretation. Although the perspective of the generalized other may be strong and even compelling, it does not determine individuals' meanings or subsequent actions. Instead, their interpretations of others' perspectives—not those perspectives themselves—guide individuals' meanings and choices of how to communicate in particular situations.

Mead was very clear about the kinds of research he thought were appropriate and inappropriate for symbolic interactionism. He firmly rejected behavioristic views of individuals as unthinking, unwilling reactors to external stimuli (Mead, 1934). Mead also scorned experimental research, since he believed that it, and most other quantitative methods, were incapable of getting at the meaning behind observable actions (Blumer, 1969). Participant observation, ethnographic study, and interpretive textual analysis are favored methods of symbolic interaction theorists.

Try it out

Apply the criteria for evaluating theory (see Chapter 2) to symbolic interactionism. How well does this theory measure up on each criterion?

1. Does the theory provide a full description and explanation of how individuals create meaning?

2. Is the theory testable?

3. Is it appropriately simple?

4. Does it have practical utility?

5. Is the theory heuristic?

Critical Assessment of Symbolic Interactionism

As is true of most theories, symbolic interactionism has both admirers and detractors. Those who find fault with this theory tend to focus on three shortcomings.

The Theory Has Conceptual Inconsistencies   First, a number of scholars complain that Mead is inconsistent in how he describes key concepts such as self, mind, and generalized other. The response of symbolic interactionists to this criticism is twofold. First, they point out that Mead himself never formally wrote out his theory. It was only years after his famous lectures at the University of Chicago that his students synthesized their lecture notes to compile the manuscript of *Mind, Self, and Society,* which is often called "the Bible of symbolic interactionism." Second, say proponents of the theory, the concepts Mead emphasized are inherently complex and appropriately take on different nuances in varying contexts. For instance, in describing the generalized other as both society and social groups in different portions of his book, Mead was being faithful to the complicated and multifaceted nature of social life.

The Theory Is Too Vague and Broad   A second charge is that symbolic interactionism is too vague and general to be a useful theory. Critics assert that Mead's ideas are highly abstract and don't provide much insight into the specific processes by which individuals construct meanings and sculpt communication behaviors. Responding to this, symbolic interactionists argue that the criticism is unfair because it disparages Mead and his followers for not doing something they never set out to do. Mead's goal was to understand how "society got into individuals" so that they constructed meanings with reference to those commonly endorsed in the culture as a whole. Mead was successful in providing a coherent account of the role of symbols in socializing individuals and in allowing meanings to be shared by members of a society.

Calvin and Hobbes

by Bill Watterson

The Theory Neglects Self-Esteem   The third indictment made of symbolic interactionism is that it virtually ignores self-esteem, which many communication scholars consider a centrally important concept. Symbolic interactionism describes how we come to see ourselves, but has little to say about how others' labels for us and how various experiences enhance or diminish self-esteem. Symbolic interactionists agree that self-esteem is not a focus, but they don't agree that this is a weakness of the theory. Instead, they point out that Mead's goals were to describe and explain how society gets into individuals. He was not attempting to provide a critical theory. Thus, he didn't offer critical analysis of processes that affect self-esteem, and he didn't criticize ways in which the generalized other's perspective may oppress individuals and groups outside of the cultural mainstream. Like all theorists, Mead limited his attention to only some dimensions of communication and social life.

To place these criticisms in perspective, it's important to recognize that symbolic interactionism has remained healthy, vibrant, and popular for over 60 years—a record that few theories can match. In addition, this theory provides the foundation for countless other more specific communication theories. In this book, you'll hear echoes of symbolic interactionism as you study dramatism, narrative theory, constructivism, rules, cultural studies theory, theories of mass communication, muted group theory, and standpoint theory. The scope and endurance of symbolic interactionism's influence are impressive.

Dramatism

Dramatism begins with the premise that life is a drama and that it can be understood in dramatic terms. Thus, communicators involved in situations are seen as actors performing dramatic scenes on the metaphorical stage of life. Dramatism includes both rhetorical and sociological theories. Probably the best known tradition in sociology is Erving Goffman's dramaturgy, which studies individuals as always engaging in the presentation of self in everyday life. Although Goffman's (1967) perspective is fascinating, we will not examine it here.

Our exploration of dramatism will focus on the work of Kenneth Burke, a giant among symbolic theorists. Burke's theory accords a central position to symbolic action; thus, it is particularly pertinent to the study of communication. Burke sees life as a drama, which involves conflict and division that threatens some existing form of order. For example, a strike by workers creates (or makes visible) the division between workers and factory owners and threatens the existing order in which owners define the terms of work in ways that suit them. Burke also believes that drama involves scenes that invite or discourage specific action by actors. For example, a news conference called by workers invites actions that highlight their grievances and that condemn owners' lack of concern and respect for workers. Management–labor negotiation behind closed doors is a different scene that invites more cooperative forms of communication and discourages purely one-sided views. Burke believes that the conflict inherent in drama results in suffering and gives birth to new ways of understanding self, others, and situations. Thus, in Burke's view, dramatic conflict opens new possibilities for humans.

Kenneth Burke is as unorthodox a theorist as we will meet. He spent his early adult years in Greenwich Village, a New York community that has long attracted beatniks, hippies, and others who didn't fit or want to fit into the social mainstream. Unlike most of the theorists we've studied, Burke never earned an undergraduate degree. Despite this, he educated himself well in literary criticism and, later, in philosophy, communication, sociology, economics, theology, and linguistics. Clearly, he loved learning and education, even if he didn't find academic institutions the best context for his education. In mid-life, Burke taught for nearly two decades at various colleges, including Harvard, Princeton, and the University of Chicago. His time at the University of Chicago may explain the consistency between many of Burke's ideas and those of George Herbert Mead, who for years was one of the luminaries on the faculty at the University of Chicago. Unlike Mead, Burke has published prolifically. Since 1931, he has published eight books, as well as numerous articles and chapters in books. His work is widely quoted and, even when not directly cited, often is reflected in the perspectives of most communication scholars.

Burke's theory has been called the most comprehensive of all theories of symbolic action. Because Burke himself is so well read in many fields, his ideas are complex, nuanced, and sometimes very confusing. The originality and depth of his insights into human nature and human communication, however, make it worth our while to try to understand Burke's dramatistic theory. We'll do so by examining two of the central concepts in his theory and the method that he invented to analyze human symbolic behavior.

Identification

Burke launches his theory by announcing that we must recognize that all things have **substance,** which he defines as the general nature or essence of a thing. Each person is a distinct substance, a holistic essence derived from the interaction among all aspects of that individual. Burke believes that the distinct, or unlike, substance of each person is the basis of human communication. There is a degree of overlap between the substances of individuals, but it is not complete, so we remain apart. Because people are not identical, we are divided from one another. Communication becomes the primary means by which we seek to transcend our divisions and enhance our **consubstantiality,** or identification with each other (Burke, 1950).

For Burke, consubstantiality is what makes communication possible. We can understand one another only because there is some overlap in individuals' substances (experiences, language, goals). At the same time, communication can't be perfect because there are also differences and divisions that keep individuals from being completely consubstantial. Communication is the primary way that we increase our identification, or consubstantiality, with others and diminish our division, or separateness, from others.

Reflection

What connections do you see between Burke's idea of consubstantiality and Mead's idea of significant symbols?

Whether a public speaker is trying to persuade a large audience or a couple is trying to work out a conflict, division is always present and is the impetus for communication that seeks to build identification. In all cases, Burke thought, there is an order that is threatened by divisions between people. We may fail to live up to the order, or ideal, of friendship, in which case we experience guilt and must find a way to redeem ourselves. These are the interlocking moments in the unfolding drama of human communication. In Baxter's dialectical theory, division–identification might be considered a fundamental dynamic similar to autonomy–connection. In the identification–division dialectic, each pole negates the other and, simultaneously, requires the other to exist. Identification is sought because we feel division; division makes us aware of the need for identification.

Guilt

Burke (1965, 1966) argues that **guilt** is the central motive for human action, specifically communication. Guilt, however, is defined broadly as any tension, discomfort, sense of shame, or other unpleasant feeling that humans experience. In Burke's judgment, we continuously feel guilt and are continuously attempting to purge ourselves of the discomfort it causes. In other words, guilt is the primary motivation for human action. According to Burke, the ability to feel guilt is uniquely human and is possible only because we are symbol-using animals. He identifies three ways in which symbolic abilities give rise to guilt in humans (1965, 1966).

Hierarchy   Language allows us to create categories and evaluations that are the basis of social hierarchies, such as socioeconomic classes, titles in organizations, and degrees of status and power. In turn, social hierarchies create division among people, and division provokes guilt. Guilt can be aroused both by being above some people and by not being higher ourselves in the social **hierarchy.** In both cases, we're divided from others by our position in the hierarchy. Hierarchy explains the human propensity for war and conquest, which were major concerns of Burke's social criticism. Whether as individuals or nations, we want to be on top, the winner, the conqueror rather than the conquered. At the same time, the human quest for consubstantiality makes us uncomfortable with conqueror–conquered and have–have not relationships.

Perfection   In defining humans, Burke says we are "rotten with perfection" (1966). By this he means that our symbols allow us to conceive and name perfect forms or ideals that are at the top of the hierarchy: a flawless relationship, a completely egalitarian society, your ideal weight, a perfect LSAT score, a world free of war. Guilt arises because of the gap between what is the case (personal shortcomings, imperfections in relationships, social inequities) and the **perfection** that we can imagine. Because we can identify perfection, yet can never achieve it, we feel rotten. If we couldn't conceive of perfection, we wouldn't feel guilty about falling short of ideals.

The Negative   Humans, says Burke, invented the idea of the **negative,** by which he means the moral capacity to say "no," "not," and "thou shalt not." Our ability to name the negative, or what should not be, is the basis of moral judgments, which other animals do not seem to make in any sophisticated way. Because we have invented a great many negatives and we judge ourselves by them, it's difficult to avoid

"I think you'll find that we have a fairly rigid hierarchy around here."

Reprinted from THE WALL STREET JOURNAL by permission of Cartoon Features Syndicate.

guilt from disobeying some rule we've created or in which we believe. For example, we think "We should lose weight to be attractive" and we simultaneously think "It's wrong to deprive ourselves of pleasure." You believe "I shouldn't be selfish when close friends and family want my company and time," yet you also believe "It's wrong to let others define my life." You believe everyone should have basic medical care and decent living conditions, yet you also think your tax dollars should not be used to support other people. Which "should" should you follow? Which "should not" should you disobey? In Burke's view, conflicts such as these are basic to the human condition.

Try it out   List five "shalt nots" in which you believe. Select ones you consider impor-tant to your personal code of morality. Now list particular situations in which you violated some of your shalt nots. Can you identify an alternative rule that specifies a shalt not that was honored by transgressing the rule you listed?

Purging Guilt   If guilt is the primary human motive, reasons Burke, then purging guilt becomes the principal goal of communication. Two methods of ridding ourselves of guilt are available. First, we may engage in **mortification,** which is blaming ourselves. We do this by confessing our failings and asking forgiveness. "I'm sorry," "Can you overlook what I did?" and "America was wrong to interfere in the internal affairs of another country" are examples of ways we engage in mortification. A more formal method is the Catholic ritual of confession, followed by penance to regain grace.

A second way to purge guilt is to engage in **victimage,** which involves identifying an external source for some apparent failing or sin. The 2-year-old says, "She pushed me first," whereas the 40-year-old says, "I was really stressed out by work." Either way, some source other than the individual is blamed for a wrongdoing. Victimage often takes the form of **scapegoating,** which is placing sins on a sacrificial vessel whose destruction serves to cleanse an individual or group of sin. In biblical times, a sacrificial goat carried all the sins of people and the slaughter of the goat cleansed them. In secular activities, an individual is often sacrificed to redeem many others. For example, in 1994, a nominee for a high post in the administration was found to have failed to pay social security taxes on a domestic employee. She became the sacrificial scapegoat for a great many economically privileged people who hadn't paid social security taxes for their domestic employees. Once this individual was sacrificed, all prominent officials were symbolically redeemed from the sin of not paying taxes.

Try it out   **To see Burke's theory in practice, examine articles on people accused of some kind of wrongdoing that are reported in the first section of a state or national newspaper during one week. How do the reports and the statements made by those accused of misbehavior illustrate mortification and victimage? Are there any accounts of wrongdoing that don't fit into one of the means of redemption Burke identifies?**

The Dramatistic Pentad (Hexad)

To show how his theory could illuminate symbolic activities, Burke (1945) devised a method called the **dramatistic pentad.** The pentad is a tool that provides a structure for analyzing human actions. The pentad does not perform actual analysis—it provides only the terms for conducting analysis. As the name suggests, the pentad consists of five aspects that Burke considered central to understanding and analyzing human symbolic activity. The **act** is what is done by a person (insult, caress, explanation of behavior, request for forgiveness, statement of common ground). The **scene** is the context in which interaction occurs (the physical situation, the cultural setting, the historical era). The third element of the pentad is the **agent,** which is the individual or group that performs an act (the character, history, personality, occupation, family ties). **Agency** refers to the means an agent uses to accomplish an act (channels of communication, message strategies, storytelling, physical violence). Finally, the **purpose** is the goal for the act (to gain forgiveness, to highlight common ground, to scapegoat another).

Many years after Burke developed the pentad for conducting dramatistic analysis, he added a sixth element to his model of human action, thereby revising the pentad into a hexad. **Attitude** refers to how an actor positions herself or himself relative to others and the contexts in which she or he operates (Burke, 1968). Attitude is incipient action that shapes the disposition of an actor in relation to action, specifically communication. If you've ever interacted with a person who acts superior, then you understand the importance of attitude to an overall comprehension of human activity. Examples of attitudes include equality, impartiality, personal involvement, respectfulness, and arrogance. Because these attitudes underlie and shape our communication, we need to consider them in analyzing particular symbolic activities.

Doing a dramatistic analysis of rhetorical actions involves two steps. First, it's important to identify each of the elements in a particular situation: What is portrayed as the act? (What is represented as the primary issue? What is defined as not an issue?) What scene is represented as the context for action? Who is presented as the agent? (It is not always the one speaking, as for example, in the statement "He made me do it.") What is the agency of communication? (How is the act implemented?) What is the purpose of the act? (What rationale or goal is claimed?) What is the attitude of the agent? (How does the person or group position itself in relation to others, the scene, and the act?) Asking these questions gives us insight into the dramatic structure of a particular symbolic interaction.

Dramatistic analysis also may focus on **ratios** between various elements in Burke's model. A ratio is proportion. For example, 1:10 describes a 10% proportion. In dramatistic analysis of ratios, we ask how prominent each element is in relation to the others. How often is the agent emphasized? How often is attention called to scene, act, purpose, agency, and attitude? Analyzing ratios among elements of the human drama allows us to see which elements prevail in a particular situation, and this tells us something about dramatic emphasis and point of view. In addition to considering ratios, analysts may focus on points of conflict or division (Burke called these agon) and progression in a drama from an order, to division, to suffering, to purging of guilt, and finally, to redemption.

The value of dramatistic analysis is illustrated by rhetorical critic David Ling's (1970) study of Senator Edward Kennedy's speech to the people of Massachusetts in 1969. In this speech, Kennedy wanted to persuade his constituents that he was not primarily responsible for the death of Mary Jo Kopechne, a political aide who drowned when Kennedy drove his car off a bridge. In addition, he wanted to convince his constituents to grant him forgiveness in the form of supporting his continuation as their senator. In his analysis, Ling shows how Kennedy skillfully transformed himself from an agent of Kopechne's death to a helpless victim of circumstances. After transforming the agent from himself to circumstances, Kennedy then redefined the agent as the people of Massachusetts. He offered to resign if that was their wish or to stay on as their senator if that was their desire, thereby casting the voters as the actor and their decision as the primary action in the situation. Dramatistic analysis helps us see why Kennedy's speech was remarkably effective. By understanding the metamorphosis of agent during the course of his address, we gain insight into why his constituents refused to blame him.

Critical Appraisal of Dramatism

Burke's dramatism is widely regarded as the most comprehensive theory of symbolic action. This is a source of both praise and criticism. Although serious challenges to Burke's overall views have not been advanced, two reservations have been voiced.

The Theory Is Obscure and Confusing   The most frequent criticism of Burke's theory is that it is complicated, confusing, and extremely difficult to comprehend (Foss, Foss, & Trapp, 1991). Unquestionably, Burke's writing is dense and difficult to follow. In part, this is because he commands and uses the language of many different perspectives to develop his ideas. On a single page, he may mix the vocabularies of linguistics, psychology, and religion, and garnish his discussion with liberal literary allusions. Readers who don't have Burke's vast knowledge are likely to be bewildered. For people who are committed to understanding Burke's grand theory, however, the struggle to follow his ideas can be most rewarding.

The breadth of Burke's theory also leaves it open to the charge that it lacks focus. In one sense, this is a valid criticism. In later chapters, we'll examine tightly focused theories, such as uncertainty reduction, which concentrates on the relationship between communication and uncertainty. For Burke, such a narrow focus is restrictive and inadequate for understanding the many forms of communication. His aim is to explore the expansive terrain of human society, and that means studying symbolic activity wherever, however, and whenever it occurs (Gusfield, 1989). Whether the deliberate breadth of his theory is a weakness or a strength depends on your point of view. In Burke's view, it is clearly an asset.

Is Guilt All There Is?   A more specific criticism of dramatism is its claim that guilt is the basic motive that underlies most (or all) human action. Are there no other basic human motives that impel us? Are we not motivated by compassion, desire for esteem, a drive for community, and love? Celeste Condit (1992) suggests that Burke's emphasis on purging guilt and specifically engaging in victimage reflects his knowledge of Christian theology. She suggests that there may be different basic motives for human conduct in, for example, Buddhist societies. It is possible that Burke's emphasis on universality hindered him from recognizing much of the diversity in human experience and motives (Chesebro, 1992).

Although Burke might not dismiss the idea that there could be other important human motives, he would argue that guilt ultimately underlies them. Compassion, esteem, and love, after all, reflect awareness of division and a desire to transcend it. According to Burke, these motives reflect guilt, which he defines all-inclusively as any tension. If we accept Burke's broad definition of guilt, then perhaps it is the ultimate human motive and, thus, the basis of human communication.

Difficult, frustrating, imaginative, dense, confusing, fascinating—Burke's theory is all of these. It is also an extraordinarily original analysis of the motives and manifestations of human communication. Considered by many to be the preeminent symbolic scholar of this century, Burke himself says he's a "gypsy scholar" and a "word man."

 **arrative Theory**

Kenneth Burke isn't the only "word man" among communication theorists. As an introduction to another one and the theory he developed, read the four passages on the next page and consider what they have in common:

Once upon a time there were three little bears. There was a great big bear called Papa Bear, and a middle-sized bear called Momma Bear, and a little bear called Baby Bear. . . .

———

Question: *How did your day go?*
Answer: *I had a really interesting experience. I was walking to my 11 o'clock class when a guy who is in the class came up to me and started talking. It turns out that we're both juniors and both from small towns, and we both feel overwhelmed by this huge campus. We talked more after class, and we're going out this weekend.*

———

Mommy, my shirt got dirty outside, so now we have to wash it and make it clean again. Then we can put it back in my closet for another day.

———

Professor Smith, I wanted to explain why my paper isn't ready to hand in today. I have been working on it for the last 2 weeks, not waiting until the last minute. Then just when I was finishing it last night, there was a power surge and the file got scrambled. I have an appointment after class today to work with the computer support office to retrieve the file. As soon as I do that, I'll print it out and give it to you.

What do these four communications have in common? Each one is a story. *The Three Bears* is a fairy tale told to many Western children. The other three scenarios are also stories, although they are less formal ones than the fairy tale. When asked about the day, the respondent in the second example tells a story. She doesn't just say "I met a new guy." Instead, she recounts their meeting by telling a story with a plot, a climax, and a beginning, middle, and end. The child in the third example also tells a story that gives a progressive account of events that begins by defining a starting event (the shirt got dirty), moves on to identify what must be done (wash it), and casts forward in time to predict what will then happen (it will be clean and can be hung in the closet). In the fourth exchange, a student tells the professor a story (perhaps a figurative as well as a literal one) that explains why a paper is not ready on time. The student could have simply said, "My paper isn't ready, but I will have it for you soon," but instead a story is woven to give reasons for the delay. According to communication theorist

Walter Fisher, humans are natural storytellers (1978, 1984, 1987). We continuously weave discrete events and experiences together into coherent wholes that have all the features of stories: a plot; characters; action; a sequence of beginning, middle, and end; and a climax.

In Chapter 3, we discussed different ontological beliefs that theorists have. In addition to opinions about whether human behavior is determined from outside or is motivated by free will, ontological assumptions concern the essence or crux of human nature. Mead, for instance, believed that humans are defined by their ability to use symbols. General semanticists also saw symbolic abilities as the crux of human nature. In the next chapter, we'll learn about coordinated management of meaning theory, which points to the capacity to invent, understand, and follow rules to create meanings as definitive of human nature, and constructivism, which regards the ability to form and use knowledge schemata to interpret experiences as the essence of what it means to be human.

Walter Fisher thought there was something more fundamental about humans than the capacities highlighted by other theorists. He argued that humans are by nature storytelling beings and that the narrative capacity is what is most basic and most distinctive about humans. According to Fisher, humans are storytelling animals. Fisher (1987) believed that we make sense of our experiences in life by transforming them into stories, or narrative forms. In addition, he maintained that most of our communication takes a storylike form with plot, characters, and sequences of action. To appreciate Fisher's narrative theory, we'll consider two concepts critical to this perspective.

Reflection

What are the practical implications of defining humans as storytellers?

The Narrative Paradigm

Calling his theory **the narrative paradigm,** Fisher defined narration as "symbolic actions—words and/or deeds—that have sequence and meaning for those who live, create, or interpret them" (1987, p. 58). You probably realize immediately that this is a very broad view of narration. If we accept this definition, then it's difficult to identify communication that doesn't qualify as narration. That, thought Fisher, is exactly why it is appropriate to describe and explain communication as storytelling. In his view, storytelling is not an occasional activity in which we engage. Instead, storytelling describes the continuous processes by which we perceive the world and communicate with others. Storytelling, in other words, is an ongoing human activity, one as natural and nearly as continuous as breathing.

The word *story* is often associated with only formal kinds of stories such as novels, films, fairy tales, and songs. Departing from this restrictive view of stories, Fisher claimed that narrations abound in everyday life. You go to a church, temple, or synagogue, and a religious leader tells stories. Christian preachers often weave sermons out of parables, just as those are much of the content in the Bible. Buddhist priests refer to the stories they tell as *teichos,* which is translated into English as "teaching stories"—tales designed to teach a moral lesson. Science professors describe inventions and discoveries in terms of the sequence of research and thinking that led to new insights. History professors weave stories about events and experiences in former times and the effects they had. In conversation with friends, you and they share experiences by creating sequences out of discrete events (plots); dramatizing good and bad individuals (heroes and villains); imputing motives to what you and others do, think, feel, and believe (character development); and deferring the point of a discussion or the revelation of an experience until the end (climax). Stories, stories, stories— they're continuous in everyday life, said Fisher.

Good Reasons

In Western cultures, rationality is considered extremely important. We are taught to evaluate the worth of ideas and arguments by judging how much evidence is adduced, how many facts support a claim, and how well links among evidence and claims are reasoned. Fisher thought the Western emphasis on "pure logic" and conventional ra-

Table 5.1

Rational World and Narrative Paradigms

Assumptions of the Rational World Paradigm	*Assumptions of the Narrative Paradigm*
People are basically rational beings.	People are basically storytelling beings.
We make decisions and form beliefs on the basis of arguments.	We make decisions and form beliefs on the basis of good reasons.
Arguments are determined by the nature of specific speaking situations.	What we consider good reasons depends on history, culture, personal character, and biography.
Rationality is evaluated by the quality of knowledge and reasoning.	Narrative rationality is evaluated by the coherence and fidelity of stories.
Life consists of logical relationships that can be discovered through rational logic and reasoning.	Life is a set of stories; in choosing to accept some stories and to reject others, we continuously re-create our lives and ourselves.

tionality was excessive. He also thought that logic or strictly rational thinking doesn't always explain why we believe what we do.

In his original statement about narrative theory, Fisher (1978) claimed that telling a compelling story is more persuasive than scads of statistics, expert testimony, and logical deduction. He believed that because we are naturally storytellers, we are most persuaded by good stories. Nearly a decade after introducing his narrative paradigm, Fisher (1987) wrote a book that elaborated his view that compelling stories are the basis of persuasion. In that book, Fisher contrasted what he called the rational world paradigm and the narrative paradigm. The distinctions between the two approaches are summarized in Table 5.1.

The paradigm shift that Fisher advocated opens up new ways of thinking about communication, persuasion, and belief. If we accept the rational world epistemological position, then evidence and reasoning alone should guide what we believe and do. Values, emotional arguments, and aesthetic considerations should make no difference in what we believe and do. If we adopt the epistemology of the narrative paradigm, however, then a compelling story is the basis of our beliefs and actions. Within the narrative paradigm, values, beliefs, and actions are assumed to be influenced by emotional arguments and by aesthetic matters such as verbal style and dramatic flourishes.

Narrative Rationality

Although Fisher argued that we are all natural storytellers, he didn't believe that we are all equally skilled or that all stories merit equivalent belief. To answer reservations that the narrative paradigm provided no standards for judging the quality of various stories, Fisher presented the concept of **narrative rationality.** He claimed that not all stories are equally compelling; that is, not all stories have the same power to gain our belief. We judge stories on the basis of a distinctively narrative form of rationality, which Fisher saw as quite different from conventional criteria of rationality (those in the rational world view). Fisher identified two standards for assessing narrative rationality: coherence and fidelity.

Coherence   The first question to be asked about a story (remember, Fisher meant this to refer to most, if not all, communication) is whether it is coherent. Do all of the parts of a story seem to fit together believably? Does the outcome of a story make sense given the plot and characters? In short, the coherence criterion asks whether a story makes sense.

How do you decide whether a story makes sense? Fisher suggested that we first ask whether a story has internal **coherence.** We judge whether the storyteller told us all of the important details so that the outcome is believable. We try to figure out if the storyteller distorted parts of the story. We ask whether the characters behave consistently as they should, given how the storyteller portrays them and their motivations. If we find holes in a story or think it doesn't quite hang together, we will judge it to be incoherent and, thus, not compelling of our belief.

The second way we assess coherence is to compare a specific story we are told with other stories about the same or similar situations, events, and so forth. Perhaps you have been friends with a couple that broke up. If so, you may have heard two decidedly different accounts of what happened. Pat says the relationship ended because Leigh was selfish and demanding; Leigh says it ended because Pat was unresponsive and unwilling to invest in the relationship. Although there may be some truth to each account, we usually find one more compelling than the alternative.

In the fall of 1991, we witnessed a dramatic example of conflicting stories and efforts to assess the coherence of each. As you may recall, Clarence Thomas had been nominated to be a member of the Supreme Court when law professor Anita Hill came forward to charge that he had sexually harassed her years before when they worked together. The two main characters told radically different stories about what happened. Anita Hill recounted a series of vulgar remarks, inappropriate sexual impositions, and sexist and sexual activities that she alleged Thomas had committed. She portrayed him as a man with perverted sexual interests who used gutter language. He countered with a story that portrayed him as an honorable professional and Anita Hill as a hysterical feminist.

How were the Senate committee and the millions of viewers around the nation to decide between these two dissimilar stories? Many people, both senators and laypeople, were swayed by Orin Hatch and other defenders of Thomas who argued that Hill's story was incoherent. They claimed that if Thomas had actually done to her what she claimed he had, she wouldn't have continued to work for him and wouldn't have waited years to bring charges. The Senate committee apparently found this a credible attack on the coherence of Hill's testimony, since it confirmed Thomas to the highest court in the land. However, communication scholars who analyzed the hearings point out that the reason Hill's story seemed incoherent to the committee was that all members were male and white (see Bingham, 1994, 1996; "Telling Our Stories," 1992). White men, more than women or men of color, have limited experience in being trivialized and abused by others. To men who have never been sexually harassed, it wasn't credible that Anita Hill would tolerate the egregious behaviors she charged Thomas of committing, and it wasn't believable that she wouldn't have brought charges at the time she alleged he sexually harassed her. Many women of all races, however, found Hill's tolerance of abominable harassment and her ensuing silence credible. They knew, many from personal experience with sexual harassment, that victims can't always leave a job or complain officially.

Fidelity   Fisher's (1987) second standard for narrative rationality is fidelity, which he defined as the extent to which a story resonates with listeners' personal experiences and beliefs. Fidelity concerns whether a story rings true to listeners in terms of their own experiences, values, beliefs, and self-concepts. This is reminiscent of the general semanticists' emphasis on fields of experience as the filters through which we interpret the meaning of communication. According to narrative theorists, we find stories believable when they are consistent with experiences in our lives, and we find characters believable when they act as we do or as we would like to see ourselves acting. If you've ever felt irrelevant to the world, then you can identify with Willie Loman in *Death of a Salesman*. If you see yourself as an adventurer who boldly goes into new territories, then you may identify with many of the characters in *Star Trek: The Next Generation*.

Reflection

With which film and television characters do you identify? What does this tell you about how you see yourself and the values in which you believe?

Fisher explains that the standard of fidelity involves judging the values in narration. When we identify with a character, we regard her or his actions as admirable, worthy, or understandable. When we accept a story as true and right, we judge it to reflect the values in which we believe and the ways of the world as we have experienced them. Those people who identify with the idea that black men have been subject to vindictive, violent racism may identify with Thomas's portrait of the hearings as a "high-tech lynching." People who have experienced sexual harassment and have learned that superiors will not respect their complaints are more likely to perceive fidelity in Anita Hill's story.

From the perspective of narrative theory, another telling point in the events of 1991 was when Thomas proclaimed that the hearings were a "high-tech lynching." Thomas issued this charge in the form of a story of the history of injustices to black men. He chronicled discrimination against African Americans from enslavement to violent lynchings to racist treatment and attitudes in general. In likening the hearings to a "high-tech lynching," Thomas created a story that was compelling to many who heard it. The story made sense to some listeners in terms of history, culture, biography, and character—the criteria Fisher lists for what count as good reasons.

We've now explored the narrative paradigm, Fisher's expanded idea of good reasons, and the bases of judging a story's rationality. The narrative paradigm has had considerable influence in the field of communication. In 1985, one of the major communication journals devoted an entire issue to discussing the narrative paradigm (Storytelling and Narrativity in Communication Research). Seven years later, in 1992, the *Journal of Applied Communication Research* published a symposium titled "Telling Our Stories," in which members of the field who had been sexually harassed gave accounts of their experiences. Prior to the symposium, articles on sexual harassment had been restricted to reporting the frequency of sexual harassment, analyzing personal and organizational dynamics that legitimized sexual harassment, and identifying characteristics of victims and harassers. Breaking from these traditions, "Telling Our Stories" didn't offer conventional evidence about sexual harassment. Instead, it offered compelling personal accounts of what sexual harassment is and how it affects victims. Many readers reported that the 30 stories in the symposium were more persuasive and more compelling than all of the facts and statistics they had encountered in prior research. That's one example of the power of storytelling.

Critical Assessment of Narrative Theory

What's the verdict on the narrative paradigm? As is the case with any
theory, that depends on which criteria we use to assess the theory. If
we judge it by heuristic power, then it fares very well indeed. Fisher's
ideas are original, and they have provoked new ways of thinking about
communication, the nature of reasons, and the bases of judging rationality. The theory also measures up to the criterion of parsimony, since
it uses a limited number of concepts to explain communication. Even
with these strengths, the narrative paradigm has been criticized in
three ways.

Incomplete Description   First, some scholars are skeptical that the
theory really provides, as it claims to, a comprehensive description of
all communication. Is Fisher right that all communication is narrative?
Robert Rowland (1989) argues that some forms of communication are
not narrative and don't attempt to be. For example, he points out that
science fiction and science fantasy stories don't attempt to make sense
in terms of most people's experiences and values. The very purpose of
science fiction and science fantasy is to challenge prevailing values,

experiences, and ways of being in the world. We might also ask whether storytelling is at work in exchanges between customers and clerks, in business meetings, and in technical articles in scientific and professional journals.

There are two specific kinds of communication that scholars have identified as not within the articulated scope of narrative theory. First, Kirkwood (1992) argues that Fisher's view of narrative fails to explain how stories create new possibilities, new visions of ourselves and social life. Surely some storytelling, such as that by the Reverend Martin Luther King, Jr., holds forth new ways of being that are sufficiently compelling to change how people see themselves and act. James Chesebro (1995b) also believes that the narrative paradigm seems un-mindful of the metaphorical power and harmful social consequences of storytelling. For example, narratives of injustice and the right to revenge can incite riots and killing. In developing his theory, Fisher has not fully accounted for the power of stories to create new visions or to instigate evil.

Too Broad   A second criticism of the narrative paradigm is just the opposite of the foregoing charge. This criticism is that Fisher's theory is too broad. You may recall encountering this criticism in our previous discussions of symbolic interactionism and dramatism. If Fisher is right that all communication is narration, he simultaneously says everything and nothing. If all communication is narration, then defining communication as narrative fails to distinguish among different types of communication. Do we wish to lump public speaking, group discussion, intimate talk, intercultural dialogues, and organizational negotiations into one large heap called communication or stories? Such a sweeping view of communication, charge the critics, doesn't help us recognize important distinctions among myriad forms of communication.

Reflection

If all communication is narration, then does it mean anything to describe communication as narration?

Conservative Bias   A final criticism of the narrative paradigm is that it has a distinctly conservative bias. According to William Kirkwood

(1992), Fisher's idea of good reasons privileges prevailing values and attitudes and accords less attention to the ways in which stories can promote positive changes in the human condition. This is an important criticism. Remember that Fisher says one criterion for judging narrative rationality is fidelity, which he defines as how well a story resonates with listeners' beliefs, values, and experiences.

This may explain why we find some stories more credible than others, but does it amount to a sound or adequate criterion for evaluating the goodness of a story? Kirkwood thinks not. He argues that this standard of judgment encourages us to say only what will square with others' experiences and to avoid challenging prevailing views, values, and the status quo in social life. Rather than seeing his ideas as a direct challenge to Fisher's theory, Kirkwood views himself as extending narrative theory by acknowledging the power of stories to create new possibilities for people.

Fisher denies the charge that narrative theory perpetuates the status quo. Even before Kirkwood published his critical article, Fisher (1987) wrote that humans are wonderfully creative and imaginative beings. Extending this, he claims we are able to invent and accept new stories when those better explain our lives or offer better directions for future living than the stories we have grown up hearing and believing. This may account for the stunning shift in opinion over time about the stories told by Hill and Thomas. During and immediately after the Hill–Thomas hearings, national polls reported that a majority of people found Thomas's story more credible than the one Anita Hill told. However, a year after the hearings when people had thought more about the stories, a majority of those polled reported they believed Anita Hill's account. Given time to consider and weigh both stories, people were able to accept one that initially they had not found credible. The shift in beliefs about Hill's and Thomas's stories also indicates that Fisher's criterion of fidelity may not be fixed at one time, but may shift in response to additional experience and/or reflection.

There is certainly ample evidence that we are able to do more than retell old stories and respond to stories that are familiar. History is full of examples of humans who created original narrations and of people who were captivated by stories that departed from customary values, experiences, and ways of acting. Most of the major advances in social life have come about because people told new stories, ones that contested popular views and established ideas about life. The Reverend Martin Luther King, Jr., told stories about nonviolence to his followers, whose own lives had been riddled with incidents of violence in which they were both victims and perpetrators. The stories King told gave many African Americans another way of thinking about how to resist injustice. His stories were powerful not because they reflected existing experiences of African Americans, but rather because they created a compelling alternative to what they knew.

Similarly, feminists in the 1800s and 1900s did not argue for women's rights by telling stories that resonated with existing values and experiences. Instead, their narratives were of new ways of seeing women and new kinds of relationships between the sexes. Environmental rhetoric too is most successful when it offers a counterpoint to attitudes and practices that have prevailed historically. Narratives that tell of recycling, living lightly on the planet, and respecting rather than dominating the earth invite us to see the world and ourselves in new ways.

 ummary

In this chapter, we've studied three theories of how language works. Although all three theories are centrally interested in language, they offer distinct, yet compatible views—stories, Fisher would say—of what happens when people use language to communicate.

Symbolic interactionism and dramatism are especially broad theories, which means they rate well on the criterion of theoretical scope. Both theories offer expansive descriptions of relationships between individuals and social life. Whereas Mead concentrates on how symbolic interaction allows individuals to acquire minds and selves, Burke focuses on the ways in which we use language to create identifications and to purge ourselves of guilt. Both of these theories call attention to the crucial role of communication in our perceptions of others, situations, and ourselves.

Walter Fisher, on the other hand, is not particularly interested in the development of self and mind or in the motives of human symbolic behavior. His theory is an effort to explain how language bewitches, beguiles, and compels belief. Whereas general semanticists urged people to be more rational and to be more attentive to evidence and the empirical world, Fisher claims we already accord too much emphasis to conventional rationality. He advocates greater awareness of and respect for a new kind of logic—narrative rationality—in which good reasons, culture, history, character, and aesthetics are recognized as having a legitimate influence on how we interpret communication and on how we ourselves create communication.

Reflection

Do you think Westerners rely too little, too much, or appropriately on evidence and conventional reasoning?

In different ways, symbolic interactionism, dramatism, and narrative theory enlarge understanding of how we use and misuse words and why they affect us as they do. Perhaps the theories are not incompatible, but are distinct in the aspects and effects of language they describe and explain.

Chapter Six

Theories About How Individuals Construct Meaning

Erik meets a new person and notices that she's bright, friendly, politically liberal, and concerned about social issues. Erik assumes she votes Democratic and does volunteer work in her community.

―――――

At work, Carlos's supervisor tells him teamwork is expected on the new project to which he's been assigned. Carlos understands this means he's expected to share information and coordinate with others, rather than to make himself stand out as an individual.

―――――

Shennata and her partner have a disagreement. When she sees her partner's jaw clench, Shennata knows from past experience to drop the subject for now. She's learned to wait until her partner's anger blows over before confronting conflict.

On what basis does Erik make predictions about his new acquaintance's patterns of voting and community service? How does Carlos translate the abstract term *teamwork* into a specific behavioral script that will guide his future actions? What leads Shennata to believe it is wiser to delay discussing a conflictual subject with her partner?

All of these questions revolve around the process by which individuals construct the meanings of communication. Communication theorists have generated a number of impressive theories to account for the ways we go about making sense of interactions.

In this chapter, we will consider two of the most prominent and widely endorsed theories about how individuals construct meaning. The two theories, **rules theory** and **constructivism,** extend the general premises of symbolic interactionism by providing more detailed accounts of how individuals construct meanings. These two theories are compatible with each other, and both reflect the basic framework of symbolic interactionism, which we studied in Chapter 5. Although constructivism and rules theory work well together, that isn't necessarily the case for different theories about a particular aspect of communication. These two theories are compatible because they have common philosophical foundations and they share intellectual roots in symbolic interactionism.

 **ules Theory or the Coordinated Management of Meaning**

Rules theory is concerned with how humans construct meaning for their communication. It is also called the coordinated management of meaning (CMM) theory to emphasize that we use communication rules to coordinate meanings in interaction with others. CMM emerged in the 1970s and has been continuously refined and elaborated since then. This theory owes an intellectual debt to symbolic interactionism whose fundamental assumptions it shares and uses to develop its own claims.

CMM is an interpretive theory that assumes human communication is rule guided and rule following. Rules theorists do not believe human behavior is strictly determined by external forces. Instead, they think we learn broad social patterns of interpretation that are woven into cultural life and we use those to guide our communication. Immediately, you should recognize the link between this ontological premise and symbolic interactionism's emphasis on learning social meanings through interaction with others. To understand CMM, we'll focus on its three key concepts.

Hierarchy of Meanings

Barnett Pearce and Vernon Cronen (1980) believe that we rely on a **hierarchy of meanings** to interpret experiences. The hierarchy consists of multiple levels of meaning, and each level is contextualized by higher levels in the hierarchy. Thus, how we interpret experience at a lower level of meaning is influenced by higher, or more general, levels of meaning in the overall hierarchy.

Rules theorists have identified six levels of meaning in the hierarchy. They are quick to note, however, that there may be additional levels of meaning that have not yet been recognized.

Content   Consider a simple comment: "You are a jerk." The words "You are a jerk" are the **content** of communication, the lowest level of meaning in the hierarchy. We understand the dictionary meanings of *you, are, a,* and *jerk,* but that doesn't tell us how to interpret the statement. What does it mean when someone says "You are a jerk"? To construct the meaning of this content, we have to refer to higher levels of meaning in the hierarchy.

Speech Act   According to CMM theorists, communication is action. In other words, we do things when we speak: We plead, demand, promise, threaten, joke, apologize, and so forth. The action emphasis of CMM is captured in the concept of **speech acts,** which are "actions we perform by speaking" (Pearce, 1994, p. 104). Speech acts provide a context for interpreting the raw content of communication. They tell us how to view particular comments.

If a friend says "You are a jerk" and smiles while speaking, you're likely to interpret the comment as the speech act of joking. If you just told a sexist joke and a woman who is a friend of yours says "You are a jerk," you would probably interpret her comment as the speech act of scolding or reprimanding. But if you bump into a stranger on the street and he says "You are a jerk," you might decide he's engaging in the speech act of hostility or threat. Of course, *which* speech act is performed isn't always clear. That's why we need higher levels of meaning in the hierarchy.

Episode　**Episodes** are larger frames for interpreting speech acts. Episodes are recurring routines of interaction that are structured by rules and that have boundaries. For example, in the episode of "friendly banter," it is acceptable to say "You are a jerk" in a joking manner. It's within the rules for friends to exchange playful insults, but it is outside of the rules to be cruel or to inflict real hurt. It violates the rules of friendly banter to attack a friend in areas where you know him or her to feel vulnerable. "You are a jerk" takes on a different meaning if it is said within the episode of an ugly argument, in which case it would probably not be interpreted as playful and friendly. Episodes are frames that help us determine what is inside and outside of a given interaction routine (Pearce, 1994).

Relationships　The fourth level in the hierarchy is **relationships,** which are somewhat scripted ways we interact with particular others. In some relationships, you have an understanding that exchanging friendly insults is a form of playing, so "You are a jerk" is appropriate within those relationships. In other relationships, that understanding may not exist. If you and a particular friend haven't established the rule that insults aren't offensive, then "You are a jerk" may be interpreted as the speech act of serious insult, rather than play. How we define a given relationship provides a context for interpreting particular content, speech acts, and episodes within it.

Jonathan Shailor (1994), a student of Barnett Pearce, explains that we define relationships as including certain rights, exclusions, freedoms, and responsibilities. Thus, I think my partner, Robbie, has a right to complain if he feels I'm not spending enough time with him. I don't grant that same right to my neighbors. If both Robbie and a neighbor I know only casually said "I want you to spend more time with me," I would interpret the statement differently because of the distinct meanings I assign in the two relationships. I might interpret Robbie's communication as the speech act "requesting intimacy" and decide it was an example of the episode "feeling distant," which each of us has experienced in our many years together. The same statement from a casual neighbor, however, I might interpret as the speech act of "being pushy" and regard it as inappropriate in the episode of neighborly interaction.

Reflection

What happens in communication when communicators don't define their relationship in the same way?

Autobiographies   Originally, Pearce labeled the fifth level in the hierarchy "life scripts." More recently, however, he and other CMM theorists refer to it as **autobiographies.** An autobiography is an individual's view of himself or herself that both shapes and is shaped by communication. In other words, how you see yourself influences how you communicate; at the same time, communication with others influences how you perceive yourself. The link to symbolic interactionism is clear here, since Mead argued that we gain a sense of self in the process of interacting with others.

Your definition of who you are influences communication in many ways. You regard some speech acts as consistent with your sense of self and others as inconsistent. For example, helping others, being responsible, and arguing about ideas are three speech acts that are consistent with my sense of who I am. Consequently, I am comfortable in episodes and relationships that I perceive as allowing or requiring these speech acts. Being rude, ignoring others, and deferring are speech acts that are not consistent with how I view myself. As a result, I feel uncomfortable when I am in relationships and episodes that evoke being rude, ignoring others, or being deferential. Just as we see certain speech acts as consistent or inconsistent with our identities, so too do we see episodes, relationships, and even specific content as congruent or incongruent with who we are. The comment "You are a jerk" may be consistent with the autobiography of people who perceive themselves as playful and sassy. The "same" words may be incongruent with the autobiography of individuals who see themselves as formal and conventionally polite.

All of the speech acts and episodes that are consistent with an individual's sense of self make up the whole autobiography. It describes a person's overall pattern of communicating, responding, and acting in the world. Some individuals consistently act out of a tragic script in which they view events as trials, focus on losses or problems, and represent themselves as martyrs, trodden upon, or otherwise victims of a tragic cosmos. Other people operate out of a comic life script in which they approach problems with a sense of humor, appreciate the irony in events, and represent themselves as jesters. My autobiography is defined by adventure. Consistently, I approach challenges, problems, and relationships as adventures: I'm always looking for new discoveries and experiences.

Reflection

How would you describe your autobiography? How has it been shaped by communication, and how does it influence your patterns of communicating?

Cultural Patterns   The final level of meaning that has been identified is **cultural patterns.** These are understandings of speech acts, episodes, relationships, and autobiographies that are shared by particular social groups or societies. "You are a jerk" is more likely to be interpreted as friendly and acceptable among college friends than among business associates: The two social groups comprise contexts that distinctly affect how the "same" words are likely to be understood. Social groups develop distinctive ways of interpreting experiences, and these make up the cultural patterns on which members of those groups rely to construct meanings.

Because different social groups develop distinct cultural patterns, communication between cultures is often laced with misunderstandings. For example, what would you think if you asked a classmate how her job interview went and she replied, "Damn! I'm good. I was so terrific that they will be begging me to take that job. They won't even look at anyone else." If you are a European American, you might identify this as the speech act of bragging within the episode of obnoxious, egotistical behavior. On the other hand, if you are an African American, you might recognize this as braggadocio, which is intended as humor not serious boasting (Gates, 1987; Houston & Wood, 1996; Smitherman, 1977), and you might perceive it as an episode of joking or wit. Different speech communities have different cultural patterns that affect how they communicate and what various forms of communication are understood to mean. We'll learn more about this in Chapter 9, which presents theories that focus on communication cultures.

Native English speakers who were socialized in Western culture are generally very individualistic. The content of native English speakers' communication includes references to *my* school, *my* parents, *my* country, and so forth. The individualism that is a cultural pattern in the West is not pronounced in many Eastern cultures. A greater sense of family, community, and collectivity infuses most Eastern cultures. The collectivism that is a cultural pattern in many other cultures explains why the content of their communication includes phrases such as *our* school, *our* parents, and *our* country (Ferrante, 1995).

Try it out   Apply the hierarchy of meanings to analyze the levels of meaning you rely on in your own communication. Think about the last time that you had a disagreement with a friend. Now recall a specific verbal statement made in that situation.

1.   What did you regard as the content?

2.   How did you define the speech act?

3.   What did you consider the episode?

continued on next page

continued from previous page

4. **How did you perceive the relationship?**

5. **How do you describe your autobiography?**

6. **What cultural patterns can you identify that influence this specific communication?**

Notice that in each of the above questions, you were asked how you defined, interpreted, described, and perceived levels in the hierarchy. You weren't asked "What was the episode?" or "What is your autobiography?" This highlights the important point that *we* construct the meaning of communication by the ways in which we define levels in the hierarchy of meanings. The levels are not objective phenomena.

Rules

The hierarchy of meanings provides the basis for social interaction. Yet to coordinate the different levels in the hierarchy, we need some ways to connect the six levels (Box 6.1). **Rules** allow us to make sense of social interaction and guide our own communication so that we coordinate meanings with others. CMM theorists refer to two kinds of rules: constitutive and regulative.

Constitutive Rules   **Constitutive rules** define what counts as what. Like the institutional facts that Searle (1976) discussed, constitutive rules tell us what certain actions constitute or mean. For example, many people count hugging, kissing, and giving support as showing affection; listening and responding often are counted as being attentive; preparing an agenda and guiding discussion count as group leadership; and dating someone other than your regular partner may count as betrayal.

We learn constitutive rules in the process of interacting with others. Consequently, our constitutive rules reflect the cultural patterns of our particular social groups, rather than universal rules of meaning. Developing shared understandings of constitutive rules is essential if we are to coordinate meanings with others. Many romantic partners have

Box 6.1

The Hierarchy of Meanings

LEVEL 6: CULTURAL PATTERNS
A norm in this group is to engage in playful insults.

LEVEL 5: AUTOBIOGRAPHY
I'm a friendly person who enjoys fun.

LEVEL 4: RELATIONSHIPS
This is a long-standing friendship.

LEVEL 3: EPISODE
This is our normal banter.

LEVEL 2: SPEECH ACT
Joke

LEVEL 1:
CONTENT
"You're a jerk."

difficulty coordinating their constitutive rules. A common example of this difficulty concerns rules for conflict. One partner thinks disagreement counts as disruption and avoiding discussion of problems counts as being loving, and the other partner thinks constructively confronting tensions counts as loyalty to the relationship.

Reflection

According to your constitutive rules, what does conflict count as?

Regulative Rules   To coordinate communication, we also rely on **regulative rules** to guide interaction. Regulative rules tell us when it's appropriate to do certain things and what we should do next in an interaction. In the episode of playful banter, friends follow a regulative

rule that says it is appropriate to match an insult with an insult. Classroom communication often follows regulative rules such as it is appropriate to raise your hand before speaking, you can (or must) speak when the professor calls on you, and it is not appropriate to hurl insults at the teacher or other students.

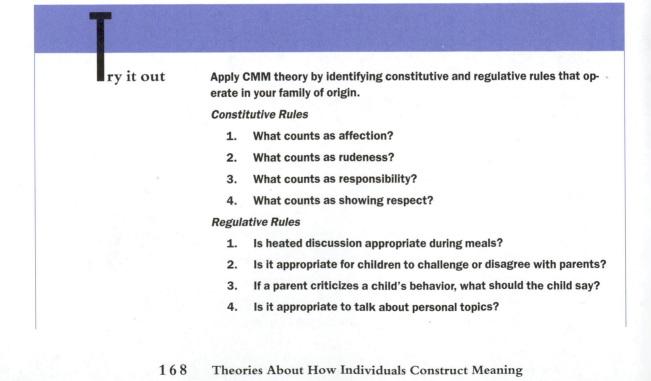

Try it out

Apply CMM theory by identifying constitutive and regulative rules that operate in your family of origin.

Constitutive Rules

1. **What counts as affection?**

2. **What counts as rudeness?**

3. **What counts as responsibility?**

4. **What counts as showing respect?**

Regulative Rules

1. **Is heated discussion appropriate during meals?**

2. **Is it appropriate for children to challenge or disagree with parents?**

3. **If a parent criticizes a child's behavior, what should the child say?**

4. **Is it appropriate to talk about personal topics?**

When constitutive and regulative rules are coordinated, interaction tends to run smoothly and comfortably. That's because the individuals agree on what various communications mean and on how to sequence their activities. But when individuals operate according to different constitutive and regulative rules, friction and misunderstandings often result. Research indicates, for instance, that men interrupt more frequently than women and that men give minimal responses ("um," "yeah") to others, whereas women typically give more extensive responses (DeFrancisco, 1991; Wood, 1994a). In a conversation among men, frequent interruptions and minimal responses may be seen as normal interaction. Women, however, may operate by constitutive rules that define interruptions as rude and minimal responses as showing indifference. This is one of many gender differences in communication. We'll learn more about these in Chapter 9.

Logical Force

As we've noted, rules theorists do not endorse a deterministic view of human nature. They view rules not as absolute and unchanging phenomena, but rather as fluid patterns that humans construct and that are more or less open to change. Some of the rules that we use to guide our communication and to interpret that of others are relatively flexible, and we may choose not to follow them at times. Yet other rules on which we rely feel binding, and we find it difficult to abandon them.

Cronen and Pearce (1981) use the concept of **logical force** to describe the felt obligation to act. The term *force* refers to the degree to which we feel we must act or cannot act in particular ways. The term *logical* reminds us that our felt obligation is tied to the logic of our overall hierarchy of meanings. We decide what we may, should, or must say based on our understandings of speech acts, episodes, relationships, autobiographies, and cultural patterns. The assumption that higher levels of meaning contextualize lower levels implies that we will feel more bound by rules that involve higher levels in our system of meanings. Thus, you might deviate from a regulative rule about how you should respond in a particular episode, but you would be unlikely to disregard a constitutive rule that is tied to your autobiography. For example, Zarina might choose not to be attentive in class (episode), but she would resist communicating in ways that undermine her view of herself as a supportive friend (autobiography).

Logical force concerns the extent to which we feel certain actions are logical, appropriate, or required in specific situations. There are different sources, or types, of logical force. Sometimes we feel we must do something because of prior actions, such as promises we've made. We may also feel logical force to act because of desired outcomes we think will result from acting. For example, mischievous children often become atypically well behaved in the period before their birthday in the expectation that good behavior will result in more or better presents. A third basis of logical force is situation demands. For instance, imagine that you attend the funeral of a relative whom you didn't like and someone who loved the deceased says to you, "Such a wonderful person, didn't you think?" The logical force of the funeral context is likely to compel you to agree that the deceased was wonderful. Finally, rules theorists say we sometimes feel impelled to change situations that are other than we think they should be. Sometimes people who grew up in dysfunctional families take it upon themselves to create very different patterns of communication in the families they create as adults. This kind of change could alter the relationship level (family) in the hierarchy of meanings. Logical force, then, comes in four different forms but has the common feature of leading us to feel that certain kinds of communication are right, appropriate, or required.

Strange Loops   Pearce's student Robert Branham and Pearce (1985) extended the theory by identifying what they called **strange loops** in interaction. Strange loops are internal conversations in which individuals become trapped in destructive patterns of thinking. Meanings at different levels in the hierarchy interact to sustain a repetitive cycle of behavior from which an individual seems unable to escape. Using this concept, therapists have helped clients deal with eating disorders and other problems.

Let's consider an example of a strange loop. Repeatedly, Marla drinks too much and suffers a hangover and impaired ability to function the next day. Marla defines her behavior as the act of getting drunk in the episode of college partying. Finally, Marla decides to get control of her problem and resolves not to drink. After 3 weeks without any alcohol, Marla concludes she can control her drinking and, thus, she doesn't have a problem. So she drinks at the next party, and the whole cycle begins anew.

Is Marla forever trapped in this destructive cycle? Not necessarily. CMM theorists would argue that if Marla wants to escape from this strange loop, she will need to revise her hierarchy of meaning. Perhaps Marla should redefine drinking episodes as "problem behavior," instead of "college partying." As long as Marla interprets her drinking as routine college partying, she's likely to regard it as acceptable and normal. It might also help Marla escape the strange loop if she redefined "college partying" as "drinking scenes" and redefined her own participation in parties as "abstaining from alcohol." Marla might also consider redefining her autobiography to include the view of herself as alcoholic or predisposed to have problems with alcohol. By altering the meanings she assigns to her drinking and to herself, Marla might be able to escape from a strange loop that is dangerous and potentially debilitating.

Try it out   **Identify a strange loop in your life. It might be a recurring cycle having to do with eating or drinking problems, or a negative repetitive pattern in a relationship.**

Once you have the strange loop in mind, answer these questions:

1.   **How do you define specific actions that make up the strange loop?**

2.   **How do you describe episodes in the strange loop?**

3.   **What views of relationships provide a context that maintains the cycle in the strange loop?**

4.   **How does your autobiography, or life script, explain and/or sustain the strange loop?**

5.   **Do any cultural patterns include meanings that justify or normalize the strange loop?**

Let's summarize what we've learned about CMM or rules theory. The fundamental premise of the theory is that individuals create meanings by relying on an organized system of meanings in which higher levels contextualize lower levels of meaning. In interaction, individuals rely on constitutive and regulative rules to guide how they communicate and how they interpret the communication of others. Like symbolic interactionism, CMM assumes that people make sense of their experiences by assigning meanings to them. Also like symbolic interactionism, CMM assumes that the meanings we assign are not entirely unique to individuals, but are nestled within larger frames of reference and meaning that operate in cultures.

Originally, CMM theory was envisioned as a theory of interpersonal communication. Since the theory's birth, however, it has been applied to intrapersonal, organizational, therapeutic, and intercultural communication. Jonathan Shailor (1994) relied on CMM principles to analyze uncoordinated communication between spouses engaged in dispute mediation. Several scholars have used CMM theory to describe and explain various aspects of communication in institutions and organizations (Barge, 1985; Harris, 1979; Williams, 1989). This theory has also illuminated lack of coordination between people from different cultures (Cronen, Chen, & Pearce, 1988).

Critical Assessment of CMM Theory

Criticism of CMM has tended to focus on three issues.

Unclear Meaning of Rule   One problem is that not all rules theorists agree on the meaning of the key basic concept of rules. Susan Shimanoff (1980, 1985) asserts that rules deal exclusively with observable behaviors. On the other hand, Pearce and his colleagues (Cronen, Chen, & Pearce, 1988; Cronen & Pearce, 1981; Pearce, 1989; Pearce & Cronen, 1980) claim that rules pertain to internal, subjective interpretation, as well as to overt activities. Because the term *rule* is used to mean different things, it's difficult to coordinate findings from rules theorists' research. Of course, the deeper issue underlying terminological confusion concerns epistemological assumptions. If we assume that only observable behaviors can be known, then we would agree with Shimanoff's definition of *rule*. If, however, we think that behaviors that aren't overt also matter and deserve scholarly attention, we're likely to find ourselves more comfortable with Pearce and his colleagues' view of rules.

Too Ambiguous   Rules theories have also been criticized for their ambiguity. Not only is there no agreed-on definition of rule, but theorists have not advanced a precise definition of how to identify whatever it is they count as rules. In other words, what are the constitutive rules for defining rules? This ambiguity leads to the related question of whether rules theory deals well with unexpected forms of communication. If rules are based on the hierarchy of meanings and are influenced by logical force, then what accounts for creativity, innovation, and violations of convention? Ambiguous responses—such as the assertion that violations follow different rules—are not convincing. Rules theorists have not developed or identified precise rules for violations, so creative behaviors remain difficult to analyze within the framework of this theory.

Too Broad in Scope   The most common and most serious criticism of CMM theory is that it is too broad in scope. Critics have asserted that CMM tries to explain the whole universe from problems between cultures to difficulties in intimate relationships (Brenders, 1987). In attempting to explain such diverse phenomena, critics charge, the theory fails to achieve sufficient precision to permit insight into specific communication activities.

CMM theorists do not deny the charge that the theory is extremely broad. They do, however, reject the idea that this is a problem or a weakness of the theory. One of the primary theorists, Vernon Cronen (1991), replies to the criticism by asserting that a good humanistic theory should shed light on the overall human condition, not just on isolated facets of human activity. CMM theorists argue that the theory is meant to offer an expansive view of human action and should be assessed in terms of whether it achieves that goal. If that is the criterion of evaluation, then CMM fares rather well. Unquestionably, it gives us new insights into how we create meanings and how our patterns of making meaning guide our communication.

Reflection

Based on the foundations of theory that you endorse, what do you perceive as values of CMM theory?

Constructivism

Symbolic interactionism gives us a broad picture of humans as interpretive beings who actively engage in the process of constructing meanings for their activities. Yet it doesn't explain in a precise way exactly how we go about interpreting the world to assign meanings. Constructivist theory attempts to do this. Working from the fundamental assumptions of symbolic interactionism, constructivist theorists have developed an account of how the interpretive process works. The roots of constructivist theory are symbolic interactionism and psychologist George Kelly's (1955) personal construct theory. Both of these foundations for constructivism focus on cognitive processes that we use to create meaning. Extending those foundations, communication theorists have elaborated the relationship of cognitive processes to communication (Delia, O'Keefe, & O'Keefe, 1982). Before studying this theory, respond to Box 6.2, which is an abbreviated version of the basic research tool used by constructivists (Crockett, 1965).

To understand constructivist theory, we will discuss three of its primary concepts. As we do so, you'll discover how constructivist theorists would interpret your descriptions of a liked and disliked peer and what they would conclude about your ways of constructing meaning.

Think of people about your age whom you know well. Select one person that you like and one person you dislike. Thinking about these two specific people, spend a moment to mentally compare and contrast them in terms of personality, habits, beliefs, and the way they treat others. Don't limit yourself to similarities and differences between the two; consider all of the qualities that make them who they are.

Please spend about 5 minutes describing the person you like so that a stranger would have an accurate picture of him or her. Don't describe physical characteristics, but do list all of the attributes, mannerisms, and reactions to others that identify who the person is. Use phrases and single words to describe the person; full-sentence descriptions aren't necessary.

When you've finished describing the person you like, repeat the procedure to describe the person you dislike.

Box 6.2
Role Category Questionnaire

_____   _____
        (liked peer)   (disliked peer)

1. _____   1. _____

2. _____   2. _____

Continue list on another sheet of paper.

Cognitive Schemata

In his original theoretical statement, George Kelly (1955) claimed that personal constructs are the building blocks for individuals' interpretations of experience. Substantial research since Kelly's formulation of the theory has supported his basic insight and identified three additional kinds of knowledge structures or **cognitive schemata.** We'll consider each of the four and how they work together to help us make sense of our experiences.

Prototypes **Prototypes,** the broadest cognitive structure, are ideal or optimal examples of a category of people, situations, objects, and so forth (Fehr, 1993). You have prototypes of "great teachers," "nasty supervisors," "good friends," and "two-faced people." For each category, your prototype is the person who most exemplifies the whole category—the ideal teacher, the nastiest boss you ever worked for, the best friend you ever had, and the most duplicitous person you know.

That person who embodies the category is your prototype. We use prototypes to interpret others who fit in particular categories. Thus, when you begin a new class, you don't interpret the professor in terms only of what he or she does. Instead, you compare that person to your prototype of great teachers. Thus, how you experience the new teacher is influenced by your prototype for teachers.

Reflection

How do prototypes help you interpret interpersonal experiences?

Personal Constructs **Personal constructs,** the second broadest knowledge structure, are the building blocks that Kelly (1955) originally identified. Kelly defined personal constructs as "mental yardsticks" that allow us to measure a phenomenon on a particular dimension. Personal constructs are bipolar, or opposite, scales of judgment. Examples of personal constructs many people use in judging others are intelligent–unintelligent, interesting–uninteresting, attractive–unattractive, ethical–unethical, and kind–unkind. Each of these bipolar scales serves as a measuring stick by which you interpret others and compare people to one another: Konya and Allison are both intelligent, and Konya is more intelligent than Allison. Whereas prototypes help us place a person or experience in a particular category (both Konya and Allison are intelligent), personal constructs allow us to go further and assess the person or experience in depth and in comparison to others along particular dimensions we consider relevant (Konya is more intelligent).

Reflection

What personal constructs are salient in your initial impressions of people?

Stereotypes **Stereotypes,** the third type of knowledge structure, are predictive generalizations. Stereotypes go beyond the description that prototypes and personal constructs provide and make predictions about how a person will behave. When we stereotype a person, we prophesy what she or he will do based on the general group into which we have classified the individual (notice that we classify people, so that too is part of our interpretive construction of meaning). For example, because you've defined Aaron as liberal, you predict he votes for pro-choice candidates; because you've interpreted Margo as an ambitious person, you predict she isn't committed to homemaking and mothering. Your predictions may be correct or incorrect. Either way, they are part of how you interpret others and decide who they are.

Scripts Finally, the cognitive schema known as **scripts** are guides to action, much like the episodes that we read about in CMM theory. Scripts are routines, or action sequences, that we have in mind about particular interactions. You have scripts for most of your daily activities such as how to talk to clerks in stores, how to discuss classwork with professors, and how to interact with friends or roommates. You also have scripts that define what kinds of behaviors and sequences of behaviors are appropriate in contexts such as classes, parties, visits with family, and so forth. Scripts are our understandings of how particular kinds of interactions are supposed to proceed—what happens, what comes first, second, and so forth. Thus, they help us organize interaction.

Among college students, researchers have found broad agreement on scripts for dating: Men are still expected (by both sexes) to initiate dates and plan activities, and women are still expected (by both sexes) to defer to men's initiatives except in the realm of sexual activities (Pryor & Merluzzi, 1985). Leslie Baxter (1992), an interpersonal communication scholar, reports that playfulness and "hanging out" with no particular purpose are important scripts for friendship. Steve Duck and Paul Wright (1993) also found that talking and working together on a project are among the most common scripts for women's and men's friendships.

Reflection

What is your script for a first date? How does your script compare with the scripts of others in your class?

Prototypes, personal constructs, stereotypes, and scripts organize how we think about others and situations and help us make sense of interpersonal experiences. These four knowledge structures provide a simple, concise description of how we interpret phenomena.

Try it out

Think about a relatively common communication activity in your everyday life. Examples are meeting with a professor to discuss your work in a class, having lunch with a close friend, and visiting with your family over the holidays.

Once you have the specific activity in mind, answer the following questions:

1. What prototypes do you apply in interpreting the activity and other people?

2. What personal constructs are salient in how you think about the other people?

3. What stereotypes do you make about how specific others will act? What is the basis of your predictive generalizations?

4. What script do you follow in this activity? Has your script ever not worked? What happened?

Cognitive Complexity

Although four kinds of knowledge structures have been identified, only one has been the focus of substantial research by constructivist scholars in communication. Personal constructs are the centerpiece of constructivist theory building, perhaps because they are the most specific interpretations we make of others.

Constructivists believe that people vary in the complexity, or sophistication, of their interpretive processes. Some of us, they claim, have more elaborate ways of organizing perceptions and interpreting phenomena. The concept of **cognitive complexity** refers to how elaborate or complex a person's interpretive processes are along the three dimensions of differentiation, abstraction, and organization. We'll discuss each of the three.

Differentiation The first facet of cognitive complexity is **differentiation.** It is measured by how many distinct interpretations (in this case, constructs) an individual uses to perceive and describe others.

Presumably, more cognitively complex individuals have and rely on a greater number of constructs to interpret others than do less cognitively complex individuals.

Constructivist theorists don't emphasize average numbers of constructs that are used by more and less cognitively complex individuals. Thus, there are no absolute scores that tell us how complex a person is. However, you can get a rough idea of how your own cognitive complexity would be scored by counting the number of distinct constructs you used in the descriptions of a liked and disliked peer. Do not count as separate constructs adjectives and adverbs that are attached to a descriptive term. For example, *kind, very kind,* and *always kind* would count as one construct, not three. Also don't count separately items that are repetitious. If you described your liked peer as *interesting* twice, that counts as only one construct. More than 30 constructs is above average in cognitive complexity.

Abstraction   The dimension of cognitive complexity referred to as **abstraction** focuses on the extent to which an individual interprets others in terms of internal motives, personality traits, and character. It shows less cognitive complexity to describe George as quiet because he doesn't talk much than to interpret George's quietness as stemming from personal insecurity. The latter explanation is rooted in internal processes that are less visible and more abstract than concrete descriptions of what appears on the surface of interaction.

To assess your abstractness, consider how many of the descriptive terms you used in Box 6.2 are surface-level observations (quiet, attractive, physically active) and how many offer more in-depth psychological impressions (secure, compassionate, spiritually centered, inconsiderate).

Organization   The final facet of cognitive complexity is organization, which is the degree to which individuals notice and are able to make sense of contradictory interpretations. For example, perhaps you know a person who is outspoken and assertive in classes, but quiet and deferential in social situations. How would you reconcile these seemingly contradictory observations? A person who is not highly cognitively complex might simply record all observations without even recognizing tensions among them. Another cognitively unsophisticated interpretation would be to say "Sometimes Logan is outspoken, and sometimes he is not." That may be true, but it provides little insight into the psychological dynamics behind what is observed on the surface. A more cognitively complex explanation would be "Logan is outspoken and assertive in academic contexts where he feels confident, but he is more quiet and passive in social situations where he feels unsure of himself." This explanation reconciles the two observations by linking both to the psychological dynamic of confidence or security.

Most constructivist research has measured cognitive complexity primarily or entirely in terms of the one facet of differentiation. Obviously, this is a convenient and easy aspect of complexity to measure, since all we have to do is count the number of distinct constructs a person uses to interpret others. But does a measure of differentiation tell us anything about cognitive abstractness and organization? According to proponents of differentiation, it does. They point out that early efforts to measure all three facets demonstrated that differentiation is moderately positively correlated with abstractness and organization (Burleson & Waltman, 1988; O'Keefe & Sypher, 1981). Thus, claim the theorists, measuring all three is redundant and unnecessary to determine how cognitively complex individuals are.

Person-Centeredness

According to constructivists, people who are cognitively complex are capable of engaging in more sensitive communication that is tailored to particular others. They refer to this as being **person-centered.** Here's the reasoning: A person who is not cognitively complex doesn't perceive many nuances in others, misses subtle differences among people, and doesn't understand surface behaviors in terms of internal, psychological dynamics that provide insight into people. On the other hand, a cognitively complex individual interprets others in detailed ways, is able to distinguish people from one another on multiple dimensions, and has insight into the psychological reasons behind specific behaviors and communication patterns (Burleson & Waltman, 1988).

If this is true about cognitively complex individuals, then the interpretations they make allow them to adapt their communication to the particular style, needs, tendencies, and so forth of other individuals. Consequently, they would be more persuasive and effective in personal and professional interactions (Applegate, 1990; Zorn, 1991). Suppose Rodriguez is a supervisor who has to have performance appraisal conferences with three of his subordinates, John, Myranda, and Suchen. If Rodriguez is not highly complex cognitively, he may express criticism and identify areas for improvement in much the same way to all three subordinates. However, if Rodriguez is cognitively complex, then we would expect him to use different communicative strategies with the three distinct subordinates. Perhaps he would be very explicit about desired changes in talking with John, whom Rodriguez perceives as a concrete thinker and someone who needs considerable guidance. With Myranda, Rodriguez might be more indirect and simply suggest general areas for improvement, because he perceives her as able to make inferential leaps and as self-initiating. He must be much more supportive and spend more time emphasizing positive aspects of Suchen's job performance, since Rodriguez perceives her as very unsure of herself. The ability to adapt communication to particular others is an earmark of effectiveness.

Reflection

Describe a person you consider person-centered in his or her communication and a second person you think is not skilled at person-centered communication. In what ways do their different levels of person-centeredness affect your relationships?

The research inspired by constructivist theory is impressive and growing. The studies conducted so far have largely supported the theoretical claims advanced by constructivism. One firm conclusion from existing research is that the link between cognitive complexity and person-centered communication is clear and strong. In a specific extension of work on person-centered communication, Brant Burleson has studied comforting communication (Burleson, 1989; Burleson, Albrecht, & Sarason, 1994). His studies indicate that more cognitively complex individuals are more skilled than less cognitively complex individuals in creating messages that are comforting to particular others.

Another important line of constructivist inquiry concerns the development of cognitive complexity in children. Ruth Ann Clark and Jesse Delia (1977), who are among the foremost constructivist theorists, first measured young children's cognitive complexity by giving them the Role Category Questionnaire (RCQ) to which you responded in Box 6.2. After taking the RCQ, the children were asked to create persuasive messages for three different listeners. Those children who were more cognitively complex showed greater flexibility in adapting their communication to listeners of different ages and interests. The less cognitively complex children either didn't recognize that listeners might differ from them or realized the differences but didn't tailor their communication to address these differences.

Critical Assessment of Constructivist Theory

Three serious criticisms of constructivist theory and research have been advanced.

Internal Validity Is Questionable First, questions have been raised about the internal validity of constructivist theory. Not all scholars are satisfied with the adequacy of the RCQ, which is the single measure on which constructivists rely in developing and testing their theory. One question is whether the RCQ actually measures what ordinary people think of as cognitive complexity (this is referred to as validity). Some scholars believe that the RCQ is largely a measure of vocabulary, rather than the actual complexity of an individual's interpretations. According to this criticism, a person with a large vocabulary could provide more elaborate and wordy descriptions of a liked and disliked other than could a person with a more limited vocabulary. There is doubt about whether the number of different words a person can use to describe others accurately reflects the complexity of her or his thinking about others. Even if we accept the RCQ as an adequate method of gauging cognitive complexity, we might still doubt the appropriateness of measuring cognitive complexity in terms of only one of three facets that are theorized.

Pragmatic Utility Is Weak   A second criticism is that constructivist work has made little effort to deal with applied communication. Not only has applied research received little attention so far, but the leaders of the theory seem to think this trend will and should continue. Jesse Delia, who is acknowledged as the founder of the theory, argues that applied research detracts from a concern with pure theory. He sees developing and testing constructivist theory as the primary, if not exclusive, goal of future research (Griffin, 1994, p. 149).

As we noted in Chapter 2, many scholars believe a good theory should have practical value—it should make a difference in the real world. Those who regard pragmatic utility as an important criterion for assessing theory reproach constructivists for ignoring practical applications. Others, including many of the prominent constructivists, argue there is value in purely theoretical research. They claim that a good theory will eventually have practical applications. Discovering and implementing the theory's practical implications is not, however, what pure theorists should do. Instead, their goal is to develop and refine the theory. Once that is done, others can apply it.

Reflection

Must all scholars concerned with theory attend to pragmatic issues?

Theoretical Scope Neglects Communication   Related to the second criticism is the recurrent charge that constructivist research and theory are more concerned with cognitive processes than with actual communication. As you read about this theory, you probably noticed that it emphasizes cognitive operations involved in perceiving and interpreting interpersonal phenomena. Although it seems safe to assume there is a link between how we think about others and social situations and how we communicate, that link has been little explored so far.

In response to this criticism, some constructivist researchers are conducting studies that advance understanding of how cognitive processes affect actual talk between people. Ted Zorn (1995) has integrated constructivism with other theories to examine how people make sense of interactions in the workplace. Brant Burleson's (1984, 1991) studies of comforting communication also apply constructivist theory and use constructivist research methods to enlarge understandings of how cognitive schema influence our efforts to communicate comfort.

 ummary

In this chapter, we've examined two theories that are centrally concerned with how individuals create meanings. Asking how we make sense of the world, ourselves, and interaction, these theories offer keen insights into the ways in which we sculpt lines of action for ourselves and assign meaning to the actions of others.

Both CMM theory and constructivism build on the rich foundations that symbolic interactionism provides. Each theory assumes that humans are interpretive beings who actively work to make sense of experiences. The humanistic premise that underlies both of these theories explains why they focus less on external phenomena than on how individuals process impressions. CMM theory is an ambitious effort to explain the multiple levels of meaning that we rely on in order to make sense of experiences and coordinate communication. Constructivist theory emphasizes different aspects of cognition (personal constructs and cognitive complexity instead of rules and the hierarchy of meaning) in its quest to describe and explain how we organize perceptions in ways that affect our communication.

Because CMM and constructivism share ontological and epistemological assumptions, the two theories are generally compatible. Each offers a particular angle of vision on the overall question of how we go about the complex, difficult, and fascinating process of deciding what things mean in our lives. Despite the high degree of compatibility between CMM and constructivism, the two theories are distinct. Theorists of the two schools identify and pursue different goals.

Whereas constructivists have historically been less interested in pragmatic applications of the theory than in developing the theory itself, CMM theorists have consistently highlighted the ways in which their theory applies to real-life situations. The uses of CMM to describe strange loops and to suggest ways of escaping their confines exemplify the commitment to making a difference in everyday life. Whether you regard immediate utility as a particularly important goal of theorizing will affect how you judge these two theories.

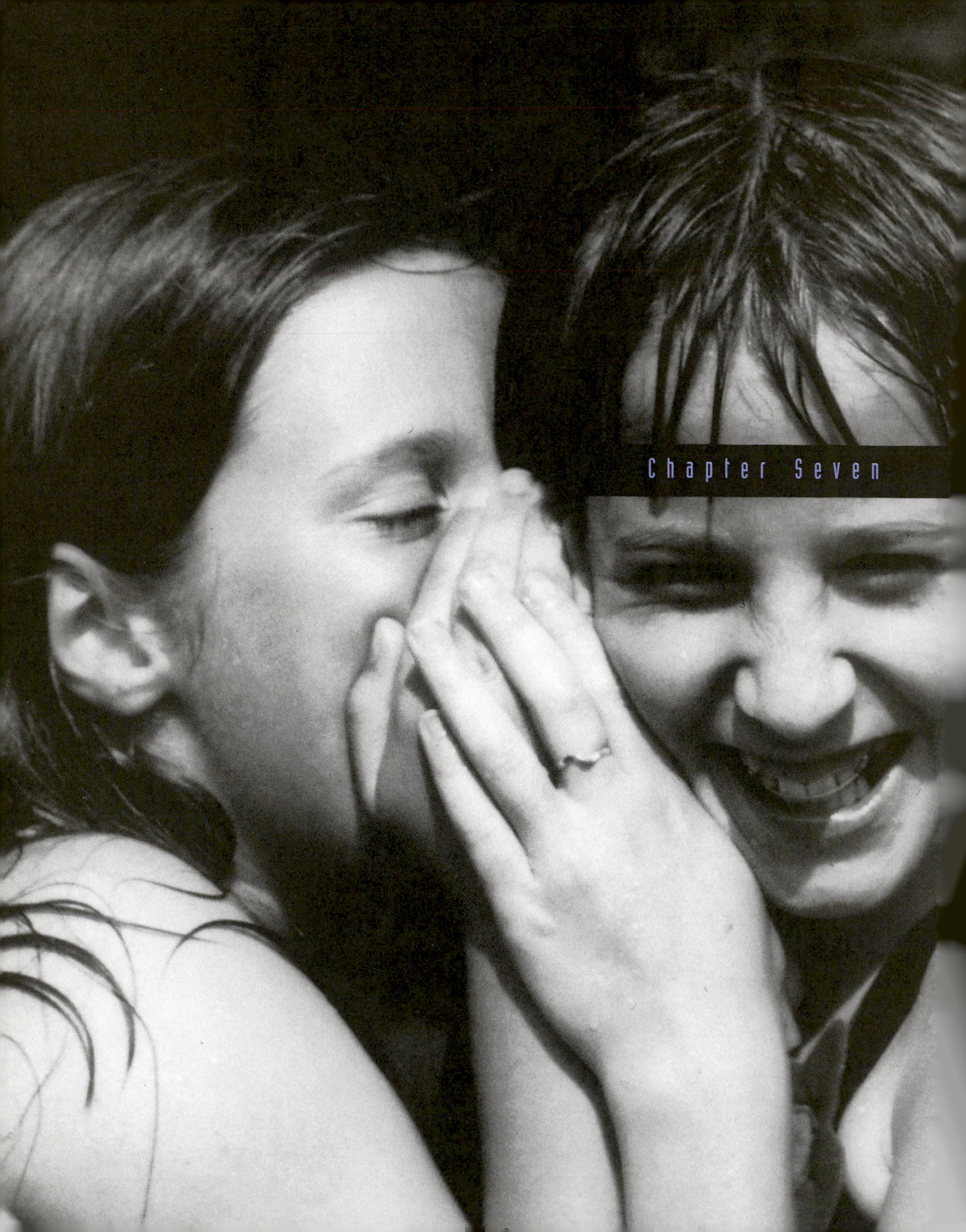

Chapter Seven

Theories of Communication Dynamics

To some extent, all communication theories deal with the dynamics of human interaction. It's not possible to ignore dynamics when communication is the topic of study. Yet only some theories focus on the dynamics of communication. For these theories, the central concern is the processes that are involved in communication and that explain some of the outcomes of interaction. Theories that emphasize processes try to get at the *how* and *why* of communication phenomena. They ask questions such as these: How does communication operate? How does communication affect satisfaction in relationships? How are patterns of communication formed and changed, and how do they affect people and relationships? How do facets of communication affect one another? In this chapter, we'll consider two theories that concentrate on communication dynamics: interactional theory and dialectical theory.

Interactional Theory

In 1967, three clinicians named Paul Watzlawick, Janet Beavin, and Don Jackson wrote a very important book titled *The Pragmatics of*

Human Communication. In it the authors advanced an original and bold **interactional theory** (also called pragmatic theory) of communication. Both immediate and long-term responses to interactional theory have been positive, and it remains influential in the field three decades after it was first formulated.

Watzlawick, Beavin, and Jackson had spent years counseling troubled families. Their clinical experiences led them to new insights about what was involved in communication and how it works. Working with nearly two dozen other clinicians at the Mental Health Institute in Palo Alto, California, Watzlawick developed interactional theory. Although the original theorists were most interested in family interaction and applied their theory to family contexts, other scholars have extended the theoretical principles of interactional theory to other types and environments of communication. To understand interactional theory, we'll discuss four of the most important concepts it includes.

Communication Systems

Prior to interactional theory, many communication professionals had concentrated on isolated aspects of communication or individual communicators: the verbal behavior of group leaders apart from the behaviors of other members and the context in which the group meets; the behaviors of an individual who was labeled dysfunctional independent of the interpersonal situation in which the person was "dysfunctional"; conflict episodes divorced from other communication patterns in relationships. According to interactional theory, investigations of this sort neglect the fact that communication occurs in contexts that affect it and what it means. Interactional theorists claim we can't understand group leaders, so-called dysfunctional individuals, or conflict episodes unless we examine them in context.

Reflection

In what ways do you think general semanticists would agree or disagree with the idea that communication can be understood only within contexts?

The idea of contexts did not originate with Watzlawick. A Viennese professor of biology named Ludwig von Bertalanffy pioneered the idea under the name of **general systems theory.** Shortly after emigrating to Canada in 1949, von Bertalanffy founded the Society for the Advancement of General Systems Theory. Von Bertalanffy's biological research led him to puzzle over basic questions about life: Why does a live sponge that is forced through a sieve spontaneously reorganize itself? Why does transplanting certain cells from the leg of a newt to its tail result in growth of a second tail instead of a new leg? Why when one organ is injured or destroyed in a living creature do other organs compensate by replacing the functions of the damaged organ (Hampden-Turner, 1982, p. 158)?

After many experiments and years of thinking, the scientist concluded that these things happen because life forms are organized wholes that seek to sustain themselves (von Bertalanffy, 1951, 1967). In other words, organisms are dynamic wholes that function and continue to exist as a result of organized interaction among parts. An organism seeks to sustain its wholeness or structural integrity. This explains why the newt grows only tails and not legs in the tail area of its body. If the original wholeness of an organism is disrupted or no longer possible, the organism generates an alternative form of holistic organization. This explains why other organs take over for damaged ones and why live sponges reconstitute themselves after being reduced to pulp.

You may be wondering why we're discussing newts and sponges in a book on communication theories. The reason is that von Bertalanffy's insights were not restricted to biology. He believed that all life forms, social as well as biological, can be understood only as complex, organized wholes that he referred to as systems. Von Bertalanffy's insights into life were considered so valuable that he was nominated for a Nobel Prize just before his death in 1971 (Hampden-Turner, 1982).

The Palo Alto Group of therapists used von Bertalanffy's ideas about life systems as the foundation of their interactional theory of communication. System thinking also quickly found its way into communication research and teaching (Fisher, 1982). Most concisely defined, a communication system is a group of interrelated and interacting parts that function as a whole (Wood, 1992, 1995b,c). There are four propositions to the systems view of communication.

All Parts Are Interrelated The elements of communication systems are not simply a heap of parts that happen to be together. Instead, as von Bertalanffy realized, the parts are interrelated and interacting. Because the parts of a system are interdependent, they affect one another. This explains one of the axioms of interactional theory: If you change any part of a system, you change the entire system. Anyone who has had a child understands how one new part (the baby) in a system (the marriage) changes all aspects of the system, including how parents interact with each other, when meals are served, and what kinds of recreation are pursued. Drawing an example from CMM theory, if you change how you define episodes and autobiographies, you may be able to extricate yourself from strange loops. The general semanticists whom we discussed in Chapter 4 relied on this systems principle (though they used different terminology) in advising people to replace intentional orientations with extensional ones in order to improve the accuracy of their thought and communication.

Systems Are Organized Wholes This second proposition of systems theory emphasizes the idea that we cannot understand any part of a system in isolation of the other interrelated parts. Because systems are organized wholes, they must be seen and studied as a totality of interacting elements (Hall & Fagen, 1956). By extension, each element of the system must be understood within the context of the overall system. Prior to the Palo Alto Group's insights, therapists often worked with disturbed members of families and tried to "fix" the individual who supposedly was the problem that was disrupting family life. Thus, an alcoholic might be separated from his family and given therapy to reduce the motivation to drink and/or to increase the desire not to drink. Often, however, the alcoholic who was "cured" resumed drinking shortly after rejoining his family.

Systems theorists believe this result is almost inevitable when therapists fail to deal with the entire family system. In many dysfunctional families, the "problem person" is assisted by other family members. Perhaps the alcoholic's wife denies he has a problem, and his children try to cover for his lapses to minimize friction in the family. The problem isn't the individual, but the whole system in which the individual's alcoholic tendencies interact with co-dependent patterns of other family members.

Now assume the man has individual therapy, then returns to his family. If he says he is an alcoholic, his wife may deny that because this is her patterned way of acting in the family system. When the man acknowledges he has a drinking problem and his wife denies that he does, the children are anxious about the friction between their parents. Consequently, they engage in their patterned responses to tension by trying to excuse or cover up for their father. With everyone else telling him he doesn't have a drinking problem and criticizing him for causing discord by saying he's an alcoholic, the man returns to drinking. He does so not because the therapy was ineffective in changing his attitudes, but because individual therapy didn't address or alter overall family dynamics that sustain his drinking.

The Whole Is More Than the Sum of Its Parts   This third proposition is an effective way to remind ourselves that living systems are more than just the aggregate of the parts that make them up. Living systems such as families, groups, organizations, and societies evolve, change, discard old parts and patterns, and generate new parts and ways of interacting. Over time, the changes in a system result in something that is more than the sum of its original parts.

A concrete example will help us understand the idea that in living systems the whole is more than the sum of its parts. Hannah and Damion meet in October and are attracted to each other. By January, each of them has come to trust the other and they have developed a number of interaction routines. On Wednesdays, they study together in the library and then go out for a snack. On Friday nights, they either go to a movie or rent a tape. Damion fixes a meal for them on

Reflection

Does focusing on an overall family system when dysfunction exists relieve individuals of personal responsibility for their actions?

Interactional Theory   **191**

Saturday night, and then they either talk or go out to a party or concert. On Sunday mornings, they attend services together and then Hannah treats them to lunch. By this point in their relationship, Damion understands that Hannah values constructive conflict and expects him to be up-front when he's upset about something. Hannah has learned that Damion has trouble dealing with conflict and needs time before he can talk about it.

Originally, this relationship was a system consisting of only two elements: Hannah and Damion. Their interactions, however, gave birth to new elements in their relationship: trust, routines, roles, dual perspective or person-centeredness, and insights into each other's meanings. All of these features that are part of the relationship system in January grew out of, but are different from, the two original parts of Hannah and Damion that were present in October. Thus, we should understand that systems include not only their original parts but also interaction among those interrelated parts and what is created as a result of the interaction.

Living systems vary in how open they are. **Openness** refers to the extent to which a system affects and is affected by factors and processes outside of it. Most human relationships are fairly open. Damion and Hannah's relationship is affected by their interactions with families, work associates, and friends, as well as by the norms and practices prevailing in society. Some tribal communities, such as those that survive in the imperiled rain forests, are virtually, though not completely, closed systems in which interaction with people and events outside of their community is extremely limited. The more open a system is, the more factors can influence what happens in it.

Systems Strive for, But Never Achieve, Equilibrium This is a paradoxical but important premise about systems. On the one hand, living systems seek to achieve a state of equilibrium or **homeostasis.** Hannah and Damion developed a number of routines to create stable, predictable patterns of interaction in their relationship. They also generated ways of balancing responsibilities for meals so that Damion cooked one night and Hannah paid for lunch on another day. The dysfunctional family we discussed earlier developed stable ways of living with an alcoholic member. In fact, the members were so committed to the balance they had achieved in the system that they pulled the man back into those patterns and, thus, back into alcoholic behavior.

Yet absolute balance or equilibrium isn't possible for living systems. Change is inevitable and continuous. Sometimes it's abrupt; at other times it's gradual. Sometimes change comes from outside a system; in other cases it arises within the system. To maintain function and to meet the system's objective of survival, members of the system, like the sponge, must continuously adjust and change. Perhaps Hannah has to quit working in order to spend more time on her studies. Without her earnings, she can't afford to buy lunches every week. She might decide she'll cook lunches on Sundays as a less expensive way of providing her half of their joint meals. Alternatively, Hannah might ask Damion to pick up the cost of lunches, a choice that would disrupt the equity they had previously maintained. Hannah and Damion could adapt in a variety of ways to her diminished finances, but change of some sort is inevitable. Because parts of systems are interrelated, a change in any one reverberates throughout the whole system.

Try it out

How do you deal with changes in your relationships? Think about one specific relationship—perhaps a long-standing friendship or a serious romantic bond or your family. Recall a time when something major happened—you and your friend or romantic partner had to separate because of jobs or school, your parents divorced or remarried, a baby was born, and so on.

The following questions will prompt you to trace how the change reverberated throughout the entire relationship and how you responded to the change.

1. How did the change affect interaction routines in the relationship?

2. How did changes in interaction routines affect trust, closeness, and understanding between people?

3. How did the change affect your relationships with other people? (Did you form or strengthen other friendships when a friend moved

continued on next page

continued from previous page

away? Did you become less close to one of your parents if they divorced?)

4. How did you try to maintain equilibrium in the face of the change? (Some couples try to call daily when they are forced to have a long-distance relationship. Younger children often deny that their parents have separated for good. Older children sometimes regress in an effort to retain their share of attention in the wake of a new baby's arrival.)

Don't stop with these questions. Go on to identify the ripple effects of the change in your relationship system and the ways in which you both resisted and adapted to the change.

Dynamic equilibrium is a term that captures the contradictory ideas of change and stability (Wood, 1995b, p. 45). Interactional theory maintains both that systems attempt to maintain a steady state by re-sisting change and that they are dynamic entities that cannot avoid changing. This helps us understand why we sometimes deny or try to avoid changes that disrupt our habitual ways of acting. At the same time, it explains why we seek novelty and appreciate changes in our lives and the new perspectives they bring.

Reflection

To what extent do you think a relationship can ever stabilize?

In sum, system is an important concept in the interactional theory of communication. System is both a theory in its own right (general systems theory founded by von Bertalanffy) and part of other theories, including interactional.

Levels of Meaning

A second significant contribution of the Palo Alto Group was the recognition that all communication involves two types of meaning. Perhaps you've had the experience of being in a conversation in which you felt the other person was trying to control you. You may have interpreted the other person's statements as ordering and dictatorial, or you may have perceived a patronizing tone of voice. Interactional theorists borrowed from the work of Gregory Bateson (1951) to emphasize the idea that all communication includes two levels, or types, of meaning. The first level of meaning is the obvious one: the content of what is said. This is the literal substance of communication. When Cassandra says to her roommate, Glenda, "Clean up this room. It's a mess," the **content meaning** of the communication is that the room looks messy and Cassandra wants Glenda to clean it up.

The second level of meaning is called relationship because it carries information about the relationship between people. The **relationship meaning** of Cassandra's statement asserts that she has the right to criticize Glenda and tell her what to do. This expresses her power in the relationship. If Glenda responds by saying "Sorry, I'll clean it up right now," the relationship level of her message is an acceptance of Cassandra's power. On the other hand, if Glenda says, "My mess is on my side of the room, and you have no right to complain," on the relationship level she communicates that she doesn't accept Cassandra's assumption of power over her. In addition to power, affection and responsiveness are also dimensions of relationship meaning (Wood, 1994a, 1995b).

Relationship level meanings may be expressed verbally and/or nonverbally. A good deal of research has focused on nonverbal indicators of relationship level meanings (Brehm, 1992; Fletcher & Fitness, 1990; Sallinen-Kuparinen, 1992). If Cassandra smiled while making her statement, it would have a much more friendly relationship meaning than if she scowled. We signal our feelings about others with facial expressions, eye behaviors, distance, touch, and vocal cues. Whatever content we express, we simultaneously communicate how we see ourselves, the other, and our relationship. The Palo Alto theorists often used the term *metacommunication* to refer to relationship level meanings. **Metacommunication** is communication about communication, or commentary on the content level. Metacommunication (that is, relationship meanings) says "This is who I am in relation to you; this is who you are in relation to me; this is who we are together."

Couple counselor Aaron Beck (1988) calls the relationship level of communication "hidden meanings." Hidden meanings are very powerful aspects of relationship systems because they express and sustain the emotional climate between people. It is the relationship level of our communication that says we do or don't pay attention to, respect, and care for another person.

Punctuation

A third contribution of interactional theory is the concept of **punctuation.** In writing, we use punctuation to define where sentences begin and end. In much the same way, we punctuate interaction by designating the start and stop of episodes of interaction. Communication functions as long as all parties agree on punctuation (CMM theorists would say there is coordinated management of meanings). Both partners in a marriage agree on when particular episodes begin and end, so they understand what is happening in interaction. But if partners differ in how they punctuate communication, misunderstanding and conflict may arise. José and Maria have an argument and eventually agree to the solution he prefers. José then assumes that episode is closed. He punctuates it with a period. Maria, however, resents José for imposing his preference, and she doesn't punctuate the episode as over. The next time she and José disagree, Maria remembers the last argument and feels it is her turn to get her way. She punctuates the two arguments as a single, continuous episode; José punctuates them as two separate episodes. Not only do Maria and José disagree about issues, but they have a more basic disagreement about when episodes of disagreement begin and end.

Relationship counselors have identified a particularly common pattern of disagreement over punctuation (Bergner & Bergner, 1990; Christensen & Heavey, 1990). Called the demand–withdraw or pursuer–distancer pattern, this occurs when one partner strives to create closeness by talking and the other partner attempts to maintain distance by avoiding interaction. The more the partner who seeks closeness pursues closeness, the more the partner who seeks distance retreats from intimacy; the more the partner wanting distance withdraws, the more the partner seeking closeness pursues. Clinicians tell us that each partner punctuates the episode as starting with the other's behavior. Thus the person who wants intimacy thinks, "I am pursuing because my partner is withdrawing." The person who desires distance, however, thinks, "I'm withdrawing because my partner is pursuing me." Each person perceives the other's actions as the cause of his or her own behaviors, and each sees his or her behaviors as a response to what the partner does. As long as partners punctuate differently and don't realize that they differ in how they punctuate, it's nearly impossible for them to alter the frustrating pattern. CMM theorists might regard this as a strange loop.

Reflection

Identify recurrent patterns in your relationships that involve differences in how you and your partners punctuate communication.

Communication and Power

The final facet of interactional theory we'll consider is the claim that communication establishes and reflects power relationships. Initially, this claim held that all communication is either **symmetrical** (reflects equal power) or **complementary** (reflects different levels of power). At first you might think it odd that a theory of communication emphasizes the issue of power. This focus makes sense when we consider the context in which the theory developed. (Systems theorists would applaud our effort to view the theory in its context.) Remember that the Palo Alto Group worked with troubled families. Power in many guises (passive-aggression, games, manipulation) is often a central issue in disturbed families and is a continuous tension in communication among family members.

Watzlawick and his associates (1967) believed that every communication expresses either equality (symmetricality) or inequality (complementarity). In our earlier example, Cassandra's demand "Clean up this room" asserted her power over Glenda. A symmetrical message would have been "Gee, don't you think this room's messy? Let's clean it up."

Of course, systems logic warns us we can't understand a system by isolating particular parts from the whole. Thus, we can't draw conclusions about the power balance in Cassandra's and Glenda's relationship based on a single statement. Interactional theorists realize that evaluations about power in relationships can be made only by observing sequences of interaction. We at least need to know how Glenda responds to Cassandra's complementary message to have any insight into the power between the two women. We might also want to observe interactions over time to see if there is a consistent power balance between Glenda and Cassandra across various situations and areas of their relationship. Does Cassandra always send complementary messages? Does Glenda always accept them? By observing communication patterns over time, we can determine whether the overall relationship is one of equality or inequality.

Since the Palo Alto Group formulated interactional theory, communication researchers have extended the proposition that all communication is either symmetrical or complementary. Edna Rogers-Millar and Richard Farace (1975) devised a way of coding the power dimension of messages between spouses. Messages that attempt to gain power or control of interaction are coded as one up (↑). Examples would be ordering, interrupting, and threatening. Messages that defer to another are coded as one down (↓). Examples of these are allowing an interruption, obeying an order, asking for advice, and yielding to another's wishes.

Based on the marital interactions they studied, Rogers-Millar and Farace identified a third kind of power message that doesn't express either equality or inequality. They labeled one across (→) any communication that neutralizes issues of power and control. Examples might include explicitly commenting on power issues ("We've both dug our heels in," "Are you comfortable with the tactics we're using in this discussion?") or inviting a move away from the struggle for control ("Let's step away from this for now"). The Palo Alto theorists might disagree with the idea that some messages can neutralize power. They might argue that "Let's step away from this for now" is a complementary message, since it asserts what should be done. Yet many communication scholars agree that both particular interactions and relationships can be neither complementary nor symmetrical. The term **parallel relationships** is used to describe relationships in which power is equal overall, but is distributed so that each individual has primary authority or control in certain realms (Wood, 1995b). For example, Robbie and I have equal amounts of power in our marriage, but each of us has primary control in certain areas. I handle our investments and any financial bargaining such as trading cars and buying homes, and Robbie defers to my authority in the area of family finances. He has primary authority over travel plans and arrangements (though I suggest the overall travel budget), and I generally defer to his recommendations for trips and don't question the schedule and reservations he makes. Robbie also takes primary responsibility for our personal and material contributions to social issues, whereas I am in charge of personal and material involvement with our relatives.

Reflection

Do you think it is possible for communication not to express equality or inequality?

Interactional theory offers an original perspective on communication and its role in sustaining patterns in relationships. Incorporating the insights of general systems theory, interactional theorists proposed that communication and relationships are systems; this is the foundation of their theory. Building on that, they added other propositions, three of which we examined: All communication has two levels of meaning; the meaning of communication depends on punctuation;

and communication expresses power relationships. Work since the Palo Alto Group's original theorizing suggests that the third proposition may be modified by the idea that some communication attempts to neutralize power issues in relationships.

Critical Assessment of Interactional Theory

Three criticisms of interactional theory merit attention.

Theory Is Not Testable   A serious criticism is that the theory resists testing. How could we test the proposition that meaning depends on punctuation? How could we determine that all parts of a system are interrelated and interdependent? How could we measure relational level meanings, especially since they may depend on hierarchies of meaning that a researcher might not know? As intuitively appealing as these propositions are, they are extremely difficult to verify or disprove through testing. Thus, on the criterion of testability, many think the theory is weak.

Theory Overemphasizes Power Between Communicators   Interactional theory also has been criticized for placing too much emphasis on power in describing relationships between people (Owen, 1995). Clearly, power is one dimension of personal relationships, yet it isn't the only one. In stressing equality and inequality so strongly, the Palo Alto clinicians obscured awareness of other, perhaps equally important, dimensions of relationships. For example, respect and affection are critical aspects of relationships. Not only were these dimensions not accented by the original interactional theorists, but they also have been neglected in research applying and extending their work. We have methods designed to code power (one up, one down, one across messages), but we don't have equivalent methods of coding affection, respect, responsiveness, and so forth. Knowing that interactional theory grew out of therapy with disturbed families may explain why power was so emphasized in the original theorizing. However, the origins of the theory don't provide a satisfactory explanation of why other scholars haven't modified the theory to make it more applicable to a range of human interaction, not all of which is disturbed or governed by power dynamics. If interactional theory is to be a useful theory of communication, scholars will need to refine it so that it applies to a greater range of relationship processes.

Theory Ignores Intent   A third criticism concerns the theory's failure to distinguish between intent and effect. Assume Yolanda says "I can't believe you did that" to a friend who forgot to do a favor she had promised. The friend hears this as a criticism and feels that the relational meaning of Yolanda's comment is disapproval or judgment. But perhaps Yolanda only felt surprised and not judgmental. Is her intent irrelevant?

Intent and effect are also interwoven in questions about power in a relationship. If Robin agrees to purchase the car Marcus wants instead of the one she prefers, we would code her agreement as a complementary one-down message. Perhaps, though, Robin doesn't care much about models of cars, and she isn't giving up any power that matters by going along with her partner's preference. Is her agreement really expressing her subordinate position in the relationship? In describing and explaining communication, interactional theorists have largely relied on the perspectives and judgments of observers (researchers or clinicians) rather than those of participants. This opens them to criticism from scholars who believe individuals' interpretations are integral to understanding communication and meaning.

These three criticisms notwithstanding, interactional theory has been and continues to be extremely influential in the field of communication. It fares well on most criteria for evaluating theory: It offers a full description and explanation of communication patterns; it is fairly simple; it has obvious practical applications and values; and it is quite heuristic. The heuristic strength of the interactional view is evident in the amount of research generated by the provocative insights of this theory. In addition, interactional theory's emphasis on systemic relations propelled new and important lines of thinking about communication as more than a linear, cause–effect sequence.

Interactional theory may be troublesome or seem inadequate to people who require formal testing. The inability to demonstrate interactional premises definitively, however, doesn't concern people who recognize other ways of assessing the value and utility of a theory. One indicator of this theory's significance is that many other communication theories incorporate propositions formulated by interactional theorists.

ialectical Theory

In your relationships, do you sometimes feel that you can't get enough of intimates, yet at other times you need your own space? Do you seek comfortable routines, but also want spontaneity? Do you ever feel conflict between wanting to share your innermost feelings and wanting to maintain a zone of privacy? If you answered yes to any or all of these questions, then **dialectical theory** has a lot to offer you.

In the opinion of many scholars of communication in personal relationships, dialectical theory is perhaps the most exciting theory to emerge in recent years. It provides an especially insightful explanation of particular dynamics in personal relationships. Leslie Baxter has headed the effort to develop and test dialectical theory in the communication field. Over the years, she and her associates have published many articles that explain, refine, and provide empirical support for the theory (Baxter, 1987, 1988, 1990, 1992, 1993; Baxter & Simon, 1993; Dindia & Baxter, 1987; Wood et al., 1994; Zorn, 1995). To appreciate the theory of relational dialectics, we'll consider its root terms, dialectics that have been identified, and empirical evidence of ways partners respond to dialectics.

Root Terms

Stated most simply, this theory asserts that in any relationship there are inherent tensions between contradictory impulses or **dialectics.** Dialectical tensions and how we respond to them are central dynamics that shed light on how relationships function, as well as how they evolve and change over time.

Dialectics   Dialectics are contradictory or opposing tensions. My 5-year-old niece Michelle wants to be grown up and independent, yet she also wants the protection of her parents. She experiences a dialectical tension between wanting independence and wanting dependence. My close friend Louise is single and cherishes her privacy and the lack of obligations that come with relationships. Yet Louise also wants the closeness and sharing of intimacy. Louise feels contradictory impulses to form intimate bonds and to avoid them. I want to tell a new friend named Larry about fears and concerns that trouble me so that he can understand me and we can be closer. At the same time, I don't want to make myself vulnerable by disclosing personal information to someone I don't yet know well. I am caught on the horns of a dialectical tension between wanting openness and wanting to preserve my privacy.

Michelle, Louise, and I are entirely normal in experiencing these tensions between contradictory impulses. The idea of dialectics is that they are natural, normal, even inevitable dynamics in human relationships. The central idea of a dialectic is not the contradictory impulses, but rather the tension between them. Thus, dialectical theorists would be less interested in individual desires for independence and dependence than in the friction generated by the contradiction between the two impulses.

Baxter's understanding of dialectics is informed by her study of work by Mikhail Bakhtin, a Russian philologist who developed a theory of personal dialogue. Bakhtin believed that dialectical tensions are inevitable and fundamental foundations of all personal relationships (Baxter, 1994). Bakhtin did not adopt the Marxist or Hegelian view of dialectics as oppositions that could ultimately be resolved into some final form. Marx and Hegel saw dialectics as involving a thesis (we are independent) and an antithesis (we are dependent) that are reconciled through a synthesis of the two opposing ideas (we are interdependent).

In contrast, Bakhtin and, following him, Baxter believe that tensions between contradictory impulses are continuous and have no ultimate resolution or end point.

Baxter and other dialectical theorists do acknowledge the possibility of periods in which the contradictory impulses of dialectics do not generate tension. They do not, however, see these as final settlings or syntheses that resolve tensions. **Dialectical moments** is the term used to describe momentary periods of equilibrium between opposing dialectics in the larger pattern of continuous change that marks relationships (Baxter & Simon, 1993; Montgomery, 1993). For dialectical theorists, change is the one constant of relationships—they are always in flux and evolving, and any times of stability are but fleeting moments in the larger pattern of ongoing change.

Contradiction Baxter credits Cornforth (1968) with identifying the two root ideas underlying the concept of dialectics. The first root idea is contradiction. The obvious aspect of contradiction is that there is conflict, opposition, contrast, or discrepancy between two things such as the desire for distance and the desire for intimacy. You want to be close to a friend, yet you also feel the need for your own space. Less obvious, but equally important to the notion of contradiction, is that the two incongruous impulses are productively interdependent and interactive. Your need to be close is fueled by times when you are separate from your friend; being intimate for a period kindles your desire for time alone. Bakhtin's philosophical position was that tensions between people promote communication, which links them together. He believed that the communication prompted by dialectical tensions allows partners to grow individually and together (Baxter, 1994).

According to this perspective, each impulse needs the contradictory one. Independence is meaningful only because there is such a thing as dependence; distance gains its meaning from the opposite notion of intimacy; privacy and openness reciprocally define each other. We couldn't appreciate spontaneous moments and novel experiences if those were all we had. We notice and enjoy novelty because it stands apart from standard routines. Conversely, we value routines as a contrast to too much novelty. If you've ever loved being home after an exciting vacation, you understand how much routine and novelty depend on each other for their meaning and value.

Process The second root idea behind dialectics is that of process. Baxter's attention to process also reflects her study of Bakhtin's ideas in which change was celebrated and viewed paradoxically as the only constant in human relationships (Baxter, 1994). Viewing dialectics as in process means that we understand they are ongoing, always in motion, forever changing. Dialectics are not static balances between contradictory impulses. Instead, they are fluid relationships that continuously evolve. Emphasizing the processual character of personal relationships, Steve Duck (1990) says they are "unfinished business." By this he means that relationships are never settled, never fixed once and for all. Always, continuously, they are moving to new places and dealing with new issues. Change, then, is a primary dynamic of intimacy—one that is normal and ongoing in relational life.

Reflection

To what extent do you agree with dialectical theory's claim that relationships are always, inevitably "unfinished business"?

Viewing dialectics as processes implies that they are moving somewhere. In other words, theorists assume that the tension between contradictory impulses is positive and productive in moving relationships forward. For example, feeling discomfort about their conflicting needs to be together and to be independent leads Derek and Bonita to redefine their routines so that needs for both intimacy and autonomy are satisfied. Because dialectical tensions are seen as productive, contradictory needs have a decidedly complementary relationship with each other.

Dialectical theory's attention to process makes it a highly dynamic theory. As such, it is especially able to consider how relationships change over time, transformations in partners' feelings and behavioral patterns, and varying forms of tensions between contradictory impulses. Rather than viewing changes as departures from the norm or standard of a relationship, dialectical theorists see changes themselves as the norm. Communication scholars Kathryn Dindia and Dan

Box 7.1

Internal and External Forms of Relational Dialectics

	Dialectic of Integration/ Separation	Dialectic of Stability/Change	Dialectic of Expression/ Privacy
Internal Form	Connection/ Autonomy	Predictability/ Novelty	Openness/ Closedness
External Form	Inclusion/ Seclusion	Conventionality/ Uniqueness	Revelation/ Concealment

Canary (1993) claim that dialectical theory is distinctive in the extent to which it highlights change as the ongoing character of personal relationships.

Relational Dialectics

You could probably think of many contradictory impulses that you experience in your relationships. Existing research suggests, however, that there are a limited number of basic dialectics. Baxter (1988, 1990, 1993) and other researchers (Dindia & Baxter, 1987; Wood et al., 1994) have identified three dialectics, each of which has both an internal form that concerns tensions within a relationship and an external form that concerns tensions between a relationship and outside systems such as society, family, work, and friends. Box 7.1 summarizes the dialectics.

Integration/Separation   This dialectic involves tension between wanting to integrate ourselves with another person or persons and wanting to be separate from others. Within relationships, partners experience both the desire to be connected to each other and the desire for autonomy. We want to be one with those we love, and we also want to be distinct, independent, our own person. Among counselors, there is virtual consensus that the most central friction in personal relationships is the dialectic of autonomy/connection (Goldsmith,

1990; Scarf, 1987). Research also indicates that this dialectic is particularly salient in relationships that endure for some time (Baxter, 1990). Michelle's desire to be both independent of and connected to her parents illustrates this dialectic.

The external form of the integration/separation dialectic involves the tension between wanting a relationship to be included in larger systems and wanting to keep the relationship secluded from the social world. Romantic partners want to be part of a community and to have their relationships recognized by others. Typically, we want to introduce a new romantic interest to members of our family and our social circles. At the same time, couples want time to themselves to nurture their closeness and to be unconstrained by pressures, expectations, and judgments others may impose.

Stability/Change   The second dialectic involves tension between wanting sameness, constancy, or familiarity, on one hand, and wanting stimulation, novelty, or change, on the other hand. Relationships require considerable stability to survive and function: Partners have to be able to count on certain routines, roles, and so forth or their lives would be chaotic. Yet, too much routine can make relationships rigid or boring. When life is too predictable, we may feel stifled or find the monotony dreary. Consequently, we want the novelty of new experiences, patterns, and surprises. Yet too much novelty can be overwhelming, leaving us feeling unanchored and out of control. The bottom line with this and the other dialectics is that both needs are natural and both should be satisfied. As you may have already guessed, tension over contradictory needs for novelty and routine tends to be more pronounced in long-term relationships than in ones that are just developing, since novelty is characteristic in the latter.

The external form of this dialectic involves tension between wanting to conform to conventional social expectations and patterns in a relationship and wanting to emphasize the relationship's uniqueness (Owen, 1984). To be accepted by others, we have to comply with many prevailing norms, expectations, and patterns of relating. Yet we don't want our relationships to be just like any others. Elaborating this point, Baxter notes that "carbon copy relationships do not provide couples with the sense of uniqueness so central to their intimacy" (1993, p. 143).

Expression/Privacy   The third dialectic pivots on tension between the desire to be open and expressive, on the one hand, and to be closed and private, on the other. Between partners, this dialectic is often felt as a struggle between self-disclosing and keeping personal information to themselves. The romantic ideal of totally open relationships would be undesirable and perhaps unbearable in reality. Partners who shared absolutely everything would soon be intolerably bored by information in which they have no interest. Total openness would also damage a relationship, since some of our private thoughts might hurt our partners.

Reflection

Is the frequently extolled ideal of total openness in relationships a dream or a nightmare or both?

We want to reveal ourselves to intimates because we feel closer when others understand and accept our innermost selves. We want the intimacy of sharing private information. Thus, we desire openness. Yet we also know that self-disclosures make us vulnerable, and we want to avoid the potential that personal information could be turned against us. In addition, many people prefer to preserve parts of themselves as completely private: They are just for us and not shared with anyone (Wood, 1995b). This dialectic tends to be most prominent in early stages of relationships when individuals are experimenting with how much personal information to reveal (Baxter, 1990).

The external version of this dialectic involves wanting to reveal a relationship to others and wanting to conceal it from public scrutiny. We want to reveal our relationship because that is a standard route to social acceptance and approval. Sometimes we also want to talk with others about particular experiences, problems, and so forth in our relationships. Yet once others know about a relationship, or particular issues in it, they can interfere. Others can offer unsolicited and unwanted advice, make judgments of our partners or patterns in our relationships, and otherwise butt into what we regard as a private relationship.

In the case of taboo relationships, such as extramarital affairs, partners may have especially strong desires to conceal the relationship from others. We may also be especially motivated to screen a relationship from outsiders when we are ashamed of something such as an alcoholic partner or abusive behaviors (Klein & Milardo, 1993; Prins, Buunk, & VanYperon, 1993). Although secrecy about problems is understandable, closing a relationship to others may actually sustain the problems. Interactional theorists would point out that by sealing the relationship system off from the outside world, the patterns that allow aberrant behavior are kept intact. Unless something is done to disrupt destructive patterns, they will continue and may damage partners and the relationship.

Try it out

One indicator of the prevalence of relational dialectics in everyday life is the number of adages or folk sayings that reflect one or the other of contradictory impulses that make up dialectics. Identify the impulse, or desire, alluded to in each of the following common expressions:

1. A rolling stone gathers no moss.
2. Don't be a stick in the mud.
3. I need some space.
4. We never seem to do anything together anymore.
5. What she/he doesn't know won't hurt her/him.
6. Honesty is the best policy.
7. Don't talk about family problems with outsiders.
8. Keep your own counsel.
9. Absence makes the heart grow fonder.
10. I feel like a fish out of water.

Can you think of other folk sayings or common expressions that reflect one or both contradictory needs in a dialectic?

Responses to Dialectics

Now that you understand what relational dialectics are, you're probably wondering how people do and should manage them in order to keep relationships healthy. Researchers too have asked this question, and they have begun to find answers at least to how people *do* respond to dialectics. We know less about the effects of different responses and, therefore, about the advisability of particular ways of managing dialectical tensions. In a recent study, Baxter (1990) interviewed 106 college undergraduates to find out how they dealt with dialectical tensions in romantic relationships. She discovered four basic methods of response.

Selection Some couples manage dialectical tensions by **selection,** which is satisfying one need and ignoring or denying the contradictory one. Gina and Elton give up all of their independent interests and activities and spend all free time with each other. This response selects the need for connection as the one to satisfy, and ignores the companion desire for autonomy.

Separation **Separation** attempts to meet both contradictory needs in dialectics by satisfying each one in separate situations or spheres of relational life. Some couples are very open about discussing personal and family topics, and they don't share much about issues in their work lives. Other couples meet the need for novelty through vacations, and have highly routinized daily patterns. Friends often affirm their connection through particular shared activities, and maintain their autonomy through independent pursuits in other areas.

Neutralization The third response to dialectics is **neutralization,** which is a compromise that meets both needs somewhat, but neither need fully. Friends are somewhat expressive about all topics, but they have no off-limits topics and none on which they share in great depth. Mark and Todd make sure their lives intersect on a daily basis, but they neither do a great deal together to fully meet needs for intimacy nor pursue any independent activities to satisfy completely their desires for autonomy.

Reframing   The most difficult and sophisticated response to dialectics is **reframing.** That may explain why it is also the least frequently employed response. According to Baxter, reframing is "a perceptual transformation . . . such that the two contrasts are no longer regarded as opposites" (1990, p. 73). In a study that my students and I conducted, we found an example of reframing (Wood et al., 1994). Several of the romantic couples we interviewed told us that preserving and arguing about differences between them fortified their intimacy by energizing the relationship. In this manner, they reframed the autonomy/connection dialectic so that it wasn't experienced as a contradiction. Another couple that are friends of mine have marked certain subjects as closed to discussion. However, they tell me that they have an agreement to respect privacy in these zones, so they are open about the closedness.

Reflection

Which of these responses to dialectics seem familiar in terms of your own experiences?

The most common response to all three dialectics is separation. Usually, this involves assigning one need to particular topics or spheres of activities and assigning the contradictory need to different topics and spheres. However, in response to the autonomy/connection dialectic, some couples in Baxter's study reported using separation responses that met each need at different times. They cycled between the two needs so that periods of high autonomy were followed by periods of extreme togetherness.

The existence or intensity of dialectics doesn't appear to have a noticeable effect on partners' satisfaction with a relationship. There is evidence, however, that satisfaction does vary, depending on how couples respond to dialectical tensions. From all of Baxter's findings about the links between response strategies and satisfaction, one stands out: The selection strategy is not a satisfying response to the dialectics of stability/change or autonomy/connection. Couples also reported being very uncomfortable with managing the openness/closedness dialectic by defining certain areas as closed. There is reason to suspect that reframing could be a very satisfying response, since it reconciles the contradiction between different needs. Yet we have little insight into the effects of reframing, since few people report using this complicated, creative strategy. Baxter (1990) has stated that reframing is a valuable and underused response to dialectical tensions.

Reflection

Can you think of ways to teach people the skill of reframing?

In sum, dialectical theory claims that relationships are continuously in flux because of tensions between contradictory needs that are inherent in relationships, as well as the interaction of relationships with larger contexts. The tensions generated by conflicting needs are regarded as a primary dynamic that explains why and how relationships change over time and circumstances.

Critical Assessment of Dialectical Theory

Response to dialectical theory has been uncommonly positive. As you know from reading Chapters 4 through 6, as well as this chapter's prior discussion of interactional theory, scholars are usually quick to point out flaws in any theory. Why hasn't that been the case with dialectical theory? One answer might be that because dialectical theory is a relatively new approach, scholars haven't yet had time to render critical judgments. Although that reason may seem credible on first glance, it doesn't hold up when we realize that criticism has been voiced about other theories in a shorter time than the 9 years since Baxter began publishing work on relational dialectics.

A better explanation for the positive reception that has greeted dialectical theory is that the theory merits admiration. Let's consider how it measures up on the standards used to evaluate theories. First, does it provide a good description and explanation of what it proposes to study? The answer is yes. The dialectics Baxter and others have identified substantially enhance our understanding of continuous tensions in relationships and the changes they generate. Is the theory testable? Again, we'd answer yes and support that answer by pointing to the impressive body of research that already exists and that supports the main tenets of dialectical theory. This theory also fares well on the criterion of simplicity. It has a limited number of concepts, and those are explained in straightforward ways.

Dialectical theory is especially strong on the criteria of practical value and heuristic power. If you are like most people, learning about dialectical tensions gave you new insights into your feelings and your relationships. You may have felt relief in learning that the contradictory needs you sometimes feel are normal in all relationships. You may have learned new strategies for managing dialectical tensions in your own friendships and romantic bonds. This is sound evidence that the theory has practical merit. Further evidence of the theory's pragmatic strength may come as it becomes better known and more available in training of counselors and teachers.

The heuristic power of dialectical theory is measured by the research it generates and the original lines of thinking it promotes. On both counts, the theory fares well. Since Baxter introduced dialectical theory in the late 1980s, many other researchers have employed it in their own investigations. In addition, a number of current textbooks in communication and personal relationships devote substantial attention to dialectical theory.

Many personal relationship scholars regard dialectical theory as a remarkably original perspective that ushers in exciting new ways of thinking about communication in relationships. Prior to Baxter's introduction of this approach, interpersonal scholars had been restricted to theories that were simplistic, focusing only on narrow aspects of relationships, and/or highly mechanical, describing relational life in terms of "inputs," "outputs," "costs," "rewards," and "exchanges." Dialectical theory offers a broader, more dynamic, and more humanistic, view of interaction than any of its predecessors.

One question sometimes raised about dialectical theory is whether the three dialectics Baxter has identified are really *the three and the only three dialectics* of all relationships. This question concerns whether the theory has adequately described the phenomena it studies, in this case dialectics. One example of different dialectics comes from Bill Rawlins

(1992), who didn't find the novelty/routine dialectic but did identify a judgment/acceptance dialectic in best friend relationships. When he studied on-the-job friendships, Ted Zorn (1995) found the dialectics Baxter identified, and he found additional ones specific to the work context in which the relationships existed.

Yet other researchers have independently found the dialectics Baxter identified, and they haven't found additional dialectics (Petronio, 1991; Werner, Altman, Brown, & Ginat, 1993; Wood et al., 1994). Limited existing reports by clinicians are also consistent with the description Baxter has advanced (Beck, 1988; Bergner & Bergner, 1990; Goldsmith, 1990; Scarf, 1987). It is clear that the majority of existing work is consistent with dialectical theory as formulated by Baxter.

Reflection

What would you consider adequate evidence of additional dialectics beyond the three Baxter has identified?

Rawlins's curious findings may reflect differences in vocabulary, rather than in the actual character of dialectics. Tension between judging and accepting a friend might be a particular instance of the larger dialectic of openness/closedness. Would the theory be invalidated if future research does reveal dialectics beyond the three Baxter has identified? No, because the theory maintains only that tensions between contradictory impulses are inherent in relationships. I know of no dialectical theorists who claim that there are only three relational dialectics, and Baxter herself has never advanced the claim that there are only three dialectics. Thus, future research may illuminate either other dialectics common to all relationships or certain dialectics in specific relationships. If so, that will refine, not invalidate, dialectical theory.

 **ummary**

This chapter allowed us to explore two distinct theories about the dynamics of communication in relationships. Both are centrally concerned with relationship patterns and processes and the ways in which those affect what happens between people. Yet they differ in terms of which processes and patterns they emphasize. Interactional theory is most concerned with levels of systemic interaction, levels of meaning, power balances, and punctuation. These emphases reflect the theory's genesis in clinical work with disturbed families. In addition, interactional theory provides some of the most focused attention to pragmatics of communication that has been associated with any theory.

Grounded in different assumptions and focused on different relational processes, dialectical theory emphasizes the continuous, inherent tensions that arise from contradictory impulses for autonomy and connection, openness and closedness, and novelty and routine. Viewing dialectics as natural, ongoing, and productive, this theory provides impressive insight into dynamics that are central, continuous, and never fully resolved parts of relational life. Dialectical theory encourages us to understand and appreciate the contradictions and the continuous changes that saturate, complicate, and enliven our relationships.

Chapter Eight

Theories About Communication and Relational Evolution

Before reading this chapter, take a moment to indicate the extent to which you agree or disagree with the following questions, using this scale: 5 = strongly agree; 4 = agree; 3 = no strong feeling; 2 = disagree; 1 = strongly disagree.

_____ 1. Relationships progress as the result of partners' reducing their uncertainty about each other.

_____ 2. People stay in a relationship if the rewards they receive equal or outweigh the costs they incur from being in the relationship.

_____ 3. Most romantic relationships follow a standard pattern in their development.

_____ 4. As we decrease our uncertainty about others, the amount we like them increases.

_____ 5. A person who receives greater or lesser rewards from a relationship than her or his partner will be dissatisfied.

_____ 6. Individuals' expectations about how relationships should progress guide their perceptions of the intimacy in their own relationships.

Certain theorists agree strongly with each of these assertions. The only problem is that a theorist who would concur with statements 2 and 5 would disagree with statement 6. A person who agreed with 6 would be likely to dispute 4. If you're beginning to suspect that there are different, even conflicting, theories of how and why relationships develop, you're right. There's also no consensus among scholars about which theory is most accurate and useful.

In this chapter, we will explore three of the most influential theories of communication and relational development. We'll look first at **uncertainty reduction theory,** which is the most simple and specific of the three. Next we'll consider **social exchange theory,** which asserts that people try to maximize rewards and minimize costs in relationships in much the same way they do when buying a car or engaging in other commercial transactions. Finally, we'll study **developmental theory,** which envisions personal relationships as evolving through stages defined by participants' expectations, perceptions, and meanings. Each theory offers an interesting point of view on the evolution of closeness, and each reflects a particular perspective on human nature. As you study these three theories, see which one or ones make most sense to you.

ncertainty Reduction Theory

When two people first meet, there is a high level of uncertainty. They don't know what each other likes, thinks, and believes; how each other responds to certain things; and how each is seen by the other. They can't predict the other's reactions, and they're unsure what the other expects of them. Because uncertainty is very high in initial encounters, reducing it is important if the relationship is to progress. That is the basic premise of uncertainty reduction theory, which was developed primarily by Charles Berger and his associates (Berger, 1979, 1987, 1988; Berger & Bradac, 1982; Berger & Calabrese, 1975).

Laws of Behavior

As its name implies, uncertainty reduction theory spotlights uncertainty as the primary issue in developing relationships. The theory's central goal is to explain how uncertainty (and its counterpart, certainty) affects communication in relationships. Consequently, this theory explains progression in relationships in terms of the communication that uncertainty motivates and the effects of increases and decreases in uncertainty on the development of interpersonal relationships.

Unlike the other theories we've analyzed, uncertainty reduction theory is a strictly laws approach (Berger, 1977). Because this is the first laws approach we've studied, we'll review what that implies. You'll recall that in Chapter 2, we discussed different types of explanation. Laws, or covering laws explanations, assume that human behavior is the result of invariant laws. In Chapter 3, we discussed different epistemological views that inform theories. Those who believe in covering laws assume that humans respond in predictable (lawlike) ways to external stimuli. In other words, we react to stimuli predictably, rather than act in varying ways on the basis of mediation, cognitive processes, rules, meanings, interpretations, and so forth. Because covering laws theories assume behavior is regulated by invariant laws, the focus of theory building is articulating basic laws that explain why we do what we do.

Theoretical Axioms

An **axiom** is a statement that is presumed to be true on its face value and, therefore, does not require proof or explanation. Examples of axioms are as follows: Life is valuable. A square has four equal sides. The earth revolves around the sun. Abusive relationships are undesirable. We accept these axioms about social and physical life as indisputably true. They form unquestioned foundations for our beliefs and actions.

Theories based on covering laws begin with axioms, which are principles that are presumed to be self-evident. From these axioms, additional principles are deductively derived. Thus, the best way to

Box 8.1

Axioms of Uncertainty Reduction Theory

1. Given the high level of uncertainty present at the onset of the entry phase [of relationships], as the amount of verbal communication between strangers increases, the level of uncertainty for each person in the relationship decreases. As uncertainty is further reduced, the amount of verbal communication increases.

2. As nonverbal affiliative expressiveness increases, uncertainty levels decrease in an initial interaction situation. In addition, decreases in uncertainty level cause increases in nonverbal affiliative expressiveness.

3. High levels of uncertainty cause increases in information-seeking behavior. As uncertainty levels decline, information-seeking behavior decreases.

4. High levels of uncertainty in a relationship cause decreases in the intimacy level of communication content. Low levels of uncertainty produce high levels of intimacy.

5. High levels of uncertainty produce high rates of reciprocity [in self-disclosing communication]. Low levels of uncertainty produce low reciprocity rates.

6. Similarities between persons reduce uncertainty; dissimilarities produce increases in uncertainty.

7. Increases in uncertainty level produce decreases in liking. Decreases in uncertainty level produce increases in liking.

Source: Based on Berger, C. R., & Calabrese, R. (1975). Some explorations in initial interaction and beyond: Toward a developmental theory of interpersonal communication, Human Communication Research, 1, *99–112.*

understand uncertainty reduction theory is by examining the axioms that form its foundations. Although axioms probably won't make your list of spellbinding reading, they do provide concise descriptions of the building blocks of laws theories. Box 8.1 summarizes the seven axioms that are the foundation of uncertainty reduction theory. As you read the axioms, imagine you are just starting a relationship with a new person. Ask yourself whether these seven statements accurately describe what you feel and do in initial interaction.

What do these axioms tell us about how people get to know one another and develop relationships? The most basic claim of the theory is that uncertainty is discomforting and we use communication to reduce our uncertainty about others. If you accept this as true, then you would expect people who are getting to know each other to engage in a good deal of communication designed to gain information and reduce uncertainty. All of the axioms build on and reflect the foundational idea that uncertainty is discomforting and we seek to reduce it.

Reflection

Can you think of instances in which uncertainty was not uncomfortable and you didn't act to reduce it?

Rather than discussing each individual axiom, we'll select just a few to illustrate what the theory proposes about relationships between communication and uncertainty. Axiom 2 suggests that nonverbal signs, such as smiles and head nods, reduce our uncertainty about others by giving us clues about what they think and feel and how they respond to us. As we become more sure of another person, axiom 2 suggests we become more friendly in our own nonverbal behaviors.

Axiom 4 claims that as we become more certain of another person, we engage in greater amounts of self-disclosure. Presumably, increased certainty makes us feel safer about revealing personal information. Each of the axioms states a generalization that presumably holds true for all or most people who are launching a new relationship.

Critical Assessment of Uncertainty Reduction Theory

Despite its simplicity and testability, uncertainty reduction theory has not gained widespread support in the field of communication.

Narrow in Scope   It has been criticized for being extremely narrow in focusing only on uncertainty, which is surely not the only influence on how relationships develop. Michael Sunnafrank (1986) faults the theory for claiming that uncertainty is the primary issue in the early stages of relationships. Sunnafrank and others (Duck, 1994a; Wood, 1993d, 1995a) argue that other issues are far greater influences than uncertainty in the developmental course of personal relationships. For instance, attraction, similarity of values and attitudes, and stimulation

are influences that we might reasonably think are as important as uncertainty in developing relationships.

Invalid   Far more serious is the accusation that the theory is invalid.
This is the most damaging indictment that can be brought against a
theory. If a theory is shown to be invalid, or false, then it is dismissed
by scholars. Critics of uncertainty reduction theory claim that some of
its basic axioms (see Box 8.1) are faulty. If so, then additional laws
derived from those axioms are also unreliable. The questions raised
about the theory's axioms and the laws deduced from them are too
numerous to review comprehensively. We will focus on only two of
the specific indictments of claims made by uncertainty reduction
theory.

One of the basic laws proposed by the theory is that as our uncertainty about another person decreases, we are less likely to seek information about that person. The theory also claims that our tendencies
to seek information decrease as our liking for another person increases.
Are these claims true? To decide, step back from the theory for a
moment and think about relationships in your life. Do you become
less interested in learning about another person as you become more
certain of what she or he is like and as you develop increasing fondness
for her or him?

If these claims were true, then enduring relationships would involve
little information seeking. In reality, however, partners continue to
seek information about each other throughout relationships that span
many years. Robbie and I have been together for more than 20 years,
and information seeking is a continuous and substantial part of our
routine interaction: How are you feeling about your new position?
How was your day? Are you making good progress on your project?
Did you work out the problem with the student who had surgery and
missed classes? At what stage are you with the book you're writing?
What's your opinion of today's ruling from the Supreme Court? Do
you have any major resolutions for the new year? How is the new

friendship coming along? Is your class going well? Also, like most people, Robbie and I change as individuals. Continuing to communicate and seek information is essential if we are to continue knowing each other in depth.

Communication to learn about each other is continuous in our relationship, as it is in most long-term relationships. Yet, according to uncertainty reduction theory, people are less motivated to seek information as they become more certain of others. It could be that this criticism is less a direct refutation of the theory than an objection to its limited scope. Uncertainty reduction theory was developed to explain initial interactions, not communication in established relationships. Thus, its dubious applicability to enduring relationships may not invalidate the theory, even though it does raise legitimate questions about whether the theory is sufficiently broad to shed light on communication in personal relationships.

Related to this criticism is the suggestion that there are other motives for communicating that are more basic and more important than uncertainty. In a stinging indictment of the theory, Kathy Kellerman and Rodney Reynolds (1990, p. 7) state that "it seems more reasonable to suggest that persons will seek information about and from those they like rather than those they dislike." Although we might initially seek information about people we don't know and/or don't like, there is no self-evident reason to assume the converse is true. In other words, it isn't sensible to assume that knowing and/or liking others decreases our interest in learning about them.

Axiom 3 is the most controversial of the seven. It declares that uncertainty motivates information-seeking behavior and that reductions in uncertainty lead to declines in information-seeking behavior. Does this ring true in your experiences? Do you invariably seek information when you are uncertain, or do you seek information only when you care about knowing someone or something? In other words, is uncertainty or interest the motive for seeking information?

Reflection

In your own relationships, how important are uncertainty and interest in motivating communication?

This is a question raised by Kellerman and Reynolds (1990) in their critical review of uncertainty reduction theory. They point out that many times we have no interest in learning about another person. Consequently, even though we are uncertain about the person, we have no motivation to reduce that uncertainty by gathering information. We communicate to gain information not because we are uncertain about people per se, but because we care about them, find them interesting, or have some reason why we need to understand them (for example, they can affect us).

Responding to the Critics   What do the proponents of uncertainty reduction theory say in response to these criticisms? To date, they haven't been able to marshal a convincing refutation. In fact, Berger has explicitly acknowledged that the theory includes "some propositions of dubious validity" (1987, p. 40). Yet, this admission doesn't lead Berger to abandon uncertainty theory. He still believes it is basically on the right track. He suggests uncertainty reduction be evaluated as a theory in progress, rather than as a fully developed perspective (Berger & Gudykunst, 1991). Most recently, Berger (1991) has argued that rather than throwing the theory out because of its flaws, communication scholars should work to modify and refine it because it has basic value. Whether uncertainty reduction theory actually has adequate scope and the basic value that Berger claims remains a matter of controversy.

ocial Exchange Theory

It's 7 P.M. and you are starving. You're too tired to fix a meal, and you don't have much money to buy one. Then you remember the student paper had coupons from several local pizza restaurants. Reviewing the paper, you discover that one restaurant offers to deliver a large pizza with five toppings for $8.99. Another pizzeria charges only $6.99 for delivering a large pizza, but only two toppings are included. The third coupon advertises a large five-topping pizza for $6.99, but you would have to go get it, since this restaurant doesn't offer delivery. Which pizza do you order?

If you're tired, you probably don't want to invest the effort to drive in to pick up a pizza. Because you're low on money, the $6.99 deal looks good, but you do love lots of toppings. You have to decide whether three additional toppings are worth the investment of an extra $2.00. The choice you make is based on economic principles in which you attempt to minimize your costs and maximize your gains.

According to social exchange theory, we apply the same economic principles to interpersonal relationships. The basic idea is that people seek to maximize rewards and minimize costs in relationships. Thus we conduct cost–benefit analyses to make sure we are getting enough out of a relationship, given what we're investing in it. We communicate and build relationships to gain rewards, and we stay with relationships that are more rewarding than they are costly and that are more rewarding than alternatives.

Reflection

Do you think of your personal relationships in economic terms?

There is no single exchange theory. Rather, there are a covey of related exchange theories that grow out of basic propositions originally formulated by George Casper Homans (1954, 1961) and elaborated by others, including Peter Blau (1967), John Thibaut and Harold Kelley (Kelley & Thibaut, 1978; Thibaut & Kelley, 1959), Michael Roloff (1981), and Caryl Rusbult and Bram Buunk (1993). Although there are distinctions among specific exchange theories, we will not unravel these nuances. Instead, our discussion will focus on general concepts and claims that are common to the group of exchange theories.

Evaluation of Relationships

Exchange theories assume humans base their behaviors on rational calculations designed to maximize individual profit. In terms of relationships, exchange theorists claim we tally our costs and benefits

Calvin and Hobbes

by Bill Watterson

(or rewards) to derive a net outcome. **Rewards** are things that have positive value to an individual. Most of us would positively value acceptance, loyalty, financial contributions, personal assistance, support, and companionship. We might also find it rewarding to have a relationship with a person who enhances our social status.

Costs are things that have negative value to an individual. For example, relationships cost us time, money, and effort. Another cost of relationships is all of the adjustments in personal behaviors we make to coordinate with another person. We may find it costly to stay in a relationship with someone who puts us down, is insecure and needs a lot of emotional support, or has health problems that require us to provide assistance. Costs also include forgone opportunities—real and possible benefits we give up by being in a relationship. The net outcome of a relationship is determined by subtracting costs from rewards: $O = R - C$. Positive net outcomes come from relationships that provide more rewards than costs; negative net outcomes result from relationships that are more costly than they are rewarding.

Standards of Comparison

Calculating rewards and costs tells us whether the net outcome of a relationship is positive or negative. However, outcome value alone doesn't really tell us much about what people will do. Some people stay in relationships in which costs outweigh rewards. In other cases, people leave relationships that have positive net outcomes. Thus, the absolute net value doesn't fully explain why we are satisfied or dissatisfied with relationships, and it doesn't explain why we choose to end or continue them.

According to exchange theory, there are two standards against which we compare our relationships (Thibaut & Kelley, 1959). These two standards measure different facets of interpersonal life: one diagnoses individuals' satisfaction; the other predicts relational stability.

Comparison Level The **comparison level,** or **CL,** is a subjective standard of what we expect in a particular type of relationship. The CL is based on an individual's past and current relationships, as well as the individual's observations of other relationships and general knowledge derived from books, films, TV, and other sources. Given all of the friendships you've had in your life, you have a general expectation of what's involved in friendships and of what is average and acceptable for you. Your history of romantic relationships and your observations of others' romantic relationships provide you with a general standard for evaluating the value of a particular romantic relationship in your life. Our CLs reflect the total of our experiences in relationships, combined with our knowledge of relationships in general.

Comparison levels vary among individuals, since they reflect our personal experiences and knowledge. If you have been blessed by highly rewarding friendships, you will have a high CL for friendships—you will have lofty standards. If your romances have been gratifying, you will have an elevated CL for those relationships. Conversely, if you have had troubled romantic relationships and consistently disappointing friendships, then you probably will have a lower standard of what you regard as normal and expected in your relationships.

Reflection

What is your CL? Do your present friendships and romances meet your CL?

The CL gauges satisfaction, and it tends to be a fairly stable standard. Because it is an aggregate value based on the totality of our relationship experience and knowledge, the CL tends not to be significantly altered by a single relationship, even one that is dramatically good or bad. According to exchange theory, we are satisfied with a relationship if it meets or exceeds our comparison level. In other words, we feel we're getting a pretty good deal if a relationship is as good as or better than other relationships of that type we have experienced. But does satisfaction lead to commitment? Not necessarily, as we will see.

Comparison Level of Alternatives   Have you ever been in a relationship that you considered very good and then met someone who was more interesting? Have you ever stayed with a relationship that wasn't very satisfying because there weren't any better options? If so, then you understand why satisfaction doesn't always lead to relational continuity and dissatisfaction doesn't necessarily translate into relational demise.

A second standard by which we assess relationships is the **comparison level of alternatives,** or CL_{alt}. This is a relative measure that evaluates how good a particular relationship is in comparison to real or perceived alternatives to that relationship. Alternatives include both other relationships that are possible or that we think are possible and also the choice not to be involved in any relationship. CL_{alt} is the perceived value of alternatives to a given relationship.

Consider a concrete example. Assume you have been dating Chris for 6 months, and you think this is a good relationship. You perceive your romance with Chris as a 7 on a scale of 1 (terrible) to 10 (perfect), and your CL is only a 6. Thus, the relationship with Chris is satisfying. But you think a romance with Kim, whom you just met, would be a 9. Your CL_{alt} is a 9, and it exceeds the net outcome of 7 in the relationship with Chris. Exchange theory predicts that in this case you would leave the relationship with Chris for the one with Kim that you imagine would be better.

Unlike the CL, the CL_{alt} is not particularly stable. It fluctuates according to alternatives that emerge. One day you may have a very low CL_{alt} because you see no options preferable to the relationship you're in. That can change the next day if you meet a new person whom you find really attractive or if you decide you would be happier being uninvolved with anyone. We should also remember that CL_{alt} isn't necessarily accurate. Many people find out, often when it's too late, that there's a big gap between what we imagine a relationship will be and what it actually is once we're in it! Kim may not be nearly as lovable or loving as Chris once the novelty and infatuation wear off.

Reflection

Have you ever left a good relationship for one that you thought would be better and then discovered it wasn't?

The concept of CL_{alt} provides insight into the reasons people sometimes stay in abusive, even dangerous relationships. Many victims of domestic violence perceive that they have no viable alternatives to the abusive relationship. A woman who has young children and few job skills may feel dependent on a man who provides an income, even though he abuses her. Even though her marriage is highly unsatisfying, she may not perceive options for supporting herself and her children.

Equity and Inequity

Homans claimed that people expect a fair exchange in relationships, and by extension, we are unhappy when we feel an exchange isn't fair. Extending this basic idea, exchange theorists have investigated the nature and effects of perceptions of **equity** in personal relationships. Equity moves beyond the notion of immediate exchanges and rigid, cost–benefit analyses of specific interaction. Equity is concerned with whether a relationship is equitable to individuals in it over time.

Reflection

Is equity a more useful measure of fairness than immediate calculations of costs and benefits?

Perceived inequity is related to both individual dissatisfaction and relational distress. Interestingly, inequity seems uncomfortable, regardless of whether it works to our disadvantage or to our advantage. Obviously, people are unhappy when they feel they aren't getting a fair shake. For example, you might be distressed if you felt you consistently invested greater effort in a friendship than your friend invested. Likewise, you'd probably be upset if you felt you did a lot more to demonstrate love to a romantic partner than the partner did to show love to you. According to research, the converse is also true: We are distressed when we feel we get more than our fair share or invest less than our partners in relationships (Brehm, 1992). Apparently it's unpleasant to love more and also to be loved more.

What are the sources of perceived inequity in romantic relationships? In-law relations, sex, emotional investments? It may surprise you to learn that none of these is the greatest source of perceived inequity and the relational instability it generates. More important than in-law relations, sex, or most other matters is perceived equity regarding the division of housework and caregiving (Fowers, 1991; Suitor, 1991). Money is the only factor that equals household equity in its importance.

The majority of couples today include two people who work outside the home. Less than 17% of current marriages in the United States have a single breadwinner (Adler, 1994; Wilkie, 1991). The sexes' equitable participation in the paid labor force, however, has not been paralleled by equitable divisions in the domestic sphere. In only about 20% of dual-worker families do men assume half of the responsibilities for housework and caregiving (Hochschild, 1989; Nussbaum, 1992).

The cost of inequity in home life is substantial and mounting. Women who work one shift in a paid job and then return home to work a second shift at unpaid labor suffer increased stress, fatigue, and vulnerability to illness and disease. In addition, they feel frustrated and resentful at the inequity of the situation (Hochschild, 1989; Suitor, 1991; Wood, 1994d). When domestic inequity is chronic, it exacts a heavy toll on individuals and it can sabotage relationships. Research on inequitable home responsibilities suggests that the concept of equity is important in understanding relationships, even if we don't accept all the tenets of exchange theory.

In summary, exchange theories suggest that we enter and stay in relationships for what we can get out of them and we will leave relationships that are less profitable than alternatives. Although social exchange theories have been used to generate a vast number of specific lawlike propositions, the social exchange view of relationships can be summarized by five basic claims it advances: (1) Individuals are rational actors who calculate rewards and costs of relationships. (2) Individuals operate to maximize rewards, minimize costs, and optimize outcomes in relationships. (3) Satisfaction with relationships is based on individuals' CLs. (4) Relational stability (and dependence on relationships) is based on individuals' CL_{alts}. (5) Equity is preferable to inequity; both being overbenefited and being underbenefited are displeasing.

Try it out

Test the value of exchange principles for understanding relationships in your life. First, think about a relationship, either a friendship or a romantic relationship, that ended. Answer these questions:

1. What rewards did you get from the relationship?
2. What did the relationship cost you?
3. Did the relationship meet or exceed your CL?
4. Did the relationship, when it was its strongest, exceed your CL_{alt}? Did it exceed your CL_{alt} at the time it ended?
5. Did you perceive the relationship as equitable?

Now think about a relationship (again either a friendship or a romantic relationship) in which you're currently involved. Answer the following questions:

1. What is your net outcome in this relationship?
2. Does the relationship meet, exceed, or not measure up to your CL? Are you satisfied?
3. Does the relationship meet, exceed, or fall below your CL_{alt}? Do you consider the relationship stable?
4. Do you perceive that the relationship is equitable?

Does applying exchange concepts to your relationships shed any new light on how they operate, how you feel, and the choices you made and are making?

Critical Assessment of Social Exchange Theory

Using the logic of exchange, it seems fair for us to conduct a cost–benefit analysis of this theory. There are four major criticisms of social exchange theory in its many forms.

Little Heuristic Value   Some scholars are sympathetic with the assumptions and claims of exchange theory, yet they fault it for providing little new insight into human behavior and human relationships. Of course people like what is rewarding and dislike what is costly, they say. So what does that tell us that we didn't already know? It's obvious that people prefer equity to inequity; where's the news in that finding? Naturally, people are satisfied with relationships that meet or surpass their expectations; why wouldn't they be? What's surprising or even interesting about the idea that people will leave a relationship if a better alternative comes along?

If the claims of exchange theory are self-evident, then they do little to enlarge or extend understanding. The principles and propositions of social exchange theory may tell us what we already know, but do they tell us anything beyond that? If not, then the theory has little heuristic value. A theory that is only self-evident also fares badly on the criteria of providing a satisfying description and explanation and having practical value.

Not Testable   A second criticism made of exchange theories is that they can't be tested. On first glance this doesn't seem valid, since there is a great deal of research that measures exchange concepts, such as stability, satisfaction, and equity, and there is equally substantial research testing propositions, such as inequity is distressing and CL_{alt} predicts relational stability. Clearly, much work has been invested in testing the claims of exchange theories.

However, some critics ask what is really being measured in these studies. Their concern centers on the vagueness of definitions of key concepts in the theory. The concept of reward, for instance, is defined as anything that is positively valued. Thus, a person might irrationally value something that shouldn't be valued and consider that something rewarding. The classic case of this is a masochist who finds pain rewarding. Is the concept of reward so vague that we count pain as rewarding as long as a person says it is? If we reject that idea, then we have to admit that exchange doesn't really offer universal explanations of human behavior, since its laws don't cover some individuals.

Exchange theory states that people seek what they find rewarding. Yet, the theory also assumes that humans are rational actors. Thus, a masochist who seeks partners who inflict pain is making an irrational choice, which violates one of the basic assumptions of the theory. But if the masochist makes what would be judged the rational choice and avoids partners who inflict pain, then she or he doesn't experience rewards, which violates a different basic tenet of the theory. If we cannot define basic concepts such as reward adequately, then it is impossible to test the theory and, thus, to determine its validity and value. One response to this criticism would be that exchange theory limits its scope only to psychologically healthy people who, presumably, would not have conflict between acting rationally and seeking rewards.

Reflection

Is it possible to quantify rewards and costs in a precise and universal manner for all individuals?

Inappropriate for Humans   Additional questions can be raised about whether exchange's focus on individuals is appropriate for a theory of relationships. For example, reward is defined as what an individual values positively. Yet in close relationships, one person's rewards (and costs) are intertwined with those of a partner. Symbolic interaction theorists, for example, assume that intimates internalize each other's perspective and so can't evaluate relationship issues in a strictly individual manner. In Burke's terminology, intimates become consubstantial and thus identify with each other. When something is costly to Robbie, it is costly to me too. When I value something, Robbie does too. Can a theory that views costs, rewards, net outcome, and satisfaction as individual phenomena really apply to what happens in relationships between people?

If relationships are something other than and more than for-profit enterprises, then it may be inappropriate to describe and explain them in terms of economic concepts and capitalistic motives. A number of scholars argue that exchange principles may well apply to commercial transactions, but they do not apply to personal relationships that are based on feelings, intangible rewards and costs, and subjective experiences. Steve Duck (1993, 1994a), a scholar of personal relationships, vigorously protests against the notion that our actions in personal relationships are motivated by crass marketplace calculations. I share his point of view and have published several essays that argue relationships are not governed and cannot be explained by economic principles or cost–benefit considerations (Wood, 1993b, 1995a,b). Duck and I have joined forces to denounce the idea that close relationships are primarily evaluated in terms of whether we're getting a good deal (Duck & Wood, 1995; Wood & Duck, 1995a). Since the most fundamental assumption of exchange theory is that in relationships we operate to maximize individual rewards, the entire theory falls if that assumption is faulty.

The criticism that exchange theories are inappropriate for human relationships can't be evaluated by scientific logic and it can't be proven or disproven by empirical research. Instead, it's a matter of belief. You either do or do not believe that we approach personal relationships with the same orientation we use to buy a car or negotiate a deal. Depending on which ontological and epistemological assumptions (see Chapter 3) you embrace, you will find social exchange theory's view of humans either credible or misguided.

Not Supported by Research   Finally, doubt about the validity of exchange theory is prompted by research that fails to confirm its claims. Investigations (McDonald, 1981; O'Connell, 1984) have found that exchange principles are not evident in close relationships in which trust and commitment exist. Partners routinely tolerate imbalances in net outcomes as long as trust and a desire to sustain the relationships are high. Research by Mary Lund (1985) confirms this by demonstrating that commitment, or relationship stability, is positively related to individuals' investments. This suggests that accepting some costs of being in a relationship may increase our commitment, not decrease it as exchange theory implies. Finally, one study of different kinds of relationships found that exchange principles do operate in marketplace interactions. In friendships and romantic relationships, however, exchange principles not only did not operate but were disparaged and undesired (Clark, Quellette, Powell, & Milberg, 1987).

Exchange theories assume people are motivated by the quest to maximize personal rewards. Based on this assumption, the theories attempt to quantify rewards, costs, and comparison levels and to calculate the satisfaction and stability of relationships. Whether relationships and our decisions to abandon or sustain them involve more than the calculus of exchange remains a controversial issue.

evelopmental Theories

The final approach to the evolution of relationships that we will consider is developmental theories. As with the social exchange perspective, the developmental viewpoint includes more than one theory. There are theories of how individuals develop cognitively and morally, how groups move through stages of decision making, and how personal relationships evolve over time. To stay with this chapter's focus on relationships, we'll trace the progression of developmental theories pertinent to personal relationships. We'll focus on ideas and claims that are common to various developmental theories of relationships.

Viewing Relationships Developmentally

Sometimes it may seem that relationships spring to life suddenly or end abruptly. In reality, however, most relationships grow, mature, and decay gradually over the course of time. You see a stranger, talk to her, learn something about her, go out to a few movies and dinners, and pretty soon that person seems naturally woven into your life. When you left for college, you and your friend pledged to remain close even though you'd be separated by many miles. At first you did call and write regularly. Then new people, experiences, and routines filled your life, and your contact lapsed. By now you hardly ever think about the person who was once a close friend.

Box 8.2
The Social Penetration Process

SUPERFICIAL LAYERS
(likes and dislikes in clothes, music, and so on)
MIDDLE LAYERS
(political views, social attitudes, and so on)
INNER LAYERS
(spiritual values, deep fears, hopes, goals, fantasies, secrets, and so on)
CORE PERSONALITY
(most basic self)

Like these examples, most of our relationships progress over a more or less lengthy span of days, weeks, months, and years. Because personal relationships wax and wane over time, a number of communication theorists have tried to map the evolutionary course of intimacy. Their work can be classified into two distinct eras of developmental theorizing (Wood, 1995b).

First-Generation Developmental Theories

The first wave of developmental theories emerged in the 1970s. One of the best known models was developed by Irwin Altman and Dallas Taylor (1973). Choosing the unfortunate label **social penetration model,** Altman and Taylor metaphorically described people as onions that have wedges, or areas, of personality, each of which has multiple layers of progressive depth. Box 8.2 illustrates the social penetration process using the onion metaphor.

They proposed that to develop a personal relationship, people penetrate through the outside layers (superficial tastes in books, music, and food), middle layers (political views and social attitudes), interior layers (spiritual values and beliefs and deeply felt fears, hopes, and goals), and finally to the inner core of the self-concept.

The social penetration model provided a starting point for thinking about development of relationships. Yet, this isn't a very sophisticated or comprehensive explanation of how intimacy evolves. It doesn't even address the question of how relationships deteriorate! The original social penetration model ties relational development to the single process of becoming increasingly open in communication.

Eight years after developing the model, Altman and his colleagues acknowledged that the original model erred in portraying relationships as developing by following an uninterrupted path toward greater and greater openness and intimacy. Influenced by dialectical theory, Altman and his colleagues (Altman, Vinsel, & Brown, 1981; Taylor & Altman, 1987) have amended their ideas to acknowledge that the developmental course of relationships involves a continuous tension between desires for greater openness and intimacy and desires for independence and closedness.

In the 1980s, more complex views of relational development emerged (Knapp, 1984; Phillips & Wood, 1983; Wood, 1982). These models accounted for multiple influences (not just increasingly personal information) on the progression of closeness. For instance, attention was paid to communication, reduction of uncertainty, dual perspective, and sharing of experiences. Models of the 1980s also described specific stages in relational development—in some cases as many as 12 stages from the first hello to the final goodbye. Relationships were depicted as escalating through phases such as acquaintance, intensification, and intimate bonding, and as deteriorating through stages including dissatisfaction, stagnation, and separation.

During the mid and late 1980s and into the 1990s, scholars of personal relationships began voicing criticisms of specific developmental models and doubts about the value of a developmental perspective in general. Critics strongly questioned the assumption that relationships develop and deteriorate in linear sequences (Baxter, 1985, 1988; Duck, 1990, 1991; Van Lear, 1992). They argued that many, perhaps most, relationships follow zig-zag paths in which moves to increase intimacy are followed by retreats from closeness. Certainly dialectical theory would regard it as natural to vacillate between seeking intimacy and seeking distance.

Another problem with linear models is that they imply an inevitability to relational development: Once you're on the upward spiral, you continue increasing intimacy; once you're headed downhill, there's no turning back. Linear models also suggest there is an ideal of intimacy to be achieved. One model, for example, defined the apex of intimate bonding as symbolized in marriage (Knapp, 1984). That view of the zenith of intimacy excludes gay and lesbian couples, as well as heterosexuals who cohabit. Any model that excludes such a substantial portion of relationships is inadequate.

Perhaps the greatest criticism of the first round of models was that they defined stages by events outside of the people who are involved in relationships. Theorists identified particular kinds of activities, forms of communication, events, and so forth to distinguish specific stages. For example, one model defined intimate bonding as a public ritual such as a marriage ceremony (Knapp & Vangelisti, 1992, p. 39). Skeptics pointed out that what binds a couple together is more likely to be private understandings and feelings than public rituals (Wood, 1993b).

Second-Generation Developmental Theories

The second wave of developmental theorizing was launched by James Honeycutt's conceptual breakthrough in 1993. Honeycutt rejected the emphasis placed on external events by prior developmental models. In place of that view, Honeycutt proposed that movement in relationships is both defined and guided by individuals' perceptions. To grasp the importance of this idea, let's consider an example. Tonya and Phyllis have been seeing each other for several weeks when Tonya confides that she once had a problem with drugs. Will this disclosure increase the intimacy between the two women?

According to early developmental models, disclosures both indicate and cause increases in intimacy. Honeycutt's reformulation, however, claims that disclosures themselves don't affect intimacy. Instead, it is *how Tonya and Phyllis perceive and assign meaning* to the disclosure that determines its effect, if any, on their relationship. If Phyllis doesn't

Box 8.3
Relationship Trajectories

Starting Event	Alternative Trajectories of Relational Development
Meet person you like	date with friends, date alone, engage in deep conversation, make commitment
	go on date, sleep together, make commitment
	engage in personal talk, date, get engaged, get married, sleep together

perceive Tonya's comment as particularly revealing, it's unlikely to affect how she feels about Tonya. If Tonya tells lots of people about her former drug problem, she may not regard it as an especially disclosive comment. Honeycutt's insight is that behaviors and external events don't affect relationships until and unless individuals assign them meanings that have relational consequences. This view is consistent with the broad trend among communication scholars to emphasize personal interpretations and meanings.

Relationship Trajectories

Extending the idea that individuals' meanings are the critical influence on relational evolution, Honeycutt proposed that individuals use their past knowledge and experiences to define movement toward increased or decreased closeness. He suggested that people have "imagined **trajectories,**" which are personal understandings of various tracks in relationships (Box 8.3). If in your relationships arguments have typically presaged deterioration of intimacy, then you may have a trajectory that presumes conflict leads to decreased closeness and eventually the end of a relationship.

Honeycutt thought the trajectories were a kind of schemata, a concept that originated with constructivist theory, that guide how we think about what's happening between us and others. Perhaps you have a trajectory that defines intimacy as intensifying when a person calls several times during the week and suggests getting together just to hang out. You probably have trajectories that outline how you see the whole range of gradations associated with closeness and distance.

You may also have **turning points,** which are key relational events or feelings that you perceive as marking changes in direction or intensity of a relationship. According to Baxter and Bullis (1986), most people do perceive definite turning points in romantic relationships. Perhaps the best example is saying "I love you." This communication can radically change how people feel about a relationship and its future.

Try it out

What are your relationship trajectories? To figure that out, think about what you consider indicators of changes in intimacy. (CMM theorists would ask you to think about your constitutive rules for different stages of intimacy.)

1. **How do you know when someone is romantically interested in you?**

2. **What do you say and do to signal another person that you're interested?**

3. **What is involved in being infatuated?**

4. **How do you tell the difference between being infatuated and being in love?**

5. **What clues you that a relationship is disintegrating?**

6. **How do you know when a relationship is over?**

Research supports and elaborates Honeycutt's claim that we develop trajectories that define relational turning points and levels of closeness. Studies have shown that we learn about relationships much as we learn about anything else—from experience, observation, and instruction. Our direct experience in relationships, as well as our reflections on that experience, is a major source of our relationship knowledge (Andersen, 1993; Honeycutt, 1993). Because experience is a powerful teacher, individuals who have been involved in serious relationships have more developed expectations and trajectories than people who haven't been seriously involved (Honeycutt & Cantrill, 1991; Martin, 1991, 1992).

In addition to direct knowledge gained from participating in relationships, our relational trajectories reflect more indirect forms of knowledge. We learn about relationships from television and films (although we may get some pretty unrealistic ideas about them from media) and from observing others and what happens in their relationships (Andersen, 1993; Honeycutt, Cantrill, & Greene, 1989). We also gain relationship knowledge from conversations in which others give us advice or opinions about relationships and share their perceptions of how relationships do and should operate.

Honeycutt's contribution redirected the course of developmental theory and research. No longer do most scholars focus on behaviors and communication patterns that characterize distinct stages in the rise and fall of intimacy. Instead, the center of current developmental work is learning more about how trajectories, or relational schemata, are formed and how they guide communication between people.

This revised view of developmental theory leads scholars to identify stages based on the perceptions, meanings, and perspectives of participants in relationships. The stages, though necessarily depicted in a particular order, are not assumed to be in a fixed sequence. Instead, scholars realize that people may skip stages, cycle more than once through some stages, zig-zag, and otherwise pursue diverse developmental paths. Box 8.4 presents one version, or one trajectory, of stages based on the relational schemata of participants. It is the model I use in my teaching (Wood, 1995b).

Emerging emphasis on subjective trajectories links developmental theorizing with a number of other theoretical lines that concentrate on individual interpretation and the ways in which we assign meaning to our experiences. The body of constructivist research, for example, is directly relevant to issues such as the prototypes, scripts, and personal constructs individuals use to define interpersonal interaction. We have prototypes, or ideals (perfection in Burke's terms), for relationships, and we have scripts both for dates and for how relationships are supposed to progress. CMM theory's concept of the hierarchy of meanings provides one way of thinking about how individuals develop coordinated understandings of episodes in relational life. For example,

Box 8.4

A Model of Trajectories in Relational Development

Ongoing Intimacy

(Perceiving routines, rhythms, and patterns in interaction; acting on basis of constitutive and regulative rules worked out between partners; engaging in everyday "small talk"; reflecting on relationship and partner; responding to changes and to dialectical tensions)

Intimate Commitment

(Believing in a shared future of intimacy; deciding to maintain the relationship)

Dyadic Breakdown

(Feeling dissatisfied; experiencing lapses in routines, rhythms, and patterns; transgressing rules)

Intensifying

(Perceiving greater frequency, depth, and value in interaction; gaining a sense of a private world shared with partner; developing personalized communication such as nicknames and private codes; idealizing; publicizing the relationship)

Intrapsychic Phase

(Brooding about relationship problems and partner; feeling negative about relationship; having lessened perception of relationship's good points)

Explorational Communication

(Perceiving increasing breadth and depth in communication; feeling increasingly confident of knowledge about other)

Dyadic Negotiation

(Discussing tensions and perceived problems in relationship or avoiding confronting problems)

Initial Interaction

(Being attracted/noticing other is attracted; communicating interest/ noticing other is interested; forming initial interpretations of the other)

Social Phase

(Experiencing dialectical tension between wanting to conceal problems from outsiders and wanting to talk about problems with friends and family; seeking others' support)

Individuals

(Increasing sense of personal identity, CL, CL_{alt}; growing level of interest in new relationships)

Grave Dressing

(Making sense of the end of a relationship; revising perceptions of the relationship, self, and partner)

Steve Duck (1984) developed the model of relational dissolution featured here. The model of intimacy and relational escalation is based on Wood (1995b).

coordination is needed if one partner avoids conflict and thinks it's unhealthy and the other partner views conflict as healthy and as best worked through. Dialectical theory suggests that trajectories for established intimacy may include both distance and closeness and both openness and closedness. An important contribution of interactional theory is the reminder that we need to consider both content and relationship levels of meaning when asking about trajectories we have for intimacy. Narrative theory would encourage us to pay attention to the overall stories people compose to describe the evolution of their relationships.

Symbolic interactionism, too, adds insights to current lines of developmental theorizing. You'll recall that symbolic interactionism claims we learn the meanings of our culture through interaction with others who are members of it. This alerts us to the importance of cultural contextualization of trajectories. Your trajectory for falling in love is probably quite different from that of an Indian person whose parents have arranged a marriage. What we expect of friends, too, reflects cultural values, and so expectations will vary among diverse cultures.

Even within Western culture there are many co-cultures, which we will discuss in Chapter 9. Gay and lesbian co-cultures have some patterns for meaning that parallel those of heterosexuals and some that are distinct (Huston & Schwartz, 1996). African Americans and Hispanics have some relationship understandings that diverge from those of European Americans (Gaines, 1995; Houston & Wood, 1996). One of the challenges for developmental theorists is to integrate cultural influences into their thinking about the evolution of personal relationships (Wood & Duck, 1995a; Wood, 1995c).

Critical Assessment of Developmental Theories

Most criticism of developmental views of relationships was leveled at the first generation of theories. Critics legitimately reproached the early models for deterministic, linear depictions of relational evolution and for reliance on external phenomena to define stages in intimacy.

As we have seen, recent work has addressed those criticisms by advancing more dynamic theories of relational growth that rely on individuals' perceptions and meanings to define movement toward greater and lesser intimacy. The refinements in the second generation of theorizing illustrate that dialogue among scholars is critical to the development of sound theories.

One question that has been raised is whether developmental views are true theories or merely perspectives. To answer this question, we can ask whether the developmental research we have considered meets the goals of theory that we discussed in Chapter 2. Does the work describe relational evolution? Yes, current models of relational development offer useful descriptions of stages in relational life and recognize that stages may be skipped, revisited, and experienced in various orders. A second goal of theories is to explain phenomena. By tying relational development to individual cognitions and meanings, the second generation of theories provides satisfying explanations of why relationships move toward greater and lesser degrees of intimacy.

The third goal of theory is to allow prediction and control or to enhance understanding. Most developmental scholars are less interested in prediction and control than in understanding, so we want to assess the understanding generated by developmental work. What is your judgment? Does what you've read about developmental theories enhance your insight into the developmental paths in your own relationships? Most people respond affirmatively to the question of whether developmental research adds to understanding of relationships.

Reflection

How does knowing about developmental theory alter your understanding of relationships in your life?

A final observation we might make about developmental theories is that they seem especially capable of synthesizing and integrating a number of other theories into a holistic view of communication and relationships. There are many interconnections, some already explored and some yet to be probed, between current developmental theory and other communication theories that assume individuals are interpretive, meaning-making beings. The ability of developmental theory to integrate other theories gives it unusual power to describe, explain, and enhance understanding of developmental dynamics of relationships.

ummary

The three theories we've studied in this chapter offer distinct perspectives on communication and relationships. The most narrow and controversial theory is uncertainty reduction, which focuses on how uncertainty influences interpersonal communication and relational development.

A far broader, yet also controversial theory is social exchange, which explains relational activities and evolution in terms of costs, rewards, and standards of evaluation. Although research generated by exchange theory has produced some interesting information about relational issues such as equity, the value of the theory itself is questioned by scholars who don't share the theory's assumption that humans are primarily rational, calculating animals whose primary goal in relationships is to maximize individual profit.

Developmental theories offer a third way of thinking about relationships. Emphasizing change and process, the developmental view aims to describe, explain, and increase understanding about alternative evolutionary paths that relationships follow. Although the first generation of developmental theorizing suffered from assuming that relational development is strictly linear and that stages are defined by external phenomena, these flaws in the theory have been corrected in the second generation of research.

Most current developmental theorists assume there are multiple possible paths of relational development. Further, most current theorists focus on subjective perceptions, schemata, and meanings to define moments in relational life. By drawing from other theories with compatible assumptions, developmental theory offers an unusually broad and rich view of the role of communication in the growth, maintenance, and deterioration of personal relationships.

Chapter Nine

Theories About Communication Cultures

Janine is planning her wedding to Drew, a man she met and fell in love with her sophomore year in college. Her parents don't approve of Drew and tried to talk her out of marrying him, but eventually accepted her choice.

———

Across the globe in India, Nanya tries to imagine what it will be like to be married to Dilip. She met him only once after her parents and his parents arranged the marriage, and she wonders whether they will like each other and what it will be like to live with this man she doesn't know.

———

In Kathmandu, Concha prepares to leave his city wife and return to Boulde and his village wife in the southern hill country. The trekking season is over, so he will no longer use Kathmandu as his home base as he does from July through December of each year when he serves as a sirdah on expeditions. For the rest of the year, Concha will join his wife and neighbors in farming and repairing dwellings.

Three different cultures, three different views of marriage, three distinct worlds of meaning and experience. At least since the time of George Herbert Mead (1934), whose symbolic interaction theory we discussed in Chapter 5, communication scholars have recognized the intricate connections between communication and culture. The relationships between the two are reciprocal and interactive: On the one hand, communication creates and sustains culture; on the other hand, communication reflects, or expresses, culture. In an ongoing cycle, communication creates, expresses, reproduces, and sometimes alters cultural life.

In this chapter, we encounter three closely related theories that focus on the ways in which communication both reflects and perpetuates particular cultures. The theories we will discuss concentrate on cultures within the United States, yet the basic perspectives they offer can be applied to communication in cultures around the world.

ommunication and Culture

Before we discuss specific theories, let's consider the overall relationship between communication and culture. Communication is closely linked to culture because communication creates, expresses, sustains, and alters cultural life. Your culture directly shapes how you communicate, teaching you whether it's polite to interrupt, how much eye contact is appropriate, whether individuality is desirable, and whether argument and conflict are healthy.

Patterns of communication reflect cultural values and perspectives. Consider, for example, that many Asian languages include numerous words to describe particular relationships: my grandmother's brother, my father's uncle, my youngest son, my oldest daughter. This linguistic focus reflects the cultural emphasis on family relationships (Ferrante, 1995). There are fewer and less specific English words to describe kinship bonds, which reflects the lesser salience of familial relationships in Western culture.

Asian cultures also revere the elderly, and this too is reflected in language. "I will be 60 tomorrow" is an Asian saying that means I have enough years to deserve respect. In contrast, Western cultures tend to prize youth and to have many positive words for youthfulness (*young in spirit, fresh*) and negative words for seniority (*has been, old fogy, over the hill, outdated, old-fashioned*).

In the process of learning language, we learn our culture's values, beliefs, and norms. Then, as we use the language of our culture, we reflect its values, norms, and beliefs. The regard that most Asian cultures attach to age is evident in Asian languages. For instance, the Korean language makes fine distinctions among different ages, and any remark to another person must acknowledge the other's age (Ferrante, 1995). To say "I am going to school" in Korean, a teenager would say "hakkyo-eh gahndah" to a peer of the same age, "hakkyo-eh gah" to a parent, and "hakkyo-eh gahneh" to a grandparent (Park, 1979).

Language also reflects cultural views of personal identity. Western cultures tend to emphasize individuals, whereas many Eastern cultures place greater emphasis on family and community than on individuals. If I were a Korean, I would introduce myself as Wood Julia to communicate the greater value placed on familial than personal identity. In the United States and many other Western societies, a person is regarded as an independent being who has an individual self that is separate from those of others. Thus, terms such as *individualism, autonomy,* and *independence* have positive connotations (Gaines, 1995; Wood & Duck, 1995a) in Western societies. In contrast, the Korean word for individual, *kaein,* connotes selfishness and interest only in one's own concerns (Ferrante, 1995), which is strongly disapproved of in Korean society. Korean and American children learn their culture's distinct attitudes toward individualism through a variety of communication practices. For instance, most European American parents provide a separate room for each child or a bedroom that children share. The American norm is not to let children sleep with parents after infancy. Korean babies often sleep with parents for several years, a practice that communicates children are inseparable from their families.

The intimate relationship between communication and culture has inspired a number of theories. Of these, we will consider three that have earned high regard. The broadest of the three is standpoint theory, which traces the ways in which the locations of distinct social groups within a society shape members' experiences, knowledge, and ways of interacting. **Speech community theory** offers a more specific analysis of the same issue with its focus on how interaction with particular social groups shapes styles of communication that differ for women, men, and members of different ethnicities. Finally, we'll consider **organizational culture theory,** which illuminates the role of communication in creating and sustaining distinct cultures in organizational life. As we will see, all three of these theories echo ideas we've explored in earlier chapters. In particular, you'll notice the influence of symbolic interactionism and narrative theory, both of which are centrally concerned with ways in which we use communication to create meaning and coherence in social life.

tandpoint Theory

Standpoint theory is one of the newer entries into the communication field, although the theory itself has a long history. Dating back to the early 1800s, standpoint theory claims that the social groups within which we are located powerfully shape what we experience and know as well as how we understand and communicate with ourselves, others, and the world. To probe the implications of this claim, we'll examine three central ideas in standpoint theory.

Locations in Cultural Life

You will recall that symbolic interactionism claims that we are socialized into cultural meanings and values that pre-exist any individual. Mead's quest was to understand how society "gets into individuals" so that members of a culture share common understandings, patterns, and values. Mead noted that there is a common social world, and his theory emphasized the ways in which individuals come to understand and participate in that common world. Yet, Mead also wrote about social communities and groups, which may not be common to all members of a society. He did not fully develop the theoretical implications of diverse social groups for personal identity and cultural life. Standpoint theory fills that gap by highlighting the diversity and inequities within an overall society.

According to standpoint theorists (Collins, 1986; Haraway, 1988; Harding, 1991; Hartsock, 1983), a culture is not experienced identically by all of its members. Instead, cultures are hierarchically ordered so that different groups within them have positions that offer dissimilar power, opportunities, and experiences to members. Thus, this theory claims that the social, material, and symbolic circumstances of a social group shape the standpoints of members of that group.

Writing in 1807, the German philosopher Georg William Fredrick Hegel provided an insightful analysis of how different positions in a society result in different perspectives on self, others, and social life. Hegel focused on the master–slave relationship to demonstrate the disparate standpoints that different social groups have on the "same" phenomena. Although slaves and masters participate in a common society, wrote Hegel, they do so from vastly different positions that affect what each group sees and cannot see.

Hegel concluded that because societies involve unequal power relationships, there can be no singular and no correct perspective on social life. Each individual perceives and understands society primarily as it is experienced from the perspective of his or her social groups, and that perspective is shaped by the group's location in the culture as a whole. Thus all perspectives are partial in what they notice and emphasize, as well as in the meanings they assign to social activities and identities.

Reflection

If all perspectives on social life are partial, how can there be any common understandings of our world?

Social groups are defined differently in different societies, but all societies have ways of defining groups and assigning disparate power to them. The universality of social hierarchies lends credence to

Burke's claim that we are goaded by the hierarchy, or the need to create ranks. Among Hindus, caste is the criterion used to assign individuals to groups. Among Native Americans and many Asians, age is a primary factor in determining an individual's status. In the United States, social groups are organized along lines of race, socioeconomic class, gender, affectional orientation, and ethnicity. The groups a society designates are defined not only as different, but as differentially worthy, valuable, or capable. Thus, arbitrarily created social groups are granted dissimilar rights, roles, and opportunities.

Situated Knowledges

Donna Haraway (1988) coined the term **situated knowledges** to emphasize that any person's knowledge is situated in his or her social circumstances and, thus, there are multiple knowledges. For Haraway and other standpoint theorists, knowledge is not singular, but plural. It refers to the overall ways of perceiving, experiencing, and knowing that are shaped by our social situations.

A useful illustration of standpoint theory's focus on situated knowledges comes from the work of Sara Ruddick (1989). Concentrating on the activities of mothers, Ruddick argued that their location in the social groups of women and mothers cultivates "maternal thinking." Ruddick argued that mothers develop values, priorities, understandings of others, and skills at nurturing that are specifically required to fulfill the role of mother. Important in Ruddick's analysis is her distinction between maternal instinct and maternal thinking. Maternal instinct is an innate capacity to mother that our culture assumes is intrinsic to women. Departing from this viewpoint, Ruddick argued that maternal thinking is a learned capacity and that more women than men learn it because the two genders occupy different locations in the society.

Reflection

To what extent do you think what has been labeled the "maternal" instinct reflects biology and/or circumstances?

Ruddick's study of maternal thinking concludes that the idea of "maternal instinct" is really a set of attitudes and behaviors that are fostered by women's more frequent location in domestic spheres and caregiving roles. If this claim is true, then we would expect that men in domestic situations and caregiving roles would also develop skill at "maternal thinking." In fact, research bears out this claim. In her study of men who are primary parents of young children, Barbara Risman (1989) found that men who are primary caregivers are more nurturing, attentive to others' needs, patient, and emotionally responsive than men in general and as much so as women in general. A separate investigation of men who care for elderly people also concluded that men in these caregiving roles become more nurturing, attentive, and interpersonally sensitive than are men in general (Kaye & Applegate, 1990).

Try it out How has your social location shaped your thinking, skills, and orientations toward others? Which of the following statements do you think describe you?

1. I am good at caring for others.

2. I like to argue for my ideas.

3. I would be unhappy if I couldn't afford my own home, car, and yearly vacations.

4. I am more comfortable eating at McDonalds than at fancy, expensive restaurants.

5. I think it's very important to sustain close ties with family throughout life. Living near family and getting together regularly is what I expect.

Now ask how your sex, ethnicity, and socioeconomic class have shaped your attitudes about the above activities and involvements. How do you think your attitudes would be different if you were of another race, ethnicity, and/or socioeconomic class?

Accuracy of Different Standpoints

We've already noted that standpoint theory claims that a group's location in the social order shapes the standpoint of members.

Consequently, there are multiple, sometimes inconsistent perspectives on social life. Yet, the theory doesn't regard different standpoints neutrally. Instead, it argues that some standpoints are more complete and, thus, more accurate than others.

Reflection

Before reading further, ask what criteria you might use to evaluate the completeness of different standpoints.

Although all social locations are partial, standpoint theorists believe that some standpoints are more limited than others. Specifically, the theory maintains that groups in positions of lesser power in a society have more comprehensive, more accurate views of social life than do groups that occupy higher positions in the social hierarchy. Sandra Harding (1991, p. 59) explains that there are two reasons for this. First, people with subordinate status have greater motivation to understand the perspective of more powerful groups than vice versa. Economic security and survival, material comforts, and so forth depend on developing insight into the motives, expectations, values, and behavioral patterns of those who hold power (Puka, 1990; Wood, 1994d).

A second reason why members of subjugated groups may have fuller insight into the social order is that they have no personal investment in maintaining, much less justifying, the status quo. Groups that are advantaged by the prevailing system have a vested interest in not perceiving social inequities that benefit them at the expense of others.

Reflection

If all standpoints are partial, can one standpoint be less partial than any other?

Both of these reasons for assuming that subordinated standpoints are more complete and accurate can be seen clearly if we return to Hegel's analysis of the master–slave relationship. Because slaves have subordinate positions of power, their comfort and well-being and perhaps their survival depend on understanding the views, values, and even the moods of masters. No reciprocal understanding of slaves is required of masters who occupy dominant positions of power in the social order. For the same reason, other subordinated groups are likely to develop keen skill in interpreting members of dominant groups. For example, children, prisoners, and women demonstrate greater skill in decoding and deciphering parents, guards, and men than vice versa (Janeway,

1971; Puka, 1990; Wood, 1994a,d). Muted group theory, which we consider in Chapter 11, elaborates this point into an analysis of the reasons that dominant groups control the language and meanings of a society.

The second reason for suspecting that members of dominant groups have more partial and limited perspectives than members of subordinate groups is that the former have an unmistakable interest in preserving a system of power relations that benefits them. It is easier to sustain and justify an inequitable system if we don't perceive its injustices and the harms it imposes on groups that aren't privileged.

Standpoint logic would suggest that whites are less likely than people of color to recognize the continuing legacy of racism and discrimination and to support affirmative action and other programs designed to equalize opportunities in education, politics, and business and industry. Because minorities in many societies have suffered historical injustices and the persisting consequences of these, they are more likely to perceive and denounce inequities and to see the need for and the justice of programs designed to reduce or eliminate inequality.

Standpoint's Relation to Communication

Standpoint theorists posit a reciprocal relationship between communication and standpoints. Consistent with Mead's analysis of socialization, standpoint theorists assume that we develop standpoints largely by interacting with others in our social groups. Through communication with members of our groups, we learn the values, meanings, and ways of interpreting the world that are common to our groups as a result of their location in the social order. In this sense, communication shapes standpoints.

At the same time, it is assumed that our standpoints influence how we communicate and how we interpret the communication of others. The ways that we talk and the nonverbal behaviors in which we engage reflect the norms, meanings, and patterns of our social groups. Thus, some African Americans engage in braggadocio, which is outrageous bragging that isn't taken seriously or perceived as arrogant in

By permission of Doug Marlette and Creators Syndicate.

Theories About Communication Cultures

their communities (Houston & Wood, 1996; Smitherman, 1977). For example, as Fred gets ready for a date with a new woman named Geneva, he might say to his roommate, "Man am I a hunk. I swear, I am the best-looking thing on the West Coast. Geneva is one lucky woman to have the pleasure of stepping out with a dude as cool as I am." This form of verbal artistry is cultivated, practiced, and admired in some African American communities. It is often misinterpreted as egregious egotism by people outside of those communities, since they don't share the communication rules and understandings of that group. Thus, standpoints also shape communication.

In sum, standpoint theory highlights social locations as primary influences on the experiences, opportunities, and understandings of group members. Further, standpoint theory maintains that the perspectives of subordinate groups are more complete and, thus, better than those of privileged groups in a society. Although standpoint logic doesn't deny individuality, it does insist that the social groups to which we belong are powerful influences on how we perceive and act in the world.

Critical Assessment of Standpoint Theory

Two important reservations about standpoint theory have been voiced.

Theory Unjustifiably Privileges Marginalized Standpoints The first reservation centers on the claim that some perspectives are better than others. Some critics ask whether it is reasonable to assert that any particular standpoint is superior, or more accurate, than any other. Because the theory itself claims that all standpoints are necessarily partial, is there any justifiable basis for privileging one partial vision over another?

In response to this question, proponents of standpoint insist that there are degrees of partiality and, thus, some standpoints are more partial, more limited, and more incomplete than others (Harding, 1991). Standpoint theorists also remind us of the reasons we've discussed why marginalized groups are likely to perceive the society from a perspective that is more layered and less distorted than groups that enjoy locations in the cultural center. Social inequities are unlikely to be seen or corrected by those who benefit from them. Consequently, marginalized standpoints have the greatest potential to provide insight into how societies operate in ways that maintain a status quo that unequally affects different social groups.

Theory Obscures Human Diversity   The second criticism of standpoint is more troublesome. In focusing on social groups, standpoint theory runs the risk of obscuring diversity within groups. Terms such as *African Americans, gays, working class, women,* and so forth suggest a homogeneity among members of those groups. Yet we know that there are differences, as well as commonalities, among members of all groups. As a European American, middle-class, professional, heterosexual woman, I have much in common with other women who are European American, professional, heterosexual, and middle class. Yet, I also differ from some of them. For instance, I am less socially conservative than many women in these groups, and I am more involved in my career than most of them. I have more in common with several gay men and lesbians and with some of my African American friends than I do with some individuals who share my own race and sexual preference. Does standpoint's emphasis on social groups diminish awareness of differences among members of groups?

Standpoint theorists have responded to this criticism in three ways. First, they argue that the concept of social groups is politically and pragmatically useful (Wood, 1993a). Most of the major reforms of discriminatory practices would not have been achieved had we been unable to speak about "women's issues" and "racial oppression." If we treat each person as an absolute individual, not affected by membership in any group, then we lose the ability to prod legal and social changes that result in greater overall equality for all people in our society.

A second response to the criticism is that emphasizing various social groups within a single culture promotes awareness of multiple bases of identity. In other words, recognizing a range of social groups is a move away from viewing individuals in terms of membership in one particular group. The concept of "women," for instance, lumps all women together, regardless of differences in race, socioeconomic status, sexual orientation, and so forth. Yet, the problems, opportunities, concerns, and experiences of poor women are not the same as those of upper-class women. Similarly, African American and European American men, as groups, have distinct pressures and prospects. Standpoint theory's attention to our participation in multiple social groups attenuates its tendencies to obscure differences among people within any specific group.

The third response made by standpoint theorists is that an emphasis on groups is not incompatible with recognition of diversity within groups. It would be inaccurate to argue that people are defined only by what is common to their social groups, yet it would be equally inaccurate to suggest that our social groups don't shape who we are in important ways. There may be value in sustaining the tension between diversity and commonality. Like other dialectical tensions, the contradiction between acknowledging differences among members of groups and also recognizing what is common to most members of particular social groups may generate new ways of thinking and organizing cultural life (Spelman, 1988; Wood, 1993c). For example, we might sustain the tension by remembering that all men are men and no man is only a man, all Native Americans are Native Americans and no Native American is only a Native American (Wood, 1993a).

In highlighting different and unequal social locations, standpoint theory usefully augments symbolic interactionism and other theories that imply society is a unified phenomenon in which we all participate in similar ways. Although scholars need to refine analysis of the dialectical tension between commonality and diversity, this theory has exciting potential to shed light on general differences in the values, understandings, and communication styles of different social groups.

Reflection

Where would the idea of social locations fit within CMM's hierarchy of meanings?

Speech Communities

In her best-selling book *You Just Don't Understand: Women and Men in Conversation* (1990), linguist Deborah Tannen translated a rich body of academic literature into language that laypeople could understand. Writing about generalizable differences between how women and men communicate, Tannen popularized the theory of speech communities. This theory, which shares much of standpoint's logic, focuses specifically on how different social groups inculcate in members distinct styles of communicating and interpreting the communication of others. This line of thinking, which is implicit in standpoint theory, emerges as the center of speech community theory.

Speech Community Theory

Nearly 60 years ago, philosopher Suzanne Langer introduced the idea of discourse communities. Like Mead, Langer saw language as the key to shared cultural life. She wrote that collective life is possible only when a group of people shares a symbol system and the meanings associated with it. Langer's early interest in the power of discourse to both create and sustain community recurred throughout her writings over the years (1953, 1979).

Building on Langer's ideas, scholars in the 1970s began studying the distinct communication patterns that reflect the circumstances of different groups and the values, understandings, experiences, and ways of perceiving that those circumstances invite and preclude. William Labov (1972), an important contributor to this theory, defined a **speech community** (or communication culture) as existing when a group of people understands goals and styles of communication in ways not shared by people outside of the group. Dell Hymes's (1974) anthropological studies led him to conclude that communication is understandable only within the cultural contexts that define the rules, meanings, and uses of communication. If you recognize the echo of CMM theory here, you're thinking like a theorist. CMM claims that communication occurs within a hierarchy of meanings, the highest of which is cultural patterns. That's very similar to the speech community theory's premise that the context of culture, or social group, shapes how we communicate and interpret the communication of others.

When we think of speech communities, we are most likely to think of groups that have different languages and live in distinct societies. It's easy to recognize dissimilar communication practices among Nepalese, Indian, and Western cultures. Distinct speech communities are less apparent when they rely on a common language, yet use it in disparate ways and to achieve varying goals. Yet, theorists maintain that speech communities are not defined by geography per se. Instead, as Labov and Hymes originally noted, they exist when members of a social group use language in ways and to achieve goals not shared by people outside of the group.

Larry Samovar and Richard Porter (1994), two intercultural communication researchers, have identified a number of different speech communities within the United States. They analyze the distinctive communication understandings and practices characteristic of gays, Native Americans, African Americans, Hispanics, people with disabilities, and women and men. To determine whether a speech community exists, we ask, "Are there communication patterns, practices, and understandings used by members of this group that are not understood and/or employed by people outside the group?"

An interesting example of a speech community and of an excellent ethnographic study was provided by Gerry Philipsen (1975, 1992). He spent 3 years doing an ethnographic study of blue-collar workers in Teamsterville, a name he gave to a multiethnic Chicago community made up exclusively of men. Within the Teamsterville community, speech is used to establish and display manhood and allegiance to the group. Thus, rules for talk in Teamsterville include using it to establish communal bonds with other members of the group and to assert loyalty to the group. Another rule in Teamsterville is not to engage in "sissy talk," which is the way the members believe you talk to women and children. The speech community in Teamsterville has distinctive rules for communication, and those rules create an identity for the men in the group. Philipsen's study highlights the importance of rules in identifying speech communities, and we turn now to that concept.

Rules of Communication

Theorists of speech communities are interested in discovering the genesis of distinct **communication rules** of different social groups. Communication rules refer to regular patterns in how communication is used and interpreted and what its functions are understood to be within a particular group. Rules are presumed to be socially constructed, rather than determined by forces beyond the control of humans. To discover and understand communication rules, scholars study interaction in particular groups, especially among young or new members of the groups. This emphasis allows researchers to learn how children and newcomers to communities learn the communication rules of specific groups.

A great deal of recent research has investigated masculine and feminine speech communities, so we'll use gender groups as an illustration of how members of different communities learn and employ distinct communication rules. The classic study in this area was conducted by Daniel Maltz and Ruth Borker in 1982. Studying young children at play, Maltz and Borker first noticed that children usually play in sex-segregated groups. They also realized that the two sexes tend to prefer different sorts of games: Many young girls favor games such as house, school, and jump rope, whereas boys typically play games such as war, football, and baseball.

If we look at the games typically favored by boys and girls, we can identify differences in their structures. Boys' games require large groups (9 players for each baseball team, 11 for each football team). Games such as house and school, however, require fewer players—two or three are sufficient for the game to work. Boys' games also tend to be competitive. The goal is to beat the other team in sports or to demolish the enemy in war. In contrast, girls' games tend to be cooperative, since all players have to get along and work out differences or the game can't continue.

A third difference in patterns of the sexes' games is that boys' games typically have clear rules and goals. Definitions of legal and illegal passes, fouls, and so forth are stipulated by rules that are external to any particular players. Also, goals such as making touchdowns or baskets and getting the enemy to retreat are independent of particular players. There are not such clear-cut and external rules to structure girls' games. There's no touchdown or other definite goal of playing school, and there's no predefined rule about what counts as a foul in playing house. Rather than pursuing an instrumental end such as gaining points, girls seem to perceive the process of interaction and the development of relationships among players as primary goals. Thus, interaction is an end in itself for girls, not a means to some other instrumental objective. The lack of external structure typical of girls' games explains why girls talk among themselves to organize their games and their relationships, whereas boys have less need to work out rules of their games through interpersonal communication.

Reflection

Think back on the games you played as a child. Can you identify the structure, goals, and degree of communication emphasized by these games?

Maltz and Borker's initial findings have been confirmed and extended by many other scholars (Aries, 1987; Beck, 1988; Inman, 1996; Johnson, 1996; Tannen, 1990; Wood & Inman, 1993). From all of this research, we have identified key communication rules cultivated by each gendered speech community. These are summarized in Box 9.1.

Misunderstandings

Speech community theory is particularly helpful in explaining misunderstandings that recurrently surface in communication between people of different social groups. Again, we'll illustrate this with gender cultures, since those have been more extensively researched than other speech communities.

One of the most common misunderstandings between women and men concerns what Tannen (1990) calls "troubles talk." Denise is upset

Box 9.1

Rules of Gendered Speech Communities

Feminine Communication Rules	*Masculine Communication Rules*
Use communication to maintain relationships.	Use communication to assert yourself and your ideas.
Use talk to cooperate with others.	Use talk to compete with others.
Avoid criticizing or outdoing others. Equality is a primary value.	Aim to outdo others in interaction. It's important to excel as an individual.
Support others by using talk to build connections and to show you understand how others feel.	Support others by using talk to accomplish instrumental goals—give advice, solve problems, and so on.
Include others in interaction; invite them to participate, and support their ideas and feelings.	Try to get and maintain the talk stage. Reroute topics to keep attention on yourself.
Speak tentatively so that others feel they can offer different points of view and ask questions about your ideas.	Speak with authority and confidence so that you appear in control and so that others don't question you.

because she just got back an exam on which her grade is a 65. When she gets together with her boyfriend, Glenn, she tells him that she feels stupid and like a failure. Glenn responds by saying, "You just need to study harder for the next exam." Denise shrugs and says, "That's not the point. I really don't understand why I did so poorly. I thought I understood the material. Maybe I'm so stupid I don't even know what I do and don't understand." Glenn replies, "You should talk with your professor and get suggestions on how to study better." In exasperation, Denise explodes, "I don't know why I even try to talk with you. You never care how I feel." Glenn is astonished by Denise's comment because he thought he was being caring and supportive by offering solutions to her problem.

Speech community theory sheds light on the reasons that underlie the misunderstanding between Denise and Glenn. Operating from a feminine speech community, Denise is using communication to build her connection with Glenn and to express her feelings to him. By the rules of her gender culture, Glenn should show support by encouraging her to talk about her feelings and by responding to her emotional concern that she is stupid. Glenn, however, is following the rules of masculine speech community, which suggest he should do something concrete with communication: He should solve the problem. Denise and Glenn, like many women and men, have different understandings of how to communicate and how to show support. They can improve their relationship by learning and adapting to each other's communication rules.

You've probably realized that speech community theory includes ideas that we've encountered before. For example, CMM theorists would analyze the interaction between Denise and Glenn in terms of the different speech acts, episodes, autobiographies, and so forth in their respective hierarchies of meaning. Interactional theorists would focus on the relational level of meanings to point out that Glenn is not responding only to the content level meaning of Denise's communication. He is dealing with the specific problem of the bad grade on an exam. What he is not addressing is Denise's relational message ("I feel stupid") and her tacit request for reassurance from him ("Please tell me you don't think I'm stupid").

Troubles talk is just one example of situations in which communication between women and men is laced with misunderstandings that arise because of their socialization in distinct speech communities. Scholars have identified a number of communicative tensions between women and men in personal relationships (Beck, 1988; Hendrick & Hendrick, 1996; Tannen, 1990; Wood, 1994a,b,c, 1996b), as well as in professional interaction (Murphy & Zorn, 1996; Natalle, 1996; Tannen, 1994; Taylor & Conrad, 1992).

Try it out Observe interactions between women and men. You may focus on your own interactions and/or those of others whom you can observe. Can you identify tensions and misunderstandings that reflect gendered speech communities into which many women and men are socialized?

1. How competitive are women and men in conversations? (Who interrupts most often, invites others into interaction, shows interest in what others say, asserts their own ideas and personalities?)

continued on next page

continued from previous page

2. **How much do women and men emphasize individuals and how much do they emphasize relationships? (Observe the frequency of terms such as *I, my, you, our,* and *we.*)**

3. **Are women and men similar in their focus on instrumental goals in communication? (Observe how much each sex proposes solutions, gives advice, and so on, and how much each focuses on feelings in conversations.)**

From your observations, is speech community theory a useful way to understand and explain generalizable differences in women's and men's communication styles?

Critical Assessment of Speech Community Theory

Because speech community theory builds on and is consistent with the assumptions and claims of standpoint theory, it's not surprising that one criticism of it parallels a criticism leveled at standpoint.

Theory Obscures Human Diversity   Specifically, some scholars think that speech community theory focuses too much on differences between groups and too little on differences within groups. Concepts such as "women's speech communities" and "men's speech communities" may foster gender stereotypes and the misimpression that all women are alike and all men are alike.

Theory Fosters Divisions Among Social Groups   An extension of this criticism is that emphasizing differences among social groups fuels divisions that are not productive for individuals or the collective society. Once we identify differences between women's and men's styles of communicating, for instance, it's tempting to make comparative judgments about which style is better. Thus, we hear competing pronouncements that men are insensitive and women are too sensitive, that men are too competitive and women lack a competitive drive, and that women focus too much and men too little on relationships and emotional issues. Such claims and counterclaims do little to encourage respect for differences among people.

Scholars who endorse speech community theory respond to this criticism by pointing out that they have consistently avoided evaluating differences. Further, they note, they have vigorously encouraged respect for and understanding of diverse styles of interaction (Tannen, 1990, 1994; Wood & Inman, 1993). If others use findings of difference to justify judgments of better and worse, say speech community theorists, that is not the fault of the theory. How adequate you consider that response depends on whether you hold a theory responsible for consequences, including ones that are not intended or supported by its originators.

Theory Is Insufficiently Critical   Ironically, a final criticism of speech community theory is that it isn't as evaluative as it should be. Some feminist critics charge that speech community theory, particularly as represented by Tannen, is both wrong and politically naive in claiming that the communication of different groups is equal. Such a claim, the critics argue, totally ignores marked and enduring inequalities between social groups. Women and men are not equal in Western culture, and so their distinct communication styles are unlikely to be granted equal respect. Senta Troemel-Ploetz, a German communication scholar, argues that the theory is wrong in assuming that the difficulties women and men experience in conversations result from misunderstandings. She asserts that men know perfectly well what women want—understanding, for instance—but men don't choose to give it to women and don't have to give it because they hold greater power than women in society (1991, p. 495). By extension, it could be argued that European Americans know perfectly well what people of color want—respect, equal opportunity, fair treatment—but they don't choose to give it. This viewpoint is shared by other scholars who worry that false claims of equality serve to sustain inequality between social groups (Penelope,

Reflection

Do you think a theory should be evaluated based on how others use and interpret findings if others' views are inconsistent with those of the people who originally developed a theory?

1990; Spender, 1984a,b; Spitzack & Carter, 1987; Wood & Cox, 1993).

To this criticism, some speech community theorists respond that assuming equality and urging equal respect for different communication styles are more likely to promote actual equality than belaboring inequalities between groups.

rganizational Culture

A third theory concerned with relationships between communication and culture focuses on the specific setting of the workplace. Studying professions, companies, labor groups, and institutional life, organizational cultural scholars attempt to describe and explain the ways in which communication creates, sustains, and expresses the values and ideology of particular work environments. As with standpoint and speech community theories, organizational culture theories assume a reciprocal relationship between cultures and communication in which each shapes and is shaped by the other.

Organizations as Cultures

Traditionally, studies of organizations have explored lines of authority, channels of communication, productivity, and so forth toward the goal of discovering how to make organizations work better. That emphasis, although still alive and well in some arenas, has been largely replaced in the field of communication by a focus on organizational cultures in which the objective is to understand how organizational life is constituted through communication (Pacanowsky & O'Donnell-Trujillo, 1982, 1983).

Study of organizational culture was strongly influenced by the work of anthropologist Clifford Geertz (1973). On first thought, the ideas of an anthropologist studying Moroccan and Indonesian cultures would seem of little relevance to organizations. As we shall see, however, Geertz's insights and extensions of them have opened up rich understandings of organizations as a kind of culture.

Geertz perceived culture as systems of shared, or common, meaning. Like standpoint and speech community theorists, Geertz realized cultures aren't homogeneous, but are honeycombed with different social groups. He claimed that cultures are ways of life that are sustained through stories, rituals, and other symbolic activities that continuously vitalize and uphold shared meanings among members.

Communication and Organizational Culture

Drawing on Geertz's general observations about cultural life, communication scholars have developed a theory that views organizations as cultures that are produced and reproduced through communication activities among members of organizations (Anderson, 1988; Pacanowsky, 1989; Van Maanen & Barley, 1985). This perspective directs scholars' attention to ways in which interactions define individual members of organizations and organize, coordinate, and normalize collective values, policies, practices, and goals. Theorists have identified a number of symbolic activities, or performances, that create and uphold important dimensions of organizational life. Of these, we will discuss vocabulary, stories, and rites and rituals, which are particularly important symbolic processes.

Vocabulary   The most obvious symbolic dimension of organizations is their vocabularies. Just as the language of an ethnic culture reflects and expresses its members' experiences and values, so does the language of an organization reflect and express the norms and ideology of the organization. The military, for example, relies on language that continuously acknowledges rank ("Yes, sir," "salute," "chain of command"), which reflects the fact that status, respect, and privilege are tied to official rank. In a study of police, researchers noted the pervasiveness of derogatory descriptions of civilians. The officers routinely called them "creeps," "dirtbags," and "maggots" to emphasize the

undesirable element with which police often deal (Pacanowsky & O'Donnell-Trujillo, 1983).

In some organizations there is a great deal of language that emphasizes interests and experiences more typical of men than women. Consider the number of phrases in the working world that are taken from sports (*home run, ballpark estimate, touchdown, develop a game plan, be a team player, the starting line up*), military life (*battle plan, mount a campaign, plan of attack, under fire, get the big guns, offensive strike*), and sexual activities (*hit on a person, screw someone, stick it to them, a person has real balls*). Whether intentional or not, such language reflects men's experiences more than those of women and serves to bind men together into a community in which many women may feel unwelcome and/or uncomfortable (Wood, 1994b).

Language in the workplace may also normalize sexist practices, including sexual harassment. From behaviors such as calling women "hon" and "sweetheart" to more egregiously sexualized comments about women's appearances, these language activities spotlight women's sexuality and obscure their professional abilities and status. Writing in 1992, Mary Strine analyzed the ways in which academic institutions define and describe sexual harassment in terms that make it seem normal and acceptable. Shereen Bingham (1994, 1996) and others (Taylor & Conrad, 1992; Wood, 1994c) have added to Strine's insights by documenting additional ways in which sexual harassment is normalized or resisted in the workplace. In related work, Carol Blair, Julie

Brown, and Leslie Baxter (1994) demonstrated that norms of thought and speech in academic communities are used to marginalize women scholars and feminist research.

Stories You'll recall that we discussed narrative theory in Chapter 5. Organizational culture theory follows Fisher's (1984, 1987) lead in assuming that humans are inveterate storytellers. Further, both groups of theorists assume that stories are coherent narratives that create meaning. Within the organizational context, Michael Pacanowsky and Nick O'Donnell-Trujillo (1983) identified three kinds of stories.

Corporate Stories. **Corporate stories** convey the values, style, and history of an organization. Just as families have favorite stories about their history and identity that are retold often, organizations have favorite stories that reflect their collective vision of themselves. Stories serve to socialize new members into the culture of an organization. When retold among veteran members of an organization, stories foster feelings of ties among members and vitalize organizational ideology. For example, both Levi Strauss and Microsoft pride themselves on their informal style of operation. New employees are regaled with narratives that emphasize the laid-back character of the companies—stories about casual dress, relaxed meetings, and nonbureaucratic methods of getting things done. These stories socialize new employees into the informal ideology of the firms.

Personal Stories. Members of organizations also tell stories about themselves. **Personal stories** are accounts that announce how people see themselves and how they wish to be seen by others. For example, if Sabra perceives herself as a supportive team player, she could simply tell new employees this by saying, "I am a supportive person who believes in teamwork." On the other hand, she could define her image by telling a story: "When I first came here, most folks were operating

Reflection

What are the stories your school tells about itself? What did you hear from school leaders during orientation? What traditions of the school are highlighted in recruiting materials and catalogs?

in isolation, and I thought a lot more could be accomplished if we learned to collaborate. Let me tell you something I did to make that happen. After I'd been on staff for 3 months, I was assigned to work up a plan for downsizing our manufacturing department. Instead of just developing a plan on my own, I talked with several other managers, and then I met with people who worked in manufacturing to get their ideas. The plan we came up with reflected all of our insights and proposals." This narrative performance gives a concrete, coherent example of the personal image Sabra wishes to project.

Reflection

How important are content and relationship levels of meaning in personal stories?

Collegial Stories.   **Collegial stories** offer an account of other members of the organization. "If you need help getting around the CEO, Jane's the one to see. Once when I couldn't finish a report by the deadline, Jane rearranged the CEO's calendar so that he thought the report wasn't due for another week." "Roberts is a real stickler for rules. Once when I took an extra 20 minutes on my lunch break, he reamed me out." "Pat trades on politics, not performance. Once Pat took several of the higher-ups out for lunch and golfed with them for the month before bonuses were decided." Whether positive or negative, collegial stories assert identities for others in an organization. They are an informal network, or rumor mill, that teaches new members of an organization how to get along with various other members of the culture.

Try it out

Think about an organization to which you belong—perhaps one in which you worked or one that you have had many opportunities to observe. Identify corporate, personal, and collegial stories that you were told when you first entered the organization. How did these stories shape your understandings of the organization?

Try extending the idea of organizational stories to your family's culture. What were the family stories you were told to teach you your family's his-

continued on next page

continued from previous page

tory and values? What were the personal stories your parents told you to define who they are and what they stand for? Did family members talk about others? If so, what were the collegial stories you heard about other relatives? Do the stories told in your family form a coherent account of its identity?

Rites and Rituals   **Rites** and **rituals** are also symbolic practices that express and reproduce organizational cultures. Rites are dramatic, planned sets of activities that bring together aspects of cultural ideology into a single event. Harrison Trice and Janice Beyer (1984) identified six kinds of organizational rites. Rites of passage are used to mark entry into different levels in organizations. Fraternity hazing, although recently under attack, was long used to initiate new pledges into the brotherhood. Engagement parties and baby showers are rites that acknowledge changes in individuals' identities. Rites of integration serve to affirm and enhance the sense of community in an organization. Examples are holiday parties, annual picnics, and graduation ceremonies at campuses.

Organizational cultures also include rites that perform the speech act of blaming or praising. Rites of degradation are used to punish members of organizations and, thus, to proclaim that the organization doesn't approve of certain identities or activities. Firings and demotions are the most common degradation rites. In the military, being put on k.p. duty is a ritual meant to punish a trainee and lower her or his status. The counterpart to degradation rites is enhancement rites that shower praise and glory on individuals or teams who represent the organization's self-image. Campuses that value teaching, for instance, bestow awards on faculty who are especially committed and gifted teachers. Many sales companies give awards for productivity—most sales of the month, quarter, year. In my department, faculty meetings always open with announcements about honors and achievements of individual faculty. This recognition rite gives each of us moments in the limelight.

Organizations also develop rites for managing change. Renewal rites aim to revitalize and update organizations. Training workshops serve this purpose as do periodic retreats in which organizational members discuss their goals and the institution's health. Another change that organizations develop ritualized ways of managing is conflicts between members of the organization. Conflict resolution rites are regularized methods of dealing with differences and discord. Examples are arbitration, collective bargaining, mediation, executive fiat, voting, and ignoring or denying problems. The conflict resolution rite that typifies an organization reflects the values of its overall culture.

Reflection

What different organizational values do you perceive reflected in the alternative methods of conflict resolution?

Rituals are forms of communication that occur regularly and that members of an organization perceive as familiar and routine parts of organizational life. Rites differ from rituals in that the latter don't necessarily bring together a number of aspects of organizational ideology into a single event. Rather, rituals are repeated communication performances that express a particular value or role definition. Within organizations there are personal, task, and social rituals. Personal rituals are performances that individuals routinely engage in to define themselves. In their study of organizational cultures, Pacanowsky and O'Donnell-Trujillo (1983) noted that Lou Polito, the owner of a car company, opened all of the company's mail himself each day. Whenever possible, Mr. Polito hand-delivered mail to the divisions of his company to communicate his openness and his involvement with the day-to-day business.

Social rituals are standardized performances that affirm relationships among members of organizations. Graduate students in my department, for instance, routinely get together for beer each Friday afternoon. Tamar Katriel (1990) identified a social ritual of griping among Israelis. (Some of us who aren't Israelis might be familiar with this ritual!) *Kiturim,* the name Israelis give to their griping, most often occurs during Friday night social events called *mesibot kiturim,* which translates into gripe sessions. Unlike much griping by Westerners, *kiturim* focuses on national issues, concerns, and problems, rather than on personal complaints. Many Jewish families engage in ritualized *kvetching,* which is personal griping that aims to air personal frustrations but not necessarily to resolve them. The point of the ritual is to complain, not to feel better.

Task rituals are repeated activities that help members of an organization perform their jobs. For example, most organizations have forms and procedures that employees must follow to do various things. These forms and procedures regularize task performance in a manner consistent with the organization's view of itself and how it operates. In their study of a police unit, Pacanowsky and O'Donnell-Trujillo (1983) identified the routine that officers are trained to follow when they stop drivers for violations. The set of questions officers are taught to ask ("May I see your license please? Do you know why I stopped you? Do you know how fast you were going?) allows them to size up traffic violators and decide whether to give them any breaks.

Thick Description

Organizational culture theory is built primarily on **ethnographic research,** which uses interpretive methods to observe social life in depth in order to describe and analyze it and to understand what it means to members of a group. Geertz (1973) referred to this method of study as thick description. By this term he meant to call attention to the method's emphasis on interpreting the intricately entwined layers of meaning that constitute organizational life. For Geertz and other cultural researchers, it isn't sufficient to gather data such as memos, statements of company policy, and statistics on who does what. Instead, the goal of research is to analyze and interpret the surface information (what Searle would call brute facts) in order to develop a coherent account of an organization's culture.

Because engaging in thick description requires learning about the details of daily rituals, rites, and other activities, it is extremely time consuming. Organizational culture researchers often spend months or even years observing, recording, and interpreting the raw data of organizational life in order to clarify central ideology and the communication activities that sustain it. Only by immersing themselves in an organization's day-to-day activities can researchers discover centrally important meanings embedded in cultural practices that create, uphold, and express the values and ideology of the organization.

The ideal role for researchers is that of a true participant who can observe and come to understand an organization from the inside (Philipsen, 1992). To learn how police trainees are socialized into their profession, John Van Maanen (1973) joined the rookie class at a police training academy. After that, he spent months riding in a police car with a novice and a veteran officer.

Critical Assessment of Organizational Culture Theory

Response to organizational culture theory has been more positive than to many theories. Only one major reservation has been voiced. In addition, there is a debate about the appropriate uses of the theory. We'll discuss both.

Theory Has Limited Generalizability Although few scholars question the validity of viewing organizations as cultures, some do doubt the theoretical power of this viewpoint. You'll recall from Chapter 2 that a traditional goal of research is to derive generalizations that describe, explain, and predict events. A major criticism of organizational culture theory is that it is incapable of doing this. Critics charge that this theory's commitment to thick description of individual organizations prevents it from generating findings that tell us much about organizations in general. This criticism extends beyond studies of organizational communication to call into question all inquiry that focuses on situated activity. Writing in 1994, Kristine Fitch warned that "approaching meaning as something that is radically localized, the product of individuals in single times and places, . . . seems to close off any possibility of understanding a *social* world" (p. 35).

At first glance, this criticism seems valid and important in identifying a weakness of the theory. Before we jump to this conclusion, however, let's inspect the charge more carefully. The claim is that case studies of individual organizations do not and cannot produce knowledge about organizations in general. That charge may be justified if we define knowledge as information about concrete aspects of organizations' cultures. Existing studies of many organizations don't identify generalizable task rituals, enhancement rites, or stories that are performed in most organizations.

On the other hand, studies of particular organizations do give us the generalizable knowledge that in most or all organizations members engage in rituals, rites, and storytelling. We have a generalization about forms of communication that seem common, if not universal, to organizational life. By analogy, we don't know the content of constructs that are salient in any individual's cognitive interpretations, but we do know with reasonable certainty that all individuals rely on constructs to interpret experiences. Similarly, we don't know the constitutive and regulative rules any person uses to guide her or his communication, but we are relatively sure that all of us have constitutive and regulative rules. If you believe that generalizable knowledge about forms of communication is valuable, then you will probably not agree with this criticism of organizational culture theory.

Reflection

Is it sufficient for a theory to identify, describe, and explain forms of communication or should it provide knowledge about the content of communication?

How Should Findings Be Used?   Finally, we want to consider a debate about the uses of findings from research on organizational cultures. This theory has been strongly influenced by anthropology, which has the goal of understanding various cultures. Anthropologists generally do not seek to control or change cultures, and few approve of efforts to use their research to alter cultural life.

Yet, those who regard organizations as cultures often do wish to induce change—sometimes to benefit management's objectives, sometimes to improve work life for line employees. The goal of changing organizational cultures obviously deviates from the purist anthropological posture. Whether that is appropriate, ethical, or valuable is a matter of current controversy. Whatever you think in terms of this debate, it is clear that organizational culture theory offers a particularly powerful way of understanding the meanings at work in organizations and the ways in which those are affirmed, sustained, and sometimes altered through communication.

ummary

In this chapter, we've focused on theories that emphasize reciprocal relationships between communication and culture. The broadest of these is standpoint theory, which extends symbolic interactionism by noting that a society is not experienced identically by everyone but differently by members of different social groups within it. Standpoint theory enhances our awareness of ways in which societies designate groups and of the effects of social location on experiences, knowledge, identity, and opportunities.

Speech community theory is compatible with standpoint, yet offers more particularistic attention to specific social groups. The central claim of this theory is that communication is a primary socializing process that teaches us how to see ourselves and others and that shapes our understandings of what communication is and of how to use it in our relationships with others. Knowledge about disparate speech communities expands our awareness of human diversity and has the potential to improve our skills in communicating with people who differ from us.

In the final portion of the chapter, we discussed organizational culture theory, which draws on the fundamental knowledge and methods of anthropology to gain insight into the ways in which communication activities produce, reproduce, and express meanings of particular organizations. Studies of organizational cultures have opened scholars'

Reflection

Do scholars have the right to prescribe and/or attempt to implement changes in organizations?

eyes to the importance of daily performances, such as rituals and storytelling, in upholding a coherent set of meanings and activities for people involved in collective enterprises.

Taken together, these three theories enlarge our understanding of the formative power of communication in constituting individual identity, social life, and organizational activities. In addition, these theories help us understand the communicative genesis of diversity in communication, meaning, identity, and social interaction.

Chapter Ten

Theories of Mass Communication

_____ 1. What percentage of people arrested for felonies in California do you think are brought to trial?

A. 10%

B. 50%

C. 30%

D. 80%

_____ 2. In an average week, what do you think is the chance that you will be involved in some form of violence?

A. 1 in 100

B. 10 in 100

C. 25 in 100

D. 1 in 200

_____ 3. On an annual basis, what percentage of crimes in the United States are violent crimes such as murder, rape, robbery, and assault?

A. 75%

B. 50%

C. 25%

D. 10%

____ 4. On an average day, how much television do you watch?

   A. none

   B. 2 hours or less

   C. 3–4 hours

   D. more than 4 hours

The correct answer for the first three questions is D. The more television you watch, the more likely it is that you overestimated the amount of violent crime in the United States and the probability that you personally would be a victim of violent crime. Heavy television viewers also tend to underestimate the number of people arrested for felonies who are brought to trial in California. The theories we'll consider in this chapter should help you understand the relationships among media, our views of the world, and our attitudes, beliefs, opinions, and actions.

In this chapter, we turn our attention to theories of mass communication. In our technological world, mass communication is a major source of information, companionship, and entertainment. Along with the news and the story line, mass media present views of human beings, cultural events, and social life. **Mass communication** is a kind of communication that is aimed at large audiences. Mass media include books, film, television, radio, computer programs and games, and magazines and other forms of visual and print communication. Mass media do not include more personal kinds of mediated communication, such as interacting with others on the Internet, browsing the World Wide Web, or participating in electronic bulletin boards and discussion groups. Many people today sustain and increasingly even form close relationships through mediated communication (Lea & Spears, 1995). These important kinds of mediated communication involve personal interactions, not messages aimed at a mass audience. In this chapter, we'll consider two of the more prominent theories of mass communication and explore what they say about media's effects on what we think and believe, as well as on how we understand collective life.

Technological Determinism

A Canadian academic trained in literary criticism seems an unlikely candidate to be a popular cultural guru. Marshall McLuhan, however, defied the odds to become a celebrity in the 1960s. Dubbed the "Oracle of the Electronic Age" and the "Prophet of the Media," McLuhan attracted a sizable following of laypersons and professionals in media industries. The causes of his popularity were both his bold proclamations about the media and his dynamic style of presenting ideas. No doubt, McLuhan would be pleased that both style and substance gave rise to his stardom, since he coined the phrase "The medium is the message."

The theory Marshall McLuhan advanced has been called **technological determinism.** As with any deterministic theory, the basic claim is that some single cause or phenomenon determines other aspects of life. Biological determinism states that biology controls human life (remember Freud's dictum: "Anatomy is destiny"), and Marxist theory asserts that economics is the central social dynamic that determines all aspects of life. McLuhan saw media as the critical force that determined other things. The theory of technological determinism states that technology—specifically, media—decisively shapes how individuals think, feel, and act and how societies organize themselves and operate.

Reflection

To what extent are deterministic theories compatible with systems theories such as interactional theory?

Media History of Human Civilization

McLuhan claimed that media are the essence of civilized life. By this, he didn't necessarily mean that media cultivate more sophisticated consciousness or civil codes of behavior. Rather, his point was that the dominant media at any given time in a society determine the basis of

Box 10.1

*Media Epochs in
Human History*

Tribal Epoch	Literate Epoch	Print Epoch	Electronic Epoch
	2000 B.C.	1450	1850

social organization and collective life. To explain his ideas, McLuhan traced the history of human societies by identifying media that emerge and dominate in particular eras. According to McLuhan (1962, 1964; McLuhan & Fiori, 1967), history can be divided into four distinct media epochs (see Box 10.1).

The Tribal Epoch   During the **tribal epoch,** the oral tradition reigned. Communication consisted of face-to-face interactions. Oral cultures were knitted together by stories that passed along the history and traditions of a culture, oral communication of information, and oral rituals, performances, and forms of entertainment. Reliance on the spoken word for information and recreation made oral cultures highly cohesive communities. The tribal epoch's emphasis on orality made hearing a dominant sense (McLuhan, 1969).

The Literate Epoch   Invention of the phonetic alphabet ushered in the **literate epoch** in which common symbols allowed people to communicate in written form and without face-to-face interaction. With written communication came changes in human life. The emergence of writing made it possible for individuals to gain information privately—away from others in their communities. Because written communication can be reread, this medium requires less memory than oral communication. The alphabet also fostered ascendance of sight as a primary sense. For those who could read and write, sight replaced hearing as a dominant sense. Written forms of communication also established a linear form for communication. In writing, letter follows letter, word follows word, sentence follows sentence. According to McLuhan, the continuous, sequential order of written communication cultivated linear thinking and, with that, the development of disciplines such as mathematics that are based on linear logic. Diminished in prominence was the more fluid, weblike communication form typical of storytelling.

The Print Epoch   Although invention of the alphabet made written communication possible, print did not immediately gain prominence as the preferred medium of communication in society. When the alphabet was first developed, monks and scribes laboriously copied individual books and other written materials. There was no way to mass-produce the written word. Thus, both reading and access to print media were restricted to the more elite classes of society. They were not immediately accessible to the majority of people.

The **print epoch** began when Johann Gutenberg invented the printing press, and literacy ascended in human history. The printing press made it possible to print thousands of copies of a single book at a moderate cost. Thus, the printed word was no longer restricted to people with status and money; instead, it was increasingly accessible to all types and socioeconomic classes, making print a mainstream medium. McLuhan asserted that the printing press was the first mechanism for mass production, which is why he credited it with inaugurating the Industrial Revolution (McLuhan, 1962).

As with other evolutions in media, the printing press changed human life. Reliance on the visual sense was no longer restricted to the elite who had access to individually copied books and print matter. The capability to mass-produce printed material made visual perception dominant and pervasive. In addition, mass-produced writing cultivated a homogeneity among people, since the same message could be delivered to many people. At the same time, widely available printed material further fostered fragmentation of communities as people no longer needed to be together to share information and tell stories. Each woman and man could read a book, newspaper, or magazine in isolation from others. No longer was face-to-face contact necessary for gaining information (McLuhan & Fiori, 1967).

Reflection

What are the personal and social implications of media that allow people to separate from one another?

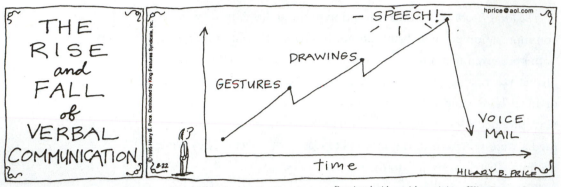

The Electronic Epoch   The dominance of print as a medium and the eye as a primary sense organ diminished with the invention of the telegraph, which was the forerunner of the **electronic epoch** in human history. Reliance on print and the fragmentation of people promoted by mass-produced written material waned, and people were once again brought together. According to McLuhan (1969), electronic media revived the oral tradition and the preeminence of hearing and touching. The telegraph made it possible for people to communicate in individual, personal ways across great distances.

The telegraph was only the first of a long line of electronic media that McLuhan believed resurrected community among people. We watch television and understand what is happening in Rwanda or Zambia; we see a newscast and know what our president said and how he looked; we use modems to "talk" with people in other places, sometimes thousands of miles away. No longer are people separated from one another by distance. Instead, claimed McLuhan, the electronic epoch creates a "global village" (McLuhan & Fiori, 1967).

Reflection

Some people agree with McLuhan's contention that electronic media bring people together into a "global village." Others, however, think electronic communication isolates people from one another with each individual hooked up to a personal computer instead of interacting with real human beings. How do you respond to these opposing views of the impact of electronic communication on human community?

McLuhan's media history of human civilization was the basis of his theory that the dominant media of an era determine the dominant human senses and the ways that humans organize their societies.

The Medium Is the Message/Massage

McLuhan's best-known idea is that "the medium is the message" (McLuhan & Fiori, 1967). For him, this phrase had multiple meanings. It implied, first, that the medium, or channel of communication, determines the substance of communication. In other words, although the content of communication is not irrelevant, it is less important than the form or medium of communication. For example, McLuhan argued that the act of watching television shapes how we think, regardless of what we watch on television. He wrote that the dominant media of an age are more influential on our lives than any specific content conveyed by those media (McLuhan & Fiori, 1967).

To understand McLuhan's point, reflect on the changes brought about with the emergence of new media in each of the epochs we just discussed. Humans adapt to their environments by developing sensory abilities that enhance their ability to survive and function. When listening and speaking were the only ways of conveying information and surviving, we developed keen oral and aural senses and prodigious memories. Once people could rely on printed matter for information and entertainment, sight supplanted hearing and speaking as the dominant sense and memory became less important. McLuhan died in 1980. Were he alive today, it is likely that he would be calling attention to ways in which new and convergent technologies are shaping how we think and how our senses are adapting in response to the media of this era.

Try it out

Call to mind a recent experience in your life. Describe that experience using a pen and a sheet of paper. Next, share the experience with another person by talking face to face. Third, recount the experience in an electronic mail message to an acquaintance.

How does the message change as you change the medium of conveying it?

How does your sense of the message vary with the different media for transmitting it?

Hot and Cool Media

McLuhan drew a basic distinction between hot and cool media. **Hot media** are those that include relatively complete sensory data. Thus, a person doesn't need to fill in a lot of information to understand the message. For example, radio, printed material, photographs, and films are hot media, since they require little involvement from us. **Cool media,** on the other hand, demand some involvement from individuals. A telephone conversation requires our participation, as do interactive computer games and face-to-face interactions. Lectures are hot, class discussions are cool; radio music is hot, rappin' is cool; newspapers are hot, crossword puzzles are cool.

Hot and cool not only describe qualities of media, but also correspond to different kinds of thinking. McLuhan believed that hot media encourage individuals to be passive. By supplying everything necessary for understanding, hot media allow us to be uninvolved in learning and thinking. Cool media, in contrast, require participation, involvement, and mental activity on our part. Cool media require imagination, effort, and emotional involvement, all of which McLuhan thought were healthy for individuals and society.

"The medium is the message" also had other meanings for McLuhan. By changing only one letter, the phrase is transformed into "The medium is the massage." This metaphor implies that media manipulate how we perceive ourselves, others, society, and the world. The media massage our consciousness and transform our perceptions. Finally, McLuhan sometimes made a play on the phrase by saying "The medium is the mass-age," by which he meant that the dominant medium has become mass communication in our age.

Reflection

To what extent do you attend to hot and cool media? How actively do you participate in creating the messages of media in your life?

Critical Assessment of Technological Determinism

McLuhan was a highly controversial thinker, and his ideas continue to be hotly debated today. Media industries applauded McLuhan's ideas, which isn't surprising, since he glamorized and popularized media. In academic circles, however, McLuhan has been less well received. A primary reason for scholarly skepticism about technological determinism is that convincing research to support McLuhan's claims has not been produced. In a sharp denunciation of McLuhan's work, communication professor George Gordon (1982, p. 42) stated flatly, "Not one bit of *sustained and replicated* scientific evidence, inductive or deductive, has to date justified any one of McLuhan's most famous slogans, metaphors, or dicta."

Hyperbolic Speculation   McLuhan's ideas are frequently criticized for being wildly exaggerated (Baran & Davis, 1995). It is hyperbolic, assert critics, to proclaim the death of literacy when reading is still a major activity in developed countries. Likewise, it seems foolhardy to dismiss linear logic as inferior when it has given rise to many of the most important capabilities in the world. Further, many believe McLuhan vastly overestimated the power of media. An alternative claim that is more qualified than the one advanced by McLuhan is that although media may influence our lives, they do not determine or transform human experience.

Lack of Rigorous Development   According to some critics, McLuhan's theory also suffers from serious underdevelopment. A number of scholars think McLuhan was far more talented at generating provocative ideas than at rigorously developing them. He promulgated fantastic claims and coined catchy phrases, but he didn't follow through by conducting systematic study to test the ideas he proclaimed. Further, when academics did test some of his ideas, they didn't find support for his claims (Baran & Davis, 1995). The lack of evidence to support McLuhan's theory led one critic to brand his work "McLuhanacy" (Gordon, 1982).

Overly Deterministic   Another criticism of McLuhan's theory is that it is highly deterministic in asserting that human consciousness is controlled and determined by media. The idea that humans are passive victims of technology is problematic for two reasons. First, believing

Pepper . . . and Salt

"It may be mindless drivel, but it's *good* mindless drivel."

Reprinted from THE WALL STREET JOURNAL
by permission of Cartoon Features Syndicate.

that we are powerless to control technology and its effects on us can function as a self-fulfilling prophecy. If we believe our fate is determined by technology, we're unlikely to attempt to control technology and its consequences. Thus, we might yield the degree of control we could have. Second, the claim that media determine human consciousness and social life obscures the complex, multiple variables that influence how we think as individuals and how we organize social life (Boulding, 1967). This objection to technological determinism has spurred development of theories that assume audiences actively participate in constructing the meanings of mass communication (DeFleur & Ball-Rokeach, 1989).

Responding to the Critics   How did Marshall McLuhan respond to his critics? As you might suspect, he dismissed them and did so with vintage McLuhan flamboyancy. Those critics, he sneered, are pedantic, left-brained academics who are able only to conduct detached, linear analyses of life. They can't appreciate imaginative, creative thinking about the "big picture." Contrasting those pedantic, left-brained academics with himself, McLuhan rather immodestly claimed that he was able to transcend linear, literary thinking and engage in more inventive, artistic right-brained thought.

Perhaps a balanced assessment of McLuhan's theorizing is that, although overstated and sloganistic, it was valuable in stimulating scholars to pay more attention to how media work and how they influence individual and collective life. Despite the excesses of his ideas and style, McLuhan contributed to both scholarly and popular awareness of the character and consequences of media in the life of a culture. If he was mistaken on many details, he still may have been insightful about the big picture. Economist Kenneth Boulding (1967, p. 57) suggested that McLuhan might be like other creative thinkers in his tendency to "hit very large nails not quite on the head." Perhaps we shouldn't dismiss McLuhan's overall views just because his aim was a little off.

Cultivation Theory

In contrast to McLuhan's speculative, colorful ideas, a second theory of media has been built on a long-term program of empirical research. **Cultivation theory** claims that television cultivates, or promotes, a view of social reality that is inaccurate, but that viewers nonetheless assume reflects real life. According to this theory, the synthetic reality of television shapes heavy viewers' attitudes, beliefs, and actions (Gerbner, 1990; Gerbner, Gross, Morgan, & Signorielli, 1986; Signorielli & Morgan, 1990).

George Gerbner and his colleagues at the Annenberg School of Communication in Pennsylvania form the center of cultivation research and theorizing. Beginning in 1967, this team of researchers systematically developed, tested, and refined cultivation theory. By now there is a solid base of research for the claims made by scholars in this school, although there are also challenges to this research and the inferences drawn from it.

Cultivation theory emerged in 1967 when George Gerbner lent his scientific expertise to two national efforts to understand media's effects: The National Commission on the Causes and Prevention of Violence, which met in 1967 and 1968, and the Surgeon General's Scientific Advisory Committee on Television and Social Behavior, which conferred during the course of 1972. Both of these counsels were concerned with violence and possible connections between televised violence and increases in both violence and tolerance of violence. The genesis of cultivation theory in national studies of violence explains why its proponents have concentrated on the ways in which television cultivates attitudes and beliefs about violence and views of the world as a dangerous place. Because these are the cornerstones of cultivation theory, in our discussion we'll focus on violence and views of dangers.

Cultivation

Cultivation refers to the cumulative process by which television fosters beliefs about social reality. According to the theory, television transmits particular and often unrealistic understandings of the world as being more violent and dangerous than statistics on actual violence indicate it is. Thus, goes the reasoning, watching television promotes distorted views of life. The word *cumulative* is important to understanding cultivation. Theorists in this school don't argue that a particular program has significant effects on what viewers believe. They do, however, claim that watching television over a long period of time has effects on viewers' beliefs and world views. By extension, the more television a person watches, the more distorted her or his ideas of life are likely to be. Simply put, the theory claims that television cumulatively cultivates a synthetic world view that heavy viewers are likely to assume represents reality.

Reflection

To what extent do you think people assume televised life equals real life?

To open this chapter, I asked you to answer questions based on surveys conducted in research on cultivation theory. Heavy television viewers are more likely to have beliefs that reflect the world view portrayed by television, which is not equivalent to a world view based on empirical data. On television, 77% of major characters who commit crimes perpetrate acts of violence. Compare this to the fact that roughly 10% of reported real crimes are violent. Analyses of prime-time programming on commercial networks reveal that 86% of the depictions of the criminal justice system in the United States portray criminals as never being brought to trial or as getting off at trial (Choi, Massey, & Baran, 1988). Yet, of the nearly 11,000 felony arrests in California in one year, 80% went to trial, and 88% of the trials resulted in convictions. Prime-time reality portrays 64% of characters involved in violence, so heavy viewing of television is likely to cultivate the belief that being a victim of violence is common. In the real world, however, the average person has a 1 in 200 chance of being involved in a violent crime in any week.

The world of television is one teeming with violence. By age 6, the average child in the United States has watched 5,000 hours of television; by age 18, the average person has watched fully 19,000 hours of television. What happens during all of the hours in front of the television set? According to one researcher (Zukerman, 1993), the average 18-year-old in the United States has viewed 200,000 separate acts of violence on television, including 40,000 murders. Given the incidence of violence on television, it's no wonder that many heavy viewers think the world is substantially more violent than crime reports indicate it is.

Why is violence so much greater on television than in real life? The answer varies with different kinds of programs. Violence in prime-time shows and cartoons may be used to increase interest and stimulation. Although most people in real life aren't shooting or mugging each other, many people might find it dull to watch shows in which there is little action. The high incidence of violence in news programming reflects, in part, the fact that the abnormal is more newsworthy than the normal. It isn't news that 99.9% of couples are either getting along or working out their problems in nonviolent ways; it is news when Lorena Bobbitt amputates her husband's penis and when Nicole Brown Simpson is murdered. It isn't news that most of us grumble about "big government" but refrain from violent protest; it is news when the Federal Building in Oklahoma is blown up. Simply put, violence is news.

Reflection

Is the goal of news programs to represent real life accurately or to selectively present what is news and, thus, by definition, atypical of real life?

Another reason for the inordinate violence shown on news programs is the breadth of coverage attempted by most news broadcasts. Approximately 15 news items are presented in a 30-minute news program. When we subtract the time for the 25 to 30 different commercials in a half-hour news program, the total time for presenting news is closer to 23 minutes (Ferrante, 1995). Because so much information is presented so quickly, there is little analysis, depth, or reflection. In his book *Amusing Ourselves to Death,* cultural critic Neil Postman (1985) argued that the fast and furious format of news programming creates the overall impression that the world is unmanageable, beyond our control, and filled with danger and violence. Consequently, reports on crime and violence may do less to enhance understanding and informed response than to agitate, scare, and intimidate us.

Try it out

Make a list of all of the news events (not sports reports or weather information) you recall from last night's news program (or the most recent news program you watched). How many specific news events do you recall? If you're like most people, you don't remember many of the events presented on television news because they are presented so quickly and superficially that viewers seldom absorb or reflect on them.

What does this experience suggest to you about the newsworthiness of news programming?

The Power of Synthetic Reality

Perhaps you are thinking that few people confuse what they see on television with real life. Research, however, indicates that this may not be the case. Children's sex-role stereotypes seem directly related to the amount of commercial television (but not educational television) that they watch. In a comparison of communities that did not have television with ones that did, one researcher (Kimball, 1986) found that children who watched commercial television had distinctly more sex-stereotypical views of women and men than children in communities without television. Further, when television was introduced into the communities that had not had it, there was an increase in children's sex-stereotypical attitudes. Equally impressive evidence of the effects of television on our views of reality is the finding that nonstereotypical portrayals of the sexes on television actually decrease viewers' sex stereotypes (Rosenwasser, Lingenfelter, & Harrington, 1989).

Research also indicates that mediated views of relationships cultivate unrealistic views of what a normal relationship is. MTV programming strongly emphasizes eroticism and sublime sex, and people who watch a lot of MTV have been shown to have expectations for sexual perfectionism in their own real relationships (Shapiro & Kroeger, 1991). Relatedly, people who read a lot of self-help books tend to have less realistic views of relationships than people who read few or no self-help guides. Investigations have also shown that people who watch sexually violent MTV are more likely to regard sexual violence as normal in relationships, and this is true of female, as well as male, viewers (Dieter, 1989). If we believe that all relationship problems can be fixed, sex can always be sublime, and couples live happily ever after, then we're likely to be dissatisfied with real relationships that can't consistently live up to these synthesized images. If we believe violence is normal in intimate relationships, we may accept it—and its sometimes lethal consequences—in our own relationships. Further, if we believe that the images broadcast by media are accurate, then we're likely to reject normal relationships in a futile quest for ones as perfect as those that exist on television but not in real life.

What accounts for television's ability to cultivate synthetic world views? Cultivation theorists identify two mechanisms to explain the cultivation process: **mainstreaming** and **resonance.**

Mainstreaming   Mainstreaming refers to the effect of television in stabilizing and homogenizing views within a society. If television programs from Saturday morning cartoons to prime-time dramas feature extensive violence, then viewers may come to believe that violence is common. It's important to realize that not just heavy viewers are affected by televised versions of reality. As they interact with others, heavy viewers communicate their attitudes and, thus, affect the attitudes of others. In this way, televised versions of life permeate the mainstream.

Describing the power of television to insinuate its views into the mainstream of cultural life, Gerbner and his colleagues (Gerbner et al., 1986, p. 18) stated that "television is a centralized system of storytelling. . . . Television cultivates from infancy the very predispositions and preferences that used to be acquired from other primary sources. . . . [T]elevision has become the primary common source of socialization and everyday information (mostly in the form of entertainment) of an otherwise heterogeneous population."

Reflection

What connections do you perceive between the idea of mainstreaming and McLuhan's claim that electronic media are making us into a "global village"?

Resonance   The second explanation for television's capacity to cultivate world views is resonance, which is the extent to which something is congruent with personal experience. For instance, a person who has been robbed, assaulted, or raped is likely to identify with televised violence. In so doing, the viewer heightens the impact of the televised message by fortifying it with her or his own real experience. In other words, we participate in creating the drama and its impact on our own thought, feelings, attitudes, and actions.

Reflection

What connections do you see between the idea of resonance and narrative theory's concept of fidelity?

We should note that resonance and mainstreaming are explanations that George Gerbner and his colleagues developed after discovering that heavy television viewers believe the world is more violent and more scary than do light viewers. The fact that these explanations were generated after data were gathered means that the explanations themselves haven't been directly tested. Consequently, although research documents a relationship between heavy television viewing and beliefs about violence, we can't be sure that mainstreaming and resonance cause or explain the correlation. Other explanations are possible.

Reflection

Can you generate alternative explanations for the finding that heavy television viewers believe the world is more violent than light television viewers do?

Assumptions of Cultivation Theory

Now that we have a basic grasp of cultivation theory and some of the research it has generated, we're ready to examine its basic assumptions. After more than two decades of research, George Gerbner (1990) summarized cultivation theory by stating six key assumptions, or claims, that guide research and development of cultivation theory.

Television Is Unique Perhaps you've been wondering why cultivation theory focuses exclusively on television in an age when there are many, many media. The reason is found in the theory's first assumption, which is that television is a unique medium of communication. Cultivation theorists believe that television is fundamentally different from other media in several ways. First, it is pervasive. In 1950, only 9% of households in the United States owned televisions. By 1991, 98.3% of Americans had at least one television in their home, and fully two-thirds of households had more than one set (Television Bureau of Advertising, 1991, p. 2). In the average home, a television set is on 7 hours each day. Thus, this medium reaches a vast number of people: 89% of 18- to 54-year-olds and 94% of people over 55 (Television Bureau of Advertising, 1991, p. 7).

Television is also uniquely accessible. It is more available than many forms of mass communication, because it doesn't require particular skills (such as literacy for reading, or computer knowledge for touring the Internet and playing computer games). Third, television is virtually free. Unlike going out to movies or buying books, we don't have to buy television time whenever we want entertainment. Other than the initial, fairly low cost of the appliance and the minimal cost of electricity, television is free. The same cannot be said for time spent browsing the World Wide Web or watching home movies. Television is also uniquely accessible to all types of people at all stages of life. Individuals with mobility impairments can view television without the exertion required to go to a library or a theater. Children who are too young to go out on their own can be entertained by television, as can people whose health problems keep them homebound. Because no other medium of communication has all of these qualities, television is unique.

Television Forms the Cultural Mainstream   Cultivation theorists claim that television is the "central cultural arm" of U.S. society (Gerbner, Gross, Jackson-Beeck, Jeffries-Fox, & Signorielli, 1978, p. 178). Because it is uniquely accessible to the vast majority of citizens, television is able to construct and project images that come to define the **cultural mainstream,** or the general view of life in the society. In heavy viewers, this cultivates (mis)understandings based more on the synthetic images of television than on real life.

To describe the process by which television achieves this, theorists identify "the three Bs": blurring, blending, and bending reality in ways that normalize a synthetic, yet coherent world view. Explaining these, Gerbner (1990) noted that television blurs traditional distinctions in world views; blends diverse realities into a single, homogeneous mainstream view; and bends that mainstream view to serve the institutional interests of television's sponsors.

Television Cultivates Basic Assumptions About Life, Rather Than Specific Attitudes and Opinions   This premise asserts that television is less influential in fostering specific beliefs and opinions than in shaping viewers' underlying assumptions about life and how it works (Gerbner, Gross, Morgan, & Signorielli, 1986). Obviously, the coherent, synthetic sys-

Calvin and Hobbes

by Bill Watterson

tem of life portrayed on television may lead to specific attitudes about groups of people, levels of violence, and so forth. The focus of cultivation theory, however, is not specific opinions and attitudes, but rather more general underlying ideas about the world.

The basic world view studied by cultivation theorists is exemplified in research on the **mean world syndrome.** The mean world syndrome is the belief that the world is a dangerous place, full of selfish, mean people who cannot be trusted and who are likely to harm us. Although on an annual basis less than 1% of the U.S. population is a victim of a violent crime, television represents the world as a mean and dangerous place in which everyone is at risk (Gerbner et al., 1986). In a study of over 2,000 children's programs aired between 1967 and 1985, Nancy Signorielli (1990) found that 71% of prime-time and 94% of weekend programs included acts of violence. On average, there were over five acts of violence per hour of prime-time programming and six per hour of weekend programming. Signorielli then surveyed people at five different times to discover their views of the world. Her findings indicate that heavy viewers are more likely to see the world as a mean place and people as untrustworthy than are lighter viewers. This study is consistent with cultivation theory's claim that television viewing has a cumulative effect on basic views of the world.

Television Is a Medium of Conservative Socialization   The fourth assumption is a logical extension of the first three. Because television reaches so many people, it is a major socializing agent for members of a culture. Further, claim cultivation theorists, television is conservative in stabilizing existing social patterns and in promoting resistance to change. Because reform, change, and activism aren't encouraged by television, it serves to normalize and preserve the status quo. A major reason that television stabilizes social patterns is that the medium itself is highly repetitive, a quality that cultivates comfort with familiar, standard patterns (Gerbner et al., 1978). In this sense, television is ritualistic, relying on generic formulas to tell stories in news, drama, and comedy programs, as well as in advertising.

Observable Effects of Television on Culture Are Relatively Small   At first you might be surprised by this assumption, since cultivation theorists seem convinced that television profoundly affects social life. To understand this proposition, consider the ice-age metaphor (Gerbner, Gross, Morgan, & Signorielli, 1980, p. 14) used to explain it: "Just as an average temperature shift of a few degrees can lead to an ice age or the outcomes of elections can be determined by slight margins, so too can a relatively small but pervasive influence make a cultural difference. The 'size' of an 'effect' is far less critical than the direction of its steady contribution." Cultivation theorists maintain that television's cumulative effect on cultural consciousness is significant, although specific measures of that effect may not reveal the full impact.

New Technologies Extend Television's Influence   The final proposition—one that was added to the theory in 1990—addresses the emergence of newer technologies such as the VCR. Gerbner (1990) argues that additional technologies will not diminish the impact of television as a medium, but will actually reinforce and magnify it. Why might this be so? To understand, let's recall the first assumption made by cultivation theorists: Television is a unique medium. The same may be said of any new technologies that offer the same kind of accessibility, economy, and range of content to appeal to various groups of people. Videos that can be viewed in the home meet these criteria; thus, they extend the mainstreaming of the television medium. Interactive and convergent computer technologies are also becoming more accessible as computers become less expensive and competition among on-line companies drives down the cost of those services.

These six propositions sum up the claims of cultivation theory. In concert, they argue that television is a uniquely accessible medium that creates and mainstreams a synthetic view of the world that heavy viewers may come to accept as representing real life.

Critical Assessment of Cultivation Theory

Debate over cultivation theory has been intense and sometimes distinctly antagonistic. We'll consider four prominent criticisms of cultivation theory and discuss responses made by Gerbner and his colleagues.

Weak Support for the Theory   One major criticism is that research has shown only a very weak relationship between television viewing and viewers' fear of violence and belief that the world is a mean, dangerous place. Some critics assert that the demonstrated relationship is so slight that the theory should be dismissed. In a fiery assault, Paul Hirsch (1980) contended that cultivation theorists have selectively reported only results that support their claims and have obscured findings that are inconsistent with the theory. For example, Hirsch claimed that his own reanalysis of the data collected by Gerbner and his colleagues indicated that many nonviewers believed the world was a dangerous, mean place and they were fearful of violence. Cultivation theorists dismissed Hirsch's charges, calling his reanalysis highly selective and certainly no basis for disregarding the cumulative results of a decade of careful research (Gerbner, 1981, p. 39). The validity of Hirsch's claims may become more clear if other researchers reanalyze data gathered by Gerbner and his colleagues at the Annenberg School of Communication.

Incompatibilities in the Theory   A second criticism is that cultivation theory mixes incompatible frameworks, relying on the traditional tools of social science to explore decisively humanistic questions. Many conventional social scientists are uncomfortable with the fifth assumption of cultivation theory, which holds that the observable, measurable effects of television are relatively small. Traditional social science is built on the idea that the effects of phenomena can be observed and measured. Traditional social scientists are also disturbed by the lack of control in much cultivation research. Instead of observing viewers in carefully controlled laboratory settings, Gerbner and his colleagues have relied primarily on self-reports of viewing habits. People might deliberately or inadvertently misestimate how much they watch television. Further, because cultivation researchers haven't observed people watching television, they haven't checked for influences of situational factors that might affect both viewing (for example, whether television is the focus or the background) and motivations (for example, whether fearful people watch more television). Thus, some social scientists think that cultivation theory is built on a shaky foundation of nonrigorous research.

Humanists, on the other hand, have a different complaint. On one level, humanists believe that the methods of social science are ill-suited to answer basic humanistic questions about "what it all means" (Newcomb, 1978). From a staunch humanistic perspective, phenomena such as meaning, values, and beliefs resist scientific measurement. At a second level, humanists criticize cultivation theory for presuming humans are powerless puppets of the media. Horace Newcomb (1978) argued that individuals have the capacity to defy the mainstreaming effect of television. They can, he insisted, resist, challenge, and redefine the intended messages of television. To assume that all viewers are taken in by the synthetic world view depicted on the tube is to reduce humans to nonhuman status. Further, Melvin DeFleur and Sandra Ball-Rokeach (1989) argue that it is naive to assume television is the singular cause of viewers' attitudes. They assert that there are very complex interactions among television, viewers, and society. If this is so, then a theory that concentrates only on a linear relationship between television viewing and attitudes is suspect.

Individual Variation   Newcomb's humanistic arguments are the basis for a third major criticism of cultivation theory. Central to the theory is the concept of "viewers" who are conceived and studied as a homogeneous group. That homogeneity, contend some scholars, may be an illusion that raises questions about the validity of the theory. In other words, despite cultivation theory's claim that television has homogenized society, some critics believe people remain quite diverse in their motives and world views, as well as their specific attitudes and opinions. By extension, individuals apply their particular and highly diverse meanings to interpret television programming. Cultivation theorists rely on very crude measures of both television (pure viewing time) and effects of television (mean world and violence indexes). These rough measures assume that all television is the same (and all violence presented on television is alike) and that all people interpret and respond to research questions in like manner. This criticism basically argues that glossing over the range of meanings people attribute to the diverse communication transmitted by television reflects an inaccurate and inappropriate view of human nature.

Correlation Versus Cause; Cause Versus Effect A final important challenge to cultivation theory is that it may be guilty of confusing correlation and cause, on the one hand, and cause and effect, on the other hand. In Chapter 2, we distinguished between causation (one thing brings about another thing) and correlation (two things go together). Some scholars believe that cultivation theorists have confused cause with correlation in suggesting that television cultivates (causes) views of violence and a mean world. The two may go together (be correlated), argue critics, but this doesn't necessarily mean one strictly causes the other.

Cultivation research suggests that heavy viewing and fearful views of the world go together. Cultivation theorists have interpreted this finding as indicating that television causes fearfulness. However, the results could equally well be interpreted to indicate that people who are fearful are more likely to be heavy viewers of television. According to the alternative interpretation, belief that the world is mean, dangerous, and violent is a direct cause of heavy viewing. Which explanation is more accurate, or more plausible? We don't know, and that's the point of this criticism: The research demonstrates only correlation, not causation. Claims for the mainstreaming, homogenizing power of television cannot be supported by correlational data.

A related criticism is that cultivation theorists have at least prematurely, if not inaccurately, labeled television the cause of certain effects. Some scholars suggest that television viewing may be an effect of other causes, rather than a primary cause in its own right. Even if research were to demonstrate that fearful views of the world follow television viewing (rather than vice versa), we could not be sure that television is the cause of those views. It's entirely possible that there is another factor or factors that cause both television watching and fearful views of the world. For example, perhaps physically frail and homebound individuals watch more television than active, healthy people. Their physical limitations may cause both feelings of fear (because they are more vulnerable than physically stronger individuals) and heavier television viewing (because that medium is most accessible to them).

Support for the idea of more basic causes of fearful attitudes was produced in a study by Anthony Doob and Glen Macdonald (1979). Studying four Toronto cities with distinct rates of crime, these researchers found that the empirical danger of neighborhoods accounted for nearly all of the variation in residents' fearfulness. In other words, the effect of television viewing was nil.

Responding to the Critics   As you might suspect, Gerbner and his colleagues do not agree with the criticisms we've discussed. Rather than seeing cultivation theory as entailing incompatible assumptions, its proponents believe that their work marks a critical nexus of two formerly separate scholarly paradigms. It is a strength of the theory, they claim, that it can bring together heretofore disparate research traditions.

In response to the humanistic criticism that cultivation theory ignores humans' ability to produce meanings and to interpret images presented to them, Gerbner and his colleagues (1986) asserted that humans learn their meanings from the culture, of which television is a major part. They went on to claim that television is the mainstream that cultivates stable images for heavy viewers. If you accept the idea that television is a primary socializing agent of the culture (the second assumption of cultivation theory), then it is reasonable to assume that we learn meanings and patterns of interpretation from television.

Reflection

How would symbolic interaction theorists regard the claim that television is a major socializing agent through which individuals are talked into humanity?

Cultivation theorists have been less effective in refuting charges that they conflate correlation with causation and cause with effect. Gerbner's response to the study by Doob and Macdonald is that it supports cultivation theory by illustrating the resonance principle: People in dangerous neighborhoods find violence on television congruent with their personal experiences. This response, however, doesn't address the central finding that the effects of television were minimal once real-life circumstances were taken into account.

Cultivation theory has been badly battered by critics and research that challenge its basic claims. Even so, many people find it intuitively sensible that there are links between television viewing and world views, especially views of violence, meanness, and danger. We should also note that even if cultivation theory is not completely correct in all of its claims, there is some evidence that television viewing is related to world views. Regardless of whether the relationship is causal or correlational, the connection is important. Whether cultivation theory is the best, or even an adequate, way of conceiving and studying those links is an open question. Ongoing research at the Annenberg School of Communication may provide more definitive answers in the years ahead.

 ummary

In this chapter, we've examined two theories about mass communication. In many respects the theories are distinct. McLuhan's technological determinism claims that the dominant media of an epoch shape how we think, take in and process information, and function as a collective society. In contrast, cultivation theory focuses on ways in which the specific medium of television cultivates basic world views.

Another distinction between the theories is scope. Technological determinism is broadly concerned with any and all media that affect individual and collective sensory adaptation. McLuhan and those who accept his ideas want to understand the effects of various media on individual and social behavior. Cultivation theory, on the other hand, concentrates exclusively on television, a medium it regards as a uniquely influential socializing agent of the culture.

A third area of divergence between the two theories is the assumed impact of media of interest. For cultivation theory, violence and beliefs about the perilous character of the world are key concerns. These theorists have focused exclusively on investigating relationships between television viewing and views of violence and the dangerousness of the world. Technological determinism, however, considers a broader range of consequences of media. Theorists in this school look at "the big picture" and advance sweeping claims about the power of media on many dimensions of cultural life.

These differences notwithstanding, there are also important similarities between cultivation theory and technological determinism. The most basic commonality is that both theories assume media (or, in the case of cultivation theory, one particular medium) do profoundly affect us as individuals and as a society. Thus, both theories assume media are extremely powerful.

A second similarity between the theories is that both place greater emphasis on media, or channels, than on the content of communication. McLuhan concentrated on the ways in which particular media advance or foster development of different human senses, such as sight, hearing, writing, and various forms of human thought, such as right and left brain specialization. Gerbner and his colleagues pursue similar lines of inquiry with their attention to the ways in which television shapes human consciousness and fundamental views of the social world.

A final similarity between the two theories is that both are primarily descriptive and explanatory. McLuhan offered a description of media epochs and an explanation of how different media shape human sensory development. Cultivation theorists describe the mainstreaming effects of television and explain how televised realities cultivate world views that, though inaccurate, are believed by heavy viewers. Thus, both of these theories are efforts to describe and explain how media operate.

Neither theory advances critical analysis of media and their effects. In different ways, both theories pursue the goals of explanation and prediction and do not attempt social reform. For example, Gerbner and his colleagues have not advanced any sustained critique of the inaccurate and potentially harmful synthetic social reality disseminated by television. They describe what exists, but do not evaluate or attempt to rehabilitate television. In like manner, McLuhan and other technological determinists note the evolution of media and human sensory skills, but they offer no critical appraisal of the developments they find.

Should theories of mass communication offer criticism? Should they instigate social reform? Not necessarily. In Chapter 2, we first noted that there are different goals for theory and not all theories pursue all goals. In examining a range of theories, we've seen examples of ones that focus on description and explanation (symbolic interactionism) and others that aim for social reform (standpoint theory). Whether you think the mass communication theories we've considered are inadequate because they fail to promote social reform reflects your own values and the theoretical priorities you endorse as much as the character of cultivation theory and technological determinism.

If you are dissatisfied with theories that describe the status quo but fail to assess it critically, then you'll be interested in the next chapter. In it we will explore three decisively critical theories that seek to provide understandings and explanations that will allow us to transform society from a brutal hierarchy in which some groups are oppressed into a more egalitarian world that respects a diversity of needs, heritages, and voices.

Chapter Eleven

Critical Communication Theories

In the opening chapters of this book, we considered the goals of theory and noted that all theories share certain goals such as describing, explaining, and understanding or predicting phenomena. Only some theories, however, embrace a fourth goal of reforming social life. These theories, collectively called **critical theories,** aim to critique prevailing social practices that create or uphold disadvantage, inequity, and/or oppression.

Scholars are divided on the question of whether it is appropriate for theories to have strong value commitments such as social reform. Behaviorists, as well as many other conventional scientists, insist that theories should be value free and that any ideological biases in theories inevitably compromise the search to discover constant truths and pure knowledge.

On the other side of the debate are critical scholars who proclaim that all theories and all theorists have values. Most theories and theorists, critical scholars assert, prefer to deny that their values affect their work in order to appear objective when they actually are riddled with subjectivity. For this latter group of scholars, the question is not whether a theory should have value commitments, but rather whether theories admit the values that inhere in them. Learning about three theories that openly profess values and seek specific social changes

311

should help you decide whether you think theories can be and should be value free.

In this chapter, we will examine three examples of critical theories. The first, **feminist theory,** is actually not a single theory, but a group of theories that focus on gender and its derivative: power. The second theory we'll discuss is **muted group theory,** which claims that certain groups, such as women, have been silenced because white men as a group have had the power to name the world. Finally, we'll look at **cultural studies theories,** another group of theories that aim to unmask the techniques by which privileged groups maintain their positions of power and use them to control cultural ideologies. Although these three theories differ in notable respects, they are alike in their common focus on criticizing and resisting existing power relations that create inequities among social groups.

eminist Theories

There are probably as many definitions of feminism as there are individuals. The meanings assigned to the word range from stereotypes of man-hating, bra-burning radicals to people who recognize the equal value of all human beings and life forms and who seek to diminish oppression of all sorts.

Reflection

How do you define feminism?

However you define feminism, you would probably agree that it is concerned with gender and gender inequities. That broad agreement would be shared by most who identify themselves as feminist scholars, although they do widely different kinds of research (Wood, 1995a).

Feminist theories have roots in Western society at least as far back as the early 1800s when some women first challenged prevailing social definitions of women. At that time, the central issues were the right to vote, own property, participate in university education, and engage in gainful employment. Today different issues are of concern to feminists. Women in the United States and other First World countries have the right to vote, own property, attend universities, and pursue paid work (Davis, 1991). What they don't yet have is equal representation in the lawmaking institutions of society, equal respect and equal treatment in the classroom, equal pay in work, and equal opportunities for professional opportunities and advancement. For the most part, women also don't have equal participation from their male partners in the responsibilities of homemaking and child care (Hochschild, 1989; Wood, 1994d).

The continuing inequities between women and men in private and public life are the focus of feminist critique and feminist theories. To understand the character, goals, and findings of feminist theories, we'll start by examining key concepts that feminist scholars use.

Gender

Many people who have not studied feminist scholarship mistakenly believe it concentrates on women and men. Although the sexes do receive attention from feminist scholars, they are not the focus of inquiry. Instead, **gender** is the primary concept of feminist work. Gender is a socially created system of values, identities, and activities that are prescribed for women and men. Unlike **sex,** which is biologically determined, gender is socially constructed. Unlike sex, which defines an individual characteristic, gender refers to socially produced meanings that are imposed on individuals, but are not an innate property of individuals. Unlike sex, which is absolute and permanent (unless radical surgery is undergone), gender is fluid, variable across cultures and eras in a single culture, and subject to continuous change (Wood, 1993a, 1994a,b, 1995a, 1996a).

Reflection

How have social prescriptions for masculinity and femininity changed from when your parents were your age to today?

Feminist theorists note that gender refers to deeply ensconced social relations that define women and men and structure relationships between them. For example, the overall society expects men to be assertive and women to be deferential, men to be independent and women to be relationship oriented, men to be physically strong and women to be physically attractive, men to be sexually knowledgeable and active and women to be sexually innocent and discriminating, men to be emotionally controlled and women to be emotionally expressive. These broad social expectations exemplify the cultural character of gender.

Patriarchy

A second key concept in feminist theorizing is **patriarchy.** Literally, the term means "rule by the fathers." This denotative definition highlights the central idea that patriarchal values, institutions, and practices reflect the experiences, values, and interests of men as a group and protect their privileges while simultaneously denying, dismissing, and/ or devaluing the experiences, values, and interests of women as a group. Patriarchy is an overall system of structures and practices that sustain inequities between the experiences, responsibilities, status, and opportunities of different social groups, especially women and men.

Contrary to popular belief, patriarchy does *not* refer to the views, values, or behaviors of individual men. Patriarchy, like gender, relates to a social system, not to individuals or their behaviors, beliefs, and status. Thus, feminist criticisms of patriarchy and patriarchal values are not attacks against individual men; instead, they are indictments of a system that reflects the views and interests of men as a group. It is a system that was originally created by men who once dominated public life in Western culture. Whether men today would create the same social system that their forefathers did is an open question.

Patriarchal Universe of Discourse

Patriarchal systems are sustained in large measure by a patriarchal universe of discourse. Stephen Littlejohn (1992, p. 243) explains that a universe of discourse is "a set of language conventions that reflect a particular definition of reality." If you remember symbolic interaction theory (Chapter 5), you'll realize that language is the key to meaning, since we learn a society's meanings and values in the course of interacting with others. Thus, the universe of discourse that prevails at any moment in the life of a culture shapes the understandings of all who participate in that universe of discourse.

Historically and today, Western culture has been dominated by a masculine universe of discourse that accords priority to masculine experiences, values, and interests. For example, the prevailing universe of discourse reflects the assumption that women should assume primary care for homes and children, regardless of whether they work in the paid labor force as much as men (Wood, 1994d). We're all familiar with terms such as *housewife, mothering,* and *maternal instinct.* But we have no parallel words to describe men's participation in family life: *househusband, fathering,* and *paternal instinct* aren't in most dictionaries. We hear about the "mommy track" in businesses, but there is no equivalent "daddy track," since it is not generally assumed that fathers will be primary caregivers of their children.

Feminist theorists, like many other communication theorists we've studied, believe that language powerfully shapes our views of the world. Consequently, a patriarchal universe of discourse encourages us to perceive the world from a decidedly masculine point of view.

Try it out

Is our language biased toward masculine perspectives and interests? Consider the following common terms and sayings and decide for yourself whether women's experiences and identities are equally captured in the prevailing universe of discourse.

1. Man and wife.
2. She kept her name.
3. I have a female lawyer.
4. Successful professionals have a competitive instinct.
5. Man on the street interview.
6. Freshman.

continued on next page

continued from previous page

7. **Headline: "Feisty blond wins election."**
8. **Mankind.**
9. **Everyone should cast his vote this November.**
10. **Mrs. Aaron Berkfield.**

Multiple Ways of Knowing

Most feminist theorists believe there are multiple ways of perceiving the world and that no one way is absolutely true or best. This is consistent with standpoint theory's emphasis on situated knowledges, which are the diverse ways of knowing that people develop in response to the particular circumstances of their lives. A good deal of research in recent years has focused on identifying feminine ways of knowing, experiencing, and acting. The emphasis on feminine ways without equal attention to masculine ways is easily understandable, since masculine ways are already well codified into the prevailing universe of discourse and the perceptions of reality it invites.

Drawing on standpoint theory, which we discussed in Chapter 9, feminist theorists point out that women and men are typically socialized in gender-segregated groups, and thus, they develop distinct ways of communicating and of experiencing life. Existing research suggests that women generally are interdependent, concerned with relationships, cooperative, egalitarian, and at least as interested in process as outcomes. Masculine orientations, in comparison, emphasize independence, competition, control, and outcome over process (Foss, Foss, & Trapp, 1991; Gilligan, 1982; Wood, 1986, 1993a,c, 1994a, 1995a,b, 1996a,b).

Here's where the critical impulse shows up in feminist theory: Although both feminine and masculine perspectives exist and are equally valid, only masculine ones are widely recognized and valued. "Women's work" is routinely devalued in Western culture, and homemaking and child care, although vital, have less status than jobs in the public sphere (Wood, 1994d). Within a patriarchal universe of discourse, women's interdependence and concern for relationships are viewed as a lack of independence—not a choice for relatedness; women's willingness to nurture children and others who need help is admired less than earning a high income; women's cooperativeness and efforts to achieve equality are recast as fear of success and lack of competitive instinct. In each case, women's ways are judged against a masculine standard, rather than being recognized and evaluated on their own terms. If we operated within a matriarchal universe of discourse, we'd be more likely to disparage men who focused on jobs to the neglect of family life, and we'd criticize men for lacking a cooperative instinct and for being too insecure to enter into interdependence with others. The oddity of phrases such as "He lacks a cooperative instinct" and "He's too independent" is good evidence that a patriarchal universe of discourse prevails in our society.

Most feminists don't want to annihilate masculine meanings and values. Nor do they aim to invert the existing hierarchy so that masculine experiences and interests are subordinated to feminine ones. Instead, the principal goal of most feminist scholarship is to diminish the gendered inequities that saturate cultural life. It is not sufficient to document inequities, since that alone doesn't change them. It's not even enough to criticize practices and structures that marginalize women and their experiences. Description and critique are the necessary starting points in the larger attempt to restructure the social world so that it recognizes and accords equal value to all who participate in it.

Sonja Foss, Karen Foss, and Robert Trapp (1991) suggest that feminist theorizing proceeds in two stages. First, there is an **inclusion stage** in which scholars attempt to increase awareness of women's contributions, experiences, values, and ways of acting, and to raise awareness of inequality between women and men. For example, one line of feminist inquiry focused on education. Researchers documented differences in how women and men are treated in schools and in the ways each sex tends to learn and participate in classrooms (Hall, with Sandler, 1982; Sadker & Sadker, 1986; Treichler & Kramarae, 1983). Over time, feminist scholars built an impressive body of research that indicated that feminine styles of communication are devalued in many classrooms and that women students are taken less seriously than their male peers. Increasing awareness of inequities is a necessary foundation for the second stage of feminist theorizing.

In the second stage, feminists work to revise the prevailing universe of discourse so that it includes women's meanings, experiences, and interests alongside those of other social groups. Feminist scholars interested in education have proposed specific teaching strategies and styles to render education equally hospitable to women and men (Wood, 1993a; Wood & Lenze, 1991a,b). During the **revisionist stage** of theorizing, feminist scholars might attempt to broaden views of significant communication beyond public speaking to include the kinds of communication activities in which women have traditionally participated, to enlarge perspectives on professional communication to incorporate cooperation and attention to relationships, and to confer value on homemaking and nurturing that is equivalent to the value accorded to income-producing activities.

Reflection

How would you go about revising the prevailing universe of discourse? Would you focus on language in private settings, the public arena, or both?

Ideas developed in the revisionist stage have theoretical importance. By identifying existing theories' failure to account for the full range of human communication (that of women as well as men), revisionist research reveals the incompleteness of these theories. In turn, this paves the way for developing theories that describe, explain, and shed light on a more complete scope of human communication. Including women's communication styles and contexts in theories also serves the heuristic value of enlarging awareness of communication goals and practices that are not visible within theories that are limited to contexts and forms more typical of men than women.

In sum, feminist theory is actually a group of related theories concerned with gender, power, and inequities. Feminist communication theorists focus especially on language as a means by which masculine perspectives, experiences, and interests are privileged while feminine perspectives, experiences, and interests are marginalized. A long-term goal of feminist theorizing is to impel changes that will yield a more equitable society for everyone.

Critical Assessment of Feminist Theories

Feminist theories are indisputably gaining stature and influence in the academic and social world. Despite the ascension of feminist thought, they have received some criticism.

Fosters Divisions Between Women and Men   One criticism of feminist theory is that its focus on binary oppositions between the sexes has the potential to reify and reinforce differences between women and men. Linda Putnam (1982), who supports feminist goals, questions the value of concentrating on masculine/feminine, male/female dichotomies. Putnam points out that such a focus oversimplifies human life by emphasizing gender to the virtual exclusion of many other influences on how people think, act, and communicate. Further, it is possible that intense attention to general differences between men and women obscures both similarities among the sexes and diversity within each sex (Wood, 1993c).

To this criticism, some feminist scholars respond it is necessary to emphasize gender differences in the short term to get beyond them in the long term. Until we fully recognize gendered disparities in social life, we cannot possibly reach a point where gender isn't an issue. Further, note some feminist scholars, a key criterion for evaluating a theory is whether it accurately and adequately describes phenomena. In pointing out gender inequities in social life, in general, and communication, in particular, feminist theorists assert they are accurately describing existing inequities between women and men.

Overstates and Distorts Gender Differences   A second and more serious criticism of feminist work is that it has exaggerated differences between the sexes. Daniel Canary and Kimberly Hause (1993), for example, claim that sex differences in social action are actually very

*"We don't believe in pressuring the children. When the time is right,
they'll choose the appropriate gender."*

small and not consistent across contexts. Other communication
scholars maintain that women and men differ very little in their self-
disclosure (Dindia & Allen, 1992), tendency to help others (Eagly &
Crowley, 1986) and leadership (Eagly & Karau, 1991). If these claims
are true—if women and men really do differ very little—then feminist
theory is inaccurate in its claims and misdirected in its goals.

Not all scholars, however, agree that gender differences are as minor
as critics of feminist work suggest. Sharon Brehm (1992), who has
devoted a long career to studying intimate relationships, maintains that
gender is probably the single greatest influence on personal relationships. Supporting Brehm's claim are numerous studies that report definite differences in how women and men view conflict and aggression
(Campbell, 1993), relationship crises (Wood, 1986), demonstrations of
love (Wood, 1996b; Wood & Inman, 1993), and appropriate styles of
interacting in work contexts (Murphy & Zorn, 1996). Counselors
agree that gendered dynamics operate in relationships and that relationships cannot be understood without recognizing differences in
how women and men think, feel, and communicate (Beck, 1988;

Gottman & Carrère, 1994; Walsh, 1993). Thus, at present, scholars disagree about whether gender differences are real and important. To decide for yourself, you might review your own experiences and read some of the studies that have been conducted.

Before leaving our discussion of feminist theory, we should note that it is not as marginal as some of the interests it studies. In recent years, feminist theories have gained increasing attention and respect from a wide range of scholars, not all of whom define themselves as feminists. Feminism is not a theory or belief system that is isolated from other intellectual currents. In fact, feminist work increasingly intersects with other lines of research and theory in the humanities and social sciences (Wood, 1995a). This allows feminist scholars both to draw from and to contribute to the larger body of knowledge that makes up understandings of the world.

Muted Group Theory

Muted group theory shares many of the concerns of feminist theories in general. The distinctiveness of this theory lies in two of its features: (1) a focus on how language names experiences and, therefore, determines what is socially recognized; and (2) close attention to the way that a dominant discourse silences, or mutes, groups that are not in a society's mainstream. Muted group theory claims that the masculine bias of Western society has silenced and marginalized women's experiences. Let's consider the research and ideas that have shaped this theory.

Masculine Bias

Anthropologists Edwin Ardener and Shirley Ardener first advanced the theory that women's experiences have been muted by biases that favor masculine perspectives and experiences. In reflecting on a large number of studies of cultures, Edwin Ardener (1975) observed that anthropologists tend to be biased toward men's perspectives. He observed that many anthropological investigations relied entirely on interviews with males to describe and understand how a culture works. Other anthropologists didn't dispute the charge that they relied on males to understand a culture. They did, however, justify this bias by explaining that women are more difficult to interview because they focus a good deal on emotions, relationships, and other topics that were not of great interest to anthropologists looking for the objective facts of a culture. Ardener agreed that women do provide perspectives and information beyond the "scientific data" anthropologists typically seek. However, he noted, women's perceptions and perspectives are as rooted in their culture as are those of men. Ardener cautioned that we should be skeptical of any description of a culture that is based on the views of only half of its members (E. Ardener, 1975).

As Edwin Ardener continued to examine this issue, he concluded that the **masculine bias** in anthropological research was deeper than he had first realized. Not only are men the ones consulted about cultural life, but also the very language of cultures has a masculine bias. Ardener reasoned that this occurred because males generally dominate public life and, consequently, they create the language and meanings of a culture.

Muted Language / Muted Experience

Working with her colleague and husband, Shirley Ardener (1978) extended the original insights about discrimination in anthropological research by tracing the implications of a masculine bias in language. She pointed out that when words and their meanings do not reflect the experiences of some groups, members of those groups are constrained in their ability to express themselves. How can people describe or fully know an experience for which there is no name? Shirley Ardener noted that women are not always silent, but they tend to be less comfortable expressing themselves in certain contexts. Because the public sphere has been predominantly populated by men and their language, women generally feel less able to participate in public discourse.

Reflection

In your experience, how articulate are women and men in private settings and public ones?

Adding to muted group theory is Cheris Kramarae's (1981) observation that Western society remains divided into public and private spheres that are occupied, respectively, by men and women. Because women and men have participated primarily in different spheres of social life, they have distinct experiences. Yet, men's experiences and priorities prevail because they have created language, and they have done so from the perspective of their experiences—ones that in some ways are distinct from those of women as a group. If language reflects masculine experiences and interests, then it gives only partial insight into a culture.

It's important to understand that not all muted group theorists assume men have deliberately conspired to silence women. A majority of scholars don't assert that men have intentionally named the world from their perspectives and deliberately obscured women's experiences and perspectives (for an exception, see Spender, 1984a,b). What the theory argues is that we all tend to see the world in terms of our own perspectives, experiences, and interests. Consequently, we are inclined to develop a vocabulary to represent what we know and consider significant and to be unaware of all that we don't name because it is unfamiliar and unimportant to us (Wood, 1992b, 1994b). Although the masculine bias in language may not be an intentional effort to mute feminine experiences, that is nevertheless the effect when one half of a society creates a language to describe the life of all members of the society.

The Power to Name

Dale Spender (1984a,b), an Australian communication scholar, added to muted group theory by highlighting the power of naming. To illustrate the ways in which language can mute experience, Spender used the example of childbirth. Giving birth, she pointed out, is described from a male point of view that emphasizes the joy and beauty of the experience. Although Spender agreed that childbirth is a miraculous and joyous experience, she observed that it is also an intensely painful one. Because men have not undergone the physical pain of giving birth, the painfulness of childbirth is not encoded into the language used to describe the experience.

Reflection

Have you had experiences, feelings, or ideas for which there is no name in our language?

For the Ardeners and for Spender, the power to name experiences is equivalent to the power to construct reality. Those who name the world have the privilege of highlighting their experiences and what they consider important by naming them and of erasing experiences they do not know or consider important by not naming those. Consequently, groups that have marginal status in cultural life are denied a vocabulary to define and express their experiences.

Try it out

If you are fluent in more than one language, identify words in the non-English language that are not found in English (for example, the French language has no word for teenager). How is your ability to think about ideas, feelings, and experiences limited by the lack of certain words in English?

If you speak only one language, talk with someone who is bilingual or multilingual to discover absences in the English language and to explore how these absences affect communication.

A clear example of the power of naming is recent recognition of sexual harassment. Prior to the 1970s, the term *sexual harassment* was not used. Thousands of women, perhaps more, endured unwelcome and inappropriate conduct of a sexual nature in the workplace and in educational institutions, but our language included no term to describe what happened to them. Without words to highlight the abuse, degradation, humiliation, and fear brought on by unwanted sexual impositions, victims had no socially recognized way to identify, much less condemn, what was happening. Coining the term *sexual harassment* conferred social reality on their experiences and gave them language to capture the meaning of and to protest against unwelcome sexual conduct.

A number of communication researchers argue that sexual harassment is made to seem normal by the dominant discourses in institutions. Mary Strine (1992), a critical scholar, showed how the universe of discourse in academia perpetuates the perception that unwanted sexual conduct is acceptable and natural. Robin Clair (1993) identified discursive strategies used in organizations to trivialize, minimize, or redefine complaints of sexual harassment so that the victim, not the perpetrator, was defined as being at fault. The same universe of discourse dismisses victims' protests as hysteria, excessive sensitivity, troublemaking, and so forth. Other communication scholars have emphasized the ways in which discourse throughout society encourages men to be sexually aggressive and women to be deferential—a pattern that supports sexual harassment (Bingham, 1994, 1996; Taylor & Conrad, 1992; Wood, 1992, 1994). By extension, terms such as *date rape* and *marital rape* name experiences that have previously not been recognized.

Resistance to Dominant Discourses

Because muted group theory is a critical theory, it aims to produce social change. In the case of this theory, one desired change is for women to assume the power to name their own experiences in ways that reflect their meanings. Women cannot rely on a language invented by men to represent their experiences. Thus, they must create words to reflect the rhythms and facets of their lives.

At first, the idea of creating a new and more inclusive language may seem implausible. However, Julia Penelope (1990), an influential critical theorist, insists that language is a dynamic, changing system of words and meanings. With other muted group theorists, Penelope believes the dominant discourse in most societies is decidedly masculine. She does not, however, think this has to remain the case. She argues that creating a more equitable society requires revising the universe of discourse to fully include and value women's experiences, interests, knowledge, values, and perspectives.

Karen Foss (1991) asked women students to create words to describe experiences they had that were not represented in existing language. *Soul rinse* was a term coined by the women to express the feeling after a big cry. *Solo wholo* was a term invented to describe a person who isn't in a romantic relationship at the moment and who is neither actively searching for a partner, nor uninterested in meeting a partner; the person is whole as a solo. Women students in my classes came up with the word *noman* to describe a man who is uncomfortable with an assertive or powerful woman. Mary Catherine Bateson (1990) coined the term *placemaking* to describe the care and skill women invest in creating homes.

Reflection

What names can you create for experiences you have had that are not represented in the English language?

There are several systematic efforts to develop and record language for women's experiences that are not yet reflected in "standard" English. Suzette Elgin (1988) invented an entire language, which she calls Laadan, to capture women's experiences and interests. Cheris Kramarae and Paula Treichler (1985) took on the ambitious task of creating *A Feminist Dictionary.* Included in the dictionary are the terms *birthing,* defined as an "archetypal experience exclusive to women," and *foremother,* defined as "an ancestor." Feminist critical theorists use the fluidity and change characteristic of language to introduce new words that resonate with women's lives.

Try it out

What experiences have you had that are not represented in the English language? Think about the examples provided in the foregoing text. What can you add in terms of feelings, experiences, thoughts, and so forth that are part of your life but not part of the common language?

continued on next page

continued from previous page

Feeling: Describe one feeling that is familiar to you but has no name. Give it a name: _____ .

Experience: Describe an experience that you have had for which there is no term. Give it a name: _____ .

Identity: Describe an aspect of your identity that's important to you but is not captured in any existing words. (*Ms.* was a term coined to describe a woman who chose not to be identified by her marital status with the terms *Miss* or *Mrs.*) Name your identity: _____ .

Others: Describe a kind of person or a pattern of attitudes and actions by persons for which there is no word. Give it a name: _____ .

Let's summarize our discussion of muted group theory. Beginning with the observation that language has a masculine bias, scholars have traced the genesis and implications of language that highlights men's experiences and interests while obscuring those of women. Current thinking is that men's experiences and perceptions are privileged because men have dominated the public life of most societies and, thus, have named the world from their perspective. One effect of this is that women are muted by a linguistic system that doesn't adequately reflect or recognize many of their experiences. Consequently, they are at a disadvantage when it comes to participating in cultural discourses.

Since language shapes meanings and cultural consciousness, a masculine bias has the potential to obscure and/or distort the experiences of half of the members of a culture. Muted group theorists believe that the need for both women's expression and a language that accurately reflects an entire society demands the remaking of our present language so that it fully recognizes and values women and their lives. Encoding women's interests and experiences into language not only would increase women's voices, but also would give men a more complete vision of cultural life.

Critical Assessment of Muted Group Theory

There are three criticisms of muted group theory.

Women's Oppression Exaggerated   First, this theory, like the more general feminist theories that we considered earlier in the chapter, is criticized for overstating women's oppression. Because we considered this indictment in closing our discussion of feminist theories, there's no need to reiterate it here.

Inappropriately Political   A second criticism, also familiar, is that muted group theory is political in its goals. Critics charge that muted group theory is being used to advance a political agenda to empower women. Muted group theorists (and other critical theorists, as well) would agree that they are committed to a political agenda—constructive change in society by reducing the inequities between women and men. Muted group theorists, however, do not see a problem with having values in theory. In their opinion, values inhere in all theories, although conventional theorists deny the values that inform their work. Further, argue critical scholars, theories about social life *should* be based on values and *should* attempt to improve society.

Unrealistic   The final criticism of muted group theory is that it is utopian. Not unique to muted group theory, this criticism has been leveled at critical theories in general (Blumler, 1983; Real, 1984). Critics claim that critical theorists in general, and muted group theorists in particular, are too idealistic in believing that the changes they desire can be realized. According to some critics of critical theories, sweeping changes—for instance, remaking language—are not possible because of existing inequities that must be recognized and accommodated.

Perhaps it is utopian to imagine remaking language to include women's experiences and perspectives. Then again, perhaps that isn't such a far-fetched idea. Think about the changes that have occurred since the 1970s when scholars began calling attention to sexist language:

Ms. is now widely accepted as a title for women.

Male generic terms (*he, chairman*) have been replaced by nonsexist alternatives (*he or she, chair*).

Many women who marry choose to keep their birth names or to hyphenate their birth names and their husbands' birth names.

Most book and journal publishers have an explicit policy prohibiting sexist language.

The newest conventional dictionaries—Webster's, for instance—reflect a conscious effort to reduce the sexism and male bias in language.

Terms such as *sexual harassment, date rape,* and *marital rape* that describe experiences nearly exclusive to women have entered into general vocabulary in society.

Maybe theorists who aim to change our language, and, thus, its effects on social relationships, aren't so utopian after all. The goal of revising language so that it includes women and men equally is an ongoing experiment whose success and impact we'll be unable to judge for many years.

ultural Studies Theories

A few years ago, an African American community in the South noticed that its residents were suffering an unusually high incidence of cancer. A decade earlier, a major chemical company had buried drums of toxic waste in this neighborhood; the drums had eventually leaked into the soil and, from there, into the land and water of citizens living in the area. Members of the community asked local officials and health agencies for help in identifying the source of their cancer and other health problems. They were told that their medical conditions came from poor diet and various other influences that they controlled. Nobody would listen to their questions about the drums, which corroded the hands of anyone who touched them.

My partner, Robbie, visited with members of the community and then used his voice as president of the Sierra Club to capture media attention. The bad publicity, in turn, came to the attention of the president of the chemical company that had dumped the waste. After months of negotiations and meetings, the grassroots leaders of the community and the president of the chemical company came to an agreement that required the company to remove all buried toxins and to compensate citizens who had been harmed or killed by the lethal chemicals.

This story has a happier ending than many instances of marginalized groups that are treated unfairly and sometimes suffer grave consequences with no moral acknowledgment and no material reparation. A poor African American community was exploited by powerful corporate interests. Further, the African Americans had difficulty getting a hearing, which suggests they were a muted group—one denied a public voice. If another agent who had a voice in the dominant universe of discourse hadn't intervened, members of this community might never have secured any justice.

The situation I've recounted is precisely the kind that interests cultural studies theorists. They examine the ways a culture is actually produced, reproduced, and changed through struggles among differing **ideologies.** Within cultural studies, much attention is devoted to analyzing the means by which dominant groups in society privilege their interests and impose their ideology on less powerful groups.

Reflection

What, if any, pragmatic value is there in analyzing how dominant groups sustain their dominance?

Like feminist scholars and muted group theorists, scholars of cultural studies embrace a reformist agenda. They differ from the other two schools of thought in that they do not regard gender, or any single factor, as sufficient to explain why some groups are able to dominate and impose their views on others in a society. To understand cultural studies, we'll consider the ideas that inform theorizing in this area.

Culture

Not surprisingly, a central concept for cultural studies theorizing is **culture.** Culture has two facets or meanings (Littlejohn, 1992, p. 252).

First, a culture consists of ideology, which includes ideas, values, beliefs, and understandings that are common to members of a society and that guide the activities and customs that occur in that society. Second, culture refers to the actual, concrete practices characteristic of a society. Concrete practices include cultural rituals that stand out such as holidays, marriage ceremonies, and funerals. In addition, cultural practices encompass the routinized activities of individuals who embody and create culture through their daily ways of living. For example, Westerners typically drive cars, shop in malls, listen to music, and watch television—these are aspects of day-to-day living that express and sustain some of the meanings of our culture.

Cultural studies scholars see these two dimensions of culture as interlinked and inseparable. They believe that practices—both occasional and daily ones—reflect and uphold the ideology of a culture, and conversely, the ideology of a culture reflects and guides what individual members think, feel, believe, and do. The democratic ideology of the United States explains the concrete practice in which individuals vote in elections. At the same time, the concrete practice of voting reflects and reinforces the democratic ideology. The capitalistic ideology so prominent in Western culture undergirds specific practices such as a competitive marketplace, individuals working to outdo one another, and the awarding of money in lawsuits for personal damage or loss—money is the measure of how much something matters in a capitalistic society. At the same time, competition for raises, prizes, athletic victories, and status involves specific practices that simultaneously express and sustain capitalistic values.

Try it out Consider your school as a miniculture. Identify the dominant code of meanings, or ideology, that is promoted by your school. For example, it might be portrayed as an "institution of higher learning," "a place for personal and intellectual growth," or "a school devoted to the liberal arts." Can you identify specific documents, school rituals, and so forth that express the dominant ideology of your school?

continued on next page

continued from previous page **Now identify specific practices that you and other students engage in that reflect and sustain the dominant ideology of your school. Going to classes, making notes, studying, taking exams, and so forth are all particular activities that support a view of your school as a place in which learning is the preeminent goal and value.**

Ideological Domination

The concept of **ideological domination** is also central to cultural studies. Stuart Hall, a British scholar who is especially prominent in cultural studies, defines ideology as a set of ideas that organize a group's, or society's, understandings of reality. He also refers to ideology as a code of meanings that shapes how a group of people sees the world (Hall, 1986a, 1989a). Hall and other cultural studies scholars believe that in any culture there are competing ideologies, or ways of understanding reality. Like standpoint theory, cultural studies theory recognizes that a culture is not homogeneous, but includes different groups whose distinct experiences, circumstances, and social identities shape understanding of the overall culture.

The dominant ideology of a culture is the one that has the greatest power and the adherence of the greatest number of people at a given moment in the life of a culture. The dominant ideology maintains its domination by virtue of the support of social institutions, such as churches and temples, schools, legislatures, and media. These institutions function both individually and in interaction with one another to legitimize the prevailing ideology and to suppress, marginalize, or silence competing ideologies. For example, the perspectives and interests of white, middle-class, heterosexual, able-bodied men are made to seem normal and distinctly important by a host of social institutions. Leaders in churches and temples are usually male; top executives in business and industry are virtually all white men; the majority of educational institutions are run by white men; media feature far more white men, and fewer women and people of color, than is representative of population statistics; and the curricular content in schools emphasizes the achievements and concerns of white, heterosexual, able-bodied men who are economically comfortable. Because prevailing interests are privileged and strongly supported by cultural institutions, it is very difficult for groups outside of the mainstream to gain a fair hearing.

Reflection

If nonprivileged groups don't have access to institutions that produce and reproduce culture, how can their voices ever be heard and their interests ever served?

In the case of the African American community that suffered the effects of toxic waste, the dominant ideology privileged corporate interests over those of poor, marginalized citizens of color. Institutions including media, health services, and the law dismissed community members' questions and criticisms of the chemical company. Until someone in a position of respect and power within the mainstream spoke out for the citizens' rights, their ideology was resisted, denied, and demeaned by cultural institutions that supported the interests and ideology of the dominant group.

The media are unusually potent tools of the dominant ideology. Although many, if not most, cultural institutions support the dominant ideology, the media are particularly powerful in representing the ideology of privileged groups as normal, right, and natural (Hall, 1986a,b, 1988, 1989b; Wood, 1994b). Television programs, from children's shows to prime-time news, represent white, heterosexual, able-bodied males as the norm in the United States, although they are actually not the majority. Despite critiques of bias in television programming, minorities continue to be portrayed most often as criminals, victims, subordinates, or otherwise less than respectable people (*Media Studies Journal,* 1994). Women continue to be shown as dependent and in the primary identity of homemaker and mother, although the majority of women in the United States now work outside of the home. In these and other respects, television presents a world view that is out of sync with "the facts," but that squarely supports the dominant white, male ideology of the culture.

Because of their influence in fortifying dominant ideologies, media receive extensive attention in cultural studies. However, media are not the only concern of scholars in this area, nor are media themselves the primary concern. Rather, cultural studies scholars are most keenly interested in how dominant ideologies secure and sustain their domination and how they can be contested and changed. Thus, media are seen as a particular site of ideological struggle, but it is the struggle, not media per se, that is of greatest interest.

Try it out

Watch 2 hours of prime-time commercial television. As you watch, pay attention to the dominant ideology that is represented and normalized in the programming. Who are the good and bad characters? Which qualities of individuals are represented as admirable and which are represented as objectionable? Who are the victims and victors, the heroes and villains? What goals and values are endorsed?

The "Theatre of Struggle"

Cultural studies theorists view culture and ideology as highly fluid—always in flux and subject to change. Culture in general and a dominant ideology in particular are not fixed, but are in continuous process. Stuart Hall (1986a,b, 1989a) refers to the ongoing battle for ideological control as a **"theatre of struggle"** or "theatre of conflict." Hall has repeatedly cautioned against thinking of cultures or power relations as absolute. Instead, he argues that they must be understood as situated in particular historical circumstances (1986a,b, 1989a). Thus, racial oppression has a different character in the United States in the 1990s than it did in the United States in the 1890s. Racial oppression means something different than either of those meanings when considered in the context of South Africa now, much less 15 years ago. This suggests that the struggle among ideologies is continuously shifting as different groups gain hearings and secure the support of cultural institutions.

Resistance to the dominant ideology and efforts to legitimize alternate world views are particularly evident in music, especially new forms of music. Lawrence Grossberg (1986) has studied rock music, including punk and rock and roll, as a practice that opposes the dominant ideology. According to Grossberg, rock music addresses an expansive set of issues, including the identity of young people and their place in society. Grossberg argues that rock and roll "energizes new possibilities" and makes these possibilities central in everyday life (1986, p. 57). More recently, punk and gangsta rap have challenged rock and roll and offered possibilities of meaning radically opposed to those supported by the dominant ideology.

A particularly interesting example of new musical forms that challenge the prevailing ideology is Riot Grrrls. In Olympia, Washington, in 1990, two new bands began to attract a following. Bikini Kill and Bratmobile, the two bands, are unusual in that the band members and fans are mostly female (D. Hall, 1995). Rather than following the conventional route of successful bands, Bikini Kill and Bratmobile, as well as other women's bands, created a support network for women musicians and their fans. The collective movement that resulted is Riot Grrrls in which fans and members of the bands are equally considered to be riot grrrls. This radically egalitarian structure opposes the practice of hierarchy that is a central part of the dominant ideology in Western culture.

Specializing in hardcore punk music, these bands insistently challenge prevailing practices. According to one of the bands (Bikini Kill, 1991, p. 1), "Riot Grrrl is . . . because us girls crave records and books and fanzines that speak to us, that we feel included in and can understand in our own ways . . . because we are angry at a society that tells us girl = dumb, girl = bad, girl = weak, because we see fostering and supporting girl scenes and girl artists of all kinds as integral." Shunning conventional prescriptions for femininity, Riot Grrrls bands embody anger, dogmatism, resistance, and assertion. They speak openly about

Reflection

To what extent do you think oppositional music forms instigate changes in Western culture's views of women and minorities?

sex and sexual experience, and they resist conventional devaluation of feminine experiences and qualities.

Overdetermination

An especially noteworthy facet of cultural studies is the assumption that no single cause determines ideological domination. Hall and others in this intellectual tradition believe that there are numerous, interlinked causes of any cultural ideology or practice (Hall, 1986a). They use the term **overdetermination** to indicate that aspects of social life, including ideological domination, are determined by multiple causes, rather than resulting from any single cause. For example, the prevailing view that white men are superior to others in the society is supported by a language that reflects and supports their interests, as well as by the preponderance of white men who make and apply the laws of our land. In addition, the normativeness of white men is supported by their prominence as anchors of newscasts, as stars in movies and television programs, and as high-ranking executives in professions. Thus, a range of cultural structures and practices sustain ideological domination. From the perspective of cultural studies, it is naive and mistaken to believe that any single cause accounts for ideology or how it is reproduced and embodied in the thought and action of individuals.

Most cultural studies scholars have been strongly influenced by Marxism, so economic class is viewed as a major influence on what individuals believe and how they act. According to Marxist theory, economic systems and structures determine all other aspects of life, including politics, religion, social status, and the overall social system of a society. The fundamental economic character of a society creates what Marx called the **superstructure,** which is composed of social institutions and practices that assist in reproducing and normalizing the underlying economic system that is at the base of a society (Becker, 1984).

Although cultural studies theorists have been deeply influenced by Marxist theory, they do not accept the Marxist notion that economics *determine* individual action. As we've already seen, cultural studies theorists believe that social life is overdetermined, which means there are multiple, often overlapping and interacting determinants of individual and collective behavior. Economics is one factor; gender is another; race is a third; age is a fourth; affectional orientation is a fifth; religion is a sixth; and so forth. And each of these factors is also determined by multiple influences, ranging from language to education. Careful analysis of complex and interrelated forces is required to understand how cultures operate so as to legitimize and reproduce dominant ideologies or to overturn them in the ceaseless "theatre of struggle."

Response to Dominant Ideologies

What are we to do when confronted with television images that tell us European Americans, heterosexuals, men, and affluent classes are better than other races, gays and lesbians, women, and poor people? Are women powerless in the face of relentless advertising that urges them to be unrealistically thin and to spend large sums of money on shoes that damage their feet and clothes that restrict their comfort? Are men helpless to argue against the unremitting social messages that their worth depends on how much status and money they earn? Are we all defenseless pawns of cultural institutions such as media?

Cultural studies scholars are not so pessimistic as to believe we are totally susceptible to efforts at ideological control. They have identified three different ways individuals may respond to communication that reflects and attempts to perpetuate the dominant ideology (Fiske, 1987; Hall, 1982, 1989b). The first two responses go along with the dominant ideology to different degrees. First, we may uncritically consume messages and their ideological underpinnings. This response is one in which we accept the view of reality that supports the interests of the privileged and is expressed by tools of the culture. A second response is to qualify our acceptance of dominant ideology as reflected in cultural institutions and practices. For example, you might agree that competition is generally good (thereby accepting the basic dominant ideology), but decide it is not appropriate in romantic relationships or friendships (thereby refusing to give unconditioned assent to the ideology).

A third response is to oppose the dominant ideology. Engaging in this response requires us, first, to see through the false claims of the dominant ideology: We must recognize that it is not unvarnished truth, but instead is partial and serves the interests of the "haves" while oppressing the "have nots" in society. Second, we must rely on an alternative ideology supplied by others, or we may invent one of our own as a substitute for the dominant ideology that we are resisting. Feminists, for example, have offered oppositional readings of television advertising that encourages women to be passive, deferential, and obsessed with weight and appearance (Rakow, 1992). Feminist scholars have also offered oppositional meanings for previously accepted practices of imposing unwanted sexual conduct on others (Bingham, 1994, 1996; Strine, 1992; Taylor & Conrad, 1992; Wood, 1994b). Riot Grrrls invented a novel universe of discourse that privileges women and their experiences and that resists a strong hierarchy between performers (stars) and fans (followers).

Most scholars working in the area of cultural studies believe that human beings can exercise considerable control over efforts to persuade them to accept dominant ideologies. They also assume that people are more likely to exercise critical control over media and other cultural institutions if they are informed about how those institutions work to sustain and normalize particular world views that serve the interests of only some groups. Thus, the goal of this program of inquiry is to increase individuals' ability to identify and respond critically to prevailing ideologies and the means by which their domination is sustained.

Critical Assessment of Cultural Studies Theories

It's interesting that the primary criticisms of cultural studies are somewhat contradictory. One criticism charges that the theory is ideologically weak in underestimating the oppressiveness of gender; a second criticism faults the theory for being too ideological.

Insufficient Attention to Gender   It is ironic that one criticism of cultural studies comes from feminists, who share many of the critical impulses and values of their colleagues in cultural studies. Where cultural studies and some feminist scholars part ways is in the emphasis placed on gender as a, or the, primary basis of ideological struggle and oppression. For many feminists, gender is a fundamental social category that structures personal and cultural relations. Although other factors may also create, sustain, and normalize oppression, feminist scholars see socially constructed gender as uniquely influential.

For cultural studies scholars, on the other hand, gender is one of many factors that influence the workings of culture (remember the idea of overdetermination). Further, cultural studies theorists assume that gender, like other social constructions, is fluid and subject to change across time and place. Some feminists think gender is too powerful an influence on identity, opportunities, and experiences to be lumped indiscriminately with a host of other influences.

Reflection

To what extent is it appropriate to view gender as one of many relatively equal influences on individual identity and individual life?

Too Ideological   By far the strongest and most frequent criticism of cultural studies is that it generates flawed theories because it is mired in ideology. Cultural studies theory is attacked on the same grounds as feminist theory and muted group theory—they are indicted by some for their explicit and unapologetic commitment to values. The value-laden nature of cultural studies, charge critics, necessarily compromises the search for truth. In response to this criticism, Hall and his associates would probably shrug and ask, "Whose truth is compromised?" The point, of course, is that scholars of cultural studies do not accept the idea that there is a single, absolute, capital-T Truth. Instead, they insist that all aspects of cultural life are subject to multiple readings that lead, inevitably, to quite different views of what is and is not true (Weedon, 1987). That is why the "theatre of struggle" never closes its doors.

Summary

In this chapter, we examined three critical theories of communication. Although they differ in some respects, they share a commitment to understanding and altering inequities in cultural life. All three are centrally concerned with the role of communication in creating, sustaining, and changing power relationships in society.

Feminist theories, and there are many of these, focus on gender as a, if not the, primary source of oppression in modern societies. This group of theories attempts to identify the ways in which communication structures and practices marginalize women and their experiences. The same focus energizes muted group theory, which concentrates more specifically on the power of dominant masculine discourses to silence women and to exclude their experiences from the so-called "common language" of the culture. Many feminist theorists and the specific subgroup of scholars who endorse muted group theory believe that historical and still present inequalities between women and men are neither inevitable nor unchangeable. Consequently, these theorists generate practical recommendations for enlarging women's presence and voice in the life of society.

The third theory we explored in this chapter is cultural studies, which shares the reformist impulses of feminist and muted group theories. It differs from the other two in not believing that gender deserves special status in explaining oppression. Cultural studies scholars believe that, along with gender, race, class, age, economic resources, and other factors overdetermine oppression of particular groups in society. They also believe that power relations in society are never fixed, but are always under negotiation in the "theatre of struggle" that includes competing voices and rival views of reality.

The goal of scholars in the critical tradition is to unmask the apparatuses that uphold and perpetuate ideological domination by those who have privileged positions in society. Because of their influence in modern life, media receive extensive attention from scholars of cultural studies. Media, however, are not viewed in isolation. Instead, they are seen as interacting with other institutions and practices that work together to sustain and legitimize a particular and partial view of social life that defines the roles of specific groups within an overall culture.

All three of these theories have gained increasing respect and influence in recent years, perhaps because there is widespread awareness and concern about the injustice and unevenness of social life. Even though critical theories have earned considerable regard in the scholarly community, two reservations about them are often expressed. First, there is disagreement about whether theories that have explicit value commitments can provide worthwhile knowledge. Although some traditional researchers believe that theories must be neutral to engage in a search for truth, an increasing number of scholars think that values inhere in all theories and are unavoidable. Further, critical scholars see value commitments and efforts to foment social change as important pragmatic contributions of theories.

A second criticism of critical theories is that they are unrealistic in assuming long-standing inequities in society can be changed. Some people think that it's futile to attempt to alter historical inequalities between women and men, European Americans and minorities, and economically comfortable and poor groups. Critical theorists don't share this pessimistic view. Without falling prey to utopian thinking, critical theorists believe that cultural life is an ongoing process that has changed many times and will change more in the future. What they hope to do is to direct that change in ways that result in a society that is more fair, more just, and more inclusive for all who participate in it. Understanding how cultures and power relations are made and sustained is the first step in remaking a culture and the power relations it authorizes.

Chapter Twelve

Communication Theories in Action:
A Final Look

Our journey through the world of communication theories has allowed us to consider a broad range of ideas and issues. We've noted similarities and differences among scholars, and we've considered theories that address everything from intimate communication to dominant and marginalized ideologies in society. After all that we've discussed, you may be wondering how all of the pieces fit together into the "big picture."

The goal of this final chapter is to construct that big picture by placing our discussions of specific theories in a larger perspective on research and social life. In the pages that follow, we'll reflect on what we've learned and what it means for scholarship and our practical activities in the world. First, we'll reconsider the nature and goals of theorizing in light of the knowledge we now have of specific theories. This will allow us to highlight themes that weave through *Communication Theories in Action* and to trace their implications for our ongoing efforts to make sense of human interactions We'll close the chapter and the book by venturing onto the frontiers of modern communication theory to see what may lie ahead in the years to come.

"By God, for a minute there it suddenly all made sense!"

Drawing by Gahan Wilson; © 1986
The New Yorker Magazine, Inc.

n Integrating Perspective on Communication Theories

We've covered a lot of territory since the opening chapter, which surveyed the field of communication and the role of theory in academic, personal, and social life. Given the span of our discussions, it may be worthwhile to summarize what we've learned about the process of theorizing and to review what we've gained from considering specific theories of communication.

The Process of Theorizing

We launched our study of theory by asking what theories are and what they attempt to do. In Chapters 2 and 3, we outlined the goals of theories and the ways that they are built, tested, and evaluated. As you'll recall, the traditional goals of theory have been to describe, explain, predict, and control phenomena. Endorsing these goals, communication researchers have attempted to specify what is involved in communication, to explain relationships among those phenomena, and to use the explanations as a basis for predicting and controlling communication. These traditional purposes of describing and explaining have generated substantial insight into how communication works (or doesn't work) and how we can influence what happens in particular communication encounters.

Reflection

What are the most useful explanations of communication that you have gained from studying theories?

Controversy Over Theoretical Goals No longer do all scholars limit themselves to the orthodox goals of theory. Although description and explanation are consensually endorsed objectives of theories, many newer scholars are less enthusiastic about the goals of prediction and control. In place of those functions, a number of theorists emphasize interpretation and understanding as important goals of theorizing. Rather than trying to predict how people will communicate or to control what happens in particular communication situations, these theorists accord priority to understanding the dynamics of interaction. That insight may or may not be a basis for controlling future communication.

Reflection

Now that you've considered theories that seek prediction and control and theories that highlight understanding, how do you evaluate these different goals?

In addition to emphasizing understanding, some theorists advocate a fourth aim of theory: positive social change. The aim of instigating social reform is not necessarily at odds with traditional theoretical objectives such as prediction and control. It is, however, inconsistent with conventional epistemologies that view science as a value-free enterprise. The debate over the role of values in research is one of the most controversial issues in communication theory today.

Historically, theories have been regarded as objective, value-free descriptions of reality. Within this perspective, theorists are supposed to observe and record what exists without imposing their own values on the process or outcomes of inquiry. It is presumed that detached, dispassionate research is feasible and that it is capable of producing objective knowledge of reality.

Beginning in the 1970s, some scholars began to question both the possibility and the desirability of value-free inquiry. Philip Wander (1983) proclaimed that all theory and all research are inherently laden with values. Wander argued that values infuse the entire process of inquiry from the choice of a topic of study (and the accompanying choice not to pursue other topics), to the methods used to gather and analyze data, to the interpretations made of raw data. Scholars are always, inevitably, unavoidably operating from values, claimed Wander. The only question is whether scholars recognize and explicate the values that inform their work at each step in the process of inquiry.

Since Wander's pivotal article was published, many researchers in communication and other fields have echoed and extended the opinion that scholarship is necessarily entwined with values (Blair et al., 1994; Conquergood, 1991, 1992; Keller, 1985; Wander, 1984; West, 1993, 1995; Wood, 1995a; Wood & Cox, 1993; Wood & Duck, 1995a). This doesn't mean that a researcher's values should be allowed to operate unchecked or that data and analysis should be distorted. Quite the contrary: Only by recognizing the presence and influence of human values on research can scholars become accountable for the ways in which their values enter into the process of inquiry. Being aware of our own biases and values enables us to qualify or compensate for them in the conduct of research.

An increasing number of scholars also believe that research and theory should be used in the service of positive social change. Although many, perhaps most, scholars historically have used their research to improve social life, critical theorists are particularly vocal in promoting the use of research for social reform. They believe that theories should increase insight into the ways that communication creates and legitimizes unequal power relations in society. Increasing awareness of dominant ideologies and the ways that they are sustained empowers individuals to resist the influence of dominant ideology in their own lives and to work toward remaking society so that it is more inclusive, progressive, and humane.

In the foregoing chapters, we encountered theories that exemplify both schools of thought on the goals of theory, specifically the appropriateness of theoretical value commitments. Based on what you've learned, you should now be able to decide where you personally stand in relation to this controversy.

Reflection

Can the process of inquiry be free of human values? Should it be?

Evaluating Theories   Chapter 2 also identified standards for evaluating theories. These standards provide us with criteria for sizing up specific theories and for comparing the values of different theories. The five gauges widely used to assess theories are scope, testability, parsimony, practical value (or utility), and heuristic strength.

Now that you've studied a number of communication theories, you know that each theory meets some evaluative standards better than others. It is possible for a theory to offer very rich description and explanation (scope) and to generate substantial new ideas (heurism), but to be difficult to test and confirm. Rules theory, or coordinated management of meaning (CMM), and dramatism are examples of exceptionally broad accounts of how humans create meanings, yet it's hard to find incontrovertible evidence that we know and use communication rules or are always motivated by guilt. On the other hand, some theories can be easily tested, but they may lack explanatory scope and practical value. Uncertainty reduction theory consists of a series of axioms and hypotheses that are easy to test empirically. Yet, some scholars regard uncertainty reduction as obvious and, thus, not very heuristic, and as severely limited in the scope of communication that it explains.

There is no agreed-on hierarchy for ranking the importance of different standards used to evaluate theories. Some people think that scope and testability are the most significant criteria. Other individuals regard the most important measure of a theory's worth as its practical value—it should make some difference in the real world. Because scholars differ in the significance they attach to various evaluative standards, they naturally disagree in their assessments of specific theories.

This suggests that our judgments of theories are influenced by the values we consider most important. Thus, evaluation of theories, perhaps like theories themselves, reflects subjective interests, commitments, and values.

Reflection

Thinking back on your responses to theories we've studied, on which evaluative standards do you place greatest weight?

Try it out

Review the theories you've studied in preceding chapters. You may wish to use the table of contents to make sure that you recall each theory. Decide which theory or theories rank highest on each evaluative standard.

Scope: Which theory or theories provide the broadest description and explanation of human communication?

Testability: Which theory or theories are most easily tested to determine their validity?

Parsimony: Which theory or theories are the most appropriately simple and understandable?

Practical Value: Which theory or theories have the greatest pragmatic value? Explain what kind of practical impact each theory has (for example, controlling organizational communication, promoting social reform, improving family relations).

Heuristic Power: Which theory or theories generate the most important new insights into communication and/or the most valuable new ways of thinking about what communication is and how it functions?

Based on your judgments about which theories most fully satisfy each criterion, can you identify a single theory that you consider the best one overall?

You have learned that both the goals of theories and the standards used to evaluate them are matters of controversy. Among scholars there is ongoing debate about what theories are and should be and, by extension, how we can best assess their merits. These disagreements are constructive because they stimulate thinking, reflection, and openness to new ideas about communication and the functions it serves.

Communication Theories in Review

Chapters 4 through 11 presented a sample of all the communication theories that exist. The theories we've discussed differ in many ways. Some, like narrative theory, dramatism, and symbolic interactionism, offer very broad views of communication in personal and social life. Other theories, such as relational dialectics or uncertainty reduction, are restricted to specific contexts or types of communication. Often, theories with different explanatory scopes work together so that, for instance, the global framework of symbolic interactionism informs theories with more specific scopes, such as constructivism and standpoint theory.

Philosophical Foundations   The theories we've studied also vary in ontological and epistemological assumptions, which are beliefs about human nature and the process by which humans come to know what they think they know. We examined a few theories that adopt the view that human behavior is relatively determined by universal, or at least very general, laws of behavior. Uncertainty reduction theory, for example, claims that individuals react in predictable and generalizable ways to greater and lesser degrees of uncertainty about others. Exchange theory posits that relationships are determined by principles of exchange by which individuals seek to maximize their profits and minimize their costs in interaction. Technological determinism and, to a lesser extent, cultivation theory suggest that human meaning is at least strongly influenced, if not completely determined, by media.

We considered a larger number of theories that presume individual actions aren't strictly determined by external stimuli. The greater attention to interpretive theories reflects the fact that a majority of communication scholars today endorse ontological and epistemological positions that presume that humans are active, interpreting agents who act on the basis of meanings that they create and assign to phenomena, including themselves, others, behaviors, and situations. This philosophical stance moves theorizing away from an emphasis on external stimuli as causes of behavior and toward a focus on the processes by which we develop and share meanings that guide what we think, feel, and do.

Interpretive philosophical assumptions are evident in many of the theories we have studied. Both symbolic interactionism and dramatism assume humans are interpretive agents who rely on symbols as the primary means by which they know and represent the world. CMM explains communication as a rule-governed and rule-guided process in which we create and follow regular, but not externally determined, patterns of interacting and interpreting interaction. Constructivism, one of the most developed theories of meaning, argues that humans construct meaning by using cognitive schemata to make sense of experiences. Another theory that views humans as interpretive agents is standpoint, which asserts that different social groups develop distinct ways of understanding the world as a function of their social locations and the experiences that those locations and experiences allow and preclude. Narrative theory portrays all communication as a matter of telling and hearing stories that aim to create coherent accounts of human experience.

If you believe human behavior is determined by external stimuli that operate in lawlike ways, then you'll be unimpressed by theories that assume individuals actively work to create meanings for the world and its happenings. On the other hand, if you think humans are pro–active beings who interpret their experiences, then it's unlikely you'll place much store in theories that rely on laws to explain human reactions to external stimuli.

Reflection

Thinking back on the theories that you found most and least useful, what can you infer about your own ontological and epistemological assumptions?

As is true of other theoretical issues, ontology and epistemology are arguable. There is no way to prove conclusively that humans do or do not have a degree of free will; there is no definitive evidence that external stimuli do or do not strictly determine our behaviors. The nature of humans and the process by which we acquire knowledge, then, are ultimately matters that cannot be scientifically tested and proven or disproven.

It is less important that scholars and laypersons agree about ontology and epistemology than that we understand different philosophical positions and what they imply for theory and its applications. We should realize that theories entail assumptions that are compatible or incompatible with our own views of what humans are and how they know what they know. What you've learned about the process of theorizing and the insight you've gained into specific theories should allow you to discern the ontological and epistemological foundations that underlie different theoretical positions. In turn, this enables you to decide whether a given theory is consistent with your own philosophical assumptions.

Reflection

How do ontological and epistemological beliefs affect tendencies to hold individuals accountable for their actions in everyday life?

Views of Communication   Another difference among the theories we've studied is the views of communication that they advance. At the heart of each theory is a basic representation, or metaphor, of what communication is. The Try It Out exercise gives you an opportunity to match fundamental views of communication with different theories that we've discussed.

Try it out

Identify the theory that advances each of the following views of human communication:

1. **Communication is a bartering of profits and costs.** *Social exchange*

2. **Communication reflects continuous tension between contradictory human impulses.** *Dialectical*

3. **Communication is storytelling.** *Narrative*

4. **Communication is a primary way people create and sustain cultures.**

5. **Communication creates and reflects positions within a given social order.** *Standpoint*

6. **Communication is a ladder of abstraction that moves us farther and farther from "raw reality."** *General Semantics*

continued on next page

continued from previous page

7. **Communication is a dance between people who are attempting to coordinate their meanings.**

8. **Communication is a tool that upholds and justifies the status quo.**

9. **Communication is how society gets into individuals so that members of a society can participate in a common social order with consensual meanings.** *Cultivation* *Speech communities*

10. **Communication includes rites, rituals, and routines that sustain a common view of reality.** *Organization*

11. **Communication is the reduction of uncertainty.** *Uncertainty reduction Chapt. 8*

12. **Communication is an exclusionary apparatus that mutes nondominant social groups.** *Muted group*

13. **Communication punctuates interaction to construct meaning.** *Interactional*

14. **Communication is a reflection of varying degrees of intimacy.** *Developmental*

15. **Communication is a symbolic dance on the stage of life.** *Symbolic Interactionism*

16. **Communication is a means of cultivating world views.** *Cultivation*

17. **Communication is the tool that shapes human sensory abilities and civilized life.** *Technological determinism*

Each view of communication in the Try It Out is advanced by one of the theories we've studied. Each of these views of communication makes sense in its own way, yet they are not all compatible with one another. That raises an important question: Which view of communication and which theory of communication should we believe?

The Value of Theoretical Plurality

As you learned about different communication theories, you may have found yourself thinking "That makes sense" again and again. Perhaps you agreed with CMM theory's claim that rules of communicating explain many of the regularities in human interaction. For example, we engage in turn taking in conversations and repetitive patterns of interaction in our relationships. Yet, it also seems true that communication is an interplay between contradictory impulses or dialectics. There are moments when we communicate to establish autonomy, and other moments when we communicate to enhance closeness with others. Sometimes we use talk to open ourselves to intimates, and at other times we use talk to protect our privacy. And who would argue with the idea that communication includes both content and relationship levels of meaning?

Reflection

What are the values and limitations of adopting a single theoretical lens through which to view communication?

Studying a range of communication theories gives you a rich reservoir of ways to think about communication. This empowers you to think about interaction from a variety of perspectives, instead of being limited to a single viewpoint or only a few viewpoints. You may find, as many scholars do, that you don't want to pledge exclusive allegiance to any one theory, but prefer to draw on multiple theories to understand your own experiences, as well as interactional dynamics in the many contexts of your life.

Every theory we've studied offers a particular way of thinking about communication. Each one is a specific set of lenses that clarifies certain aspects of what we observe, but that may not allow us to see other aspects. What a theory helps us see and what it keeps invisible reflect, in part, the philosophical assumptions of those who develop the theory. Because underlying assumptions of theories are not always compatible, only some theories fit well together (such as dramatism and narrative; symbolic interactionism and constructivism). Other theories are less compatible (such as technological determinism and CMM; dialectics and uncertainty reduction), and we must choose between them if we wish to create a coherent view of communication. Because partiality and incompatibilities are inevitable, a plurality of theories provides us with the richest reservoir for understanding the multifaceted process of communication in its many forms. That's why we may want to use—or, at least, try on—more than one set of lenses to make sense of interaction.

**P**utting Theories into Practice

To realize the value of multiple theoretical perspectives, let's consider a concrete case study to which we can apply communication theories.

Police receive an anonymous call telling them that a domestic dispute is in progress. When two officers arrive on the scene, they separately question the man and the woman about what has been happening. The man explains that he got home tired after a hard day's work and his wife provoked him until he finally beat her up to teach her a lesson. He shakes his head and mutters, "Damn it, she drives me to it. I go to work every day and earn a good income for her and the kids. If she can't appreciate that and let me have peace in my own home, then maybe she needs to be straightened out. Anyway, what happens all the time on TV is a lot worse than anything I do to her."

The woman tells the officer who questions her that she doesn't know why her husband beat her up, and that she usually doesn't have any warning before a violent episode. From her perspective, his outbursts are random and beyond her control. The officer asks if she wants to press charges and go to a shelter for abused women. Without hesitation, the woman shakes her head, explaining, "Sure he knocks me about sometimes, but he's a good provider and I don't have any other way to support myself and the kids. Once the babies started coming, I quit work. What could I do now after 10 years not working in the job market?" After a moment she adds, "Besides, I guess he's got a right to blow off steam every so often as hard as he works. And he's always sorry after he hits me, and then he's very loving for a while. Judging by what I see every day on TV, I haven't got it so bad after all."

Can communication theories help us understand this couple? Can theories diminish violence between intimates?

Theories Cultivate Understanding

One of the first insights we might have is that the spouses tell different stories about episodes of violence. The husband's narrative portrays him as an unwilling victim of her provocations—he is only responding to what she does. In contrast, the wife's narrative is a mystery story in which she sees herself as a helpless victim of random and unpredictable bouts of abuse.

Reflection

How would muted group theory explain this wife's support of her husband's "right to blow off steam"?

CMM theorists would also point out that this couple is involved in a recurring episode in which they have coordinated rules that allow him to hit her, encourage her to tolerate abuse, and provide justifications for his violence. To this analysis, interactional theorists would add that the wife and the husband don't agree on how to punctuate interaction. He sees his abuse as a response to her "provocation," whereas she sees the abuse as initiated by him independent of anything she says or does. We can also see a clear example of exchange premises in the wife's statement that the abuse (a cost of the relationship) is outweighed by the value of the economic security the marriage provides (a benefit of the relationship).

Moving beyond a focus on the interpersonal dynamics between the wife and the husband, communication theories help us see how this specific relationship is embedded in and shaped by larger cultural patterns. James West (1993, 1995), a critical scholar, has identified a number of ways in which cultural structures and practices sustain violence between intimates. He points out, for example, that many battered women seek help from clergy, only to be told that a good Christian woman knows her place is with her husband and she should keep the family together. In addition, West reports that some law enforcement officers try to avoid domestic disputes because of the cultural view that family life is in the private sphere, which should be relatively immune to intervention from outsiders.

We should also realize that social prescriptions that specify women should be primary caregivers in families can restrict women's economic freedom and, thus, their options to remaining in a dangerous relationship (Wood, 1994d). Because the woman in our example is a full-time homemaker and mother, she has no independent source of support for herself and her children. Thus, the recourse of leaving an abusive spouse is constrained by economic realities that arise partially from cultural views of gender and the social standpoint into which those views place the wife.

Cultivation theory would note that both spouses see the husband's abuse as relatively minor in comparison to the perception of violence cultivated by their viewing of television. Both spouses seem to have the "mean world syndrome," which leads them to see the world as a violent, dangerous place. Judged relative to this synthetic reality, the husband's violence is perceived as insignificant.

Critical theories help us see that this woman's experiences, as well as her ability to express them, are muted by a dominant ideology to which both she and her husband subscribe. The stories that each of them tells indicate that the husband's role as breadwinner entitles him to certain prerogatives, including "blowing off steam" by beating his wife. As West (1993, 1995) and other critical scholars (Bingham, 1994, 1996; Strine, 1992; White & Bondurant, 1996) have pointed out, Western ideology esteems dominance and control, particularly by men. The prevailing ideology also socializes both sexes to see it as appropriate for men to be dominant and powerful and women to be subordinate and deferential. Despite significant changes in sex roles, the basic pattern remains one in which it is presumed that men do and should have greater power than women.

Cultural studies scholars would call our attention to the role of media in legitimizing violence against women. Pornographic* films and magazines are not consumed only by a few people. Wolf (1991) reports that three pornographic films are made for every one nonpornographic one, and that pornographic films gross a whopping $365 million a year in the United States. Pornographic media feature sex, violence, and domination of one person (usually a woman or child) by another (usually a man). Over 80% of X-rated films include scenes of domination, 75% of X-rated films show physical violence, and fully

---

* Pornography is not the same as erotica. Pornography favorably portrays subordination and degradation of individuals and represents sadistic actions as pleasurable. Erotica, in contrast, portrays consensual sexual activities that are pleasurable to all involved parties.

50% of X-rated films include explicit rape scenes (Cowan, Lee, Levy, & Snyder, 1988).

Reflection

How would symbolic interactionists explain the finding that watching violence leads to increased tolerance of violence?

Research documents connections between pornographic media and violence in real relationships. Several studies have found that women who view sexually violent material have greater tolerance, or even approval, of violence in their own relationships (Dieter, 1989; Russell, 1993). Other investigations indicate that men who read or view sexually violent media are more likely to believe rape myths (she really wants sex; men have uncontrollable sexual urges; rape occurs only between strangers), to be less sensitive to rape, and even to believe that forced sex is acceptable in their relationships (Demare, Briere, & Lips, 1988; Donnerstein, Linz, & Penrod, 1987). The links between media's positive portrayals of sexual aggression and violence and individuals' acceptance of sexual violence in their relationships are convincing evidence of the claim that media are powerful instruments of ideological control.

Reflection

What individual and institutional actions could alter media portrayals of sexual violence?

This case study of violence between intimates illustrates the value of knowing and using multiple theories to gain insight into human communication. Narrative, exchange, CMM, cultivation, and interactional theories all contribute to our understanding of the abuse in this relationship. Critical and interpretive theories enhance our insight by contextualizing this specific marriage and its dynamics within broader horizons of cultural meaning. Thus, we don't need to commit ourselves to only one specific theory. The more theories we understand and can use, the greater potential we have to analyze the complexities of human communication.

Multiple Theories Promote Social Progress

But does understanding facilitate positive social change? Will knowledge about why some individuals abuse intimate partners make any difference? Can it reduce or eliminate domestic violence? A number of counselors make use of theories we've discussed to understand how communication dynamics sustain oppressive and abusive relationships. Insight into the interactional patterns that normalize and support abuse allows clinicians to teach clients to recognize how their communication sustains destructive patterns and how they might alter their communication in ways that transform what happens in their relationships (Goldner, Penn, Scheinberg, & Walker, 1990).

In addition, identifying cultural practices that allow or even support violence against intimates guides our thinking about changes that might diminish domestic brutality. For example, research that we've discussed suggests violence would be decreased if there were less sexually violent pornographic media. Violence between intimates could be further redressed if law enforcement agencies designed training programs to reduce officers' reluctance to enter domestic battlefields and to teach officers how to intervene safely and effectively. It seems reasonable to conclude that understanding the role of communication in sustaining or changing unjust and unhealthy relations is a necessary foundation for instigating positive change. By extension, the greater the number of theories from which we can draw, the greater resources we have for addressing social problems.

Try it out

Identify an issue or problem that you consider especially important and that has both social and personal dimensions. Possibilities include the AIDS/HIV crisis, the drug problem, prejudice and hate crimes, breakdown of families, and increasing violence in all spheres of life.

Apply at least four of the theories we've studied to the social issue you selected. What does each theory contribute to your overall understanding of the issue or problem? Which aspects of the issue are highlighted by each theory? Which facets of the issue are obscured or neglected by each theory?

The Try It Out exercise illustrates the value of knowing and using multiple theories in your efforts to understand the complex, multifaceted process of human communication. As we have seen, every theory is a useful, yet partial, view of communication. Because no single theory is comprehensive, we often find that integrating several philosophically compatible theories allows us to arrive at the richest and most satisfying insights into communication. The more ways we have of thinking about communication, the greater breadth and depth of understanding we can achieve.

Communication Theories in Social Contexts

By now you should realize that theorizing is not a process that has a fixed end or finite resolution. It's unlikely that there is one right theory of communication that will one day be discovered and accepted by everyone. Instead, theorizing is and should be an ongoing activity that evolves and changes in response to personal and social circumstances. In other words, theories arise within—not outside of—social life. Thus, they reflect the urgencies and issues of particular eras (Epstein, 1988; Keller, 1985; Wood & Duck, 1995a).

Consider a few examples of the interaction between social life and academic theories. In the 1940s, theorists were concerned with understanding obedience, conformity, and prejudice, topics that were salient in the aftermath of the World Wars. Scientists in the 1940s didn't study HIV and forms of communication that promote safer sex, either because HIV didn't exist or because it wasn't identified at that time. Both natural scientists and social scientists in the 1990s do study HIV. From their research, they have generated useful theories about the effects of different communication strategies on partners' willingness to practice safer sex (Bowen & Michal-Johnson, 1995, 1996).

The majority of theories about communication in personal relationships are based on and pertain to the romantic relationships of college-age, European American, middle-class, able-bodied heterosexuals who live close to or with one another. Only in recent years has growing awareness of cultural diversity prompted scholars to study and develop theories about gay and lesbian commitments (Huston & Schwartz, 1996), relationships between members of cultural minorities (Gaines, 1995), enduring marriages between mature individuals (Dickson, 1995), relationships conducted over electronic communication systems (Lea & Spears, 1995), and long-distance relationships (Rohlfing, 1995). As we create and participate in new kinds of relationships, scholars develop theories that describe and explain the emergent relational forms.

Another example of cultural influences on theory building is the emphasis on individuality, individualism, and individual rights that characterizes most Western theories of communication. In some societies, notably many Asian ones, collective or communal values are esteemed more highly than individualism. Thus Eastern theories perceive the smallest unit of life as the collective, not the individual person (Wenzhong & Grove, 1991). Interdependency is a more salient theoretical and practical issue than independence (Chang & Holt, 1991). By extension, dominant ideologies in collectivist cultures emphasize harmony, conformity to the group, humility, and deference in contrast to individualist cultures' emphasis on assertion, self-confidence, autonomy, and conflict (Berg & Jaya, 1993; Klopf, 1991).

In contrast to Western communication theorists' substantial attention to self-disclosure, Eastern theorists have shown little interest in personal revelations and displays of emotions, which are frowned upon in many Eastern societies (Ishii & Bruneau, 1991; Johnson & Nakanishi, 1993; Ting-Toomey, 1991). These examples highlight the extent to which cultural ideologies and concerns shape the character of theories at any given moment in the life of a society.

The Frontiers of Communication Theory

Because social life influences theoretical concerns and perspectives, it's reasonable to ask what current social trends imply for communication theory. It's safe to predict that many of the theories we've studied in previous chapters will endure and be developed further by additional research. At the same time, current social conditions and academic developments are converging to bring forth new ways of thinking and theorizing about human communication. The two most important emergent lines of theorizing are the interpretive, critical emphasis and **postmodern** and **poststructural** perspectives.

The Critical Edge in Theorizing

One of the more prominent developments in recent communication scholarship is the increasing emphasis on critical theories. In Chapter 11, we discussed three specific critical theories, so you understand that they share an explicit and unapologetic commitment to reforming society. The growing prominence of critical perspectives on communication influences and is influenced by concurrent general awareness of inequities in the prevailing social order.

In the 1960s, the civil rights movement and the second wave of American feminism emerged as major social movements that compelled attention to pervasive inequalities between different social groups in the United States. Now, nearly four decades later, our society is still riddled by disparities between the status, opportunities, and experiences available to women and men and to European Americans and citizens with other ethnic heritages. Ordinary people in the work-a-day world wonder why it is that women earn, on average, only about 70 cents for every dollar a man earns. We wonder why traditionally black schools still receive less generous financial support than do predominantly white schools. We question vociferous claims of sexual equality when four women in the United States are beaten to death each day by an intimate. And we are skeptical of announcements that racial discrimination is a thing of the past when the Ku Klux Klan still gathers and toxic waste dumps are routinely located in poor communities populated by people of color while middle- and upper-class white communities enjoy healthier environments.

The aching inequities that still infect our society highlight the unevenness of social life. Scholars, like people in other walks of life, are not immune to growing social awareness of disadvantage and injustice.

Yet, scholars cannot fully respond to these problems within traditional theoretical frameworks that emphasize scholarly detachment and objective attitudes. Instead, response to savage inequalities demands passionate engagement by scholars who strive to identify and alter communication structures and practices that sustain disparities in social life. Critical theories, then, reflect enlarged awareness of and scholarly activism toward inequities among social groups.

The critical turn in theorizing is accompanied by the pronounced ascendancy of interpretive forms of research. Although experimental, quantitative studies continue to be conducted and to add to knowledge, there is clearly increasing support for qualitative, interpretive research and the deep understandings it fosters. When interpretive studies are appropriately rigorous and sensitive, they allow insights into cultural practices and meanings that are not likely from more quantitative research. Taken together, critical and interpretive impulses are enlarging the terrain of scholarship and the means by which scholars go about their work.

Postmodern Puzzlings

A second marked development in recent theorizing is the emergence of postmodern–poststructural views of individual identity and social life. This is a complicated and increasingly influential emphasis in modern scholarship and theorizing.

Postmodernity is a term used to distinguish our era from the prior modern period in Western social life. The modern era was characterized by belief in the constancy and stability of individual identity and the coherence of social life. Within this world view, it was assumed that individuals have relatively stable selves that endure and unify them throughout life. Society was also assumed to have a continuing, relatively fixed character. Belief in a stable self and a stable society are reflected in theories that emphasize order, logic, and continuity. Uncertainty theory and exchange theory, for instance, assume there are predictable, durable patterns in how people interact across time and situations.

Relational Selves   In contrast to the modern mind-set, postmodern thinking proclaims that there is no stable, core self. Instead, it is assumed that individuals are continuously changing, in both large and small ways. Rather than presuming identity is a constant that we carry with us wherever we go, postmodern theorists believe that our identities are fluid and flexible; they emerge and continuously re-form as we enter specific situations and relationships. Consequently, we are not one constant self, but a kaleidoscope of always forming and re-forming selves. Kenneth Gergen (1991) refers to this as a **relational self** because identity comes into being as we participate in particular relationships. Thus, identity is emergent and variable, not established and unvarying.

Many people, scholars and laypersons alike, are uncomfortable with the claim that there is no core to the human self, but only various performances of identity that emerge and dissolve in response to particular relationships. In fact, Gergen acknowledges that even as he writes about relational selves, he is uneasy with the idea that there is no stable, enduring core of identity. He suggests that his discomfort and that of many others reflect the fact that we grew up in the modernist period, which instilled in us a strong belief in a unified, stable self.

Modernist foundations, however, may not be the only reason to be skeptical of the claim that there is no constant nucleus to each of us. Certainly, many of the theories we have studied assume that there is something relatively stable and enduring about the self. Symbolic interactionism, for example, shares with postmodern theory the idea that selves are acquired. However, symbolic interactionists do not think the self an individual builds up through interaction with others is only a superficial role or roles that a person slips on and off in various situations. According to some critics, postmodern theory is at least hyperbolic and perhaps inaccurate in claiming that the stable, core self is dead in our era.

Localized Action   Postmodern scholars regard social life as being as fragmented and fluid as individual identity. Words such as *society* and *culture* are abandoned as fictional representations of a homogeneous social order that doesn't really exist. Instead, claim postmodern thinkers, society is actually a collage of many different communities, each with its own experiences, understandings, and ways of living, and each in dynamic flux. College students don't think and act like middle-aged professionals, nor like college students of the 1970s; Asian Americans don't rely on the same values as European Americans; lesbians don't endorse the same patterns of relating that their heterosexual sisters do, nor do they communicate as their lesbian foremothers did; and members of the working class operate by values and customs that don't parallel those of middle- and upper-class citizens. When people differ so greatly in experiences, values, and communication goals and rules, it makes little sense to speak about *the* culture or *the* society.

Consistent with the postmodern era are poststructural theories, which mark a frontier of current scholarship in many fields, including communication. The foundation of poststructural theories is the idea that social life is structured by social institutions and practices. Given this, poststructural theories pay far less attention to personal motives and actions than to social structures that shape how individuals think, feel, and act. Yet, postmodern theory is not rigidly deterministic, since it sees social life and individuals as ever-changing and ever-changeable. Within poststructural theory, individual consciousness is linked to social structures, and both are subject to change, change, and more change (Sarup, 1989; Weedon, 1987).

Postmodern–Poststructural Communication Theories

The postmodern character of our era prompts the development of poststructural theories that attempt to be as fluid, dynamic, and inconstant as the human phenomena they study. In the field of communication, where postmodern and poststructural perspectives have been especially influential, this emergent perspective revises how we think about subjects, language, meaning, and social relations.

Subjects Postmodern and poststructural theorists use the term **subject** to refer to persons. This is a deliberate effort to move away from modernist connotations associated with the term *individual*. A subject is a way of being, not a fixed essence (Weedon, 1987). For example, a person might be, in different moments, a parent, child, spouse, worker, and friend. Each of these subjects, or subject positions, is constructed in specific social interactions. Thus, the parent subject is most likely to emerge in relationships with a child, whereas the friend subject may arise in interactions with close peers. Each subject is a position that is formed within particular relationships and may fade when those relationships are dormant.

Yet, the postmodern–poststructural perspective extends the idea that humans are formed in interaction to claim that each of us is, at different times, constructed differently in different situations. Subjects, then, are positioned within social processes that define status, rights, and appropriate codes of conduct. Especially important is the idea that we often simultaneously experience competing social structures and practices that invite us to assume inconsistent subject positions (Weedon, 1987). Recently, Rebecca, a student of mine, came to talk with me about her upcoming marriage. "I think I want to keep my name," she began, "but my fiancé says that a wife should take her husband's name." I nodded and she continued, "But a lot of my girlfriends tell me that I should keep my name so that I have an identity independent of his." Rebecca was struggling with competing efforts to define her subject position—should she be a wife, an identity that exists in relation to a husband, or should she be an independent person? Are there other options for Rebecca's subject position that do not force a choice between an identity based on relationship and one based on autonomy?

When she completes college, Rebecca will meet co-workers who define her as a woman or wife or mother and who invite her to assume a subject position based on her gender. She will also meet others who signify she is a professional, colleague, or boss and who invite her to assume a subject position reflective of her professional abilities. Like most of us, Rebecca is continuously immersed in different, often contradictory, efforts to construct her as a subject in social life.

Language Postmodern–poststructural theories consider language to be perhaps the most important means by which subjects and the social order are constituted. Along with many of the theories we have studied in previous chapters, this one assumes that communication creates reality. Many of the European philosophers who have developed poststructural theory (Derrida, 1973, 1974; Foucault, 1967, 1977, 1980; Habermas, 1971, 1984; Lacan, 1977, 1981) insist that knowledge of the world, ourselves, and others is determined by language: It shapes what we can and do perceive. This is consistent with views expressed by general semanticists, yet postmodernism provides a far more rigorous analysis of the implications of the idea that language shapes human life.

Within this perspective, the self arises in language and is possible only because of language (Lacan, 1977; Sarup, 1989). This is because humans are continuously immersed in language and can never escape from a realm that is inevitably symbolically mediated. In other words, it's impossible to think about ourselves, others, or situations without language. Further, the language that we use reflects and reproduces the values, social relations, and subject positions endorsed by our culture. In many Asian cultures, terms to describe individuals include references to their place within their families. Thus, the language used to name themselves includes relationships to family members. This is not necessarily true for Westerners, since the English language uses highly individualistic terms to describe persons.

Reflection

Can you reflect on your identity without using language?

Although theorists insist that we exist as subjects only in and through language, they do not assume that any term or terms can completely describe a person. Instead, they believe that we can neither escape linguistic definition nor be totally described by it (Sarup, 1989, p. 15). For example, the term *African American* describes an individual's ethnicity–race, but it does not define gender, socioeconomic class, sexual preference, religious beliefs, or many other aspects of an individual. This insight beckons communication theorists to explore the ways in which language both highlights and obscures facets of subjects.

Meaning   Jacques Derrida (1973, 1974) is particularly interested in the precarious character of meanings that are constituted by language. He argues that no meaning can ever be adequately represented by a single word, even though we do depend on single words in our daily interaction. (Remember the general semanticists' advice to use *etc.*?) To emphasize both the inadequacy of words and the necessity of them, Derrida speaks of "sous rature," a term that means under erasure. He sometimes places an X through a word (lonely, friend, angry) to indicate that the term is both necessary and inadequate to describe its referent. For Derrida, meaning is scattered throughout extensive chains of symbols in which each symbol bears the traces of other symbols that precede and follow it. Thus, a word can point to, or indicate, meanings, but it can never fully capture them.

Try it out   To understand Derrida's argument that meaning is scattered throughout symbolic chains, read the words below by looking at only one line at a time.

I am

going

to the bank

to withdraw everything from our account

before I leave you for good.

The two words on the first line make sense all alone, yet to understand what they mean we have to grasp all of the other words in the entire sentence. The I that is cleaning out a bank account and then leaving someone is not the same as an abstract I without a specified purpose. Likewise, "going to the bank" is a phrase with meaning, but what it means changes when we read the words that follow it.

Neither single words nor even whole chains of words can explain the meanings we create. Instead, meaning arises from interaction between a subject and language. In other words, the experiences that we have and the subject positioning we accept in a moment shape how we interpret communication. If a man says to a woman, "You have great legs," how will she interpret his meaning and respond to it? That depends on how the woman constitutes her subjectivity and that of the man in the particular situation. If the man is a romantic partner, she may interpret the words as a compliment and respond affirmatively. On the other hand, if a colleague at her workplace makes the statement, she is likely to take offense at the "same" words. She defines herself and her romantic partner as subjects between whom seductive remarks are welcome; at her workplace she defines herself and her colleague as professionals between whom comments of a sexual nature are unwelcome and inappropriate.

Social Relations   Like subjects and meaning, poststructural and postmodern theorists assume that social relations are constructed by social institutions and practices. Michael Foucault (1967, 1972, 1977, 1980) has been particularly influential in advancing the idea that the world view of a society is determined by what he calls the predominant **discursive structures** of the era. For Foucault, discursive structures are deeply ensconced ways of thinking about and expressing identity and conducting social life. For example, in Western societies, gender is a primary discursive structure that shapes both individual and cultural activities. Likewise, European Americans are deeply wedded to individualism and notions of independence, whereas African Americans, Hispanics, and many Asians act according to a cultural emphasis on collective identity and responsibility.

If discursive structures influence human behavior, it follows that what we notice and think in any era and social location depends on the discursive structures that organize and direct knowledge. This claim, like others in poststructural theory, resists the idea of any constancy in social life. Instead, social relations are presumed to be fluid, continuously shaped and reshaped by the prevailing world view that is sculpted by discursive formations.

Foucault and other poststructural theorists contend that discourses are controlled by rules that specify who may talk and who may not, define which topics can and cannot be discussed, and designate when (in which circumstances) particular kinds of talk are appropriate and inappropriate. If you remember muted group theory's claim that women have been silenced in Western culture, then you'll appreciate Foucault's point. This connection also explains why power is an issue of central concern to poststructuralists. They seek to understand the origin and operation of discursive rules that allow and prohibit voices to different social groups. In this respect, they share impulses of critical theories.

Postmodern–poststructural theories take us to the edge of current communication theorizing. They extend the interpretive and critical impulses of many recent theories to chart new territory and new ways of thinking about familiar issues in the field of communication. At the same time, they decisively challenge many of the claims, and even the fundamental assumptions, of many existing theories. Most notably, postmodern and poststructural theories have been criticized for being **nihilistic,** which means that they deny there is any firm basis for values, meanings, moral conduct, and social orders. Nihilism is so radically relativistic that it rejects any distinctions among diverse beliefs, codes of ethics, and ways of being. Postmodern–poststructural theories are yet too new to have received thorough critical evaluation and response. So, we'll end our exploration of communication theories by noting that radically new views of communication, identity, and social life mark the frontier of current scholarship.

ummary

Throughout this book, we've seen that theorizing is both a specialized scholarly endeavor and a routine activity that each of us engages in every day. Scholars develop and test theories by conducting research, including observation, experiments, ethnographic analyses, and measurement. From these specialized ways of gathering and interpreting data about many people, scholars formulate descriptive and explanatory accounts of human communication. In turn, these accounts guide academic efforts to predict, control, and understand communication and to intervene to change communication structures and practices that are harmful, unjust, or otherwise undesirable.

Perhaps the introduction to communication theory that you've gained from this book and the course it accompanies has whetted your appetite for further study of theory. If so, you can look forward to an exciting and very rich advanced study of theories and theoretical controversies whose surface we have only scratched in this introductory textbook. Perhaps you will choose an academic career in which you work continuously with theories, both ones generated by others and ones you develop to explain the aspects of communication of greatest interest to you.

Even if you don't choose to pursue further academic study of theory, theorizing will be an ongoing process in your life. You will enter situations, decide what they mean and how they operate, and analyze the probable consequences of various communication strategies you might choose to advance the goals or social change you favor. You'll then select a particular course of action, put it in practice, evaluate what happens and why, and then move forward in the ongoing process of human communication. Each of these familiar daily activities involves theoretical thinking.

In both routine and dramatic interactions, you will continue to theorize about communication and act on the basis of theories you hold. You will approach situations with certain assumptions about how communication works and what various communication strategies will accomplish, and you will test and refine your theoretical propositions by putting them into practice in your life. What you have learned in this book and the course it accompanies should allow you to be more informed, rigorous, and effective in your everyday theorizing.

Whether as scholars engaged in theorizing as a vocation or as non-academics using theories to understand our own lives and our environments, all of us are theorists. This is why theories are eminently practical. They are the best tools we have for creating order and meaning in our lives and for improving the human condition. Each of us is a theorist, forever engaged in trying to make sense of what happens in our personal lives and our social world and trying to communicate in ways that foster relationships that nourish us and that promote a society that is humane and just. And that is why theories matter.

Glossary

abstraction   One of three measures of cognitive complexity. Abstraction refers to the extent to which an individual interprets others in terms of internal motives, personality traits, and character versus more concrete factors, such as actions, physical appearance, and so forth.

act   One element in the dramatistic pentad. Act is what is done.

agent   One element in the dramatistic pentad. Agent is who performs an act.

agency   One element in the dramatistic pentad. Agency is the means or channel of performing an act.

attitude   One element in the dramatistic pentad. Attitude is incipient action based on how an actor positions herself or himself relative to others and the contexts in which she or he acts. Attitude is a sixth element that Kenneth Burke added to the original dramatistic pentad, making it a hexad.

autobiography   One of six levels in the hierarchy of meanings. An autobiography is an individual's view of himself or herself that both shapes communication and is shaped by communication.

axiom   A statement that is presumed to be true on face value and, therefore, does not require proof or explanation.

behaviorism   Form of science that focuses on observable behaviors and assumes human motives, meanings, feelings, and other subjective phenomena either don't exist or are irrelevant to behavior.

brute facts   Objective, concrete phenomena unadorned by interpretations of what they mean.

causal   Form of explanation that asserts one phenomenon directly causes another.

cognitive complexity   Concept in constructivist theory. Cognitive complexity refers to how differentiated, abstract, and organized an individual's interpretive processes are.

cognitive schemata   Knowledge structures on which individuals rely to interpret experience and construct meanings. There are four types of cognitive schemata: prototypes, personal constructs, stereotypes, and scripts.

coherence   One standard for judging the quality of a story in narrative theory. Coherence refers to whether a story is internally consistent, complete, and believable.

collegial stories   An account about one member of an organization told by a different member of the organization to a third person.

communication   A systemic process in which individuals interact with and through symbols to create and interpret meanings.

communication rules   Regular patterns in how communication is used and interpreted and what its functions are understood to be within a particular group.

comparison level (CL)   A subjective standard of what we expect in a particular type of relationship such as friendship or romance. CL is a concept in social exchange theory.

comparison level of alternatives (CL$_{alt}$)   A relative measure that evaluates how good a particular relationship is in comparison to real or perceived alternatives to that relationship. CL$_{alt}$ is a concept in social exchange theory.

complementary   A form of communication and a type of relationship in which power is unequal between individuals.

constitutive rules   Used in CMM theory. Constitutive rules define what counts as what in communication (for example, what counts as support, meanness, a joke, praise).

constructivism   Point of view that claims humans construct meanings by relying on four basic cognitive schemata, or knowledge structures.

consubstantiality   Concept in dramatism. Consubstantiality is identifying with another or becoming common in substance.

content   One of six levels in the hierarchy of meanings. Content concerns the denotative or literal meanings of words in communication.

content meaning   One of two levels of meaning identified by interactional theorists. The content level of meaning is the literal significance, or denotative meaning, of communication.

control   Using explanations and predictions to govern what a phenomenon actually does.

cool media   McLuhan's term for media that are incomplete and, thus, require human involvement and participation.

corporate stories   Narratives that serve to convey the values, style, and history of an organization. Told to newcomers, stories perform socialization; told among veteran members of an organization, stories serve to bind members together and vitalize the organization's ideology.

correlational Form of explanation that asserts two things go together, but that does not assert one causes the other.

costs Anything that has negative value to an individual. Costs are one of the concepts of social exchange theory.

critical analysis Form of research that goes beyond description and explanation to argue for changes in communicative practices that are judged to be oppressive, wrong, or otherwise undesirable.

critical theories Group of theories that seek to produce change in oppressive or otherwise undesirable practices and structures in society.

cultivation Cumulative process by which television fosters beliefs about social reality including the belief that the world is more dangerous and violent than it actually is.

cultivation theory Point of view that claims television cultivates, or promotes, a view of social reality that may be inaccurate, but that viewers nonetheless assume reflects real life.

cultural mainstream General view of life in a society. Cultivation theorists argue that television constructs and presents images that define the cultural mainstream.

cultural patterns One of six levels in the hierarchy of meanings. Cultural patterns are understandings of speech acts, episodes, relationships, and autobiographies that are shared by some groups and some societies.

cultural studies theories Group of related theories that seek to unmask the techniques by which privileged groups maintain their privilege and power in society.

culture Both the ideology of a society and the actual, concrete practices that occur in that society.

description One goal of theory. Description is a process of using symbols to represent some phenomenon or phenomena and to identify its/ their parts.

descriptive statistics Numerical representations of human behavior. Descriptive statistics describe populations, proportions, and frequencies.

determinism The belief that human behavior is governed by forces beyond individual control, usually biology, environment, or a combination of the two.

developmental theory Point of view that claims relationships evolve through stages defined by participants' expectations, perceptions, and meanings.

dialectical moments Momentary periods of equilibrium between opposing dialectics in the larger pattern of continuous change that marks relationships.

dialectical theory Point of view that claims that certain tensions between contradictory desires are inherent in personal relationships.

dialectics Points of contradiction that cause tension and impel change in relationships. Three relational dialectics have been identified: autonomy–connection, openness–closedness, and novelty–routine.

differentiation One of three measures of cognitive complexity. Differentiation refers to how many distinct interpretations (constructs) an individual uses to perceive and describe others. More cognitively complex individuals have and rely on a greater number of constructs to interpret others than do less cognitively complex individuals.

discursive structure Deeply ensconced ways of thinking about and expressing identity and conducting social life. Gender, race–ethnicity, and socioeconomic class are examples of discursive structures that reflect and embody cultural ideologies.

dramatism Point of view that regards life as a drama that can be understood in dramatic terms such as act, agent, scene, agency, and purpose. Identification is viewed as the primary goal of symbolic interaction, and purging guilt is viewed as the ultimate motive for communication.

dramatistic pentad Method for conducting dramatistic analysis of communication by analyzing act, scene, agent, agency, and purpose. Later, attitude was added as a sixth element of the method, making it a hexad.

electronic epoch Fourth era in media history of civilization. The electronic epoch was ushered in by the invention of the telegraph, which made it possible for people to communicate personally across distance.

episode One of six levels in the hierarchy of meaning. An episode is a recurring routine of interaction that is structured by rules and that has boundaries.

epistemology Branch of philosophy that deals with the nature of knowledge, or how we know what we know.

equity A concept in social exchange theory. Equity refers to whether a relationship is equitable, or fair, to individuals over time.

ethnographic research Interpretive methods for observing social life in depth in order to describe and analyze it and to understand what it means to members of a group.

ethnography Qualitative research method that relies on careful, thorough observation to discover what behaviors mean to people from their perspectives, not from the perspective of researchers.

experiments Controlled studies that systematically manipulate one thing (called an independent variable) to determine how that affects another thing (called a dependent variable, since what it does depends on the independent variable).

explanation One goal of theorizing. An explanation is an effort to account for why and/or how something works.

extensional orientation View of meaning and communication that is based on objective particulars of phenomena.

external validity Generalizability of a theory across contexts, especially ones beyond the confines of experimental situations.

fantasy theme Ideas that spin out in a group and capture its social and task themes.

feedforward Process of anticipating the effects of communication and adapting it in advance of actually engaging in communication. This concept was advanced by general semantics theory.

feminist theories Group of theories that are related by their focus on gender and its derivative, power.

fidelity One standard for judging a story's quality in narrative theory. Fidelity refers to whether a story "rings true."

gender Socially created system of values, identities, and behaviors that are prescribed for women and men. Unlike sex, which is biologically determined, gender is socially constructed.

general systems theory Founded by Ludwig von Bertalanffy. Claims that all living organisms are dynamic wholes that function as a result of organized interaction among parts.

generalized other The organized perspectives of a social group, community, or society.

guilt Concept in dramatism. Guilt is any tension, discomfort, sense of shame, or other unpleasant feeling that humans experience. In dramatism, guilt is regarded as the ultimate motive for all human action.

heurism A criterion for evaluating theories. Heurism is assessed by asking whether a theory provokes new insights, thoughts, and understandings.

hierarchy Concept in dramatism. Hierarchy is a social ordering in which phenomena, including people, are classified into groups with different value, status, or rank.

hierarchy of meanings Concept in rules theory (coordinated management of meaning). The hierarchy consists of multiple levels of meaning, and each level is contextualized by higher levels in the hierarchy. We rely on the hierarchy of meanings to interpret communication.

homeostasis A steady state, equilibrium, balance. General systems theory claims that living systems (relationships, for example) strive for, but never fully achieve, homeostasis. Dialectical theory, on the other hand, claims that continuous change is the very nature of relationships.

hot media McLuhan's term for relatively complete media that do not require significant human participation.

humanism Form of science that focuses on human choices, motives, and meanings and that assumes the reasons or causes of human behavior lie within humans, not outside of them.

hypothesis   Carefully stated prediction of a theoretical relationship or outcome. A hypothesis must be testable.

I   Concept in symbolic interaction theory. I is the phase, or part, of self that is impulsive, creative, and unconstrained by social norms and knowledge.

ideological domination   The set of meanings, values, and concrete practices that has the greatest power and the adherence of the greatest number of people at a given moment in the life of a culture.

ideology   Ideas, values, beliefs, and understandings that are common to members of a social group and that guide the activities and customs that take place in a society.

inclusion stage   First stage in feminist theorizing. The work of this stage is to raise consciousness of gendered inequities.

indexing   Associating referents (such as names) with specific dates, situations, and so forth to remind ourselves that meanings change. General semanticists advocate indexing as a remedy for misunderstanding.

institutional facts   The meaning of an act, event, or other phenomenon. Institutional facts are interpretations of brute facts.

intensional orientation   View of meaning and communication that is based on factors inside individuals (biases, experiences, etc.).

interactional theory   Built on the premise that communication and relationships are systems in which meaning is established through contexts, punctuation, and content and relationship levels of meaning.

intercultural communication   Branch of communication field that studies communication between people from different cultures, including distinct cultures within a single country.

internal validity   Refers to whether the design and methods used to test a theory actually measure what they claim to measure.

interpersonal communication   Communication between individuals. Interpersonal communication exists on a continuum ranging from impersonal (between social roles) to highly personal.

intrapersonal communication   Communication with oneself, including self-talk, planning, and reflections.

law   An inviolate, unalterable fact that holds true across time and space. Also called universal law and covering law.

laws-based explanations   One form of theoretical explanations. Laws-based explanations argue that anytime x happens, y will invariably follow; or x and y always go together.

literate epoch   Second era in media history of civilization. Invention of the phonetic alphabet inaugurated the literate epoch in which common symbols allow people to communicate with writing.

logical force   Concept in CMM theory. Logical force refers to the degree to which a person feels he or she must act or cannot act in a situation.

looking glass self   Concept in symbolic interaction theory. The looking glass self refers to the image of oneself that a person gains by seeing the self reflected in the mirror of others' eyes.

mainstreaming   The effect of television in stabilizing and homogenizing views within a society. Mainstreaming is one of two processes used to explain television's cultivation of synthetic world views.

masculine bias   Research that gives primary or exclusive attention to men's behaviors, beliefs, and contexts and uses these phenomena to describe and explain social life. Bias exists because roughly half of the social world (that is, women) is not studied and therefore not represented in theories that are developed.

mass communication   Form of communication aimed at large audiences.

ME   Concept in symbolic interaction theory. Phase or part of self that is socially aware, analytical, and evaluative.

meaning   Significance that is conferred on experiences and phenomena; meaning is constructed, not intrinsic in communication.

meanings   Communication has two levels of meaning: the report (or command) level that concerns the information in a message; and the relational level that concerns what communication implies about the power, liking, and responsiveness between communicators.

mean world syndrome   Belief that the world is a dangerous place, full of selfish, mean people who cannot be trusted and who are likely to harm others. Cultivation theorists assert that the mean world syndrome is fostered by heavy viewing of television.

metacommunication   Communication about communication.

mind   Concept in symbolic interaction theory. Mind is the ability to use significant symbols. Mind is acquired through symbolic interaction with others.

monitoring   Observing and managing our own thoughts, feelings, and actions. Monitoring is possible because humans are symbol users.

mortification   Concept in dramatism. Mortification is a method of purging guilt by blaming ourselves, confessing failings, and seeking forgiveness.

muted group theory   A specific feminist theory that claims women (and other groups) have been silenced because (white, heterosexual, middle-class) men have had the power to name the world and, thus, constitute experience and meaning.

narrative paradigm/narrative theory   Point of view that asserts humans are natural storytellers and that most, if not all, communication is storytelling.

narrative rationality   Concept in narrative theory that includes coherence and fidelity as criteria for judging the quality of narratives, or stories.

negative   Concept in dramatism. The negative is the capacity to say no and is regarded as the basis of moral conduct and thought.

neutralization   One method of responding to the tension of relational dialectics. This method is a compromise that meets both dialectical needs to a degree, but satisfies neither need fully.

nihilistic   Empty of meaning and, more radically, of any basis for making meaningful distinctions among values, moral codes, and forms of social organization.

objectivism   The belief that reality is material, external to the human mind, and the same for everyone.

objectivity   Quality of being uninfluenced by values, biases, personal feelings, and other subjective factors.

ontology   Branch of philosophy that deals with the nature of humans.

openness   Refers to the extent to which a system affects and is affected by factors and processes outside of it. Living systems may be more or less open to outside influence and more or less influential on their contexts.

operational definition   Precise description that specifies how to observe the phenomena of interest. Operational definitions provide clarity and precision to research hypotheses and research questions used to test theory.

organizational culture   Understandings about identity and codes of thought and action that are shared by members of an organization.

organizational culture theory   Point of view that focuses on the ways in which communication creates and sustains distinct customs, understandings, and perspectives within particular organizations.

overdetermination   The idea that aspects of social life, including ideological domination, are determined by multiple, often overlapping and interacting, causes, rather than resulting from any single cause.

parallel relationships   Relationships in which individuals have equal power overall, but power is distributed so that each person has greater power in particular spheres of activity.

parsimony   One criterion for evaluating theories. Parsimony refers to whether a theory is as simple as it appropriately can be.

particular other   Concept in symbolic interaction theory. A particular other is a specific individual who is significant to another person.

patriarchy   Literally means "rule by the fathers." Patriarchy refers to cultural values, institutions, and practices that reflect and normalize the experiences of men as a group while denying, dismissing, and/or devaluing the experiences, values, and interests of women as a group. Patriarchy does *not* refer to individual men, but to a cultural system established by and reflective of men as a group.

perfection   Concept in dramatism. Perfection is the ideal or perfect form of things and ourselves that we can imagine. The inability to achieve perfection is a source of guilt.

personal construct   One of four cognitive schemata used to interpret experience. Personal constructs are bipolar scales of description (for example, happy–unhappy).

personal stories   Accounts that announce how people see themselves and how they wish to be seen by others in an organization.

person-centered   The ability to tailor communication to particular individuals with whom we interact. Individuals who are highly complex cognitively seem capable of more person-centered communication than do less cognitively complex individuals.

postmodern   Refers to era of social life that emerged after modernism. Postmodern society is described as fragmented, uncertain, and continuously in flux; individuals are described not as a core self, but as a range of selves that are brought forth by and embodied in particular contexts.

poststructuralism/poststructural theory   Point of view that emphasizes relationships among language, subjectivity, social organization, and power.

prediction   Projecting what will happen to a phenomenon under specified conditions or when exposed to particular stimuli.

print epoch   Third era in media history of civilization. Invention of the printing press made it possible to mass-produce written materials so that reading was no longer restricted to elite members of society.

process   Quality of being ongoing, in flux, ever changing. Communication is a process.

prototype   One of four cognitive schemata. Prototypes are ideal or optimal examples of a category of people, situations, objects, and so on.

punctuation   A concept advanced by interactional theorists. Punctuation refers to subjective designations of the start and stop of particular communication episodes.

purpose   One element in the dramatistic pentad. Purpose is the reason for an act.

qualitative methods   Forms of conducting study that involve probing and interpreting subjective meanings for experience.

quantitative methods   Forms of conducting study that involve gathering data that can be quantified.

ratio   Concept in dramatism. Ratios refer to proportions among different elements in the dramatistic pentad.

reform   One goal of theorizing. Also called producing positive social change, this goal is pursued by using theory to instigate change in pragmatic life.

reframing   A method of responding to, or managing, relational dialectics. This method involves transforming the perception of dialectical needs as opposing and reframing them as unified, complementary, or otherwise allied.

regulative rules Concept in CMM theory. Regulative rules tell us when it's appropriate to do certain things and what we should do next in an interaction.

relational self Term in postmodern theory that refers to a self that has no stable core, but rather is formed in particular relationships and changes as it enters and leaves relationships.

relationship meaning One of two levels of meaning in communication identified by interactional theorists. The relational level of meaning is what communication reflects about feelings and relationships between people. Relationship level meanings may express liking, power, and/or responsiveness.

relationships One of six levels in the hierarchy of meanings. Relationships are scripted forms of interaction that we engage in with particular others.

reliability Criterion for evaluating theoretical research that concerns the consistency of particular behaviors, patterns, or relationships.

research question Question that specifies the phenomena of interest to a scholar, but does not predict relationships between phenomena. Research questions are less formal than hypotheses.

resonance The extent to which something (specifically, phenomena on television) is congruent with personal experience. Resonance is one of two mechanisms used to explain television's ability to cultivate synthetic world views.

revisionist stage Second stage in feminist theorizing. During this stage, the goal is to re-vision (or revise) cultural practices, structures, and modes of interpreting experiences in ways that do not marginalize women and their activities.

rewards Anything that has positive value to an individual. Rewards are a concept in social exchange theory.

rite Dramatic, planned set of activities that bring together aspects of cultural ideology into a single event.

ritual Communicative performances that are regularly repeated in an organization and that members of an organization come to regard as familiar and routine.

role taking Concept in symbolic interaction theory. Role taking occurs when an individual internalizes and perceives experiences from the perspective of another person or persons.

rule Regularity in behavior that is consistent within a particular situation or situations but is not assumed to be universal. Rules are guides for behavior, rather than determinants of behavior.

rules-based explanations A form of theoretical explanation that asserts there are regularities, or patterns, in human behavior that are routinely followed in particular types of communication situations and relationships.

rules theory   Point of view that claims socially constructed and learned rules guide communication. Also called coordinated management of meaning (CMM) theory.

scapegoating   Concept in dramatism. Scapegoating is placing sins on a sacrificial vessel whose destruction serves to cleanse an individual or group of its sins.

scene   One element in the dramatistic pentad. Scene is the context in which an act is performed.

scope   One criterion for evaluating theories. Scope refers to the range of phenomena a theory describes and explains.

scripts   One of four cognitive schemata that we use to interpret experience. Scripts are routines, or action sequences, that reflect our understandings of how particular interactions are supposed to proceed.

selection   One means of managing relational dialectics. This method involves satisfying one need and ignoring or denying the contradictory one in a dialectic.

self   Concept in symbolic interaction theory. Self is the ability to reflect on oneself from the perspective of others. Self is not present at birth, but is acquired through symbolic interactions with others.

self-fulfilling prophecy   Behaving and seeing ourselves in ways that are consistent with how others label us.

separation   One means of managing relational dialectics. This method attempts to meet both contradictory needs in dialectics by satisfying each one in separate situations or spheres of relational life.

sex   Biological and genetic quality. Sex refers to being male or female. Sex is not the same as gender.

significance   The importance of a theory in terms of conceptual or pragmatic value.

situated knowledges   A concept within standpoint theory that refers to the idea that any individual's knowledge is situated within her or his particular circumstances and, thus, there are multiple knowledges, not a singular one.

social exchange theory   Point of view that claims that in relationships, people try to minimize costs, maximize rewards, and ensure equity.

social penetration model   One of the first-generation theories of relational development. This theory likened the development of personal relationships to peeling the layers of an onion to move progressively toward the center, or core self.

speech act   One of six levels in the hierarchy of meaning. A speech act is an action that is performed by speaking (for example, pleading, joking, apologizing, inviting).

speech community   A group of people who share understandings of communication that are not shared by people outside of the group.

speech community theory   Point of view that explains the communication styles of particular social groups (women and men; African Americans and European Americans) with reference to the cultures in which members of the groups are socialized.

standpoint theory   Argues that the material, social, and symbolic circumstances of a social group shape what members of that group experience, as well as how they think, act, and feel.

stereotype   One of four cognitive schemata. Stereotypes are predictive generalizations that predict how a person will behave based on general knowledge about the group to which we classify the person as belonging.

strange loop   Concept in CMM theory. A strange loop exists when a person engages in an internal conversation (intrapersonal communication) in which the individual is trapped in destructive patterns of thinking and/or acting.

subject   Term used to describe persons. This term, put into usage by postmodern–poststructural theorists, is used to distinguish persons as individuals and to call attention to subjectivity as a way of being—a process, not a fixed essence.

substance   Concept in dramatism. Substance is the general nature or the essence of some thing or person.

superstructure   Social institutions and practices that assist in reproducing and normalizing the underlying economic system that is at the base of a society.

surveys   Quantitative method of research that relies on instruments, questionnaires, or interviews to find out about feelings, experiences, and so forth.

symbolic interactionism/symbolic interaction theory   Point of view that claims society predates individuals who acquire minds and selves in the process of interacting symbolically with other members of a culture. Symbols are also necessary to the functioning and continuation of collective life.

symbols   Arbitrary, ambiguous, and abstract representations of other phenomena. Symbols are the basis of language, much nonverbal behavior, and human thought.

symmetrical   A form of communication and relationships in which power is equal between partners.

systemic   Related to systems, which are organized and interacting wholes in which all parts interrelate. Communication is systemic.

technological determinism   Point of view that claims that media decisively influence how individuals think, feel, and act, as well as how they view collective life.

testability   Ability to test claims advanced by a theory. Testability is one criterion for evaluating a theory.

texts   A form of data popular in qualitative research. Texts include all symbolic activities that are written, oral, or nonverbal.

theatre of struggle   Term used by cultural studies theorists to describe the ongoing battle for ideological control of cultures.

theory   An account of what something is and/or how it works and/or what it produces or causes to happen and/or what should be the case. Theories are points of view, human constructions.

thrownness   The arbitrary conditions of the particular time and place into which an individual is thrown for her or his life.

trajectories   Personal understandings of various tracks in relationships. Trajectories define relational courses based on past experiences and observations.

tribal epoch   First era in a media history of civilization. During the tribal epoch, the oral tradition reigned and face-to-face talking and listening were primary forms of communication.

turning point   Critical event, process, or feeling that individuals perceive as marking a new direction or intensity in a personal relationship.

uncertainty reduction theory   Point of view that claims uncertainty motivates communication and certainty reduces the motivation to communicate.

understanding   One goal of theorizing. Understanding involves gaining insight into a process, situation, or phenomenon, not necessarily with the goal of predicting or controlling it.

unobtrusive methods   Means of gathering data that intrude minimally on naturally occurring interaction.

utility   A criterion for evaluating theories. Utility is assessed by asking whether a theory has practical merit or applied value.

validity   A criterion for evaluating whether a theory measures what it claims to measure. Validity has both internal (the theory measures what it claims to measure) and external (the theory applies to real life beyond the laboratory) dimensions.

victimage   Concept in dramatism. Victimage is a method of purging guilt by identifying an external source (also called a scapegoat) for some apparent failing or sin.

References

Acitelli, L. (1988). When spouses talk to each other about their relationship. *Journal of Social and Personal Relationships, 5,* 185–199.

Adler, J. (1994, January 10). Kids growing up scared. *Newsweek,* pp. 43–49.

Allan, G. (1989). *Friendship: Developing a sociological perspective.* London: Harvester Wheatsheaf.

Allan, G. (1993). Social structure and relationships. In S. Duck (Ed.), *Understanding relationship processes, 3: Social context and relationships* (pp. 1–25). Newbury Park, CA: Sage.

Altman, I., & Taylor, D. (1973). *Social penetration: The development of interpersonal relationships.* New York: Holt, Rinehart & Winston.

Altman, I., Vinsel, A., & Brown, B. (1981). Dialectical conceptions in social psychology: An application to social penetration and privacy regulation. In L. Berkowitz (Ed.), *Advances in experimental social psychology, 14* (pp. 135–180). New York: Academic Press.

Andersen, P. (1993). Cognitive schemata in personal relationships. In S. Duck (Ed.), *Understanding relationship processes, 1: Individuals in relationships* (pp. 1–29). Newbury Park, CA: Sage.

Anderson, J. A. (Ed.). (1988). *Communication yearbook 11* (pp. 310–405). Newbury Park, CA: Sage.

Applegate, J. (1990). Constructs and communication: A pragmatic integration. In R. Neimeyer & G. Neimeyer (Eds.), *Advances in personal construct psychology, 1* (pp. 203–230). Greenwich, CT: JAI Press.

Ardener, E. (1975). Belief and the problem of women. The problem revisited. In S. Ardener (Ed.), *Perceiving women* (pp. 1–27). London: Malaby Press.

Ardener, S. (1978). *Defining females: The nature of women in society.* New York: Wiley.

Aries, E. (1987). Gender and communication. In P. Shaver (Ed.), *Sex and gender* (pp. 149–176). Newbury Park, CA: Sage.

Baird, J. E. (1976). Sex differences in group communication: A review of relevant research. *Quarterly Journal of Speech, 62,* 179–192.

Baran, S., & Davis, D. (1995). *Mass communication theory: Foundations, ferment, and future.* Belmont, CA: Wadsworth.

Barge, J. (1985). *Effective leadership and forms of conversation: A field descriptive study.* Unpublished master's thesis. University of Kansas, Lawrence, KA.

Basow, S. (1992). *Gender: Stereotypes and roles* (3rd ed.). Belmont, CA: Brooks-Cole/Wadsworth.

Bateson, G. (1951). Information and codification. In J. Reusch & G. Bateson (Eds.), *Communication.* New York: W. W. Norton.

Bateson, M. C. (1990). *Composing a life.* New York: Penguin/Plume.

Baxter, L. A. (1985). Accomplishing relationship disengagement. In S. W. Duck & D. Perlman (Eds.), *Understanding personal relationships: An interdisciplinary approach* (pp. 243–265). Beverly Hills, CA: Sage.

Baxter, L. A. (1987). Symbols of relationship identity in relationship cultures. *Journal of Social and Personal Relationships, 4,* 261–279.

Baxter, L. A. (1988). A dialectical perspective on communication strategies in relationship development. In S. W. Duck, D. F. Hay, S. E. Hobfoll, W. Iches, & B. Montgomery (Eds.), *Handbook of personal relationships* (pp. 257–273). London, UK: Wiley.

Baxter, L. A. (1990). Dialectical contradictions in relationship development. *Journal of Social and Personal Relationships, 7,* 69–88.

Baxter, L. A. (1992). Forms and functions of intimate play in personal relationships. *Human Communication Research, 18,* 336–363.

Baxter, L. A. (1993). The social side of personal relationships: A dialectical perspective. In S. Duck (Ed.), *Understanding relationship processes, 3: Social context and relationships* (pp. 139–165). Newbury Park, CA: Sage.

Baxter, L. A. (1994). Thinking dialogically about communication in personal relationships. In R. Conville (Ed.), *Structure in human communication.* Westport, CT: Greenwood.

Baxter, L. A., & Bullis, C. (1986). Turning points in developing romantic relationships. *Human Communication Research, 12,* 469–493.

Baxter, L. A., & Simon, E. P. (1993). Relationship maintenance strategies and dialectical contradictions in personal relationships. *Journal of Social and Personal Relationships, 10,* 225–242.

Beck, A. (1988). *Love is never enough.* New York: Harper & Row.

Becker, S. (1984). Marxist approaches to media studies: The British experience. *Critical Studies in Mass Communication, 1,* 66–80.

Berg, I., & Jaya, A. (1993). Different and same: Family therapy with Asian-American families. *Journal of Marital and Family Therapy, 19,* 31–38.

Berger, C. R. (1977). The covering law perspective as a theoretical basis for the study of human communication. *Communication Quarterly, 25,* 7–18.

Berger, C. R. (1979). Beyond initial interaction: Uncertainty, understanding, and the development of interpersonal relationships. In H. Giles & R. St. Clair (Eds.), *Language and social psychology* (pp. 122–144). Oxford, UK: Basil Blackwell.

Berger, C. R. (1987). Communicating under uncertainty. In M. Roloff & G. R. Miller (Eds.), *Interpersonal processes: New directions in communication research* (pp. 39–62). Newbury Park, CA: Sage.

Berger, C. R. (1988). Uncertainty and information exchange in developing relationships. In S. Duck (Ed.), *A handbook of personal relationships* (pp. 239–255). New York: Wiley.

Berger, C. R. (1991). Communication theories and other curios. *Communication Monographs, 58,* 101–113.

Berger, C. R., & Bradac, J. (1982). *Language and social knowledge: Uncertainty in interpersonal relations.* London: Arnold.

Berger, C. R., & Calabrese, R. (1975). Some explorations in initial interaction and beyond: Toward a developmental theory of interpersonal communication. *Human Communication Research, 1,* 99–112.

Berger, C. R., & Gudykunst, W. B. (1991). Uncertainty and communication. In B. Dervin & M. Voigt (Eds.), *Progress in communication sciences, 10* (pp. 21–66). Norwood, NJ: Ablex.

Berger, P., & Kellner, H. (1964). Marriage and the construction of reality: An exercise in the microsociology of knowledge. *Diogenes, 46,* 1–24.

Bergner, R., & Bergner, L. (1990). Sexual misunderstanding: A descriptive and pragmatic formulation. *Psychotherapy, 27,* 464–467.

Bikini Kill. (1991). *Bikini Kill 1,* n.p.

Billig, M. (1987). *Arguing and thinking: A rhetorical approach to social psychology.* New York: Cambridge University Press.

Bingham, S. (1994). (Ed.). *The discursive construction of sexual harassment.* Westport, CT.: Praeger.

Bingham, S. (1996). Sexual harassment: On the job, on the campus. In J. T. Wood (Ed.), *Gendered relationships.* (pp. 233–252). Mountain View, CA: Mayfield.

Blair, C., Brown, J., & Baxter, L. (1994). Disciplining the feminine. *Quarterly Journal of Speech, 80,* 383–409.

Blau, P. (1967). *Exchange and power in social life.* New York: Wiley.

Blumer, H. (1969). *Symbolic interactionism: Perspective and method.* Englewood Cliffs, NJ: Prentice-Hall.

Blumler, J. (1983). Communication and democracy: The crisis beyond and the ferment within. *Journal of Communication, 33,* 166–173.

Bormann, E. G. (1975). *Discussion and group methods: Theory and practice.* New York: Harper & Row.

Bormann, E. G., Putnam L. L., & Pratt, J. M. (1978). Power, authority and sex: Male response to female dominance. *Communication Monographs, 45,* 119–155.

Boulding, K. (1967). The medium is the massage. In G. E. Stearn (Ed.), *Hot and cool* (pp. 56–64). New York: Dial Press.

Bowen, S., & Michal-Johnson, P. (1995). HIV/AIDS: A crucible for understanding the dark side of sexual interactions. In S. Duck & J. T. Wood (Eds.), *Understanding relationship processes, 5: Confronting relationship challenges* (pp. 150–180). Thousand Oaks, CA: Sage.

Bowen, S., & Michal-Johnson, P. (1996). Being sexual in the shadow of AIDS. In J. T. Wood (Ed.), *Gendered relationships.* (pp. 177–196). Mountain View, CA: Mayfield.

Bradbury, T. N., & Fincham, F. D. (1990). Attributions in marriage: Review and critique. *Psychological Bulletin, 107,* 3–33.

Brandt, D. R. (1980). A systematic approach to the measurement of dominance in human face-to-face interaction. *Communication Quarterly, 28,* 21–43.

Branham, R., & Pearce, B. (1985). Between text and context: Toward a rhetoric of contextual reconstruction. *Quarterly Journal of Speech, 71,* 19–36.

Brehm, S. (1992). *Intimate relationships* (2nd ed.). New York: McGraw-Hill.

Brenders, D. (1987). Fallacies in the coordinated management of meaning: A philosophy of language critique of the hierarchical organization of coherent conversation and related theory. *Quarterly Journal of Speech, 73,* 329–348.

Burke, K. (1945). *A grammar of motives.* Englewood Cliffs, NJ: Prentice-Hall.

Burke, K. (1950). *A rhetoric of motives.* Englewood Cliffs, NJ: Prentice-Hall.

Burke, K. (1965). *Permanence and change.* Indianapolis: Bobbs-Merrill.

Burke, K. (1966). *Language as symbolic action.* Berkeley: University of California at Berkeley Press.

Burke, K. (1968). Dramatism. In D. L. Sills (Ed.), *The international encyclopedia of the social sciences, 7* (pp. 445–452). New York: Collier Macmillan.

Burleson, B. (1984). Comforting communication. In H. E. Sypher & J. L. Applegate (Eds.), *Communication by children and adults: Social cognitive and strategic processes* (pp. 63–104). Beverly Hills, CA: Sage.

Burleson, B. (1986). Communication skills and childhood peer relationships: An overview. In M. L. McLaughlin (Ed.), *Communication yearbook 9* (pp. 143–180). Beverly Hills, CA: Sage.

Burleson, B. (1987). Cognitive complexity. In J. C. McCroskey & J. A. Daly (Eds.), *Personality and interpersonal communication* (pp. 305–349). Newbury Park, CA: Sage.

Burleson, B. (1989). The constructivist approach to person-centered communication: Analysis of a research exemplar. In B. Dervin, L. Grossberg, B. O'Keefe, & E. Wartella (Eds.), *Rethinking communication, 2* (pp. 29–46). Newbury Park, CA: Sage.

Burleson, B. (1991, November). *Communication skills that promote the maintenance of friendships: Contributions of comforting and conflict management.* Paper presented at the Speech Communication Association Convention, Atlanta, GA.

Burleson, B., Albrecht, T., & Sarason, I. (1994). *Communication of social support.* Thousand Oaks, CA: Sage.

Burleson, B., & Waltman, M. (1988). Cognitive complexity: Using the role category questionnaire measure. In C. Tardy (Ed.), *A handbook for the study of human communication* (pp. 1–35). Norwood, NJ: Ablex.

Campbell, A. (1993). *Men, women and aggression.* New York: Basic Books.

Campbell, K. (1995). In silence we oppress. In J. T. Wood & R. B. Gregg (Eds.), *Toward the 21st century.* Cresskill, NJ: Hampton Press.

Canary, D., & Hause, K. (1993). Is there any reason to research sex differences in communication? *Communication Quarterly, 41,* 129–144.

Canary, D., & Stafford, L. (Eds.). (1994). *Communication and relational maintenance.* New York: Academic.

Chang, H., & Holt, R. (1991). *The challenge of facework: Cross-cultural interpersonal issues.* Albany, NY: State University of New York Press.

Chesebro, J. W. (1992). Extensions of the Burkean system. *Quarterly Journal of Speech, 78,* 356–368.

Chesebro, J. W. (1995a). Communication technologies as cognitive systems. In J. T. Wood & R. B. Gregg (Eds.), *Toward the 21st century.* Cresskill, NJ: Hampton Press.

Chesebro, J. W. (1995b, May). Personal communication.

Choi, Y. S., Massey, K. K., & Baran, S. J. (1988). *The beginnings of political communication research in the United States: Origins of the "limited effects" model.* Paper presented to the Annual Convention of the International Communication Association, San Francisco, CA.

Christensen, A., & Heavey, C. (1990). Gender and social structure in the demand/withdraw pattern in marital conflict. *Journal of Personality and Social Psychology, 59,* 73–81.

Clair, R. P. (1993). The use of framing devices to sequester organizational narratives: Hegemony and harassment. *Communication Monographs, 60,* 113–136.

Clark, M. S., Quellette, R., Powell, M., & Milberg, S. (1987). Recipient's mood, relationship type, and helping. *Journal of Personality and Social Psychology, 53,* 93–103.

Clark, R. A., & Delia, J. (1977). Cognitive complexity, social perspective-taking, and functional persuasive skills in second- to ninth-grade students. *Human Communication Research, 3,* 128–134.

Collins, P. H. (1986). Learning from the outsider within. *Social Problems, 23,* 514–532.

Condit, C. (1992). Post-Burke: Transcending the substance of dramatism. *Quarterly Journal of Speech, 78,* 349–355.

Conquergood, D. (1991). Rethinking ethnography: Toward a critical cultural studies politics. *Communication Monographs, 58,* 179–194.

Conquergood, D. (1992). Ethnography, rhetoric, and performance. *Quarterly Journal of Speech, 78,* 80–97.

Conrad, C. (1995). Was Pogo right? In J. T. Wood & R. B. Gregg (Ed.), *Toward the 21st century.* Cresskill, NJ: Hampton Press.

Contarello, A., & Volpato, C. (1991). Images of friendship: Literary depictions through the ages. *Journal of Social and Personal Relationships, 8,* 49–75.

Cornforth, M. (1968). *Materialism and the dialectical method.* New York: International Publishers.

Cowan, G., Lee, C., Levy, D., & Snyder, D. (1988). Dominance and inequality in X-rated videocassettes. *Psychology of Women Quarterly, 12,* 299–311.

Crockett, W. H. (1965). Cognitive complexity and impression formation. In B. A. Maher (Ed.), *Progress in experimental personality research, 2* (pp. 47–90). New York: Academic Press.

Cronen, V. (1991). Coordinated management of meaning theory and postenlightenment ethics. In K. Greenberg (Ed.), *Conversation on communication ethics* (pp. 21–53). Norwood, NJ: Ablex.

Cronen, V., Chen, V., & Pearce, B. (1988). Coordinated management of meaning: A critical theory. In Young Yun Kim & W. Gudykunst (Eds.), *Theories in intercultural communication* (pp. 66–98). Newbury Park, CA: Sage.

Cronen, V., & Pearce, B. (1981). Logical force in interpersonal communication: A new concept of the "necessity" in social behavior. *Communication, 6,* 5–67.

Cronen, V., & Pearce, B. (1982). The coordinated management of meaning: A theory of communication. In F. E. X. Dance (Ed.), *Human communication theory* (pp. 61–89). New York: Harper & Row.

Dance, F. (1970). The concept of communication. *Journal of Communication, 20,* 201–210.

Davis, F. (1991). *Moving the mountain: The women's movement in America since 1960.* New York: Simon & Schuster.

DeFleur, M. L., & Ball-Rokeach, S. (1989). *Theories of mass communication* (5th ed.). White Plains, NY: Longman.

DeFrancisco, V. (1991). The sounds of silence: How men silence women in marital relations. *Discourse and Society, 2,* 413–423.

Delia, J., O'Keefe, B., & O'Keefe, D. (1982). The constructivist approach to communication. In F. E. X. Dance (Ed.), *Human communication theory* (pp. 147–191). New York: Harper & Row.

Demare, D., Briere, J., & Lips, H. M. (1988). Violent pornography and self-reported likelihood of sexual aggression. *Journal of Research in Personality, 22,* 140–153.

Derrida, J. (1973). *Speech and phenomena, and other essays on Husserl's theory of signs.* Evanston, IL: Northwestern University Press.

Derrida, J. (1974). *Of grammatology* (trans. G. Spivak). Baltimore: Johns Hopkins University Press.

Derrida, J. (1978). *Writing and difference.* London, UK: Routledge & Kegan Paul.

Dickson, F. (1995). Mature relationships. In J. T. Wood & S. Duck (Eds.), *Understanding relationship processes, 6: Understudied relationships: Off the beaten track* (pp. 22–50). Thousand Oaks, CA: Sage.

Dieter, P. (1989, March). *Shooting her with video, drugs, bullets, and promises.* Paper presented at the meeting of the Association of Women in Psychology, Newport, RI.

Dindia, K., & Allen, M. (1992). Sex differences in self-disclosure: A meta-analysis. *Psychological Bulletin, 12,* 106–124.

Dindia, K., & Baxter, L. A. (1987). Strategies for maintaining and repairing marital relationships. *Journal of Social and Personal Relationships, 4,* 143–158.

Dindia, K., & Canary, D. (1993). Definitions and theoretical perspectives on maintaining relationships. *Journal of Social and Personal Relationships, 10,* 163–174.

Dixson, M., & Duck, S. W. (1993). Understanding relationship processes: Uncovering the human search for meaning. In S. W. Duck (Ed.), *Understanding relationship processes, 1: Individuals in relationships* (pp. 175–206). Newbury Park, CA: Sage.

Donnerstein, E., Linz, D., & Penrod, S. (1987). *The question of pornography: Research findings and policy implications.* New York: Free Press.

Doob, A., & Macdonald, G. (1979). Television viewing and fear of victimization: Is the relationship causal? *Journal of Personality and Social Psychology, 37,* 170–179.

Duck, S. (1984). A perspective on the repair of personal relationships: Repair of what? When? In S. W. Duck (Ed.), *Personal relationships, 5: Repairing personal relationships.* London: Academic Press.

Duck, S. (1991). *Friends for life.* Hemel Hemstead, UK: Harvester Wheatsheaf.

Duck, S. W. (1990). Relationships as unfinished business: Out of the frying pan and into the 1990s. *Journal of Social and Personal Relationships, 7,* 5–24.

Duck, S. W. (1992). *Human relationships* (2nd ed.). Newbury Park, CA: Sage.

Duck, S. W. (Ed.). (1993). *Understanding relationship processes, 1: Individuals in relationships.* Newbury Park, CA: Sage.

Duck, S. W. (1994a). *Meaningful relationships.* Thousand Oaks, CA: Sage.

Duck, S. W. (1994b). Steady as (s)he goes: Relational maintenance as a shared meaning system. In D. Canary & L. Stafford (Eds.), *Communication and relational maintenance* (pp. 45–60). New York: Academic Press.

Duck, S., & Pond, K. (1989). Friends, Romans, countrymen, lend me your retrospections: Rhetoric and reality in personal relationships. In C. Hendrick (Ed.), *Close relationships* (pp. 17–38). Newbury Park, CA: Sage.

Duck, S. W., & Wood, J. T. (Eds.). (1995). *Understanding relationship processes, 5: Confronting relationship challenges.* Thousand Oaks, CA: Sage.

Duck, S., & Wright, P. (1993). Reexamining gender differences in same-gender friendships: A close look at two kinds of data. *Sex Roles, 28,* 709–727.

Eagly, A., & Crowley, M. (1986). Gender and helping behavior: A meta-analytic review of social psychological literature. *Psychological Bulletin, 100,* 283–308.

Eagly, A., & Karau, S. (1991). Gender and the emergence of leadership: A meta-analysis. *Journal of Personality and Social Psychology, 60,* 685–710.

Eakins, B. W., & Eakins, R. G. (1976). Verbal turn-taking and exchanges in faculty dialogue. In B. L. DuBois & I. Crouch (Eds.), *Papers in southwest English, IV: Proceedings of the conference on the sociology of languages of American women* (pp. 53–62). San Antonio, TX: Trinity University Press.

Elgin, S. (1988). *A first dictionary and grammar of Laadan* (2nd ed.). Madison, WI: Society for the Furtherance and Study of Fantasy and Science Fiction.

Ellis, A., & Harper, R. (1977). *A new guide to rational living.* North Hollywood, CA: Wilshire Books.

Entman, R. M. (1994). Representation and reality in the portrayal of blacks on network television news. *Journalism Quarterly, 71,* 509–520.

Epstein, C. F. (1988). *Deceptive distinctions: Sex, gender and the social order.* New Haven: Yale University Press.

Evans, D. (1993, March 1). The wrong examples. *Newsweek*, p. 10.

Fehr, B. (1993). How do I love thee? Let me consult my prototype. In S. W. Duck (Ed.), *Understanding relationship processes, 1: Individuals in relationships* (pp. 87–122). Newbury Park, CA: Sage.

Ferrante, J. (1995). *Sociology: A global perspective* (2nd ed.). Belmont, CA: Wadsworth.

Fisher, B. A. (1982). The pragmatic perspective of human communication: A view from system theory. In F. E. X. Dance (Ed.), *Human communication theory* (pp. 192–219). New York: Harper & Row.

Fisher, W. R. (1978). Toward a logic of good reasons. *Quarterly Journal of Speech, 64,* 376–387.

Fisher, W. R. (1984). Narration as a human communication paradigm: The case of public moral argument. *Communication Monographs, 51,* 1–22.

Fisher, W. R. (1987). *Human communication as narration: Toward a philosophy of reason, value, and action.* Columbia, SC: University of South Carolina Press.

Fishman, P. (1978). Interaction: The work women do. *Social Problems, 25,* 397–406.

Fiske, J. (1987). *Television culture.* London: Methuen.

Fitch, K. (1994). Criteria for evidence in qualitative research. *Western Journal of Communication, 58,* 32–38.

Fletcher, G. J., & Fincham, F. D. (1991). Attribution in close relationships. In G. J. Fletcher & F. D. Fincham (Eds.), *Cognition in close relationships* (pp. 7–35). Hillsdale, NJ: Lawrence Erlbaum.

Fletcher, G. J., & Fitness, J. (1990). Occurrent social cognition in close relationship interaction: The role of proximal and distal variables. *Journal of Personality and Social Psychology, 59,* 464–474.

Fletcher, G. J., & Fitness, J. (1993). Knowledge structures and explanations in intimate relationships. In S. Duck (Ed.), *Understanding relationship processes, 2: Learning about relationships* (pp. 121–142). Newbury Park, CA: Sage.

Fletcher, G. J., Rosanowski, J., & Fitness, J. (1992). *Automatic processing in intimate settings: The role of relationship beliefs.* Unpublished manuscript.

Foss, K. (1991). Personal communication cited in S. Littlejohn (1992). *Theories of human communication* (4th ed., p. 241). Belmont, CA: Wadsworth.

Foss, K., & Foss, S. (1991). *Women speak: The eloquence of women's lives.* Prospect Heights, IL: Waveland.

Foss, S., Foss, K., & Trapp, R. (1991). *Contemporary perspectives on rhetoric.* Prospect Heights, IL: Waveland.

Foucault, M. (1967). *Madness and civilization.* London: Tavistock.

Foucault, M. (1972). *The order of things.* London: Tavistock.

Foucault, M. (1977). *Discipline and punish.* London: Penguin.

Foucault, M. (1980). *Power/knowledge: Selected interviews and other writings: 1972–1977.* Edited by C. Gordon. Brighton, UK: Harvester.

Fowers, B. J. (1991). His and her marriage: A multivariate study of gender and marital satisfaction. *Sex Roles, 24,* 209–221.

Gaines, S., Jr. (1995). Relationships between members of cultural minorities. In J. T. Wood & S. W. Duck (Eds.), *Understanding relationship processes, 6: Off the beaten track: Understudied relationships* (pp. 51–88). Thousand Oaks, CA: Sage.

Gates, H. L., Jr. (1987). The blackness of blackness: A critique of the sign and the signifying monkey. In H. L. Gates, Jr. (Ed.), *Figures in black* (pp. 235–276). New York: Oxford.

Geertz, C. (1973). *The interpretation of cultures.* New York: Basic Books.

Gerbner, G. (1981). A curious journey into the scary world of Paul Hirsch. *Communication Research, 8,* 259–280.

Gerbner, G. (1990). Epilogue: Advancing on the path of righteousness (maybe). In N. Signorielli & M. Morgan (Eds.), *Cultivation analysis: New directions in media effects research* (pp. 250–261). Newbury Park, CA: Sage.

Gerbner, G., Gross, L., Jackson-Beeck, M., Jeffries-Fox, S., & Signorielli, N. (1978). Cultural indicators: Violence profile No. 9. *Journal of Communication, 28,* 176–207.

Gerbner, G., Gross, L., Morgan, M., & Signorielli, N. (1980). The "mainstreaming" of America: Violence profile No. 11. *Journal of Communication, 30,* 10–29.

Gerbner, G., Gross, L., Morgan, M., & Signorielli, N. (1986). Living with television: The dynamics of the cultivation process. In J. Bryant & D. Zillmann (Eds.), *Perspectives on media effects* (pp. 17–40). Hillsdale, NJ: Lawrence Erlbaum.

Gergen, K. (1991). *The saturated self: Dilemmas of identity in contemporary life.* New York: Basic Books.

Gerstel, N., & Gross, H. (1985). *Commuter marriage.* New York: Guilford Press.

Gilligan, C. (1982). *In a different voice: Psychological theory and women's development.* Cambridge: Harvard University Press.

Goffman, E. (1967). *The presentation of self in everyday life.* New York: Doubleday.

Goldner, V., Penn, P., Scheinberg, M., & Walker, G. (1990). Love and violence: Gender paradoxes in volatile attachments. *Family Process, 19,* 343–364.

Goldsmith, D. (1990). A dialectic perspective on the expression of autonomy and connection in romantic relationships. *Western Journal of Speech Communication, 54,* 537–556.

Gordon, G. (1982, January). An end to McLuhanacy. *Educational Technology,* pp. 39–45.

Gottman, J. M., & Carrère, S. (1994). Why can't men and women get along? Developmental roots and marital inequities. In D. Canary & L. Stafford (Eds.), *Communication and relational maintenance* (pp. 203–229). New York: Academic Press.

Gouran, D. S. (1982). *Making decisions in groups: Choices and consequences.* Glenview, IL: Scott, Foresman.

Griffin, E. (1994). *Communication: A first look at communication theory.* New York: McGraw-Hill.

Grossberg, L. (1986). Is there rock after punk? *Critical Studies in Mass Communication, 3,* 50–73.

Gusfield, J. R. (Ed.). (1989). Introduction. *On symbols and society.* Chicago: University of Chicago Press.

Habermas, J. (1971). *Knowledge and human interests* (Trans. J. J. Shapiro). Boston: Beacon.

Habermas, J. (1984). *The theory of communicative action, I: Reason and the rationalization of society* (Trans. T. McCarthy). Boston: Beacon.

Hall, A. D., & Fagen, R. (1956). Definition of a system. *General Systems, 1,* 18–28.

Hall, D. (1995). *Revolution grrrl style now! The rhetoric and subcultural practices of Riot Grrrls.* Unpublished master's thesis in the Department of Communication Studies at the University of North Carolina at Chapel Hill.

Hall, R. M., with Sandler, B. R. (1982). *The classroom climate: A chilly one for women?* Washington, DC: Association of American Colleges, Project on the Status and Education of Women.

Hall, S. (1982). The rediscovery of "ideology": Return of the repressed in media studies. In M. Gurevitch, T. Bennett, J. Curran, & J. Woollacott (Eds.), *Culture, society, and the media* (pp. 56–90). London: Methuen.

Hall, S. (1986a). Cultural studies: Two paradigms. In R. Collins (Ed.), *Media, culture, and society: A critical reader.* London: Sage.

Hall, S. (1986b). The problem of ideology—Marxism without guarantees. *Journal of Communication Inquiry, 10,* 28–44.

Hall, S. (1988). *The hard road to renewal: Thatcherism and the crisis on the left.* London: Verso.

Hall, S. (1989a). Ideology. E. Barnouw et al. (Eds.), *International encyclopedia of communication* (Vol. 2, pp. 307–311). New York: Oxford University Press.

Hall, S. (1989b). Ideology and communication theory. In B. Dervin, L. Grossberg, B. O'Keefe, & E. Wartella (Eds.), *Rethinking communication theory* (Vol. 1, pp. 40–52). Newbury Park, CA: Sage.

Hampden-Turner, C. (1982). *Maps of the mind: Charts and concepts of the mind and its labyrinths.* New York: Macmillan/Collier.

Hansen, C. H., & Hansen, R. D. (1988). How rock music videos can change what is seen when boy meets girl: Priming stereotypic appraisal of social interactions. *Sex Roles, 19,* 287–316.

Haraway, D. (1988). Situated knowledges: The science question in feminism and the privilege of partial perspective. *Signs, 14,* 575–599.

Harding, S. (1991). *Whose science? Whose knowledge? Thinking from women's lives.* Ithaca: Cornell University Press.

Harris, L. (1979). *Communication competence: Empirical tests of a systemic model.* Unpublished doctoral dissertation. University of Massachusetts, Amherst, MA.

Hartsock, N. (1983). The feminist standpoint: Developing the ground for a specifically feminist historical materialism. In S. Harding & M. B. Hintikka (Eds.), *Discovering reality* (pp. 283–310). Boston: Ridel.

Harvey, D. (1989). *The condition of postmodernity.* London: Basil Blackwell.

Harvey, J., Weber, A., & Orbuch, T. (1990). *Interpersonal accounts: A social psychological perspective.* Oxford, UK: Basil Blackwell.

Hayakawa, S. I. (1978). *Language in thought and action.* Orlando, FL: Harcourt Brace Jovanovich.

Hegel, G. W. F. (1807). *The phenomenology of mind* (Trans. J. B. Braillie). Germany: Wurtzburg & Bamberg.

Heidegger, M. (1927, original publication). *Being and time* (Trans. J. Macquarrie & E. S. Robinson, 1962). New York: Harper & Row.

Hendrick, C., & Hendrick, S. (1996). Gender and the experience of heterosexual love. In J. T. Wood (Ed.), *Gendered relationships* (pp. 131–148). Mountain View, CA: Mayfield.

Hirsch, P. (1980). The "scary world" of nonviewer and other anomalies. *Communication Research, 7,* 403–456.

Hochschild, A., with Machung, A. (1989). *The second shift.* New York: Viking.

Hojat, M. (1982). Loneliness as a function of selected personality variables. *Journal of Clinical Psychology, 38,* 136–141.

Homans, G. C. (1954). Social behavior as exchange. *American Journal of Sociology, 62,* 594–617.

Homans, G. C. (1961). *Social behavior: Its elementary forms.* New York: Harcourt, Brace, & World.

Honeycutt, J. M. (1993). Memory structures for the rise and fall of personal relationships. In S. W. Duck (Ed.), *Understanding relationship processes, 1: Individuals in relationships* (pp. 30–59). Newbury Park, CA: Sage.

Honeycutt, J., & Cantrill, J. (1991). Using expectations of relational actions to predict number of intimate relationships: Don Juan and Romeo unmasked. *Communication Reports, 4,* 14–21.

Honeycutt, J., Cantrill, J., & Greene, R. (1989). Memory structures for relational escalation: A cognitive test of the sequencing of relational actions and stages. *Human Communication Research, 16,* 62–90.

Houston, M. (1994). When black women talk with white women: Why dialogues are difficult. In A. González, M. Houston, & V. Chen (Eds.), *Our voices: Essays in culture, ethnicity, and communication* (pp. 133–139). Los Angeles: Roxbury.

Houston, M., & Wood, J. T. (1996). Difficult dialogues, enlarged horizons: Friendships among members of different social groups. In J. T. Wood (Ed.), *Gendered relationships* (pp. 39–56). Mountain View, CA: Mayfield.

Huston, M., & Schwartz, P. (1996). Relationships of lesbians and gay men. In J. T. Wood & S. W. Duck (Eds.), *Understanding relationship processes, 6: Off the beaten track: Understudied relationships* (pp. 89–121). Thousand Oaks, CA: Sage.

Hyde, M. J. (1995). Human being and the call of technology. In J. T. Wood & R. B. Gregg (Eds.), *Toward the 21st century.* Cresskill, NJ: Hampton Press.

Hymes, D. (1974). *Foundations in sociolinguistics: An ethnographic approach.* Philadelphia: University of Pennsylvania Press.

Inman, C. (1996). Friendships among men: Closeness in the doing. In J. T. Wood (Ed.), *Gendered relationships* (pp. 95–110). Mountain View, CA: Mayfield.

Ishii, S., & Bruneau, T. (1991). Silence and silences in cross-cultural perspective: Japan and the United States. In L. Samovar & R. Porter (Eds.), *Intercultural communication: A reader* (6th ed., pp. 314–319). Belmont, CA: Wadsworth.

Janeway, E. (1971). *Man's world, woman's place.* New York: Dell.

Johnson, F. (1996). Friendships among women: Closeness in dialogue. In J. T. Wood (Ed.), *Gendered relationships* (pp. 79–94). Mountain View, CA: Mayfield.

Johnson, K., & Nakanishi, M. (1993). Implications of self-disclosure on conversational logics, perceived communication, competence, and social attraction: A comparison of Japanese and American cultures. *International and intercultural communication annual* (Vol. 17, pp. 204–221). Newbury Park, CA: Sage.

Jones, W. H., & Moore, T. L. (1989). Loneliness and social support. In M. Hojat & R. Crandall (Eds.), *Loneliness: Theory, research, and applications* (pp. 145–156). Newbury Park, CA: Sage.

Judicial Council of California. (1986). *1986 Annual report to the governor and legislature.* San Francisco, CA.

Katriel, T. (1990). "Griping" as a verbal ritual in some Israeli discourse. In D. Carbaugh (Ed.), *Cultural communication and intercultural contact* (pp. 99–114). Hillsdale, NJ: Lawrence Erlbaum.

Kaye, L. W., & Applegate, J. S. (1990). Men as elder caregivers: A response to changing families. *American Journal of Orthopsychiatry, 60,* 86–95.

Keller, E. F. (1985). *Reflections on gender and science.* New Haven: Yale University Press.

Kellerman, K., & Reynolds, R. (1990). When ignorance is bliss: The role of motivation to reduce uncertainty in uncertainty reduction theory. *Human Communication Research, 17,* 5–75.

Kelley, H. H., & Thibaut, J. (1978). *The social psychology of groups.* New York: Wiley.

Kelly, G. A. (1955). *The psychology of personal constructs.* New York: W. W. Norton.

Kimball, M. (1986). Television and sex-role attitudes. In T. M. Williams (Ed.), *The impact of television: A natural experiment in three communities* (pp. 265–301). Orlando, FL: Academic Press.

Kirkwood, W. (1992). Narrative and the rhetoric of possibility. *Communication Monographs, 59,* 30–47.

Klein, R., & Milardo, R. M. (1993). Third-party influence on the management of personal relationships. In S. Duck (Ed.), *Understanding relationship processes, 3: Social context and relationships* (pp. 55–77). Newbury Park, CA: Sage.

Klopf, D. (1991). Japanese communication practices: Recent comparative research. *Communication Quarterly, 39,* 130–139.

Knapp, M. L. (1984). *Social intercourse: From greeting to goodbye.* Boston, MA: Allyn & Bacon.

Knapp, M. L., & Vangelisti, A. (1992). *Interpersonal communication and human relationships* (2nd ed.). Boston: Allyn & Bacon.

Korzybski, A. (1958). *Science and sanity: An introduction to non-Aristotelian systems and general semantics.* Lakeville, CT: Institute of General Semantics.

Kramarae, C. (1981). *Women and men speaking.* Rowley, MA: Newbury House.

Kramarae, C., & Treichler, P. (1985). *A feminist dictionary.* Boston: Pandora.

Kuhn, T. (1970). *The structure of scientific revolutions* (2nd ed.). Chicago: University of Chicago Press.

Labov, W. (1972). *Sociolinguistic patterns.* Philadelphia: University of Pennsylvania Press.

Lacan, J. (1977). *Ecrits: A selection.* London: Tavistock.

Lacan, J. (1981). *The four fundamental concepts of psycho-analysis.* London: Penguin.

Langer, S. (1953). *Feeling and form: A theory of art.* New York: Scribner's.

Langer, S. (1979). *Philosophy in a new key: A study in the symbolism of reason, rite and art* (3rd ed.). Cambridge, MA: Harvard University Press.

Lea, M., & Spears, R. (1995). Love at first byte: Building personal relationships over computer networks. In J. T. Wood & S. W. Duck (Eds.),

Understanding relationship processes, 6: Off the beaten track: Understudied relationships (pp. 197–233). Thousand Oaks, CA: Sage.

Lee, W. S. (1993). Social scientists as ideological critics. *Western Journal of Communication, 57,* 221–232.

Lichter, S. R., Lichter, L. S., Rothman, S., & Amundson, D. (1987, July/August). Prime-time prejudice: TV's images of blacks and Hispanics. *Public Opinion,* pp. 13–16.

Ling, D. A. (1970). A pentadic analysis of Senator Edward Kennedy's address to the people of Massachusetts, July 25, 1969. *Central States Speech Journal, 21,* 81–86.

Littlejohn, S. (1992). *Theories of human communication* (4th ed.). Belmont, CA: Wadsworth.

Lund, M. (1985). The development of investment and commitment scales for predicting continuity of personal relationships. *Journal of Social and Personal Relationships, 2,* 3–23.

Maltz, D., & Borker, R. (1982). A cultural approach to male–female miscommunication. In J. J. Gumpertz (Ed.), *Language and social identity* (pp. 196–216). Cambridge, UK: Cambridge University Press.

Martin, R. W. (1991). Examining personal relationship thinking: The relational cognition complexity instrument. *Journal of Social and Personal Relationships, 8,* 467–480.

Martin, R. W. (1992). Relational cognition complexity and relational communication. *Communication Monographs, 59,* 150–163.

McBath, J. H., & Burhans, D. T., Jr. (1975). *Communication education and careers.* Falls Church, VA: Speech Communication Association.

McDonald, G. (1981). Structural exchange and marital interaction. *Journal of Marriage and the Family, 43,* 825–839.

McLuhan, M. (1962). *The Gutenberg galaxy.* Toronto: University of Toronto Press.

McLuhan, M. (1964). *Understanding media.* New York: McGraw-Hill.

McLuhan, M. (1969, March). Interview. *Playboy,* pp. 53–54, 56, 59–62, 64–66, 68, 70.

McLuhan, M., & Fiori, Q. (1967). *The medium is the message.* New York: Random House.

McLuhan, M., & McLuhan, E. (1988). Culture and communication: The two hemispheres. In *Laws of media* (pp. 67–91). Toronto: University of Toronto Press.

Mead, G. H. (1934). *Mind, self, and society.* Chicago: University of Chicago Press.

Media Studies Journal. (1994). Special issue: Race—America's rawest nerve. Vol. 8.

Mitchell-Kernan, C. (1972). Signifying, loud-talking, and marking. In T. Kochman (Ed.), *Rappin' and stylin' out* (pp. 315–335). Urbana, IL: University of Illinois Press.

Montgomery, B. (1993). Relationship maintenance versus relationship change: A dialectical dilemma. *Journal of Social and Personal Relationships, 10,* 205–224.

Mulac, A., Wiemann, J. M., Widenmann, S. J., & Gibson, T. W. (1988). Male/female language differences and effects in same-sex and mixed-sex dyads: The gender-linked language effect. *Communication Monographs, 55,* 315–335.

Murphy, B. O., & Zorn, T. (1996). Gendered interaction in professional relationships. In J. T. Wood (Ed.), *Gendered relationships* (pp. 213–232). Mountain View, CA: Mayfield.

Nakayama, T. (1995). Continuing the dialogue of evidence. *Western Journal of Communication, 59,* 171–175.

Natalle, E. (1996). Gendered issues in the workplace. In J. T. Wood (Ed.), *Gendered relationships.* Mountain View, CA: Mayfield.

Newcomb, H. (1978). Assessing the violence profile studies of Gerbner and Gross. *Communication Research, 5,* 264–282.

Nofsinger, R. (1991). *Everyday conversation.* Newbury Park, CA: Sage.

Nussbaum, M. (1992, October 18). Justice for women! *New York Review of Books,* pp. 43–48.

O'Connell, L. (1984). An exploration of exchange in three social relationships: Kinship, friendship, and the marketplace. *Journal of Social and Personal Relationships, 1,* 333–346.

Ogden, C. K., & Richards, I. A. (1923). *The meaning of meaning: A study of the influence of language upon thought and of the science of symbolism.* New York: Harcourt Brace and World.

O'Keefe, B., & Sypher, H. (1981). Cognitive complexity measures and the relationship of cognitive complexity to communication: A critical review. *Human Communication Research, 8,* 72–92.

Owen, W. F. (1984). Interpretive themes in relational communication. *Quarterly Journal of Speech, 770,* 274–287.

Owen, W. F. (1985). Thematic metaphors in relational communication: A conceptual framework. *Western Journal of Speech Communication, 49,* 1–13.

Owen, W. F. (1995, July). Personal communication.

Pacanowsky, M. (1989). Creating and narrating organizational realities. In B. Dervin, L. Grossberg, B. O'Keefe, & E. Wartella (Eds.), *Rethinking communication: Paradigm exemplars* (pp. 250–257). Newbury Park, CA: Sage.

Pacanowsky, M., & O'Donnell-Trujillo, N. (1982). Communication and organizational cultures. *Western Journal of Speech Communication, 46,* 115–130.

Pacanowsky, M., & O'Donnell-Trujillo, N. (1983). Organizational communication as cultural performance. *Communication Monographs, 30,* 126–147.

Park, M. (1979). *Communication styles in two different cultures: Korean and American.* Seoul: Han Shin.

Pearce, B. (1989). *Communication and the human condition.* Carbondale, IL: Southern Illinois University Press.

Pearce, B. (1992, November). *Bringing news of difference: An application of systemic and social constructionist communication theory in conflict consultation.* Paper presented to the Speech Communication Association, Chicago, IL.

Pearce, B. (1994). *Interpersonal communication: Making social worlds.* New York: Harper Collins.

Pearce, B., & Cronen, V. (1980). *Communication, action, and meaning: The creation of social realities.* New York: Praeger.

Penelope, J. (1990). *Speaking freely: Unlearning the lies of the fathers' tongues.* New York: Pergamon Press.

Petronio, S. (1991). Communication boundary management: A theoretical model of managing disclosure of private information between married couples. *Communication Theory, 1,* 311–335.

Philipsen, G. (1975). Speaking "like a man" in Teamsterville: Cultural patterns of role enactment in an urban neighborhood. *Quarterly Journal of Speech, 61,* 13–22.

Philipsen, G. (1992). *Speaking culturally: Exploration in social communication.* Albany, NY: SUNY Press.

Phillips, G. M., & Wood, J. T. (1983). *Communication and human relationships.* New York: Macmillan.

Planalp, S., Rutherford, D., & Honeycutt, J. M. (1988). Events that increase uncertainty in personal relationships, II: Replication and extension. *Human Communication Research, 14,* 516–547.

Postman, N. (1985). *Amusing ourselves to death: Public discourse in the age of show business.* New York: Penguin.

Prins, K., Buunk, B., & VanYperon, N. W. (1993). Equity, normative disapproval, and extramarital relationships. *Journal of Social and Personal Relationships, 10,* 39–54.

Pryor, J. B., & Merluzzi, T. V. (1985). The role of expertise in processing social interaction scripts. *Journal of Experimental Social Psychology, 21,* 362–379.

Puka, B. (1990). The liberation of caring: A different voice for Gilligan's different voice. *Hypatia, 5,* 59–82.

Putnam, L. (1982). In search of gender: A critique of communication and sex-roles research. *Women's Studies in Communication, 5,* 1–9.

Rakow, L. (1992). "Don't hate me because I'm beautiful": Feminist resistance to advertising's irresistible meanings. *Southern Journal of Speech Communication, 36,* 11–26.

Rawlins, W. (1992). *Friendship matters: Communication, dialectics, and the life course.* New York: Aldine de Gruyter.

Real, M. (1984). The debate on critical theory and the study of communications. *Journal of Communication, 34,* 72–80.

Richards, I. A. (1936). *The philosophy of rhetoric.* London: Oxford University Press.

Richards, I. A. (1955). *Speculative instruments.* Chicago: University of Chicago Press.

Richards, I. A. (1968, February 3). The secret of "feedforward." *Saturday Review,* pp. 14–17.

Riessman, C. K. (1990). *Divorce talk: Women and men make sense of personal relationships.* New Brunswick, NJ: Rutgers University Press.

Risman, B. (1989). Can men mother? In B. Risman & P. Schwartz (Eds.), *Gender in intimate relationships* (pp. 155–164). Belmont, CA: Wadsworth/Brooks-Cole.

Rogers-Millar, E., & Farace, R. (1975). Analysis of relational communication in dyads: New measurement procedures. *Human Communication Research, 1,* 222–239.

Rohlfing, M. (1995). "Doesn't anybody stay in one place anymore?" An exploration of the under-studied phenomenon of long-distance relationships. In J. T. Wood & S. Duck (Eds.), *Understanding relationship processes, 6: Off the beaten track: Understudied relationships* (pp. 173–196). Thousand Oaks, CA: Sage.

Roloff, M. (1981). *Interpersonal communication: The social exchange approach.* Beverly Hills, CA: Sage.

Rosenwasser, S. M., Lingenfelter, M., & Harrington, A. F. (1989). Nontraditional gender role portrayals on television and children's gender role perceptions. *Journal of Applied Developmental Psychology, 10,* 97–105.

Rowland, R. C (1989). On limiting the narrative paradigm: Three case studies. *Communication Monographs, 56,* 39–54.

Ruberman, T. R. (1992, January 22–29). Psychosocial influences on mortality of patients with coronary heart disease. *Journal of the American Medical Association 267,* 559–560.

Ruddick, S. (1989). *Maternal thinking: Towards a politics of peace.* Boston: Beacon Press.

Rusbult, C., & Buunk, B. (1993). Commitment processes in close relationships: An interdependence analysis. *Journal of Social and Personal Relationships, 10,* 175–204.

Rusk, T., & Rusk, N. (1988). *Mind traps: Change your mind, change your life.* Los Angeles: Price Stern Sloan.

Russell, D. E. H. (Ed.). (1993). *Feminist views on pornography.* Cholchester, VT: Teachers College Press.

Sadker, M., & Sadker, D. (1986, March). Sexism in the classroom: From grade school to graduate school. *Phi Delta Kappan,* pp. 512–515.

Sallinen-Kuparinen, A. (1992). Teacher communicator style. *Communication Education, 41,* 153–166.

Samovar, L., & Porter, R. (Eds.). (1994). *Intercultural communication: A reader* (7th ed.). Belmont, CA: Wadsworth.

Sarup, M. (1989). *An introductory guide to poststructuralism and postmodernism.* Athens, GA: University of Georgia Press.

SCA (Speech Communication Association). (1993). *Pathways to careers in communication.* Annandale, VA: Author.

Scarf, M. (1987). *Intimate partners: Patterns in love and marriage.* New York: Random House.

Schaef, A. W. (1985). *Women's reality.* St. Paul, MN: Winston Press.

Searle, J. R. (1976). *Speech acts: An essay in the philosophy of language.* London: Cambridge University Press.

Seligman, M. E. P. (1990). *Learned optimism.* New York: Simon & Schuster/ Pocket Books.

Sexism in the schoolhouse. (1992, February 24). *Newsweek,* p. 62.

Shailor, J. (1994). *Empowerment in dispute mediation: A critical analysis of communication.* Westport, CT: Praeger.

Shannon, C., & Weaver, W. (1949). *The mathematical theory of communication.* Urbana, IL: University of Illinois Press.

Shapiro, J., & Kroeger, L. (1991). Is life just a romantic novel? The relationship between attitudes about intimate relationships and the popular media. *American Journal of Family Therapy, 19,* 226–236.

Shattuck, T. R. (1980). *The forbidden experiment: The story of the wild boy of Aveyron.* New York: Farrar, Straus & Giroux.

Shimanoff, S. B. (1980). *Communication rules: Theory and research.* Beverly Hills, CA: Sage.

Shimanoff, S. B. (1985). Rules governing the verbal expression of emotions between married couples. *Western Journal of Communication, 49,* 147– 165.

Shotter, J. (1993). *Conversational realities: The construction of life through language.* Newbury Park, CA: Sage.

Sights, sounds, and stereotypes. (1992, October 11). *Raleigh News and Observer,* pp. G1, G10.

Signorielli, N. (1990). Television's mean and dangerous world: A continuation of the cultural indicators perspective. In N. Signorielli & M. Morgan (Eds.), *Cultivation analysis: New directions in media effects research* (pp. 85–106). Newbury Park, CA: Sage.

Signorielli, N., & Morgan, M. (Eds.). (1990). *Cultivation analysis: New directions in media effects research.* Newbury Park, CA: Sage.

Skinner, B. F. (1971). *Beyond freedom and dignity.* New York: Knopf.

Smitherman, G. (1977). *Talkin' and testifyin': The language of black America.* Boston: Houghton Mifflin.

Spelman, E. (1988). *Inessential woman: Problems of exclusion in feminist thought.* Boston: Beacon Press.

Spencer, T. (1994). Transforming personal relationships through ordinary talk. In S. W. Duck (Ed.), *Understanding relationship processes, 4: Dynamics of relationships* (pp. 58–85). Thousand Oaks, CA: Sage.

Spender, D. (1984a). Defining reality: A powerful tool. In C. Kramarae, M. Schultz, & W. O'Barr (Eds.), *Language and power* (pp. 195–205). Beverly Hills, CA: Sage.

Spender, D. (1984b). *Man made language.* London: Routledge & Kegan Paul.

Spitzack, C., & Carter, K. (1987). Women in communication studies: A typology for revision. *Quarterly Journal of Speech, 73,* 401–423.

Stacks, D., Hill, S., III, & Hickson, M. (1991). *Introduction to communication theory.* New York: Holt, Rinehart & Winston.

Stewart, J. (1991). A postmodern look at traditional communication postulates. *Western Journal of Speech Communication, 55,* 354–379.

Stewart, L. P., Stewart, A. D., Friedley, S. A., & Cooper, P. J. (1990). *Communication between the sexes: Sex differences and sex role stereotypes* (2nd ed.). Scottsdale, AZ: Gorsuch Scarisbrick.

Storytelling and narrativity in communication research. (1985). *Journal of Communication, 4,* entire issue.

Strine, M. S. (1992). Understanding how things work: Sexual harassment and academic culture. *Journal of Applied Communication Research, 20,* 391–400.

Suitor, J. J. (1991). Marital quality and satisfaction with the divison of household labor across the family life cycle. *Journal of Marriage and the Family, 53,* 221–230.

Sunnafrank, M. (1986). Predicted outcome value during initial interactions: A reformulaton of uncertainty reduction theory. *Human Communication Research, 13,* 3–33.

Tannen, D. (1990). *You just don't understand: Women and men in conversation.* New York: William Morrow.

Tannen, D. (1994). *Talking 9 to 5.* New York: William Morrow.

Taylor, B., & Conrad, C. (1992). Narratives of sexual harassment: Organizational dimensions. *Journal of Applied Communication Research, 20,* 401–418.

Taylor, D., & Altman, I. (1987). Communication in interpersonal relationships: Social penetration processes. In M. Roloff & G. R. Miller (Eds.), *Interpersonal processes: New directions in communication research* (pp. 253–285). Newbury Park, CA: Sage.

Television Bureau of Advertising. (1991). *Media comparisons* (SRI Rep. A9055–4). New York: Author.

Telling our stories: Special symposium. (1992). *The Journal of Applied Communication Research, 20.*

Thibaut, J., & Kelley, H. H. (1959). *The social psychology of groups.* New York: Wiley.

Ting-Toomey, S. (1991). Intimacy expressions in three cultures: France, Japan and the United States. *International Journal of Intercultural Relations, 15,* 29–46.

Treichler, P. A., & Kramarae, C. (1983). Women's talk in the ivory tower. *Communication Quarterly, 31,* 118–132.

Trice, H., & Beyer, J. (1984). Studying organizational cultures through rites and ceremonials. *Academy of Management Review, 9,* 653–669.

Troemel-Ploetz, S. (1991). Review essay: Selling the apolitical. *Discourse and Society, 2,* 490–499.

Van Lear, C. A. (1992). Testing a cyclical model of communicative openness in relationship development: Two longitudinal studies. *Communication Monographs, 58,* 337–361.

Van Maanen, J. (1973). Observations on the making of policemen. *Human Organization, 32,* 407–418.

Van Maanen, J., & Barley, S. (1985). Cultural organization: Fragments of a theory. In P. J. Frost et al. (Eds.), *Organizational culture* (pp. 31–54). Beverly Hills, CA: Sage.

Vocate, D. (Ed.). (1994). *Intrapersonal communication: Different voices, different minds.* Hillsdale, NJ: Lawrence Erlbaum.

von Bertalanffy, L. (1951). *Problems of life.* New York: Harper & Row.

von Bertalanffy, L. (1967). *Robots, men and minds.* New York: Braziller.

Walsh, F. (1993). Conceptualization of normal family processes. In F. Walsh (Ed.), *Normal family processes* (2nd ed., pp. 3–69). New York: Guilford.

Wander, P. (1983). The ideological turn in modern criticism. *Central States Speech Journal, 34,* 1–18.

Wander, P. (1984). The third persona: An ideological turn in rhetorical theory. *Central States Speech Journal, 35,* 197–216.

Warnick, B. (1987). The narrative paradigm: Another story. *Quarterly Journal of Speech, 73,* 172–182.

Watzlawick, P., Beavin, J., & Jackson, D. (1967). *The pragmatics of human communication.* New York: W. W. Norton.

Weedon, C. (1987). *Feminist practice and poststructuralist theory.* London: Basil Blackwell.

Weiner, N. (1967). *The human use of human beings.* New York: Avon.

Wenzhong, H., & Grove, C. (1991). *Encountering the Chinese.* Yarmouth, ME: Intercultural Press.

Werner, C., Altman, I., Brown, B., & Ginat, J. (1993). Celebrations in personal relationships: A transactional/dialectical perspective. In S. Duck (Ed.), *Understanding relationship processes, 3: Social context and relationships* (pp. 109–138). Newbury Park, CA: Sage.

West, C., & Zimmerman, D. (1987). "Doing gender." *Gender and Society, 1,* 125–151.

West, J. (1993). Ethnography and ideology: The politics of cultural representation. *Western Journal of Communication, 57,* 209–220.

West, J. (1995). Understanding how the dynamics of ideology influence violence between intimates. In S. W. Duck & J. T. Wood (Eds.), *Understanding relationship processes, 5: Confronting relationship challenges* (pp. 129–149). Thousand Oaks, CA: Sage.

White, J., & Bondurant, J. (1996). Gendered violence between intimates. In J. T. Wood (Ed.), *Gendered relationships* (pp. 197–210). Mountain View, CA: Mayfield.

Wilkie, J. R. (1991). The decline in men's labor force participation and income and the changing structure of family economic support. *Journal of Marriage and the Family, 53,* 111–122.

Williams, S. (1989). *A description of the rules for the performance appraisal interview utilizing the coordinated management of meaning theory.* Unpublished master's thesis. University of Northern Iowa, Cedar Falls, IA.

Wolf, N. (1991). *The beauty myth.* New York: William C. Morrow.

Wong, W. (1994). Covering the invisible "model minority." *Media Studies Journal* (Special issue: Race—America's rawest nerve), *8,* 49–60.

Wood, J. T. (1982). Communication and relational culture: Bases for the study of human relationships. *Communication Quarterly, 30,* 75–84.

Wood, J. T. (1986). Different voices in relationship crises: An extension of Gilligan's theory. *American Behavioral Scientist, 29,* 273–301.

Wood, J. T. (1992a). *Spinning the symbolic web.* Norwood, NJ: Ablex.

Wood, J. T. (1992b). Narratives as a basis for theorizing sexual harassment. *Journal of Applied Communication Research, 20,* 349–363.

Wood, J. T. (1993a). Bringing different voices into the classroom. *National Women's Studies Association Journal, 5,* 82–93.

Wood, J. T. (1993b). Diversity and commonality: Sustaining their tension in communication courses. *Western Journal of Communication, 57,* 367–380.

Wood, J. T. (1993c). Engendered relations: Interaction, caring, power, and responsibility in intimacy. In S. W. Duck (Ed.), *Understanding relationship processes, 3: Social context and relationships* (pp. 26–54). Newbury Park, CA: Sage.

Wood, J. T. (1993d). Enlarging conceptual boundaries: A critique of research on interpersonal communication. In S. P. Bowen & N. J. Wyatt (Eds.), *Transforming visions: Feminist critiques in speech communication* (pp. 19–49). Cresskill, NJ: Hampton Press.

Wood, J. T. (1993e). From "woman's nature" to standpoint epistemology: Gilligan and the debate over essentializing in feminist scholarship. *Women's Studies in Communication, 15,* 1–24.

Wood, J. T. (1994a). *Gendered lives: Communication, gender, and culture.* Belmont, CA: Wadsworth.

Wood, J. T. (1994b). Saying it makes it so: The discursive construction of sexual harassment. In S. Bingham (Ed.), *Discursive conceptions of sexual harassment* (pp. 17–30). Westport, CT.: Praeger.

Wood, J. T. (1994c). Gender and relationship crises: Contrasting reasons, responses, and relational orientations. In J. Ringer (Ed.), *Queer words, queer images: The construction of homosexuality.* New York: New York University Press.

Wood, J. T. (1994d). *Who cares?: Women, care, and culture.* Carbondale, IL: Southern Illinois University Press.

Wood, J. T. (1994e). Gender, communication, and culture. In L. Samovar & R. Porter (Eds.), *Intercultural communication: A reader* (7th ed., pp. 155–164). Belmont, CA: Wadsworth.

Wood, J. T. (1995a). Feminist scholarship and the study of personal relationships. *Journal of Social and Personal Relationships, 12,* 103–121.

Wood, J. T. (1995b). *Relational communication: Change and continuity in personal relationships.* Belmont, CA: Wadsworth.

Wood, J. T. (1995c). The part is not the whole. *Journal of Social and Personal Relationships, 12,* 563–567.

Wood, J. T. (Ed.). (1996a). *Gendered relationships.* Mountain View, CA: Mayfield.

Wood, J. T. (1996b). She says/he says: Communication, caring and conflict in heterosexual relationships. In J. T. Wood (Ed.), *Gendered relationships* (pp. 149–162). Mountain View, CA: Mayfield.

Wood, J. T., & Cox, J. R. (1993). Rethinking critical voice: Materiality and situated knowledges. *Western Journal of Communication, 57,* 278–287.

Wood, J. T., Dendy, L., Dordek, E., Germany, M., & Varallo, S. (1994). Dialectic of difference: A thematic analysis of intimates' meanings for differences. In K. Carter & M. Presnell (Eds.), *Interpretive approaches to interpersonal communication* (pp. 115–136). New York: SUNY Press.

Wood, J. T., & Duck, S. (1995a). Off the beaten track: New shores for relationship research. In J. T. Wood & S. Duck (Eds.), *Understanding relationship processes, 6: Understudied relationships: Off the beaten track* (pp. 1–21). Thousand Oaks, CA: Sage.

Wood, J. T., & Duck, S. (Eds.). (1995b). *Understanding relationship processes, 6: Off the beaten track: Understudied relationships.* Thousand Oaks, CA: Sage.

Wood, J. T., & Inman, C. C. (1993). In a different mode: Masculine styles of communicating closeness. *Journal of Applied Communication Research, 21,* 279–295.

Wood, J. T., & Lenze, L. F. (1991a). Gender and the development of self: Inclusive pedagogy in interpersonal communication. *Women's Studies in Communication, 14,* 1–23.

Wood, J. T., & Lenze, L. F. (1991b). Strategies to enhance gender sensitivity in communication education. *Communication Education, 40,* 16–21.

Zorn, T. (1991). Construct system development, transformational leadership, and leadership messages. *Southern Communication Journal, 56,* 178–193.

Zorn, T. (1995). Bosses and buddies: Constructing and performing simultaneously hierarchical and close friendship relationships. In J. T. Wood & S. W. Duck (Eds.), *Understanding relationship processes, 6: Off the beaten track: Understudied relationships* (pp. 122–147). Thousand Oaks, CA: Sage.

Zuckerman, M. B. (1993, August 2). The victims of TV violence. *U.S. News and World Reports,* p. 64.

Name Index

Subject Index

Pages on which terms are defined are indicated by **boldface** *type.*